Reusability and Software Construction: C and C++

Reusability and Software Construction: C and C++

Jerry D. Smith

Iris Computing Laboratories
Signal Mountain, Tennessee

JOHN WILEY & SONS

New York • Chichester • Brisbane • Toronto • Singapore

Library of Congress Cataloging in Publication Data:

Smith, Jerry D., 1951-
Reusability and software construction: C and C++ / Jerry D. Smith.
p. cm.
Includes bibliographical references.
1. C (Computer program language) 2. C++ (Computer program language) 3. Computer software—Reusability. 4. Computer software—Development. I. Title.
QA76.73.C15S57 1990
005.13'3—dc20
ISBN 0-471-52411-5

89-28896
CIP

Printed in the United States of America

10 9 8 7 6 5 4 3 2 1

In Memory

TCS

Contents

Preface **xiii**

1 Introduction **1**

1.1 What Software Crisis? 1
1.2 Software Construction and Software Engineering 2
1.3 Topics of Interest in Software Construction 3
1.4 Reusable Software Modules 3
1.5 Choose Your Language 5
1.6 Object-oriented Programming—Here to Stay? 5

2 Practical Considerations in Software Construction **7**

2.1 External and Internal Factors 7
2.2 Surface Complexity of a Program 8
2.3 External/Global Variables 9
2.4 Private/Local Variables 10

2.5 Legitimate Uses of External Variables 11
2.6 Using Static Local Variables for Information Hiding 12
2.7 Competing Strategies for Module Design 14
2.8 Designing Compiled Software Modules with C 15

3 MS-DOS, IBM PC, and C Language Fundamentals 19

3.1 Background and Motivation 19
3.2 MS-DOS Basics 20
3.3 Keyboard Operations 21
3.4 Screen Management 22
3.5 Memory Models 24
3.6 Pointer Arithmetic 26
3.7 OS Function Calls 28
3.8 Managing Multiple Compiled Modules 30
3.9 Using Function Prototypes 32

4 Project Design Considerations 35

4.1 A Window-based Interface 36
4.2 Editor Input 36
4.3 Basic Editor Features 37
4.4 File Processing Support 38
4.5 Edit Buffer Design 38
4.6 Breakdown into Compiled Modules 39
4.7 Summary of Components 39

5 Designing the Application-dependent Modules 41

5.1 Use of External Variables 42
5.2 Abstract Data Structures and External Variables 42
5.3 The Primary Application Module 43
5.3.1 The Importance of Header Files 43
5.3.2 Program Initialization, Error Handling, and Termination 44
5.3.3 Mapping Keystrokes to Editor Commands 46
5.3.4 Two Public Variables for Color Attributes 47
5.3.5 Using **puts()** Versus **printf()** 48
5.3.6 Abstraction and Window Allocations 49
5.3.7 Inter-module Flexibility and Module-level Abstraction 50
5.3.8 The Keyboard Interface 53
5.4 The Supporting Application Modules 54

6 Basic MS-DOS Software Components **57**

6.1 Header Files with Shared Constants 57
6.2 The Keyboard Module 59
6.3 Procedure Abstraction in the Keyboard Module 62
6.4 The Character Display Module 63
6.5 The Screen Management Module 65

7 Developing a General-purpose Windowing System **71**

7.1 Background 71
7.2 Abstract Data Structures and Window Handles 72
7.3 Abstract Data Structures and External Variables 74
7.4 The Window Descriptor Table Array 74
7.5 Window Instantiation 77
7.6 Miscellaneous Window Operations 81
7.7 Window Input and Output 85
7.8 Access Functions 89

8 A Window Interface to the Edit Module **91**

8.1 Buffer-related Window Management 91
8.2 Displaying a Buffer in a Window 92
8.3 Managing Horizontal Scroll Operations 95

9 Developing a General-purpose Edit Module **99**

9.1 Overall Design for the Edit Module 99
9.2 Management of Critical Editing Variables 101
9.3 Buffer Management Operations 106
9.4 A General Message and Prompt Facility 110
9.5 Calculating Buffer Offsets 112
9.6 Providing Support for Search-and-replace Operations 115
9.7 Insertion and Deletion with Provisions for Undo 118
9.8 Canonical Breakdown of Cursor Movement Operations 125
9.9 High-level Cursor Movement Operations 127

10 Overview of C++ **133**

10.1 Background 133
10.2 Syntactic Components of C++ 134
10.2.1 Comments 134

10.2.2 Flexibility in the Placement of Variable Definitions 134
10.2.3 **enum**, **class**, **struct**, and **union** Qualifiers 135
10.2.4 The Scope Resolution Operator 135
10.2.5 The **const** Specifier 136
10.2.6 Type Conversion 136
10.2.7 Reference Parameters 137
10.2.8 Default and Unspecified Parameters 138
10.2.9 Overloaded Function Definitions 138
10.2.10 Language Support for Memory Management 139
10.2.11 **cin** and **cout** 140
10.2.12 The **class** Specifier 141
10.3 Elements of Object-oriented Programming 144

11 Designing C++ Interface and Implementation Files 149

11.1 Designing the **rectangle** Class 149
11.2 Designing Class Hierarchies 152
11.3 Controlled Access to Class Components 155
11.4 Nested/Hierarchical Inclusion of Interface Files 159

12 Basic MS-DOS Software Components in C++ 161

12.1 The Keyboard Module 161
12.2 The Screen Module 164

13 Designing a Window Class Hierarchy 171

13.1 Advantages of Class Hierarchies 171
13.2 Abstract Classes 172
13.3 A Window Hierarchy for Prompting and Editing 175
13.4 **window**: The Root Window Class 177
13.4.1 The Interface to **window** 177
13.4.2 Supporting Objects: Allocated Globally or Passed by Pointer? 179
13.4.3 Protecting against Direct Invocation of **window()** 181
13.4.4 Defining **window**'s Attributes 181
13.4.5 An Overview of **window**'s Methods 182
13.5 **msg_window**: A Class for Managing Messages 186
13.6 **query_box**: A Simple Yes-no Prompt Box 189
13.7 **num_box**: A Prompt Box for Numeric Responses 191

14 A Window Hierarchy with Editing Facilities **193**

14.1 **buf_window**: Adding Buffer Support to **window** 193
14.2 **browser**: A Read-only Window with Restricted Cursor Movement 199
14.3 **text_window**: Adding Text Editing Support 204
14.4 **edit_window**: A Concrete Class for Full-scale Text Editing 208
14.5 **edit_window**'s Friends: A Buffer Hierarchy 214
14.6 **prompt_window**: A Prompt Box Class with Editing Capabilities 217
14.7 Global Constructors 221
14.8 Critique of Our Class Hierarchies 222

15 ed: Using Recursion to Implement Nested Edit Windows **225**

15.1 Application Modules that Support **main()** 225
15.2 **help**: ed's Help System 226
15.3 ed: Some Assembly Required 228
15.4 Nested Edit Sessions Using Recursion 233
15.5 **dos_cmd**: A DOS-command Prompt Box 235
15.6 Wildcard File Processing—an Exercise for the Reader 237

16 Designing a Reusable Editor Class **239**

16.1 **editor**: A Self-contained Multi-window Editor 240
16.2 **dispatcher()**: Scheduling and Overseeing Editor Operations 242
16.3 Methods for Managing Multiple Windows 245
16.4 Providing for Graceful Program Termination 248
16.5 Use **dispatcher()**, not **process_cmd()** 249
16.6 Using **editor** 251

17 A Registration System for Objects and Functions **253**

17.1 The Notifier Concept in Object-oriented Windowing Environments 254
17.2 A SunView Example 254
17.3 Implementing a Callback Mechanism for Objects 258
17.3.1 Callback Object Tables 258
17.3.2 Callback Object Methods 259
17.3.3 Standard Protocols 263
17.3.4 Other Modifications and Enhancements to **editor** 264
17.3.5 Polymorphism and the Role of Virtual Methods 265
17.3.6 An Example: Adding a Pop-up, Read-only Browser 267
17.4 Implementing a Callback Mechanism for Functions 268

17.4.1 A Callback Function Table 269
17.4.2 Callback Function Methods 270
17.4.3 An Example: Having the Object Perform Clean-up Operations 271
17.4.4 An Exercise 273
17.5 Object-oriented Programming and Registration Systems 273
17.6 Class Refinement 274

18 Informal Guidelines for Enhancing Software Reusability 277

18.1 Use Encapsulation To Hide Details 277
18.1.1 Traditional Languages 277
18.1.2 Object-oriented Languages 279
18.2 Use Access Methods for Inter-module Communication 279
18.3 Use Message-passing for Inter-object Communication 281
18.4 Take Advantage of Built-in Support for Array Indexing 282
18.5 Provide Multiple Constructors for the Appropriate Classes 282
18.6 Identify Abstract and Concrete Classes 283
18.7 Hierarchies Require Fine-tuning 284
18.8 Hide Low-level Classes within High-level Classes 284
18.9 Put the Flow of Control in the Objects 284
18.10 Use Virtual Methods Where Necessary 285

Appendix A The C Version of ed 287

Appendix B The C++ Version of ed 383

Appendix C The C++ Source Code for the Multi-window Version of ed 501

References 529

Index 533

Preface

The ongoing, worldwide software crisis emphasizes the importance of advanced planning for medium- and large-scale software projects. Many of the problems that plague the software industry at present can be addressed by properly applying the principles of traditional software engineering, for example, careful project management, use of software metrics, and so on.

Improper programming practices, however, have contributed to the software crisis as well. Old-style coding techniques continue to cripple the industry. Defense contractors, large corporations, and even microcomputer software development companies all suffer from the long-term problems that accrue from:

- widespread use of global variables
- large procedures with many local variables
- improper modular decomposition of software components

It's easy to blame these problems on the relative youth of the computing industry; eventually, however, the software crisis must be met head on.

The techniques and tools for solving many of today's software problems have existed for some time. Languages such as PL/I and Pascal support modern, structured programming. Newer languages such as C and Modula-2 provide even more tools for scaling large software projects. Finally, object-oriented programming languages offer greatly enhanced support for data encapsulation, information hiding, and more—supporting a new approach to programming in the large.

The primary goal of this book is to provide a discussion, plus demonstration, of software construction techniques that promote reusability. We don't propose the ultimate approach to software development—it doesn't exist. Software development efforts take place daily for an incredible variety of applications. Different applications demand different techniques. There are, however, a number of principles that are useful across many software projects.

In this book we focus on a small subset of issues that have widespread ramifications. We consider circumstances in which global variables may be justified, yet we argue against their usage in general. We provide techniques for minimizing the use of global variables—without producing functions burdened by long parameter lists. We consider a number of issues that arise in decomposing software into multiple compiled modules.

Our interest in software construction techniques is practical, not theoretical. As a conversation piece for our discussion, we've chosen a window-based editing environment—complete source code is provided. Although choice of language is somewhat arbitrary, we've chosen C and C++ because of their current popularity and widespread availability across hardware platforms. One premise of this book is that an object-oriented programming system (OOPS), in this case, a C++ environment, provides better software development support than one based on a traditional language, such as C.

C and C++ have much in common—C++ is a superset of C. This relationship makes it particularly convenient to introduce several programming topics with examples in C. Moreover, many of the steps that a programmer can take to enhance code reusability are equally applicable to C and C++. At present, more programmers are familiar with C than C++. We assume that you are quite comfortable with C.

By the time the editor project in C is complete, our programming philosophy has been exposed. With a number of programming issues out of the way, we are free to get on to our discussion of C++. We do so by developing the same editor using C++. Having prior, hands-on knowledge of where we're going makes it easier to focus on the specifics of C++. We should note that this approach is consistent with what takes place in practice—a number of programming shops are in the process of migrating from C to C++. To some extent, you can view this book as a demonstration of what's required to convert a software project from C to C++, even though code migration is of secondary importance in our discussion.

Object-oriented programming (OOP) differs from traditional programming in its approach to program design, problem decomposition, and so on. For programmers who are new to OOP, there's a lot more to adjust to than new syntax. In some ways, switching from C to C++ is easier than switching from C to an object-oriented language that is radically different from C, say, Smalltalk. On the other hand, studying the class hierarchies that are provided with most Smalltalk environments helps to emphasize the non-language-specific aspects of OOP.

Object-oriented programmers often characterize OOP as differing from traditional programming in that a programmer typically devotes considerably more time up front to design considerations—designing data structures, developing class hierarchies, and so on.

It's not that object-oriented languages force the programmer to do something that traditional languages do not; it's simply a matter of "pay me now, or pay me later."

One of our primary concerns in the second half of the book is up-front design of classes. In particular, we want to focus on factoring a large number of related windowing and editing tasks into a class hierarchy that can be used in subsequent applications. In our class hierarchy we adopt an intermediate position with respect to the use of abstract versus concrete classes.

At present, many C++ books do not emphasize the importance of abstract classes. On the other hand, the importance of abstract classes has been well documented in object-oriented research applications and in commercial applications. For our editor project we employ fewer abstract classes than we would in designing a windowing environment for in-house applications.

We believe this intermediate position is justified because many readers are new to OOP. We do not want to obscure the fundamentals of object-oriented programming by presenting an overly complex class hierarchy. The reader may consult the *Journal of Object-oriented Programming* for additional information on class decomposition. An extensive discussion of various strategies for class decomposition and class reorganization is simply beyond the scope of this book.

We have no particular interest in MS-DOS. However, it is reasonable to assume that more readers are familiar with MS-DOS than any other operating system. With this in mind, we've developed our editor in a DOS environment. At several points in our discussions, specific information is given about MS-DOS, for example, screen management and keyboard processing. In relative terms, this information constitutes a small portion of the book, and therefore it shouldn't hinder DOS veterans or readers who have no interest in DOS. On the other hand, we've tried to provide enough information to allow programmers with minimal background in MS-DOS to understand the modules at a low-level, that is, to provide continuity across all components of our software project. Some readers may want to refer to one of the many books on MS-DOS, for example, Duncan (1988).

In general, we feel no obligation to discuss every module that is necessary to implement a full-screen editor, nor do we feel obligated to cover all aspects of programming in MS-DOS environments. At the same time, after covering many of the details of programming a medium-scale software product, we would like to leave the reader with a working product. Thus, Appendices A and B provide complete source code for the editor, in C and C++, respectively. As discussed in subsequent chapters, the C source code has been tested with a variety of C compilers, and the C++ source code has been tested with C++ 2.0.

Overall, the editor has proved to be reasonably efficient, considering its implementation in a high-level language. In fact, we use it, with some extensions, on a daily basis. Having relegated the source code to the appendices, we are free to pick and choose demonstration source code from the editor, as it relates to our focus on reusable software construction.

We made the decision not to strive for the ultimate in portability. Here's why. It's possible to develop a set of *small-scale* windowing and editing modules that are portable across hardware/operating system platforms, say, IBM PCs running MS-DOS and Sun workstations running UNIX. However, recent advances in user interface design have created a situation in which *low-level* portable code simply isn't efficient enough—it isn't commercially viable.

At present, commercial developers are taking the initial steps toward providing common user interfaces across hardware platforms and operating systems. Developing common user interfaces across computing systems requires considerable cooperation among vendors. It isn't easy to develop common user interfaces that are efficient and that maintain portability in high-level source code for window-based applications. In general, developers use a "layered" approach, wherein portability is abandoned in low-level, hardware-specific source code; window-system toolkits are provided that maintain portability at the highest levels. In this book, we develop an editor, that is, an application; providing the source code for a large-scale, operating environment isn't feasible.

With this in mind we've attempted to maintain a reasonable level of portability in our design by isolating hardware dependencies on a compiled module level. For example, the editor modules are quite portable. By replacing the screen-handling, keyboard-processing, and windowing modules with those from another hardware platform, it's possible to port the editor to a very different machine.

We've outlined several of the primary topics of this book: programming practices that directly affect reusability, a C implementation of the editor, class hierarchy decomposition using C++, and a C++ implementation of the editor. Lastly, we provide an introduction to what some have called notification-based programming (Sun Microsystems, 1988). With this approach, the flow of control in the application is inverted. For example, a windowing system can be designed that is capable of high-level control of the low-level activities that it implements.

The movement toward sophisticated user interfaces, sometimes for even the most basic operations, places a potentially heavy burden on the programmer. Programmers often claim that 50 percent (or more) of the development effort for a application may be devoted to implementing the user interface.

It's not enough to develop libraries of functions that support windowing operations. In practice, a programmer runs into the problem that, even with existing windowing software, an inordinate amount of time may be required to coordinate windowing activities. Traditionally, the application-dependent modules have taken on the responsibility of providing this coordination. That is, the application provides a big case structure within a loop that coordinates activities by issuing calls to functions imported from other compiled modules—the main control loop exists within the application.

Alternatively, the user interface modules could provide these services, relieving each application of a considerable burden. In our first editor implementation, we illustrate the traditional approach with a dispatching routine in the application-dependent source file. In the C++ version we illustrate that a large portion of this work can be hidden in the reusable compiled modules, but with the application retaining control of overall processing. Finally, we provide a demonstration of the currently preferred approach, whereby the windowing system has primary control of program execution. In this case, the application-dependent modules must take special steps to inform the windowing system of every event wherein control must be returned to the application.

A number of individuals have contributed to the development of this book. First, I would like to thank the staff of Guidelines Software Incorporated for providing me with Version 1.2 of **cfront**, the C++ translator. Second, I would like to acknowledge the help provided by the staff of Zortech Incorporated. Bob Swarm, in particular, provided valuable information, plus software, so that I could test the source code in this book with a beta version of Zortech C++. Once C++ 2.0 became available, the switch to the commercial version was quite painless.

At various stages during the development of the manuscript, I received comments and suggestions from both friends and anonymous reviewers; I would like to acknowledge their contribution. Their input was very important in shaping the final manuscript. Next, I would like to thank the entire staff at John Wiley for their efforts toward the overall process.

During the development and production of this book I worked closely with four individuals at John Wiley. I would like to acknowledge their special contributions to this project. First, Yvette Ho Sang and Isabel Stein, my production editors, made sure that the entire production process progressed according to schedule. Second, Terri Hudson coordinated the day-to-day developmental operations—minor crises didn't stand a chance. Third, I would like to thank my editor Diane Cerra for her invaluable contributions to the production of this book, for her guidance throughout the project, and for her map of the French Quarter.

JERRY D. SMITH

Signal Mountain, Tennessee
November 1989

The C and C++ source code for the projects given in Appendices A, B, and C, plus the source code for Chapter 17, is available on diskette(s) for $30.00, including shipping and handling charges. If you would like to order the source code, photocopy this page, fill in the order form, and send a check or money order for $30.00 to the address given below.

Your order will be processed promptly and professionally.

This offer is being made solely by Iris Computing Laboratories. John Wiley & Sons, as publisher of this book, is not responsible for orders placed with Iris Computing Laboratories.

Mail to:

Editor Source Offer
Iris Computing Laboratories
2439 Wood Sorrell Lane
Signal Mountain, Tennessee 37377

Name: ______________________________

Address: ______________________________

____

____

Diskette: 5.25" — 360K_____ 3.5" — 720K_____

Reusability and Software Construction: C and C++

1

Introduction

This chapter provides a brief motivation for an investigation into a number of software construction principles. Our discussion is mostly informal; however, at various points we point out the literature in which you can find more formal and more theoretical coverage of several aspects of software construction.

Initially, we discuss the rationale and motivation behind a book devoted to software construction issues. Subsequently, we overview several issues that will help set the stage for later chapters, in which we address these topics in more detail.

1.1 What Software Crisis?

No one can realistically deny the present software crisis. Its significance is apparent throughout government and private industry. Indeed, even managers in moderate-sized industries are plagued by chronic software problems.

Our objectives do not include a formal study of the traditional statistics that interest many software engineers—the national averages regarding months until delivery for various categories of software products, the inordinate amount of time devoted to software maintenance, the problems that arise in team programming for large products, and so on. In contrast, we are primarily interested in how tools, and our use of tools, either contributes to or provides solutions for the current software crisis.

Indeed, it is these tools and techniques for software construction that concerned early visionaries in the computing industry, as evidenced by the well-known plea by M.D. McIlroy in 1968 (see McIlroy, 1976) for catalogs of softwarc components/modules. The current trend toward object-oriented software technology is a direct attempt to provide mechanisms for building and maintaining such catalogs of software modules. Our principal goal is to provide an in-depth, concrete demonstration of various programming strategies that can enhance reusability of software components.

1.2 Software Construction and Software Engineering

In this book we focus on software construction, as opposed to software engineering. What are the differences? For our purposes, the term *software construction* carries a connotation of concern for the physical, source code-level aspects of software development; it emphasizes the issues that arise on a daily basis among those who construct software, principally programmers. Of course, individuals other than programmers often share an interest in software construction.

As a discipline, software engineering is, perhaps, still choosing its direction. There is some variability in the extent to which programming languages and techniques play a part in, say, undergraduate software engineering courses, graduate software engineering programs, and so on. We define *software engineering* to be that which is covered in a typical software engineering textbook! That is, software engineering refers, primarily, to the non-programming aspects of the software development process, including the study of the software development life cycle, data processing management, systems analysis and design, and so on.

It's true that some software engineering texts address software construction as well (Wiener and Sincovec, 1984). However, the software industry faces an enormous number of critical problems, many of which have taken precedence over programming-related issues in traditional software engineering discussions. In any case, our discussion focuses on a number of fundamental programming issues, such as code generalizability, global versus local variables, dependencies among procedures, and so on.

Proper techniques for software construction are becoming increasingly important throughout the computing industry, partly due to a change in view regarding the long-term (economic) impact of poorly conceived software products. In the past, "good programming" all too often meant knowing how to take advantage of a particular computer's architecture. Today, most programmers are more concerned with writing source code that is readable, maintainable, and reusable—"trick" programming is passé.

In large part, this change in attitude is due to the availability of new languages, optimizing compilers, and powerful hardware. A programmer is free to write a loop such that readability, maintainability, and portability are maximized, because the compiler takes on the responsibility of, say, removing invariant expressions from the loop. Powerful hardware makes the use of more modern, CPU-taxing programming environments quite feasible, even on personal computers and workstations.

1.3 Topics of Interest in Software Construction

There is no shortage of significant developments in computing for those of us who construct software. First, we should acknowledge the importance of software engineering principles to the actual software construction process, even though these principles are not discussed here.

The major advances in recent years in computing hardware have significant ramifications for software professionals. Why hardware? Primarily, the availability of extremely powerful hardware configurations has made compute-intensive software more viable. In particular, reasonably priced hardware platforms are now available to support the advances in programming languages and programming techniques made over the past 20 or so years. For many applications, it's becoming less important to deliver a product in FORTRAN, or even C. Moreover, even when delivery in FORTRAN is necessary, we now have the technology to prototype software in an alternative language, using FORTRAN as an intermediate language in the translation process that produces a machine-executable product.

For the first time, software professionals can "take for granted" the availability of powerful hardware and thus focus directly on the importance of programming language design for, say, software maintenance, as opposed to being preoccupied with performance concerns. This freedom is welcomed; it's widely estimated that as much as 70 percent of the time devoted to a software product is spent performing some type of maintenance.

Moreover, some of the language issues that formerly were of interest only to computer scientists are now surfacing in the software used to deliver products for industrial applications. As evidence, consider the use of functional programming principles in LISP-based languages, commonly used to deliver so-called expert system applications. Hayes-Roth et al. (1983) covers early advances in this area.

Traditional, procedural programming languages have been blamed for some of the problems associated with the current software crisis. As a solution, some experts have advocated the use of declarative and/or logic-based languages, such as PROLOG (Maier and Warren, 1988). Declarative languages, for example, allow a programmer to specify *what to compute*, as opposed to *how to compute*. Proponents of the declarative approach believe that programming in this paradigm can be superior, because it allows you to focus on analyzing a problem in terms of its constraints—its unknown and known conditions—leaving procedural details to the language translator per se.

The third and final advance in software technology that we mention is object-oriented programming (OOP). Proponents of object-oriented programming believe that it provides the best mechanisms for building software systems at present, because object-oriented programming systems (OOPS) provide the best tools for promoting abstraction and derivation. A fundamental notion of object-oriented programming is that of factoring an application in terms of its critical data structures, or objects, and then bundling these objects with the mechanisms, or methods, that are required for their manipulation.

1.4 Reusable Software Modules

Reusability issues are on almost everyone's mind these days because the software crisis has come to a head—software maintenance costs are staggering. The software engineering discipline has proposed a number of important approaches to handling maintenance problems. Our focus here, as mentioned earlier, is on the software tools and technologies that enhance software reusability.

What is the link between reusability and object-oriented programming? Surface level complexity of the source code is one of the critical problems in software development and maintenance. That is, traditional languages and programming practices have encouraged program designs in which the critical data structures, or their components, are (1) defined globally, or (2) passed around from procedure to procedure—like a hot potato. The main problem with this type of design is that a change in the make-up of a data structure can send tidal waves throughout the program, often rendering the software useless. Object-oriented programming provides a powerful mechanism for hiding data structure details in self-contained modules—a mechanism for packaging data and related operations.

Of course, data-hiding principles are not new. With traditional languages such as C, it's possible to package data and related procedures. For example, a programmer can hide a data structure inside a function (as a static variable), forcing data to be accessed by way of a function call. We investigate the merits of this approach in later chapters.

C, in particular, makes it convenient to control the availability, or scope, of data at both the procedure and file level. With file-level scoping a programmer can, perhaps, make judicious use of global variables in a manner that promotes data abstraction and program maintenance. The use of global variables is, of course, much debated in computing circles. Object-oriented languages provide better mechanisms for controlling variables that are common to many procedures.

Encapsulation of data and procedures is just one benefit of object-oriented programming. Typically, object-oriented languages provide two additional facilities for enhancing software reusability. The second principal feature provided by object-oriented programming is hierarchical program structure, that is, inheritance. Using inheritance, a programmer can define a system of classes, or user-defined (data) types, wherein it is convenient to define subsequent classes in terms of their similarities to (and differences from) existing classes. In this manner, existing source code can be reused by deriving new classes (and defining class instantiations called objects) that accommodate changes in the application.

The third feature of object-oriented programming is dynamic binding. For a number of reasons, which we touch on in later chapters, it's convenient to have the capability of building software systems in which some aspects of the relationship between data and procedures are not resolved until run-time. For example, generalized procedures could be provided for, say, calculating employee wages, along with specific procedures that handle a number of special employee categories. Depending on employee type, the proper combination of procedures can be invoked at run-time to produce the desired payroll check.

This approach is quite different from traditional case analysis, which would require updates to (typically) a number of case structures to accommodate new employee types. An OOP environment makes it easy to derive a new employee data type from existing ones, supplementing existing procedures with a new procedure that accommodates wage calculation differences.

In some cases, this type of *programming by difference* can be accomplished completely at compile-time; however, at other times, it's convenient to use dynamic binding to override existing compile-time defaults. For example, a library could be built to provide default actions with respect to an employee database, but with provisions for substitution of alternative actions. In this manner, existing code can be reused, and perhaps more importantly, changes can be accommodated without modifying (and recompiling) the existing library.

1.5 Choose Your Language

The my-language-can-beat-your-language war wages on. Although a few individuals still argue for one "be all" language, most programmers recognize the importance of having a variety of languages/tools. Certainly, a significant portion of the software problems that presently exist in government and industry is the result of imposing one programming language on many different types of computing applications, in particular either COBOL or FORTRAN.

The fault lies not with these languages, for they have served the industry well, but with those who are reluctant to move on. Invariably, up-front software conversion costs are cited as the motivation for continuing with (for many applications) out-of-date languages. Overall, the current software crisis is uncomfortably reminiscent of past reluctances to modernize a number of heavy industries.

There is some tendency to view new developments in programming technology as just "more of the same," thereby justifying management's reluctance to modernize. That is, new languages come and go, so why switch to a new language only to see it succumb to yet another language? In our view, there is little justification for this argument, even with respect to the first wave of high-level languages to follow COBOL and FORTRAN, in particular ALGOL, Pascal, and PL/I.

These languages provided a number of significant enhancements to high-level programming that directly, or indirectly, promote structured programming. Although government regulations now mandate the use of structured programming in many programming environments, the amount of goto-based programming that still exists is quite unbelievable. Eliminating these problems will require the use of modern programming languages *and* modern programming techniques.

In our opinion, the abstraction facilities provided by newer traditional languages, such as Ada, C, and Modula-2, can be used to solve a number of problems that contribute to the ongoing software crisis. Moreover, for many applications, object-oriented languages such as C++ (Stroustrup, 1986), Flavors (Moon, 1986), and Smalltalk (Goldberg and Robson, 1983) can provide a substantially improved programming environment in comparison with traditional languages. While the data abstraction facilities provided in, say, C, are important, it's the combination of data abstraction, inheritance, and dynamic binding features that makes object-oriented programming technology more than an incremental improvement.

1.6 Object-oriented Programming—Here to Stay?

Object-oriented programming methodology is not new; Simula 67 (Dahl and Nygaard, 1966) is the most widely accepted progenitor of object-oriented programming. One magazine (*Byte*) devoted an issue to object-oriented programming in 1981, and again in

1986. C++ and Smalltalk, in one form or another, have been around since the early 1980s, and Objective-C™ (Cox, 1986) since the mid-1980s. There are newer object-oriented languages such as Eiffel™ (Meyer, 1988b) and C_talk™ (CNS, 1987), a hybrid programming environment based on C and Smalltalk.

In general, object-oriented languages tend to be somewhat more CPU-taxing than languages such as C or Modula-2—there is a great amount of variability in the run-time efficiency of object-oriented languages. Widespread acceptance of object-oriented programming has been delayed, due to these hardware demands. As mentioned, the recent availability of sufficiently powerful hardware platforms at quite reasonable prices removes any disincentives to object-oriented programming. In general, the advantages offered by object-oriented programming outweigh both compile- and run-time performance considerations. Moreover, some object-oriented languages, for example, C++, are quite efficient, even with their provisions for run-time binding of objects and procedures.

The staying power of object-oriented programming can also be gauged by looking at currently available systems. Smalltalk is in widespread use in many university and industrial research laboratories, as is Flavors, a LISP-based programming language cited above. Also, C++ is widely used within AT&T (where it originated) and elsewhere; it's beginning to replace C as a systems programming language in microcomputer and workstation software development environments.

In addition to these OOP languages, object-based windowing environments are under development. There is little question that object-oriented programming and OOPS environments are here to stay.

2

Practical Considerations in Software Construction

In this chapter we address several topics that arise in day-to-day programming. Our discussion serves primarily as an overview and motivation for subsequent chapters.

This book deals with practical programming fundamentals as they relate to software reusability. Biggerstaff and Perlis (1989) provide a more theoretical discussion of reusability. We are concerned with a range of basic issues, such as the advantages/disadvantages of global variables, the overuse of local variables (as opposed to the use of a more functional programming style), and modular decomposition. In addition, however, we're concerned with topics such as surface-level complexity of a program, techniques for information hiding, and code generalizability.

2.1 External and Internal Factors

A number of factors must be considered in developing any software product; however, it's convenient to evaluate software according to two broad categories: external and internal. In the simplest sense, *external factors* are those software characteristics that directly impact the user, that is, the extent to which the software is easy to use, easy to maintain, compatible with other products, and so on. Professional programmers have responsibilities to both users and employers with respect to such external factors.

However, beyond the user's immediate concern for obtaining "good" software, there is the programmer's concern for producing software from source code that is readable, maintainable, extensible, portable, and reusable. These concerns are somewhat distinct from a number of other program characteristics such as modularity, complexity of a function's interface, code generalizability, and so on. Certainly the latter, more tangible, issues contribute to what are collectively called *internal factors*—the user simply can't tell if the internal design of an editor makes good use of modular programming principles.

Meyer (1988b) classifies portability and reusability (among others) as external factors. We prefer to think of these rather hard-to-nail-down factors as lying somewhere between the two broad classifications. Consider product upgrades. If a software developer can't deliver error-free upgrades on a timely basis, the user may recognize that a problem exists; in this sense, the former criteria are external factors.

On the other hand, it's not uncommon for a developer to "come through at the last moment" with upgrades and enhancements, even though a number of problems exist internally that may not be perceptible to the user. In this case, the impact of source code readability, portability, and the other criteria is limited primarily to the development effort—loss of profits, plus grief and despair among programmers. Regardless of how we classify these factors, they are important to the development of reusable software modules.

2.2 Surface Complexity of a Program

The term *module* has a variety of meanings in computer science. Sometimes *module* is used as a synonym for procedure, or function. On occasion, we need to refer to a collection of functions and data, manipulated as a unit. With C, it's convenient to divide a program into collections of related functions and data structures; each such collection is stored in a file and can be compiled separately, hence the term *compiled module*. We depend on context to distinguish different types of "modules," although we're mostly concerned with the latter type of module.

We use the term *surface complexity* to characterize how easy or difficult it is to understand the relationships among the modules that make up a program. Cox (1986) discusses several issues that contribute to the surface area of a program, concluding that large "surface area is bad." He suggests that the surface area of a program can be reduced by using information-hiding techniques and abstract data types.

We're using the term surface complexity to emphasize that there are other issues besides size that contribute to the readability, or lack of readability, of a program. Sometimes, as program size increases at a linear rate, understandability of the program decreases at a geometric rate! Clearly, if this happens, there is a major problem with the program design. If all programs had this characteristic, we would never be able to develop significant software products, or maintain them once developed.

Designing a good interface for each function in the program can go a long way toward reducing the overall complexity of a software product. Typically, functions must communicate with other functions. Communication between functions, in particular the passage of data to another function, can take place in two ways:

- by passing arguments to the called function
- by storing data at some "external" location before the call

Likewise, most languages provide multiple ways for "returning" the result of a function's computations to the calling function:

- by using a **return** statement
- via an argument (if call by address is supported)
- by storing data at some "external" location before the return

Most experts agree that passing information to the called function as an argument and passing information back to the calling function as a returned value are the preferred methods of inter-function communication. In general, even if the language supports call by address, passing a local variable to a called function, so that the latter can store its result there, adds to the complexity of the program. Greater readability can be achieved by having each function return its result and by using the returned value directly in an expression, as opposed to allocating local variables to hold intermediate results.

2.3 External/Global Variables

The use of a data structure external to the two cooperating functions for passing information is one example of *programming by side-effect*. That is, as a side-effect of performing some computation, a function may store its result in an external variable so that it is subsequently available to other functions. We refer to this type of common storage location as a *external*, or *global*, variable. In some cases, the use of externals may be necessary; typically, anything other than very limited use of external variables is poor programming.

It's not uncommon for computer science instructors to deplore the use of external variables, and lower a student's grade severely if he or she uses them. However, once you've made your escape from the educational environment, it's easy to develop bad habits.

There are a number of reasons for avoiding the use of external variables. Perhaps, the foremost reason is the increased likelihood of introducing bugs into a program during modification, if external variables are used to communicate between functions. That is, a programmer may have accounted for all possible side-effects (modifications) to the variable **x** during initial software development, but may inadvertently overlook one of these function-variable relationships at a later date in attempting to extend the software. In this sense, externals can severely restrict the readability, maintainability, and extensibility of software; see Figure 2.1. Visually speaking, using an external to communicate between functions introduces an agent, operating at a remote location, whose activity is hard to track from page to page in the source code.

Another problem with externals that we mention elsewhere is their impact on generalizability of the source code. If, for example, in developing an editor, an external variable is used to record the current location of the cursor in the edit buffer, it becomes difficult to generalize the edit module to a situation where multiple edit buffers must be managed.

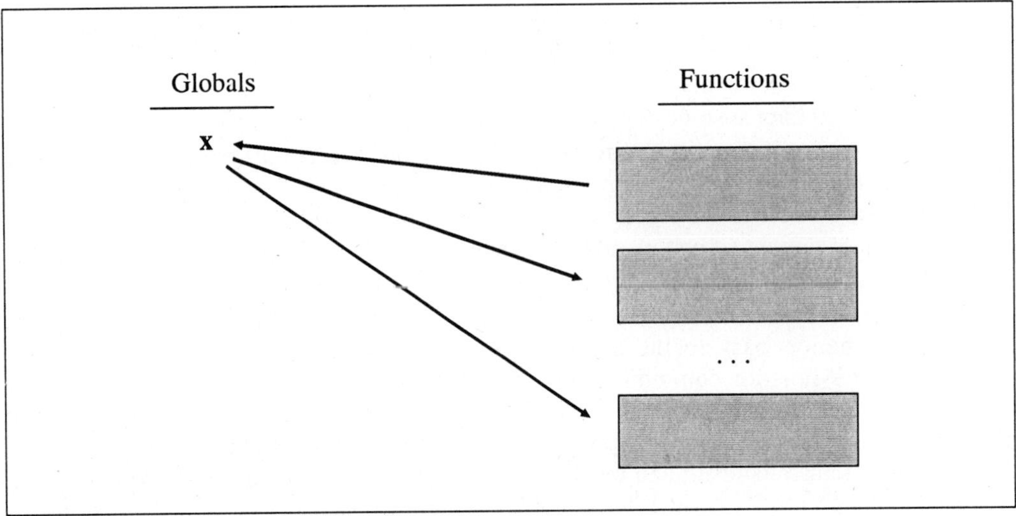

Figure 2.1 Remote Operations on a Global Variable

2.4 Private/Local Variables

We use the phrase *proliferation of local variables* to refer to the practice of overusing locals when the same computational result could be achieved by the proper combination of function calls. In fact, a number of languages do not provide call-by-address parameter passing, in order to encourage the proper use of functions and return values.

There are instances in which local variables are necessary, of course, for example, developing a program that requires composite variables. Many languages support the return of scalar values by functions, but not composite (aggregate) values, such as strings or arrays. In this case, returning information via the argument/parameter list may be essential—but only if the result is a composite value. Typically, two local variables must be managed: (1) a local must be established in the calling function to provide a communication channel between functions, and (2) a parameter must be established in the called function to reference the local variable being passed as an argument by the calling function.

With C, for example, a function that converts each element of a null-terminated character array named **temp** to uppercase could be used as follows:

```
...
char *temp = "abc123ABC";    /* a local variable */
...
str_upper(temp);     /* temp will be modified (call-by-address) */
...
```

where **str_upper()** is defined as:

```
void str_upper(char str[])
{
    int i;

    for (i = 0; str[i]; i++)
        str[i] = toupper(str[i]);
}
```

This is not the normal way to write a C function for converting a string to uppercase; however, it provides a simple demonstration of the legitimate use of local variables in dealing with arrays. (Note that if we're willing to work at a lower level, namely with pointers, we can drop the local variable in **str_upper()** and just increment a pointer:

```
void str_upper(char *str)
{
    while (*str = toupper(*str++))
        ;
}
```

Most C programmers would prefer some variation of the latter.)

In looking at a function that you've written, if there are numerous local variables and/or a number of different things going on in the function, it's likely that readability can be enhanced by breaking the function into several functions with meaningful names, each having a minimum number of local variables. For the editor project that we develop beginning with the next chapter, the average number of local variables per function is less than 1.3, not counting parameters. Of course, reducing the number of local variables by moving them to external locations is an inferior solution! Our editor project averages less than one external variable per compiled module.

2.5 Legitimate Uses of External Variables

There are other circumstances in which some programmers feel that external variables are warranted. If, for example, a number of different routines must share a common data structure, there is some merit to defining/declaring the data structure as **extern**, C's official name for an external variable. With C, the lexical scope of an external variable is the entire source code file in which it is defined. (If an external variable's scope is to be extended to other source files, external declarations for the external variable are required in those modules as well.)

Isn't this the same situation we discussed earlier, namely, inter-function communication by using external variables? The difference is a matter of degree. Setting up an external variable, simply to pass information between two functions, is a frivolous use of externals, especially considering that argument/parameter lists are provided for this purpose.

The complexity of the data structure may have a bearing on whether or not an external is warranted. If, for example, 20 or 30 functions are set up to process a complex, aggregate structure such as a window, the use of an external definition for the window may be warranted. In particular, if, in order to avoid an external, you must pass a data structure by address on numerous occasions, you may be better off with a well-documented external variable, from the standpoint of readability and maintainability. For example:

```
window_frame window[5];      /* external array of windows */
...
...
main()
{
    ...
    window_activate(1,...); /* activate the second window */
    ...
}
```

Programmers sometimes use external variables for inter-file communication. If, for example, a set of window management routines is developed and maintained as a stand-alone compiled module, many C programmers would *declare* the window data structure as an external data structure. (See the next chapter, if you aren't clear as to the difference between a definition and a declaration.) In this manner, the window routines can be tested, compiled, and stored in a library without regard for a particular application.

This approach allows any application that uses the window data structure and its related procedures to *define* a window as it sees fit. For example, one application may require a single window, whereas another may require multiple windows, say, an array of windows. Done properly, this approach can greatly enhance the extensibility and reusability of a function library. We use this approach with the C version of our editor.

2.6 Using Static Local Variables for Information Hiding

Although we've cautioned against the proliferation of local variables in a function, sometimes it's quite useful to surround a data structure with a procedural interface. Consider the situation we alluded to earlier in which it's necessary to keep track of the cursor position in an edit buffer. We could design the routines around an external variable called **buffer_cursor_position**. However, what if we later decide to generalize our editor routines to accommodate multiple edit buffers?

This particular use of externals works against extensibility and reusability, since all functions that reference the external variable would have to be modified. Moreover, consider *how* these functions would have to be modified. In order to generalize them to process multiple edit buffers, either (1) a parameter must be added to each function that is affected, or (2) another external variable must be added to represent the current (active) edit buffer. The first alternative requires numerous modifications of functions, due to ripple effects in function calls. The second alternative requires considerable program modification *and* can result in difficult-to-maintain source code.

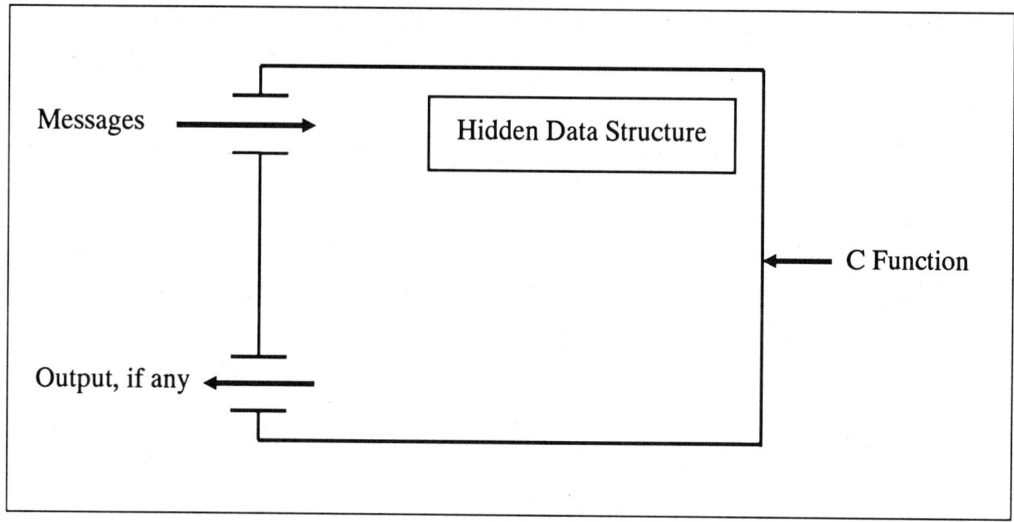

Figure 2.2 Using a Function for Information Hiding

Sometimes a better alternative is to hide a critical data structure, such as a buffer-position variable, inside a function definition. In this case, all access to the data structure must occur by way of a function call, as depicted in Figure 2.2. Some programmers balk at this suggestion, due to the overhead of adding an additional function with a local variable, where in some cases a single external variable would suffice. However, in many situations the ability to generalize the source code more than compensates for the function overhead. Moreover, function overhead for languages such as C is quite minimal.

With this approach, information hiding can be promoted by restricting the programmer to high-level communication with critical variables. For example, consider the function **buf_cursor_pos()** that performs the operation we've been discussing, namely, management of the cursor position in an edit buffer:

```
int buf_cursor_pos(int message)
{
    static int buffer_cursor_position;

    if (message == TEST)
        return buffer_cursor_position;
    else if (message == INCR)
        return ++buffer_cursor_position;
    else if (message == DECR)
        return --buffer_cursor_position;
    else
```

```
        return (buffer_cursor_position = message);
}
```

Here, an integer message that doesn't match the first three cases is interpreted as a request to update **buffer_cursor_position** to an arbitrary buffer offset. (This version assumes that error checking is done elsewhere.) Defining **buffer_cursor_position** as a **static** variable ensures that its value will persist from one function invocation to the next.

This type of information hiding helps to localize the impact of changes to a data structure. Also, in terms of code generalizability, it may be prudent to define an array of cursor positions and pass an additional value that represents the cursor of interest.

There are other reasons for adopting this approach instead of using an external variable, for example, initiating associated operations. Suppose for the editor example that we would like to update an on-screen indicator of buffer offset, for every user operation that results in cursor movement. In this case, the operations that perform the screen update should be initiated from within **buf_cursor_pos()**. In particular, this eliminates the potential for inconsistency in these two cursor values, the actual position and the on-screen offset indicator—one update occurs automatically as a function of the other.

2.7 Competing Strategies for Module Design

Meyer (1988b) provides a somewhat formal, but quite readable, discussion of software construction principles. Our discussion has been considerably shorter, allowing us to get started with our project as soon as possible. However, before doing so in Chapter 3, we should make the point that a number of the basic principles of software construction tend to compete (actually conflict) with each other.

In general, a function is easier to understand if the number of other functions that it communicates with is small. This statement is just common sense, of course. Obviously, a function that prints the message "Hello, world." is easier to understand than one that coordinates the operation of a system of windows.

It's important to recognize that *procedural abstraction* plays a role in this issue. The principle of procedural abstraction states that each individual function should be designed so that it hides the nitty-gritty details of performing its task. In this manner, when other functions call upon a function to perform its specialty, the function call appears quite intuitive. In our case, if an editor is designed such that it uses one function to dispatch keystroke commands to the respective editor functions, then the dispatcher should be quite straightforward and easy to follow, regardless of the number of calls to editor functions (the number of legal editor tasks).

Another design principle states that functions should interchange as little information as possible, that is, the number of parameters in each function should be minimized. Often, this principle competes directly with the principle that external variables should be minimized. In fact, we can often reduce the number of parameters to zero, if we add enough external and local variables. As is often the case, the surface complexity of our program should be considered in determining inter-function communication. Object-oriented languages provide an important mechanism for reducing the size of parameter lists, as we'll see in the second half of this book.

Generally speaking, if a lot of parameters are being passed, you should consider reorganization. Two disadvantages of a large interface between procedures are (1) increased surface complexity, and (2) potential ripple effects during program modification. Sometimes, a variable that is being passed around from function to function can be relocated to reduce information flow. In some cases, it may be useful to manage this information in a separate function using a static local data structure, as outlined above.

Another fundamental design rule is that relationships (interfaces) among functions should be explicit. Breaking out information that is shared among functions and managing it with a separate function may at first seem to conflict with this principle. However, this type of factoring of functions and data can provide quite *explicit* relationships, as opposed to setting up external variables. In general, it is easier to understand, in isolation, the intended usage of data that's held within a small function than to understand the usage of an external variable. Hiding a critical program variable in a function helps the reader understand the limits on how that variable can be used. If a critical variable is defined as an external, its usage can be understood only after searching out every reference to it in the program.

There are no definitive rules, of course, when it comes to program design and resolving these apparent conflicts. For the time being, programmers are responsible for a number of important program design decisions that can't be dictated by analysts from an external setting.

2.8 Designing Compiled Software Modules with C

One of the reasons that C is so popular is the flexibility that it provides. An abundance of low-level, high-level, and syntactically powerful operators makes C suitable for a wide range of applications. It is particularly well suited for an editor project because of the mixture of high-level and fairly low-level programming activities.

C's most important feature for developing reusable software modules is its support of file-level lexical scope for external variables. With C, a variable may be defined (or declared) as an external variable at the file level; it is then available to all the functions defined in that file (compiled module).

For many long-term massive software projects it is desirable to control access to a compiled module strictly. That is, once a module is developed and deemed bug-free, it should be closed, in order to prevent tinkering or proliferation of numerous versions of the module. Depending on the nature of the module, there are a number of possibilities with respect to the compiled module interface.

Suppose that you must develop a self-contained screen-handling module for a hardware (and operating system) environment where it's necessary to manipulate the screen buffer directly. In skeleton form, your design could appear as follows:

```
/****  screen.c  ****  screen handling routines  ****/


/* #includes and #defines go here */


/* function prototypes go here */


char *screen;                 /* pointer to video RAM */


int video_initialize(void)
{
    ...
    screen = /* set it to the proper starting address */
    ...
}


/* related functions go here */
```

screen, a pointer to the beginning of video memory (the screen buffer), is defined as an external variable. That is, because it is defined external to the module's functions, its lexical scope is the entire file. Hence, any function defined in *screen.c* can reference **screen**. In our example, **video_initialize()** has the responsibility of assigning the proper value to **screen**.

The previous definition of **screen** permits public access. That is, functions in another module can reference **screen** as well, if that module provides a declaration. For example, in

```
extern char *screen;
```

extern simply tells the compiler that **screen** is allocated storage and given a value elsewhere—**screen** is a *public* variable.

In some cases, it may be necessary to limit the level of access to an external variable such as **screen**. With C, adding the **static** modifier to an external definition makes that variable private. That is, if we replace the original definition above with

```
static char *screen;         /* pointer to video RAM */
```

only those functions defined in *screen.c* can reference **screen.**

The former definition can be quite dangerous; the latter definition is quite restrictive. In general, if you allow other modules to modify a variable whose value is critical to the operation of the functions in its "home" module, then you simply can't guarantee the performance of that module. At best, this level of openness can only be justified in special circumstances.

If a private definition is too restrictive, one alternative is to provide read-only access. With C, the most straightforward way to allow other modules to use a value in a "closed" module, while protecting its integrity, is with an access function. For example, suppose a module defines a commonly used variable as private:

```
static int video_mode;
```

In this case, an access function can be used to provide read-only access to **video_mode**:

```
int get_video_mode()
{
    return video_mode;
}
```

get_video_mode() provides access to the value stored in **video_mode**, but provides no syntactic mechanism for disturbing that value.

Although this approach breaks down somewhat with functions that return pointers, it's still useful for protecting data against accidental modification. For our video memory example, the following function could be added to *screen.c*:

```
char *get_screen_addr()
{
    return screen;
}
```

Since function definitions are external by default, **screen**'s value will be available to any function in any module that's linked with the screen-handling module, even if **screen** is a private variable.

The main point is that with C a programmer has a number of choices. If, for example, speed is critically important in an application, a public definition may be justified; otherwise, you can opt for the higher level of protection afforded by either of the latter two alternatives. In any event, these facilities are important in developing reusable software modules because they give the programmer considerable flexibility in deciding how open or closed a compiled module should be. C++, with its constant specifier, **const**, provides additional control over modification to variable values.

3

MS-DOS, IBM PC, and C Language Fundamentals

In the chapters that follow we'll be developing a window-based editor. Developing an editor is fundamentally different from developing, say, an engineering application program, for which portability, or some other issue, would be the most important consideration.

We begin this chapter with a discussion of several MS-DOS and IBM-compatible PC topics that are important in developing traditional PC software. Later, we mention several aspects of the C language, and our particular style of programming, that are important for medium- and large-scale projects.

3.1 Background and Motivation

An editor must be reasonably efficient. For this reason, portability must take a back seat to a number of other issues, including performance and window design. Users, especially IBM-compatible PC users, have become accustomed to a type of on-screen display of information that's vastly different from what was available several years ago. In order to provide this type of user interface, the programmer must take advantage of several features of the PC's architecture. Thus, even though C itself is quite portable across hardware platforms, our application requires a number of non-portable routines.

We should note that a similar situation has existed with UNIX-based, graphics workstations. Namely, windowing systems, and the applications developed with them, are typically not portable across different manufacturers' hardware platforms. Currently, there is a cooperative effort among many manufacturers to provide a common user interface, and common user-interface toolkits for programmers. However, it remains to be seen whether or not portable code, designed to operate across different hardware platforms, will be efficient enough to satisfy users. That is, will there be a significant performance penalty due to "lowest common denominator" programming?

There are several ways to handle the problems associated with introducing non-portable code into a reasonably large software product. We would like, of course, to design our editor such that a substantial amount of the source code is usable elsewhere, say, in developing a UNIX editor for a workstation. If, however, we were to take an extreme position with respect to code generalizability, we could end up with an editor unfit for any environment. On the other hand, we don't want to make unwarranted use of MS-DOS, IBM PC, or a specific C compiler's features. And from a tutorial perspective, there are some steps that we could take to enhance generalizability that would obscure our intent in this book.

For our editor we adopt a design position somewhere between the two extremes. The machine-dependent routines can be isolated in separate compiled modules. Moreover, most of these routines can be written using system call facilities that are common to most MS-DOS C compilers, as opposed to using a particular compiler's library enhancements. In fact, the source code given in Appendix A has been compiled and tested with Microsoft® C (Microsoft, 1988), Turbo C® (Borland, 1988), and Zortech C (Zortech, 1989). (Compiler-specific topics are discussed in Appendix A.) Turbo C, for example, provides a library function called **bioskey()** for performing keyboard operations. Microsoft C and Zortech C provide similar functions. However, we can easily avoid compiler-specific source code by writing our own routines with the proper system calls, using the **int86()** facility provided with most MS-DOS C compilers.

There are two basic activities in our editor that require non-portable system calls: keyboard processing and screen management. Both of these activities are handled in separate compiled modules. There are a number of file-related activities, such as checking the remaining disk space before attempting to save a file, that you might like to add to the editor. Again, these activities can be performed with compiler-specific library functions, or you can write your own using the **int86()** system call. Within reason, we attempt to maximize portability and reusability in each compiled module that comprises the editor.

3.2 MS-DOS Basics

DOS is partitioned into two components: low-level and high-level. The low-level, or basic, component is responsible for hardware-dependent, operating system activities. This component is commonly called the BIOS, or *basic input/output system*. Much of the BIOS is implemented in ROM (read-only memory), hence, the term *ROM-BIOS*. Storing these routines on a chip enhances the overall efficiency of the operating system; however, there must be some mechanism for incorporating modifications to DOS, even for low-level routines. DOS is designed so that extensions and/or modifications of the ROM-BIOS routines are automatically loaded during DOS start-up operations from a hidden file, called *ibmbio.com* for IBM PCs, on the start-up, or boot, disk.

The high-level component of DOS is sometimes called the BDOS, or *basic disk operating system*. A more technically appropriate term for this component is the *DOS kernel*. The kernel is loaded into memory during DOS start-up operations from a hidden file, called *ibmdos.com* for IBM PCs.

3.3 Keyboard Operations

For older, terminal-based microcomputers, keyboard processing was performed by the central processor with minimal assistance from the terminal itself. For this type of machine, keyboard programming is quite straightforward—to read a character, the programmer simply calls a built-in language primitive, such as C's **getchar()**.

Modern architectures, however, endow the various peripheral devices with more local autonomy; the current trend is to provide each peripheral with its own processor/controller. IBM-compatible PC keyboards are equipped with a specialized processor that supports a number of sophisticated operations. Our editor software doesn't require low-level keyboard programming. We are, however, interested in taking advantage of the numerous keystroke combinations provided with the function keys and the **<Alt>** key. Specifically, we can use a key combination such as **<Alt>-S** to represent an editor command, in this case, the command to save the contents of the edit buffer to disk.

For the older machines with simple keyboards, each keystroke mapped directly to an ASCII character; for example, **<Shift>-A** represented an uppercase "a" and the **A** key represented a lowercase "a". The advantage of this approach is its simplicity; keyboard communication can be handled by a dumb terminal. With the introduction of the function keys and the **<Alt>** key, there are too many possibilities to associate each keystroke combination directly with a character from the ASCII character set.

Consequently, modern keyboards provide a special controller that handles keystroke operations. The process of interpreting each keystroke and delivering the proper information to the keyboard buffer is handled jointly by the keyboard controller and low-level DOS (ROM-BIOS) routines. We are interested in this topic only to the extent that we must extract keystrokes from the keyboard buffer. (Keyboard operations are described in detail in numerous IBM PC-related books.)

The encoding scheme is quite simple. For each keystroke, a two-byte sequence is generated. The first byte indicates whether or not the user has pressed an ASCII key, that is, a key that represents an ASCII character—a Boolean condition. If the depressed key represents an ASCII character, then that byte contains the corresponding ASCII value; otherwise, that byte contains zero. In the latter case, a non-ASCII key, the second byte can be examined to determine the (physical) keyboard code for the depressed key—called the *scan code*. In other words, the second byte is primarily useful for key identification for non-ASCII keys.

We can provide a simple union in a header file for representing keystrokes:

```
union keystroke {                          /* represents a key's    */
    unsigned char byte[2];                 /* data and scan code    */
    int word;
};
```

A union is useful because it allows us to get at the bytes individually during keystroke interpretation, and it provides a convenient mechanism for manipulating keystrokes as a unit, for example, returning a keystroke from a function.

Why not just use C's built-in function **getchar()** to read a keystroke, avoiding these low-level details? The main reason is that we want our editor to take charge of keyboard interpretation directly, instead of requesting keyboard services through normal operating system (OS) function calls. Under some conditions, MS-DOS will terminate an executing program, if the user presses **<Ctrl>-C** or **<Ctrl>-<Break>**. In our case, we don't want the editor to be terminated with unsaved changes, just because the user entered one of these keystrokes by accident! By developing our own keyboard module, we can enhance our ability to build software from reusable modules.

3.4 Screen Management

If we use C's built-in function for character output, namely, **putchar()**, a character can be routed to the standard output device, normally, the monitor. In this case, the screen serves as a sequential output device. The screen management requirements for a full-screen, window-based editor can't be satisfied using the standard output facilities. We must be able to direct the cursor to random screen locations, in order to display individual characters as the user makes editing changes to the text. Also, we must be able to display pop-up windows at arbitrary locations on the screen.

Each IBM-compatible PC has a dedicated bank of video memory, sometimes called video RAM (random-access memory); this block of memory stores the image that appears on the screen. (We prefer *not* to use the term *screen buffer* for video RAM. This terminology leads to confusion between RAM that's dedicated to video operations by the system and RAM that's dedicated to video operations by our programs, for example, a screen buffer that's used to maintain the DOS-level screen image that exists prior to the start of an application.)

The video hardware is responsible for displaying the contents of video RAM on the monitor screen. Screen updates occur many times per second; consequently, software can modify the screen simply by modifying the contents of video RAM. Alternatively, MS-DOS provides several low-level, screen management routines that can be used to manipulate video memory. However, working through these OS primitives is simply to inefficient for software having a window-based user interface; hence, we must manipulate video RAM directly.

The practice of assigning a value to a cell in video memory in order to produce output on the screen is sometimes called *writing directly to the screen.* For some applications, accessing video RAM directly is unnecessary and should be avoided—since this practice isn't portable to different architectures. However, virtually all IBM-compatible PC software that employs pop-up windows and/or pull-down menus uses direct video write operations. PC users have become accustomed to the snappy user interfaces that result from direct video write operations.

The process of writing directly to the screen is quite straightforward. Computer memory is addressed as a simple, linear data structure—a one-dimensional array in which each element is a byte. Video memory is unique only in terms of how the hardware interprets its contents. Specifically, each character that appears on the screen corresponds to two bytes of video memory—that is, a character is produced from two one-byte array elements. The first byte represents the character that appears on the screen; the second byte encodes its attributes, for example, foreground color, background color, steady or blinking display, and so on. Thus, in order to display a character on-screen, a program must (1) calculate the proper offset in the array, (2) copy (assign) the character to the proper address, and (3) copy the attribute setting to the next higher memory address.

Calculating the offset is simple. On-screen characters are represented in video memory in row-major order; that is, rows are stored end to end in memory. To calculate a character position in video memory, we can use the standard array roll-out formula used by high-level language compilers to store two-dimensional arrays. Using *zero-based array indexing* the formula is

```
character_offset = row_position * 160 + column_position * 2
```

That is, since there are 80 characters per row on a normal screen and two array elements per on-screen character, in order to get to the second row, 160 array elements must be skipped. For any row, the column of interest is determined by adding the on-screen column position, multiplied by 2, to the row offset. Thus, the array position corresponding to the third row and fifth column on-screen, that is, row position 2 and column position 4 (both zero-based), is

$$2 * 160 + 4 * 2 = 320 + 8 = 328$$

The following macro is taken from one of our editor modules:

```
#define char_addr(base, r, c) ((base) + ((r) * 160) + ((c) * 2))
```

Here, **r** is the row coordinate and **c** is the column coordinate. (We prefer to think of the screen as a two-dimensional array, indexed by these two variables, as opposed to using Cartesian coordinates with (0,0) located at one corner.) **base** is the starting address of video RAM, returned by the function **get_screen_addr()**, which we mentioned in the previous chapter. Extensive coverage of these issues can be found in books such as Duncan (1988). We discuss the screen-handling module in complete detail in a subsequent chapter.

We've outlined the process for determining a character's position; let's consider the attribute byte that accompanies each character. In text mode, an IBM PC has fairly limited, but normally sufficient, character/text representation. Each character that's displayed on the screen has several attributes:

- foreground color
- background color
- foreground intensity (low or high)
- foreground blinking (on or off)
- underlining (on or off, monochrome monitors only)

For the editor, we need to manipulate foreground and background color, in order to provide normal video for text (light characters on a dark background) and reverse video for certain window borders (dark characters on a light background).

The following function shows the traditional technique used by programmers to display a character:

```
void display_char(int row, int col, char ch, int attr)
{
    char far *scrn_ptr;

    scrn_ptr = get_screen_addr();
    scrn_ptr = char_addr(scrn_ptr, row, col);
    *scrn_ptr++ = ch;
    *scrn_ptr = attr;
}   /* display_char */
```

First, a local pointer variable is set to the base address of video RAM using **get_screen_addr()**, as described earlier. Next, its value is updated to the proper offset using the previously mentioned macro. Third, the character in **ch** is stored in the array at the position indicated by the pointer variable. Also, the increment operator (++) is applied to increment the pointer to the address of the attribute byte. Lastly, the attribute is stored in the array. (The attribute is a simple integer value, for example, 7 stands for normal video.)

3.5 Memory Models

The most annoying aspect of working with IBM-compatible PCs has to be the complications introduced by the use of segmented memory without operating system support for a linear address space. Fortunately, the combination of segmented architecture and real mode addressing has minimal impact on our editor application. (Compiler designers aren't so fortunate.)

In essence, computers with segmented memory are designed such that (logically) main memory is composed of banks, or segments, of memory, as opposed to being designed as one linear address space. That is, memory is a system of small arrays, not a single, large one-dimensional array. Thus, a memory address has two components: a segment (bank) and an offset.

A robust operating system hides these details from the programmer by presenting memory as a single, linear address space. DOS, however, isn't sophisticated enough to tackle this chore. As a consequence, most high-level language compilers for DOS provide some assistance in this area. For example, we can usually define a variable **x** local to some function without worrying about how the compiler generates an address for it.

Complications arise, however, if a variable spans more than one segment, for example, an array of characters. In this case, the segment and offset values may not be incremented properly while iterating over the array, having implications for expressions that perform address comparisons (or address arithmetic) with pointer variables; see Figure 3.1. (Pointer variables contain addresses—either a segment-offset combination or just an offset.)

As an example, suppose that an editor routine(s) is provided to allow the user to perform basic search-and-replace operations. If a search is performed and the user-specified text string is located, the cursor must be advanced to that position. How do we calculate the new cursor location—the buffer offset?

An edit buffer can be represented as an array of characters in C. Typically, a C programmer uses pointer variables to manipulate an array. For example, many of the functions in the C string processing library return addresses, not an offset into the string:

```
char *strstr(const char *search_string, const char *search_text)
{
    ...
};
```

Thus, if the beginning address for the edit buffer is held in one pointer variable and the address of the "found" text is held in another pointer variable, the difference between them should be the offset—the new location for the cursor. For example:

```
    ...
    char *edit_buf_addr, *search_text_addr;
    long offset;
    ...
    ...
    offset = strstr(edit_buf_addr, search_text_addr) - edit_buf_addr;
    ...
```

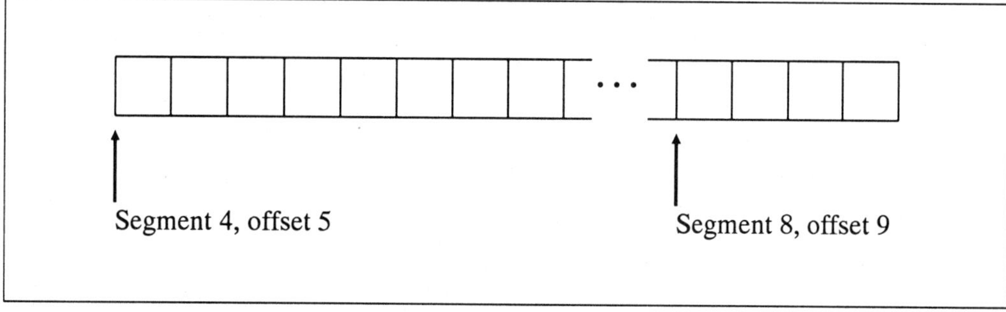

Figure 3.1 An Array That Spans Logical Segments

Pointer arithmetic (in this case pointer subtraction) may not work, however, due to the segment-offset combination. In part, the success of this type of pointer calculation depends on the OS, the C compiler, and the memory model used to compile the program. (The next section discusses pointer arithmetic.)

These issues are particularly significant in developing an editor, because the amount of data, chiefly the edit buffer(s), may be large. If all the data for a program can be managed in one segment, address calculations are simple. In particular, the segment number is immaterial and the compiler can build a program that uses segment offsets only. In this case, pointer arithmetic and pointer comparisons work as expected.

For MS-DOS C compilers, a program built with the assumption that all data will fit into one data segment (during execution) is said to use *a* small memory model. In particular, the compiler generates code that uses 16-bit (data) pointers—large enough for the offset only, since all data is stored in one segment. A 16-bit pointer is also called a *near* pointer. By default, most MS-DOS C compilers use *the* small memory model during code generation. Other models for code generation include the tiny, medium, compact, large, and huge models.

The various memory models differ with respect to whether or not the executable (program) code and/or the data will fit into one segment. The tiny model packs everything into one segment. The small model uses one segment for program code and one segment for data. With the compact model, the program code must fit in one memory segment (the code segment), while data may span multiple segments. The compact model, for example, is ideal for an editor with multiple edit buffers, that is, its data storage requirements are large relative to its program storage requirements. The terminology is a little confusing; any model based on the small data assumption is called *a small memory model*. For example, both *the* small memory model and *the* medium memory model are small memory models.

We can now explain the **far** keyword, which accompanies MS-DOS C compilers. Pointers come in two sizes: 16- and 32-bit; far pointers are 32-bit pointers. They are necessary any time that near pointers are too small. In general, a calculator, or any other small program, could be implemented with the small memory model. If, however, the calculator must reference video memory (our earlier variable **screen**), the **far** keyword can be used to force the compiler to use a 32-bit pointer (for that particular variable). A far pointer to video memory is always necessary because video memory is physically located at a high (large) memory address.

3.6 Pointer Arithmetic

There are two issues related to memory models that should concern us in developing an editor: (1) compiler reliability, and (2) address/pointer arithmetic.

Most compilers provide a memory model option for compiling programs using a particular memory model. Just because a particular compiler provides for compilation with multiple memory models doesn't mean that the generated code will work properly. Typically, you won't have any problems with the small memory model, since all pointers consist of address offsets only. You may encounter problems with the other models (where 32-bit pointers are involved), depending on (1) the compiler you've chosen, and (2) how you use pointers.

In the previous section we alluded to the problems that can occur in using pointer arithmetic to calculate buffer offsets. If, for example, you compile your program with a model that uses far data pointers (by default), you must be careful with statements such as:

```
...
char *buffer_start, *current_buffer_ptr;
long offset;
...
offset = current_buffer_ptr - buffer_start;

...
```

Here, the starting address of an edit buffer is held in **buffer_start** and another pointer variable holds a memory address that is important to editor operations, say, the location of a tag, sometimes called a bookmark, or just a mark.

In theory, the integer offset of the tag in the edit buffer can be calculated by pointer subtraction. However, for machines with segmented memory the result may be incorrect if 32-bit pointers are used. Consider the following (hexadecimal) values:

```
buffer_start == 2000:0130
current_buffer_ptr == 2013:000A
```

Memory addresses are represented in the composite form *segment:offset*; in particular, memory addresses are not interpreted as a single, 32-bit integer.

Pointer arithmetic is applied to the offset only. For example,

```
0000:FFFF + 1 -> 0000:0000
500B:0000 - 1 -> 500B:FFFF
```

(See a PC assembly language book for a complete discussion of address arithmetic.) Thus, even though buffer management doesn't involve low-level address calculations, the PC's segmented architecture has ramifications for how MS-DOS compilers handle pointer arithmetic, and how programmers must use pointer variables.

The *segment:offset* address is based on a logical memory addressing scheme—there is no absolute/physical segment number 500B. Hence, a particular memory location can be represented by multiple *segment:address* combinations. For example, A000:0340, A030:0040, and A034:0000 all correspond to the same physical location in memory. Hence, pointer arithmetic problems can be avoided in many cases by shifting as much as possible of the offset value into the segment half of the address; this process is called *pointer normalization*. Some C compilers provide library functions for normalizing pointers; others provide automatic normalization with certain memory models. Thus, for many medium- or large-scale programming projects you must "know your compiler." (Note that pointer normalization can slow some applications to a crawl.)

Sometimes programmers create memory model problems for themselves unnecessarily; in fact, it's quite easy to do so with our editor project. However, for our editor, we'll demonstrate how to avoid potential pointer arithmetic problems without resorting to manual pointer normalization or to memory models with automatic normalization. Taking this approach, where possible, enhances source code portability and program efficiency.

We should note that, typically, pointer normalization is not required in manipulating the contents of video memory, since display adapters have fixed, normalized addresses. For example, the starting address of video memory for a monochrome monitor is B0000000 (hexadecimal). In particular, a string can be displayed by calculating the memory offset for the first character, displaying the character and its attribute, and subsequently incrementing a pointer to video memory for successive characters in the string. Chapter 6 discusses this issue further.

3.7 OS Function Calls

Operating systems provide a number of services that programmers can call upon directly, or indirectly, through a programming language. Two components of MS-DOS provides OS services: (1) the MS-DOS kernel, and (2) the ROM-BIOS, the low-level OS component.

A programmer must use hardware registers to communicate with the DOS functions. MS-DOS C compilers provide two features that simplify DOS function calls: (1) the **REGS** structure, and (2) the **int86()** library function. By convention, each compiler library contains a declaration similar to

```
union REGS {
    struct WORDREGS x;
    struct BYTEREGS h;
}
```

where **WORDREGS** and **BYTEREGS** are defined as

```
struct WORDREGS {
    unsigned int ax, bx, cx, dx, si, di, cflag, flags;
}

struct BYTEREGS {
    unsigned char al, ah, bl, bh, cl, ch, dl, dh;
}
```

IBM-compatible PCs have 16-bit registers. (Newer processors have 32-bit registers, but most DOS software doesn't take advantage of this feature.) The **WORDREGS** component **ax** corresponds to the AX register. Defining **REGS** as a union of **WORDREGS** and **BYTEREGS** provides a programmer with easy access to either a 16-bit register value or an

8-bit value, low- or high-order. (**al** is the low-order byte of the AX register; **ah** is the high-order byte.)

A complementary compiler feature for communicating with DOS is the **int86()** library function. **int86()**, which is used to make a DOS service request, has the following call structure:

```
int86(int intrpt_#, union REGS *input_regs, union REGS *output_regs);
```

where *intrpt_#* is a software interrupt (DOS function), *input_regs* is a pointer to a **REGS** structure initialized with the properly register values, as required by a particular DOS function, and *output_regs* is a pointer to a **REGS** structure where a DOS function can deposit information concerning the result of its operation.

DOS service requests from a C program are straightforward. For example, suppose that an editor function must position the cursor at a particular screen coordinate. The following C function, **cursor_rc**, can position the cursor to any on-screen coordinate (zero-based):

```
void cursor_rc(int row, int column)
{
    union REGS r;

    r.h.ah = 0x02;             /* interrupt 10H, sub-function # 2 */
    r.h.dh = row;
    r.h.dl = column;
    r.h.bh = 0;                /* page # 0 */
    int86(0x10, &r, &r);       /* interrupt 10H == video function */
}
```

("0x02" means 2 hexadecimal in C. Where necessary, we use the conventional trailing letter to indicate numeric base, for example, 10H means 10 hexadecimal.)

For the C function **cursor_rc** there are two parameters representing the new row and column coordinates. Although **int86()** requires the addresses of two **REGS** structures, we don't need to make an input/output distinction in **cursor_rc**, we simply create one structure, **r**, and pass its address, **&r**, for both arguments: "int86(0x10, &r, &r);". In **cursor_rc** we must provide the video function with the necessary information. In this case, four half-register (byte) values must be set using the respective structure components.

There are numerous MS-DOS service functions. For the DOS-dependent editor modules, we frequently need to call interrupt 10H, the video function, and interrupt 16H, the keyboard interrupt. Many MS-DOS functions have sub-functions; for example, sub-function 2 of the video function handles cursor setting operations. The proper sub-function is requested by number, using the register indicated in the DOS documentation. (Again, Duncan [1988] is a standard reference for DOS technical information.)

3.8 Managing Multiple Compiled Modules

The source code for most software products is simply too large to be contained in one file—if not physically, then practically. Consequently, languages that support medium- and large-scale software products must provide a convenient mechanism for building a program from multiple compiled modules.

In terms of multiple-module program building, C is one of the most supportive languages. Earlier, we discussed C's facility for file-level lexical scoping, which is extremely important in providing communication among modules. In addition, C, through the compiler's preprocessor, allows the programmer to include project-dependent, or *header*, data during compilation. In particular, the **#define** preprocessor construct can be used to establish values for various program parameters, while the **#include** construct can be used to incorporate files containing sets of program parameters into a particular compiled module.

For example, in discussing screen management we mentioned that character attributes are specified as integer constants. Different programming projects typically require different color combinations for on-screen display of information. To handle a variety of projects, a programmer can store various color definitions in a separate file, and then pick and choose from that file as necessary for a particular project. For example, consider the file *vidconc.h*, which contains *header* (h) information, specifically, *video* (vid) *constants* (con):

```
/****   vidconc.h  ****  some video attribute constants   ****/

#define NOR_WHITE        0x07 /* normal video -- white on black   */
#define REV_WHITE        0x70 /* reverse video -- black on white */
...
#define NOR_RED_HIGH     0x0c /* red foreground, high intensity   */
#define NOR_BLUE_LOW     0x01 /* blue foreground, low intensity   */
...
#define NOR_CYAN_LOW     0x03 /* lgt. blue frgnd., low intensity */
#define REV_CYAN_LOW     0x30 /* lgt. blue bkgnd., low intensity */
...
#ifndef NORMAL_VIDEO
    #define NORMAL_VIDEO NOR_WHITE
#endif

#ifndef REVERSE_VIDEO
    #define REVERSE_VIDEO REV_WHITE
#endif
```

(Tables and explanations for video attributes are given at length in books such as Duncan [1988].)

A programmer can build a header file *once*, and then pick and choose information from it as necessary by using the proper combination of **#include** directives and conditional compilations statements, such as the **#ifndef** directives given above. For the editor program, we follow the convention that any header file whose name matches "*c.h", for example, *vidconc.h*, contains header (preprocessor) constants that are used by one or more C source code files.

Most programmers have personal preferences regarding the best way to factor program information among header files. Essentially, there are three approaches: (1) put all header information for a particular project in one header file, to be shared by all compiled modules, (2) associate a separate header file with each compiled module, as needed, or (3) a combination of (1) and (2).

Typically, approach (1) is practical only with small projects. Also, it doesn't promote reusability, since the header file serves a collection of compiled modules, only some of which will be reused in upcoming programming projects. Approach (2) is ideal for many projects in which there is a one-for-one correspondence between module parameters and modules of C functions. Approach (3) works well in a reasonably large project in which compiled modules break down into subsets, for example, DOS-related modules. For our editor, we prefer the third approach.

Programmers sometimes disagree over what should appear in header files. Without exception, header files should never contain storage *definitions*. Generally, header files should contain a sensible subset of the following:

- external variable declarations
- external function declarations
- constants/parameters established with a **#define** macro
- a limited number of argument-taking macros
- type definitions (**union**s and **typedef**s)

For the editor project we require minimal use of the latter two. In general, macros, except for constant definitions, should be avoided. We require only one macro, **char_addr**(), as described earlier. If we were developing software that required various container structures, such as stacks and queues, we would make extensive use of **typedef**s to promote reusability (data abstraction—stacks of integers, reals, characters, and so on). However, for the editor and window buffers, simple character arrays will be sufficient. Lastly, the keystroke data structure, described earlier, will be declared in a header file.

If function calls occur across compiled modules, the compiler should know about it. For example, if a compiled module contains a function definition with parameters, such as:

```
void some_editor_function(char *buffer, long offset)
{
    ...
}
```

then the compiler will generate code that pops four bytes from the stack (long integer) for the second argument in a call to **some_editor_function**(). If a different compiled module contains a function that calls **some_editor_function**() with inconsistent argument types, say,

```
some_editor_function(ed_buffer, 0);
```

the programmer is in for a debugging nightmare, unless the compiler is made aware of **some_editor_function()**'s requirements.

Without prior knowledge of **some_editor_function()**'s parameters, the compiler will generate code for the call to **some_editor_function()** that pushes two, not four, bytes onto the stack. Of course, **some_editor_function()** will pop four bytes from the stack when it begins execution. What happens at this point is almost never amusing (at least not at the time).

Some programmers depend exclusively on source code listings for the functions in all supporting compiled modules, as reminders that they should write, for example,

```
some_editor_function(ed_buffer, 0L);
```

to force argument/parameter agreement. If they forget to consult the listing, they pay the "ultimate" price. Modern C compilers support the use of function prototypes and provide strong type checking to minimize data conversion errors.

The best way to prevent this type of scenario is to provide a header file for each compiled module that declares the return type and parameter types for each function in the module. For the editor project we follow the convention that every source file, say, *edit.c* is accompanied by a similarly named header file, say, *edit.h*, that contains declarations describing each function in the source file. Every module that makes use of functions from *edit.c* should contain an **#include** directive, for example,

```
#include "edit.h"
```

to assist the compiler in generating code for function calls to *edit.c*.

As another measure of precaution, every source file should contain an **#include** directive for its function-declaring header file to ensure that no incompatibilities exist—other modules depend exclusively on these header files during compilation. Obviously, this type of cross-checking among modules enhances reusability. Moreover, a header file containing all function declarations for a compiled module provides "summarizing" documentation.

To reiterate our file-naming convention, filenames that match "*c.h" contain **#define** constants, and, in one case, a parameterized macro. Other "*.h" files contain function declarations, and any external variable declarations, for their respective compiled modules.

3.9 Using Function Prototypes

There are two ways to declare, and define, functions in C. The older style is covered in the earlier books on C, including the classic book by Kernighan and Ritchie (1978). The following function definition uses the old style:

```
int some_function(any_char, any_int)
char any_char;
int any_int;
{
    ...
}
```

If a declaration were used elsewhere in a program to refer to this definition, it would be written:

```
extern int some_function();
```

Since no information is given about parameters, the compiler can provide very little of the error checking across modules that we advocated in the previous section.

For this reason, the C community, with support from modern C compilers, advocates the use of *function prototypes*:

```
extern int some_function(char, int);
```

Specifically, for a function declaration the data types (without parameters) are provided, by position, where arguments would occur in a function call. Minimally, if a function is not used outside its compiled module, and if it is defined prior to any function that references it, a function definition alone is sufficient for proper type checking:

```
int some_function(char any_char, int any_int)
{
    ...
}
```

If a function is referenced prior to its definition, or if inter-module function calls are expected, a function declaration should be included as well. For the editor project, we will place function declarations in a separate header file, *for every function in the module.* Invariably, if declarations are provided in a header file only for those functions participating in inter-module communication at the time the module is developed, when a change is made in the program at a future date, the programmer may neglect to provide a critical function declaration, leading to numerous debugging problems.

It's interesting to note that C++ 2.0 requires function prototypes. In particular, you can't depend on functions having default integer return types, and so on.

4

Project Design Considerations

In this chapter we begin the development of **ed**, our window-based editor. We discuss a number of topics including the user interface, the capabilities included in the editor, and the project breakdown in terms of compiled modules.

Quite naturally, programmers tend to satisfy their own personal preferences in developing an editor. We've tried to remain cognizant of this fact and refrain from introducing superfluous editor functions that reflect our preferences. We've made reasonable attempts to avoid design considerations that would compromise editor generalizability.

Overall editor size is another consideration. In order to keep our project reasonably small, we've avoided specialized data structures and/or functions designed to optimize various aspects of editor operations. For example, our windows module implements a simple windowing system that works with any size window up to 25 rows and 80 columns. In contrast, it's not uncommon for a commerical editor to employ a fixed size edit window, so that screen refresh operations can be optimized. In subsequent chapters, we discuss extensions that we've made in developing our own, larger version of the editor, some of which do reflect personal preferences.

4.1 A Window-based Interface

Window-based user interfaces are the norm in the DOS community; overall, our design reflects the accepted standard. Given this standard, there is, however, considerable room for variability in how we use windows. We have several goals/considerations:

- to provide the user with an intuitive editor front-end
- to work exclusively with a high-level language (C)
- to accommodate future enhancements/modifications
- to promote reusability of most of the compiled modules

With these goals in mind, we've chosen a simple, general-purpose design that uses four windows:

- a "permanent" edit window
- a pop-up help window
- a pop-up message window
- a pop-up combination find-text and search-and-replace window

The edit window occupies the entire screen, except for the top and bottom rows. It is permanent in the sense that it appears automatically when an edit session is initiated, and it can't be removed from the screen. Figure 4.1 demonstrates the screen layout for the editor with the pop-up message/prompt window overlapping the edit window.

The top row is reserved for displaying status information. For example, **ed** displays the name of the file that's currently being edited on the top row. Other information, for example, the status of a print operation, a copyright statement, and so on, can be displayed across the top as well, if this is desirable. The bottom row is reserved for an on-screen legend of the most common editor commands, plus status indicators of insert/overwrite mode and whether or not the buffer has been modified since the last save operation.

A pop-up help window can be invoked to allow the user to page through a description of **ed**'s commands, plus a summary of **ed**'s limitations and general characteristics. The help window pops up over the edit window.

The third window is a general-purpose editor window that's used to display messages and, in some cases, prompt the user for a response. The same window can be used to inform the user of critical editor conditions, for example, attempting to exit without saving changes to the file, and for obtaining information on demand, for example, a filename. The latter operation is being performed in Figure 4.1. This window pops up in the middle of the edit window. Although similar in size to the message window, the find-text window pops up at a different location, closer to the top of the screen.

All text within a window is displayed in normal video. Lastly, each editor window has a border, and border colors are window-dependent. In Figure 4.1 the top and bottom status lines are displayed in reverse video, while the window borders are displayed in normal video.

4.2 Editor Input

In general, communication with a user can be keystroke-based, mouse-based, or a combination of the two. For our purposes, keystroke input is preferable. Mouse-based input would

```
 1 File: MYFILE.C                                          ed - 1.0
This sentence occupies the
first four lines of the
edit
window.



                    ------ Enter a Filename ------
                    File: _



F1-Help F2-Tag F3-Cut F4-Paste F5-DW F6-DEOL F7-DL F8-Undo F9-Quit F10-End MI
```

Figure 4.1 Overall Window Design for **ed**

introduce too many complications and machine dependencies for our purposes here. Moreover, most programmers, based on our own experiences and the currently available commercial editors, prefer keystroke-based editor commands, especially with small editors.

Cursor movement commands are assigned to the supplemental keys in the normal manner, for example, **<PgUp>** moves the cursor one page closer to the beginning of the buffer, **<down-arrow>** moves the cursor one line closer to the end of the buffer, and so on.

Non-cursor movement commands are assigned (1) to function keys, (2) to combinations of the **<Alt>** key and alphabetic keys, and (3) to combinations of the **<Alt>** key and function keys. For example, **<F2>** sets a tag (bookmark), **<Alt>-S** saves the edit buffer to disk, and **<Alt>-<F2>** exchanges the tag and the cursor.

4.3 Basic Editor Features

All of the basic editor features are provided. Cursor movement can occur at the character, word, page, screen, and buffer level. A number of delete operations are supported: character, word, previous word, remainder of line, and line, along with a simple undelete capability.

A clipboard is provided with copy, cut, and paste operations. The clipboard is designed to accommodate the entire edit buffer, so that the user doesn't have to estimate whether or not a block of text is too large for the clipboard.

Our editor includes support for tab operations. The editor module is general enough to handle dynamic changes in tab size. Tabs are always expanded on-screen and displayed as blanks. Also, carriage returns display as blanks at the end of each line.

ed supports horizontal scrolling. In particular, lines that are too long for the edit window to display should *not* wrap around to the next line. For this situation the **<Home>** and **<End>** keys provide manual horizontal scrolling; some editor operations may invoke automatic window scrolling, for example, cursor placement during search-and-replace operations.

Our editor provides a simple search-and-replace facility that can be enhanced. At present, it makes the requested replacement without first checking with the user. A repeat facility allows the user to make multiple replacements. In order to control the size of our project, we'll design the editor such that the undelete buffer is shared by the search-and-replace facility. Although this technique might be unacceptable in a commercial editor, some steps must be taken to enhance "page economy" for our editor project.

4.4 File Processing Support

File processing support for editors is: somewhat machine-specific, supplemental to and distinct from the editing process itself, and somewhat messy. For the editor project, we provide basic file processing support that can be enhanced. The supported file operations include: (1) saving the edited text to disk and continuing the edit session, (2) saving the edited text during editor termination, (3) abandoning edited text upon editor termination, (4) saving selected text to disk in a named file, and (5) merging an external file at the current cursor position in the edit window. You are free to provide (as we have) additional facilities in a separate compiled module based on your personal preferences.

4.5 Edit Buffer Design

ed is designed for processing ASCII files where each line is terminated by a carriage return. In particular, it doesn't include word-wrap and automatic hyphenation capabilities, as found in word processors. Essentially, our software serves as a foundation for developing a more sophisticated programmer's editor.

There are essentially two approaches to managing an edit buffer: (1) string-based, using a one-dimensional array, and (2) line-based, using a composite data structure that maintains information about each line of text, such as line length. Both approaches are used in commercial editors. The former approach is simpler to implement and quite efficient; for example, search-and-replace operations take place against a string. The latter approach provides unnecessary complications, since our primary focus is a discussion of software reusability, contrasting C and C++.

4.6 Breakdown into Compiled Modules

There are numerous approaches to factoring an editor project in multiple source code files. One approach would be to partition the program based solely on the functions/operations required to implement the editor, that is, without regard for future programming projects. This form of highly customized design has some advantages but is becoming harder and harder to justify.

Although taking every conceivable effort to, say, optimize code size, can produce a very space-efficient program, the space saved on disk usually can't be justified in terms of software reusability. An increasing percentage of software development is being done in high-level languages for similar reasons. Although a talented assembly language programmer can often produce a more efficient program, the potential costs in software maintenance are often too high to justify the effort.

Our approach for the editor project is to place more importance on reusability and extensibility (and the other "*ability"s) than on overall efficiency. As a result, our editor with minimal capabilities should be approximately 10 percent less efficient that a highly optimized editor. However, as you add enhancements to the editor, the comparative efficiency of the editor can be improved. That is, the steps that have been taken to enhance extensibility at the expense of efficiency are offset, in a comparative sense, due to efficient reuse of existing code. Moreover, our modules will be useful for providing editing capabilities as a component of various applications.

Given our interest in reusability, we can develop **ed** from the following modules:

- *ed.c* - reflects a particular editor implementation
- *edfile.c* - includes the file routines for the editor
- *edhelp.c* - handles the help system
- *edit.c* - provides the general-purpose editing routines
- *editwin.c* - hides some of the details of *windows.c*
- *windows.c* - provides the windowing functions
- *screen.c* - provides the screen management functions
- *keyboard.c* - provides the keyboard handling functions
- *display.c* - contains the basic screen display functions

The sizes of the modules differ greatly, since we're focusing on reuse of modules, as opposed to arbitrary factoring of our source code. Two of these files, *keyboard.c* and *display.c*, are very small, whereas one file, *edit.c* is quite large. The size of *edit.c* will help motivate our discussion of C++ and class hierarchies in a later chapter.

4.7 Summary of Components

At this point, we can summarize selected characteristics of each module, in order to provide a feeling for the overall scope of the project. Complete discussion of each module is deferred until subsequent chapters. In this chapter we overview the modules as we've listed them, in top-down order. Later, we discuss the editor operations in a bottom-up fashion.

ed.c is the primary module for implementing the user interface for **ed**. In general, a completely different editor could be build by replacing *ed.c*, and either one or both of its associated modules. These support modules, *edfile.c* and *edhelp.c*, are directly related to *ed.c*; a change in one file could affect either or both of the other two files.

To summarize overall editor operations, *ed.c* contains functions that manage editor initialization and termination. The initialization process includes checking command line arguments, allocating and initializing windows, and initializing the screen. Editor termination includes saving the edit buffer to disk, deallocating windows, and restoring the screen. Editor initialization and termination errors are handled in *ed.c* also. Lastly, *ed.c* contains the routines that dispatch keystrokes to the edit module.

All help-related data and functions are handled by *edhelp.c*. **ed**'s help data is built into the executable file—**ed** does not require a separate help file during execution.

There are many file-related support tasks that can be provided in *edfile.c*. File processing is distinct from normal editor operations; hence, each file-related task that's supported by **ed** adds directly to the size of the executable file. For MS-DOS editors these tasks can be closely related to the editing process per se, or quite distinct from normal edit operations. For example, allowing the user to include, that is, merge, a file at a specific location in the edit buffer might be seen as an essential editing function, whereas checking whether or not a floppy disk drive door has been properly closed is a more peripheral task.

The source file *edit.c* includes all the data and functions that are central to the editing process. All critical editing variables, such as cursor position in the edit buffer, are maintained here. A number of window-related editing tasks have been isolated in a separate file, *editwin.c*. These tasks include filling the edit window with text and managing horizontal scrolling within the edit window. *editwin.c* serves as an interface between *edit.c* and *windows.c*. The functions in *editwin.c* must call upon editing functions in *edit.c*, such as those that support tab operations, and functions in *windows.c*, for example, functions related to displaying a character in a window.

The source file *windows.c* provides window-management functions, but not the window data structure. Specifically, it treats the window data structure as an external that must be defined elsewhere, in another program component. This module would be replaced, or modified extensively, in porting **ed** to another operating system, or if an alternative, commercial windowing package were preferred.

Likewise, the last three modules, *screen.c*, *keyboard.c*, and *display.c*, provide hardware-dependent routines as discussed in earlier chapters. In porting **ed** to an alternative hardware platform, these modules would be replaced as well.

5

Designing the Application-dependent Modules

A number of critical decisions must be made in designing reusable software components, such as a window-management module. However, designing application-dependent program components is important as well, because quite often these components are subjected to ongoing modification during a software product's life cycle.

At this point, we can discuss several aspects of our project design that could be important in developing other software products. We use a significant portion of the source code for **ed** to motivate our discussion. Moreover, the calls to functions in other modules provide a peek at what's to come in subsequent chapters. In other words, this chapter motivates the material in subsequent chapters by taking a top-down look at our application through black-box views of functions from other modules.

We should reiterate that our primary goal is to discuss various aspects of practical software construction, especially reusability and maintainability. Our design for **ed** is just one of a variety of legitimate designs for a simple editor; it is quite different from the C++ design that we'll discuss later.

5.1 Use of External Variables

One of our premises has been that external/global variables should be avoided as much as possible. It's important to emphasize that there are legitimate uses for externals. Moreover, whether or not external variables are legitimate can vary, depending on the programming language that's being used.

Despite the outright ban on external variables imposed by some computer science curriculums, we don't believe that it makes sense to outlaw *all* uses of external variables with a language such as C. On the other hand, we've seen software written by professional programmers in which there are so many public variables, spread over so many source files, that it's simply impossible for an outsider to understand the program. Inheriting a program littered with public variables can be a nightmare.

There must be some common ground—a legitimate compromise. In fact, the editor project reflects our feelings concerning what circumstances warrant the use of external variables, while demonstrating how easy it is to avoid their proliferation. The basic version of **ed** that we're developing here spans approximately 4000 lines. There are a total of five external variables, public and private, for the entire project. A ratio of 5 to 4000 (external variables to lines of source code) represents a conservative use of external variables.

5.2 Abstract Data Structures and External Variables

If we can get by with only five externals, why not ban them entirely? Because program design should be driven by considerations for reusability, readability, and so on. Consider the external variable used in our main source file, *ed.c*:

```
window_frame wframe[MAIN_EDIT_WIN + MIN_NUM_WINS];
```

wframe is an array of **window_frame** elements. For now, **window_frame** is an abstract data structure that includes the critical variables necessary for managing a window, such as current row and column coordinates, window border coordinates, and so on. The details of its implementation are not important to the programmer implementing *ed.c*.

The previous definition implies that the programmer who wants to use the windows package must know something about that package, for example, the name to use in defining the window array, the name and function of certain window routines, the functions' call syntax, and so on. This information constitutes the so-called programmer's interface to the windows package—essentially, high-level information.

Although the definition of the window(s) is external, the internal structure of a window (the window descriptor table) is hidden from the programmer. In particular, a programmer who uses the windows package is isolated from any changes to low-level details associated with the storage and manipulation of windows by the window functions. Keeping such low-level details hidden is essential in developing modules that couple data structures with their associated procedures. (We'll address the pointer versus array index approach to accommodating window handles in Chapter 7.)

Conceivably, **wframe** could be placed local to some function in *windows.c*, or could even be designed as a private external in *windows.c*. The latter approach would require the addition of a number of access functions to *windows.c*, so that other modules, such as *edit.c*, could manipulate critical window variables. The former approach is quite difficult to justify; it produces a very awkward programming situation and a high level of surface complexity.

Regardless of the mechanism, defining (allocating storage for) **wframe** within *windows.c* conflicts with one of our primary goals, namely, "sealing off" certain modules in order to minimize, if not totally eliminate, day-to-day tampering with completed modules. Specifically, a programmer shouldn't have to modify the window-management module in order to allocate windows for a particular application. This consideration is important both when programmers share source-level libraries, and when a module is compiled to object code.

5.3 The Primary Application Module

There are many legitimate approaches to delegating tasks for a project such as **ed**. We believe that our design is legitimate, and more importantly, that it reflects a number of standard programming practices. We won't discuss every function in every source file for **ed**—doing so would be too space-consuming and laborious. We can, however, use the external declarations in *ed.h* to generate a discussion of the most important issues.

5.3.1 The Importance of Header Files

The header file *ed.h* that accompanies *ed.c* can be used to emphasize the importance of matching declaration and definition files. The source listing for *ed.h* is:

```
/****  ed.h  ****  external declarations for ed.c  ****/


/*
wframe is the window data structure required by windows.c.
See windowsc.h.
*/

extern window_frame wframe[];


extern void main(int, char **);
extern char *check_args(int, char **);
extern int allocate_support_buffers(void);
extern int allocate_windows(void);
extern void issue_error_messages(int, char *);
extern int edit_main(int, char *);
extern int edit_text(int, char *, char *);
extern void dispatch_extended_code(int, unsigned char,
                                   char *, char *);
```

```
extern void display_edit_info(void);
extern void display_filename(int, char *);
```

We mentioned earlier that we always follow the practice of including a declaration for each function in the header file associated with that program module; in this case, *ed.h* is associated with *ed.c*. With this approach, every module in the project that must access *ed.c* can do so safely, provided that it includes the proper declaration header file during compilation. We utilize these header files *during* project development, not just afterward.

More importantly, once a module has been closed, a programmer can get a good idea of how to reuse an existing module, just by consulting its header file. It's been our experience that over the lifetimes of several projects this practice can save countless debugging hours related to inter-module function calls.

If you're concerned about the possibility for discrepancies between function prototypes in header files and function definitions, once a module has been "completed," you can regenerate the header file of external declarations from the source file itself, stripping out the function bodies and parameters. This practice produces programmer-level documentation of the module that's 100-percent compatible with the source code file and quite useful in developing other applications.

5.3.2 Program Initialization, Error Handling, and Termination

As you can judge from the number of functions and their names given in *ed.h*, *ed.c* is reasonably small and concerned with implementing the editor interface. These functions must call other functions in *edfile.c* and *edhelp.c* for file- and help-related support.

Let's look at **main()**:

```
/*
main() sets up a pointer variable for the incoming file specification,
performs some screen handling, initializes the windows, and invokes a
file specification routine, check_args().
*/

void main(int argc, char *argv[])
{
    char *file_spec;
    int edit_status;

    if ((file_spec = check_args(argc, argv)) == NULL)
        exit(1);
    if (!allocate_support_buffers()) {
        issue_error_messages(CANT_ALLOCATE_BUFS, DUMMY);
        exit(1);
    }
    if (!allocate_windows()) {
```

```
            issue_error_messages(CANT_ALLOCATE_BUFS, DUMMY);
            exit(1);
        }

        if (video_initialize() == MONO_MODE)
            rev_border_color = REVERSE_VIDEO;
        display_edit_info();
        edit_window_count(1);
        edit_status = edit_main(MAIN_EDIT_WIN, file_spec);
        release_edit_buffers();
        restore_exit_screen();
        if (edit_status == QUIT || edit_status == EXIT)
            exit(0);
        else {
            issue_error_messages(edit_status, file_spec);
            exit(1);
        }
}   /* main */
```

main() starts off by performing three categories of error checking; an error in any category results in program termination and a message to the user. If **main()** gets past the initial error checking, it initializes the video system (the screen). If the video adapter is monochrome, an external variable, **rev_border_color**, is modified. (Some reverse video color settings display as normal video on a monochrome screen.) A simple conditional test is adequate for our purposes here, serving as a place-holder for a more elaborate approach to dynamic adjustment to the hardware's video characteristics.

Subsequently, **display_edit_info()** displays information for the top and bottom status rows, as described earlier. Then, the number of edit buffers is recorded in **edit_window_count()**, and **edit_main()** is called to start the edit session, returning the result of its efforts in **edit_status**. If an error condition is returned in **edit_status**, **issue_error_messages()** is called:

```
/*
issue_error_messages() issues messages for a number of errors
that can occur during file initialization.
*/

void issue_error_messages(int edit_status, char *file_spec)
{
    switch (edit_status) {
        case NO_MATCH:
            puts("Couldn't find any files:");
            puts(file_spec);
            break;
```

```
        case CANT_WRITE:
            puts("Couldn't write file:");
            puts(file_spec);
            break;
        case CANT_ALLOCATE_BUFS:
            puts("Couldn't allocate memory for editing space.");
            break;
        case TOO_LARGE:
            puts("File is too large (64K max) OR can't be opened:");
            puts(file_spec);
            break;
        default:
            break;
    }
}   /* issue_error_messages */
```

Some programmers may prefer to set up an array of error messages; however, for our purposes, the case structure is adequate.

In this book we follow the C tradition of coding all **#define** constants in uppercase characters, for example, **TOO_LARGE**. The editor module, *edit.c*, has its own associated constant file, *editc.h*, with editing-related constants. The application-specific editor constants are stored in *edc.h*. For example, the error constants in **issue_error_messages()** are defined there:

```
...
#define NO_MATCH            -1      /* arbitrary error constants */
#define CANT_READ           -2
#define CANT_WRITE          -3
#define TOO_LARGE           -4
#define CANT_ALLOCATE_BUFS  -99
...
```

5.3.3 Mapping Keystrokes to Editor Commands

edc.h also defines the constants that represent each editor command; *ed.c* then maps each constant to an editing function. Earlier we described DOS keystrokes in terms of their two-byte sequences. For ASCII keys, the first byte encodes the ASCII value. All keys generate a physical scan code for the second byte that can be used for keystroke identification. For our editor, it's convenient to map each scan code directly to a **#define** constant, so that they can be used to interpret keyboard input and to map keystrokes to editing commands. For example, consider several of the keystroke mappings in *edc.h*:

```
/*
keyboard- and function-related constants appear next.  Note that
a function is represented by its keyboard extended code.  That is,
the (decimal) extended byte code for F1 is 59, which is used to
represent the HELP function.
*/

#define HELP         59              /* F1      */
#define TAG          60              /* F2      */
...
#define QUIT         67              /* F9      */
#define EXIT         68              /* F10     */
#define TAG_CURSOR   105             /* Alt-F2  */
#define COPY         106             /* Alt-F3  */
#define DWORD_LEFT   108             /* Alt-F5  */
#define UNTAG        111             /* Alt-F8  */
#define CHANGE_TEXT 46               /* Alt-C   */
#define FIND_TEXT    33              /* Alt-F   */
...
...
#define CTRL_PGUP    132             /* top of file          */
#define CTRL_PGDN    118             /* end of file          */
#define CTRL_LEFT    115             /* left one word        */
#define CTRL_RIGHT   116             /* right one word       */
```

You might prefer to add more indirection by mapping scan codes to key-top values, for example,

```
#define F1           59
```

and then mapping the latter **#define**s to mnemonic editing commands, for example,

```
#define HELP         F1
```

Later in this chapter when we look at the dispatching routines, we illustrate how **ed** maps these constants to editing commands.

5.3.4 Two Public Variables for Color Attributes

We should explain the second external variable at the point. For a number of reasons, including the requirement for run-time color modification, C (preprocessor) constants are inadequate for managing the window border colors. Hence, two public color variables are defined in *edit.c* and initialized with default values for normal and reverse border colors.

These two variables can be used by any module; for example, **main()** conditionally modifies one color variable.

In our opinion, passing color variables from function to function is unacceptable. We could create a separate color function to control access to them, but this seems like overkill. Since these color variables are referenced quite often, yet provide little opportunity for introducing hard-to-detect errors, external definitions are adequate. (We've used three of our five, self-allotted external variables.)

5.3.5 Using puts() Versus printf()

check_args() and **issue_error_messages()** are the only two routines that use standard I/O library functions. Consider **check_args()**:

```
/*
check_args() checks to make sure that the proper number of arguments
is present.  It returns NULL for an error, or a character pointer
to the file spec if the argument list is OK.
*/

char *check_args(int arg_count, char *arg_vector[])
{
    if (arg_count != 2) {                      /* file_spec present? */
        puts("Usage: ED <file_spec>");
        return NULL;
    }
    if (!file_exists(arg_vector[1])) {         /* check its validity */
        if (write_to_disk(TEST, "", DUMMY, arg_vector[1]) ==
                CANT_WRITE) {
            puts("Couldn't create file:");
            puts(arg_vector[1]);
            return NULL;
        }
        else
            remove(arg_vector[1]);             /* just testing */
    }
    return arg_vector[1];
}   /* check_args */
```

Since our project requires very little standard I/O, we've elected *not* to link in the run-time code for **printf()**, or **fprintf()**, simply to print error messages related to editor initialization and termination. We can save considerable space in our executable file by using **puts()**. (**write_to_disk()** is defined in *edfile.c* in Appendix A.)

5.3.6 Abstraction and Window Allocations

Next, consider the window allocations, performed by **allocate_windows()**:

```
/*
allocate_windows() handles allocation of all windows.
*/

int allocate_windows(void)
{
    return (make_window(MAIN_EDIT_WIN, "", 1, 0, 23, 79) == TRUE &&
            make_window(HELP_WIN,
                "ed 1.0 - Help", 2, 1, 22, 78) == TRUE &&
            make_window(ATTN_WIN,
                "Attention", 11, 16, 13, 16 + POPUP_WIDTH) == TRUE &&
            make_window(FIND_WIN,
                "Find/Change", 3, 16, 7, 16 + POPUP_WIDTH) == TRUE);
}   /* allocate_windows */
```

The windows module (*windows.c*) provides **make_window()** for allocating and initializing a window; it has the following call structure:

```
    make_window(<array_pos>, <header>, <start_row>, <start_col>,
                <end_row>, <end_col>);
```

The functions in *windows.c* are designed to reference a particular element from an array of windows, hence our earlier external array definition. There are a variety of other approaches to window allocation; however, allocating the windows externally is, perhaps, the most common.

You may have inferred from the array definition and the call to **edit_window_count()** in **main()** that our edit module is designed to accommodate any number of edit windows. The array-of-windows data structure makes this particularly easy to do. For example, consider a few lines from our editor parameter file *editintc.h* (editor interface constants):

```
/****  editintc.h ****  constants for the edit interface  ****/

#define MAIN_EDIT_WIN       0       /* window array positions   */
#define HELP_WIN            1
#define ATTN_WIN            2
#define FIND_WIN            3
#define MIN_NUM_WINS        4
...
```

A second edit window can be added, say, **ALT_EDIT_WIN**, as the 0th array element, pushing **MAIN_EDIT_WIN** forward to array position 1. A third edit window would push

MAIN_EDIT_WIN forward to array position 2. That is, **MAIN_EDIT_WIN** serves as a "floating" constant that, combined with **MIN_NUM_WINS**, improves the generalizability of the editor module. These window number constants are sometimes called *window handles*.

5.3.7 Inter-module Flexibility and Module-level Abstraction

Should the edit module be responsible for low-level details such as mapping keystrokes to commands and saving edit buffers? Or, should the application welcome the opportunity to gain control of basic edit module functions? With the former approach the application programmer's task is, perhaps, easier. However, with the latter approach the programmer has greater control over, for example, how to proceed when the user invokes the **quit** command.

Consider **edit_main()**, our entry point to the editor. If the edit module were designed with a small interface, **edit_main()** would call a keystroke-dispatching function hidden within the edit module. With a more "open" module design, the programmer might be given responsibility for deciding which editor functions to implement, and so on. There are advantages and disadvantages to both approaches; we'll contrast both approaches in our C and C++ implementations of the project.

For the C implementation, the edit module is designed as a supplier of editing functions. Hence, the application program is saddled with the responsibility of initiating each editing task. Consider how **edit_main()** handles editing operations:

```
/*
edit_main() maintains a pointer to the active edit buffer.  In
addition, it reports/returns error codes for a number of file
errors that can occur during editor initialization.
*/

int edit_main(int n, char *filename)
{
    char *ed_buffer;
    int edit_status;
    long file_length;

    activate_window(n, "", nor_border_color, nor_border_color);
    initialize_edit(n);
    if ((ed_buffer = create_buffer(MAX_BUF_SIZE)) != NULL) {
        file_length = read_from_disk(ed_buffer, filename);
        if (file_length == TOO_LARGE)
            edit_status = TOO_LARGE;
        else {
            if (file_length == CANT_READ) {      /* a new file */
                edit_buf_len(n, 0);
```

```
                strupr(filename);
            }
            else
                edit_buf_len(n, file_length);
            display_filename(n, filename);
            edit_status = edit_text(n, ed_buffer, filename);
            if (edit_status == EXIT)
                write_from_buffer(n, ed_buffer, DUMMY, filename);
        }
        free(ed_buffer);
    }
    else
        edit_status = CANT_ALLOCATE_BUFS;
    deactivate_window(n);
    return edit_status;
}   /* edit_main */
```

First, **edit_main()** calls **activate_window()** from *windows.c* to open the editing window. Next, it calls **initialize_edit()** from *edit.c* to set/reset a number of critical edit buffer variables. Third, it allocates the edit buffer and proceeds to read in the text file. If it can't read the file, it assumes that the file doesn't exist and creates it. (You might prefer a different approach.)

read_from_disk() is a general-purpose function. In the C (UNIX) tradition, it returns -1 upon error, and a useful value otherwise. In this case, the file size is returned and **edit_buf_length()** is called in order to set the buffer length. **edit_text()** manages editing tasks per se. Depending on the value returned by **edit_text()**, a call to **write_from_buffer()** may be necessary to save changes to the text.

Note that the buffer number (the window handle) is being passed around from function to function; this is part of the generalizability of the modules. It's possible to maintain this type of information in a global variable; however, we're trying to minimize the use of C external variables. More importantly, depending on your editor preferences, passing the buffer number may offer some advantages. For example, passing arguments makes it easy to process edit buffers in a nested manner. In particular, as currently designed, we can take advantage of indirect recursion among several of these functions to manage primary and secondary edit buffers. (Which functions would be involved?)

Although each of these operations is straightforward, there is room for debate over which module should be given responsibility for managing file operations and edit-loop operations. Some programmers would prefer that the edit module take care of the read and write details. Other programmers prefer the flexibility that results from making these operations external to the edit module. In our opinion, these trade-offs between flexibility and procedural abstraction are critically important for reusability. We're emphasizing these issues by using contrasting designs for the C and C++ edit modules.

For example, as written, **edit_text()** has to provide fairly specific, low-level management of editing operations:

```
/*
edit_text() analyzes incoming characters and calls the
appropriate routines.
*/

int edit_text(int n, char *buffer, char *filename)
{
    union keystroke key;

    window_fill(n, 0, 0, buffer, 0);
    do {
        do {
            key.word = window_getche(n);
            if (key.byte[0])
                switch (key.byte[0]) {
                    case BKSP:
                        backspace(n, buffer);
                        break;
                    case EOF_CHAR:
                        break;
                    default:
                        insert_char(n, key.byte[0], buffer);
                        break;
                }
            else
                dispatch_extended_code(n, key.byte[1], buffer,
                                        filename);
        } while (key.byte[0] || !(key.byte[1] == QUIT ||
                                key.byte[1] == EXIT));
    } while (key.byte[1] == QUIT && buffer_modified(n, TEST) &&
                !message_query(ATTN_WIN, ",
                            "Abandon changed text (y/n): "));
    return key.byte[1];
}   /* edit_text */
```

Specifically, **edit_text()** must know about keystrokes, as discussed in an earlier chapter, and it must know which edit and window module functions to call in order to keep the edit session going. These operations could be placed in the edit module, with some loss of flexibility (for functions external to *edit.c*).

Is this type of low-level programming justified, in order to use the edit module? Should the builder of an application that requires editing facilities have to know the interfaces for **window_fill()**, **window_getche()**, **insert_char()**, and so on? In fairness to the current design, note that it reflects a reasonable level of procedure abstraction. That is, although the programmer must understand the interface to several window and edit module functions, the view of their operations is abstract. At issue is whether or not additional structure should be imposed on the programmer to reduce the size and complexity of the interface to the edit module.

With the current design, a programmer has considerable flexibility in choosing among various high-level functions in the edit module. For example, the programmer can choose whether or not to prompt the user regarding unsaved changes, how to interpret the user's response, which cursor functions to implement (see **dispatch_extended_code()**), and so on. In our view, this type of module "openness" is becoming less acceptable. Flexibility notwithstanding, modern software toolkits often minimize access to many of the functions in a module, by providing high level functions that implement default functionality.

5.3.8 The Keyboard Interface

Let's consider some of the keyboard-related operations that appear in *ed.c*. (Recall that Chapter 3 discussed a number of keyboard issues.) **edit_text()** must call a window function, **window_getche()**, to retrieve keystrokes from the edit window, storing the returned value in **key**, defined from the union data type described in Chapter 3. Recall that if the first byte is non-zero ("key.byte[0] != 0"), the user pressed an ASCII key. In this case, (with two exceptions) it is passed on to **insert_char()**. On the other hand, if the first byte equals 0, the user pressed a supplemental key and the scan (extended) code is used to indicate the desired editor command. Chapter 6 provides our rationale for direct handling of the two-byte sequence **key**.

For example, **<Alt>-W** is the command for writing the contents of the edit buffer out to an alternate disk file. **dispatch_extended_code()** takes care of these operations:

```
/*
dispatch_extended_code() processes commands by calling the
appropriate routines.
*/

void dispatch_extended_code(int n, unsigned char command,
                            char *buffer, char *filename)
{
    switch (command) {      /* 8-bit command codes ==> unsigned */
        case DEL:
            del_char(n, buffer);
            break;
        case LEFT:
            cursor_left(n, buffer);
            break;
        ...
        ...
        case HELP:
            present_help_screens(HELP_WIN);
```

```
            break;
        ...
        ...
            case INSERT_FILE:
            insert_file(n, buffer, get_alt_file_spec(ATTN_WIN));
            break;
        case SET_TABS:
            tab_size(SET);
            break;
        default:
            break;
    }
}   /* dispatch_extended_code */
```

dispatch_extended_code() is easy to follow; it simply dispatches recognized keystrokes to the appropriate editing function. However, note that in order to write this function, you must have information about the interface to each of the editing functions.

At this point we've provided a brief overview of the primary application module given in Appendix A and raised a number of design questions related to reusability. Chapter 6 addresses the DOS-specific modules in more detail. The editor implementation in the second half of the book employs a very different design.

5.4 The Supporting Application Modules

An editor that requires an accompanying help file, which must be read during program initialization, can present problems, particularly for new users. If the installation isn't handled properly, the editor can't find its help data. (Any user who goofs up the installation is likely to need the help system.) If the editor is passed along from user to user, at some point the help file will get left behind. In cases like this, it may be advantageous to hard-code the help system inside the editor. This approach isn't practical, however, if the help system is large.

edhelp.c contains the help-related functions for **ed**. The help text is stored in *edhelp.hlp*—during compilation this file is included using the **#include** directive. The most straightforward method for hard-coding the help text is to set up an array of strings, where each string represents one page of help text. However, since some compilers have a fairly restrictive limit for the maximum length of string constants, we've split each help page into two adjacent array elements. *edhelp.hlp* contains a static array of strings:

```
/****    edhelp.hlp    ****/

/*
This file contains the text for ed's help screens.  See the file
edhelp.c.  Each help screen is split into two strings to accommodate some
compilers' limits on the length of string constants.
```

```
*/

#define MAX_HELP    8          /* number of help screens * 2 */

    static char *help[MAX_HELP] = {
" Commands:\n\
\n\
   F1 (Help)   - invokes this help system.\n\
    ...
   F7 (DL)     - deletes the entire line.\n",

"   F8 (Undo)  - recovers text from the previous DW, DEOL, or DL.\n\
    ...
   Alt-F8 - removes (undoes) a tag (set by F2).",
    ...
    ...
};
```

Typically, it's more awkward to update a file like *edhelp.hlp* than a "strictly text" help file. However, the time saved with naive users sometimes makes this approach worthwhile. We'll use a different approach in the second half of the book.

The other application-dependent module *edfile.c* contains the file-related support functions for *ed.c*. Putting them in a separate file is convenient. Many of the enhancements that you might anticipate for **ed** would be placed in *edfile.c*, with modifications in *ed.c* limited to the **switch** in **dispatch_extended_code()**. Their respective declaration header files provide safe inter-module communication.

One of the intents of this chapter has been to emphasize the tremendous number of fairly far-reaching design decisions that must be made in factoring a project into many compiled modules. You may or may not agree with the approach we've taken here. As we've alluded to already, the C++ implementation does several things quite differently.

The remaining function definitions for the editor application require no special consideration here; you can find complete definitions for *edit.c*, *edfile.c*, and *edhelp.c* in Appendix A. At this point, we can proceed with a bottom-up investigation of the other modules.

6

Basic MS-DOS Software Components

Depending on your programming requirements, there are a number of DOS operations that can be encapsulated into compiled modules for reuse. For example, a DOS programmer employed by a telecommunications company could design a system of data structures and functions that support serial communications.

In this chapter we describe software components for keyboard processing and screen management, two activities that are central to many DOS applications, including an editor. You may want to refer to the overview of DOS given in Chapter 3.

6.1 Header Files with Shared Constants

We mentioned that header files are used to store external declarations for each C source file and to store commonly used constants. *scrnprnc.h* is one of our header files for constants. It contains a variety of constants that are useful for DOS screen, printer, and keyboard operations, plus the keystroke data structure discussed in Chapter 3.

We're combining these constants into one file to keep the total number of header files at a manageable level. You might prefer a different categorization of constants; however, we've found this combination to be satisfactory, since we typically require screen, printer, and keyboard operations in all of the DOS applications that we develop. Of course, using only a portion of header file has no negative impact on the size of the executable file that's generated for an application. Also, we don't have a sufficient number of data structure type definitions to warrant separation of constants and type definitions into two different header files.

Consider a subset of *scrnprnc.h*:

```
/**  scrnprnc.h  **  used by screen, printer, and keyboard routines  **/

#define VIDEO_INT           0x10     /* interrupts */
#define KEYBOARD_INT        0x16
#define DOS_FUNCTION        0x21
#define CONTROL_BREAK_FUNC  0x33
...
...
#define SET_CURSOR_POS  0x02         /* Int 10 function 2      */
#define READ_CURSOR_POS 0x03         /* Int 10 function 3      */
...
...
#define SCREEN_SIZE     4000         /* screen size @ 4000 bytes */
#define MONO_MODE       7            /* monochrome video mode #  */
#define MONO_SCREEN     0xb0000000   /* address of mono screen   */
#define COLOR_SCREEN    0xb8000000   /* address of color screen  */
...
...
/*
a data structure for keystrokes
*/

union keystroke {                    /* represents a key's     */
    unsigned char byte[2];           /* data and scan code     */
    int word;
};
```

In Chapter 3 we discussed the basics of using DOS interrupts (service requests). MS-DOS provides an extensive number of functions that applications can reference by number. In the beginning of *scrnprnc.h* we give meaningful names to three common DOS functions. Two of these represent low-level (BIOS) functions and one represents a high-level (kernel) function.

BIOS functions are accessed *individually* by number. We use the constant **VIDEO_INT** for the BIOS routine that handles video activities. We've mentioned that BIOS video routines are too inefficient in displaying text on the screen for typical DOS user interfaces, such as those used for word processors, spreadsheets, and so on. We can, however, use the video interrupt for other aspects of screen management, for example, determining the type of video system in the PC, moving the cursor, setting the cursor shape, and so on.

The keyboard interrupt, **KEYBOARD_INT**, is the other low-level function that we need for DOS applications. Both of these functions have sub-functions that must be specified any time that a request is sent via an **int86()** function call. For example, we've defined the constant **SET_CURSOR_POS** to represent the **VIDEO_INT** sub-function that positions the cursor.

Unlike the BIOS functions, each of which has a number that must be passed as the first argument to **int86()**, DOS kernel functions are collected under a single DOS interrupt, specifically, interrupt number 21H. **DOS_FUNCTION** is a useful identifier for accessing these high-level functions; each specific kernel function, for example, **CONTROL_BREAK_FUNC**, must then be specified by a register argument. Henceforth, the constants in *scrnprnc.h* are discussed as necessary.

6.2 The Keyboard Module

There are, of course, many operations that can be performed by way of the keyboard. For our purposes, it's convenient to provide a source file with a minimum number of keyboard operations. In practice, this module would grow to include more functions than required for a specific application. At some point, the source module could be compiled and stored as a library, so that only those functions required by a particular application would be linked into the executable file.

The declarations for our keyboard module are:

```
/****  keyboard.h  ****  external declarations for keyboard.c  ****/

extern int get_keystroke(void);
extern int keyboard_alt_depressed(void);
extern void set_cntl_break(int);
```

Now let's take a look at the individual functions. First, consider **get_keystroke()**, which we discussed in Chapter 3:

```
/*
get_keystroke() reads and returns the 16-bit scan code for a key.
*/

int get_keystroke(void)
{
    union REGS r;

    r.h.ah = KEYBOARD_READ;
    int86(KEYBOARD_INT, &r, &r);
    return r.x.ax;
```

```
}    /* get_keystroke */
```

The **r.h.ah** component of the **REGS** data structure **r** must specify the requested operation. After the keyboard interrupt returns, **r.x.ax** contains the two-byte keyboard code. **get_keystroke()** provides an interface to the low-level function required to read a keystroke. In particular, its task is to deliver the keystroke, not interpret it. Hence, there is no need for a **keystroke** data structure anywhere in **get_keystroke()**. Specifically, if **get_keystroke()** were designed to return a pointer to **keystroke**, its usefulness would be compromised. Returning an integer gives the programmer more flexibility.

Parenthetically, whether **get_keystroke()** should return an **int** or a **short** is, in our opinion, debatable, and depends on a number of issues, including programmer's preference, types of architecture you port software across, and so on. Note that in this module we're designing functions that are hardware-specific; hence, the assumption that **int** is a 16-bit data structure is not unreasonable.

For our editor application we always use the value returned by **get_keystroke()** with a variable of type **keystroke**, for example:

```
    ...
    union keystroke key;
    ...
    key.word = get_keystroke();
    ...
```

This approach is convenient because the function that defines **key** can use its individual components, **key.byte[0]** and **key.byte[1]**, and then pass along the 16-bit interpretation as either a **keystroke** or **int** data structure. If **get_keystroke()** were designed to return a **keystroke**, some of this flexibility would be lost.

We've elected to include two support functions in our module that would be useful in developing a larger version of **ed** (or for some other application). First, **keyboard_alt_depressed()** is a function that returns a Boolean value, indicating whether or not the **<Alt>** key has been pressed:

```
/*
keyboard_alt_depressed() determines whether or not the <Alt> key
is depressed--this can be used to allow a signal from the user.
*/

int keyboard_alt_depressed(void)
{
    union REGS r;

    r.h.ah = 0x2;
    int86(KEYBOARD_INT, &r, &r);
    return (r.h.al & 0x08);
```

```
}   /* keyboard_alt_depressed */
```

A lengthy description of keyboard shift states is beyond the scope of this book. You can, if interested, find more information on this topic in one of the PC books, such as Duncan (1988). In any case, this function is useful if you add, say, printing facilities, to an application, and you want to allow the user to terminate an operation. In particular, you can poll the keyboard simply by inserting a call to **keyboard_alt_depressed()** at the apropriate location in a function, say, in a loop test condition.

Many applications make use of the high-level DOS kernel functions that we mentioned earlier. If an application uses a DOS function that is capable of detecting a **<Ctrl>-<Break>** keystroke, the application will terminate when the DOS function is called. Needless to say, allowing this type of program termination to occur is a no-no with many applications, including an editor in which changes to the edit text may be unsaved. Using ROM-BIOS functions allows us to bypass this problem, at least during keyboard processing.

Nevertheless, there are a number of support routines that you might choose to add to **ed** that would use DOS functions. For example, if you use C library routines to perform I/O, say, for a printer routine, the C compiler will generate calls to DOS functions to perform the I/O. Hence, it's a good idea to disable **<Ctrl>-<Break>** checking. The function **set_cntl_break()** performs this task:

```
/*
set_cntl_break() stores the current status of the break flag, and
then turns it off.  It can also be used to restore the break status.
*/

void set_cntl_break(int operation)
{
    static int break_status;
    union REGS r;

    if (operation == OFF) {
        r.h.ah = CONTROL_BREAK_FUNC;
        r.h.al = 0;              /* get status function */
        int86(DOS_FUNCTION, &r, &r);
        break_status = r.h.dl;
        r.h.ah = CONTROL_BREAK_FUNC;
        r.h.al = 1;              /* set status function */
        r.h.dl = OFF;
        int86(DOS_FUNCTION, &r, &r);
    }
    else {
        r.h.ah = CONTROL_BREAK_FUNC;
        r.h.al = 1;              /* set status function */
```

```
        r.h.dl = break_status;
        int86(DOS_FUNCTION, &r, &r);
    }
}   /* set_cntl_break */
```

If **set_cntl_break()** is called with the argument **OFF**, for example, "set_cntl_break(OFF);", it first records the current break status in the static variable **break_status**, and then sets the break status to "off." A subsequent call to **set_cntl_break()** with any argument value other than **OFF** can be used to reinstate the previous break state.

As a exercise, consider the modifications required in *ed.c* to provide this measure of protection. (Hint: You only need to add two lines of source code to *ed.c*.)

6.3 Procedure Abstraction in the Keyboard Module

In Chapter 5 we mentioned the importance of abstraction and information hiding in designing a window module, so that the user of the windows package is isolated from the low-level details associated with the physical implementation of a window. Is this an important issue for keystrokes?

For the modules in this book, we've made the decision *not* to encapsulate keystrokes and keystroke operations. Let's consider the ramifications of allocating keystrokes on demand, and accessing **keystroke** components directly, in light of our arguments for a high-level interface to the windows package.

Principally, our decision means that the programmer is forced to deal directly with the components of the keystroke data structure, namely, **key.byte[0]**, **key.byte[1]**, and **key.word**—information about the structure of a keystroke is not hidden. In particular, a programmer must provide a statement such as

```
if (key.byte[1] == QUIT) {
    <ask the user if he/she is sure, before terminating>
}
```

The implication is that the programmer must know that the second byte **(byte[1])** encodes the scan code for a keystroke.

As an alternative, we could provide high-level functions for hiding these details:

```
if (scan_code(key) == QUIT) {
    <ask the user if he/she is sure, before terminating>
}
```

Here, **scan_code()** takes a keystroke as an argument and returns its scan code (physical keyboard identification).

In principle, providing this type of abstraction seems like a good idea. However, some programmers would object to the latter approach, arguing that an additional procedure call is too high a price to pay for the enhanced readability, especially with a data structure that

(1) is inherently simple, (2) is primarily associated with one function (**get_keystroke()**), and (3) isn't going to be changed in the future. In contrast, a structure that stores the attributes of a window (1) is quite complex, (2) has numerous operations performed against it, and (3) is very likely to be changed in the future.

The performance consideration may indeed be important for this particular data structure, given the likely use of the auto-repeat feature of a keyboard with certain applications (such as editors). Although we've argued for readability over performance considerations in many cases, it doesn't make sense to build an application that's I/O bound by the keyboard.

There is another issue besides performance that must be considered, namely, flexibility. Our primary reason for rejecting the use of abstraction and/or encapsulation for hiding the details of keystrokes is our desire to take advantage of the integer nature of key codes (both ASCII and scan). That is, we want the flexibility of developing functions that conditionally return either the integer interpretation of a keystroke (**key.word**) or Boolean false—this is a C tradition.

If we were to adopt a more abstract approach, the rules of consistency would have us restrict direct access to keystroke internals, such as **key.byte[0]**, to functions in the keyboard module. Thus, other modules, such as the window module, would be restricted to passing and returning a (whole) keystroke data structure. This approach severely inhibits our ability to design flexible keyboard-related functions (in other modules), say, a function that returns a key's scan code under normal conditions, and returns **FALSE** for one or more special conditions. (This issue is especially important in the second half of the book where we encapsulate the dispatchers for keystrokes with the functions that implement the dispatched activities.)

Although each of our reasons for not taking a more abstract approach carries some weight in our decision, the desire for flexibility in manipulating keystrokes is the overriding concern. We'll address this issue again in subsequent chapters.

6.4 The Character Display Module

The window system manages (almost) all screen I/O operations for **ed**; hence, we could locate all the functions for writing to the screen in *windows.c*. There are, however, other applications that require screen-writing operations, but not windowing capabilities. One example would be a sliding-bar menu system. Thus, we can enhance reusability by isolating display operations in a separate module.

The source file for our character display functions is *display.c*:

```
/****  display.c  ****  direct video display routines  ****/

#include "screen.h"
#include "display.h"


#define BLANK        ' '
```

```
#define char_addr(base, r, c) ((base) + ((r) * 160) + ((c) * 2))
...
...
```

We've made an exception to our normal rule for locating **#define** macros in a separate file, say, *displayc.h*. Since there are only two **#defines**, we've included them directly in *display.c*.

There are two **#include** directives for *display.c*. *screen.h* is included to provide access to screen-management information. In this case, the access function **get_screen_addr()** returns a pointer to video memory. In addition, each module includes its associated header file of external declarations. As mentioned earlier, this practice provides an extra measure of error detection, since the compiler will flag any discrepancies between *display.h*'s declarations and *display.c*'s definitions.

One useful function is **display_string()**, which can be used to display a string beginning at an arbitrary location on the screen:

```
/*
display_string() displays a string on the screen with the
specified attribute.
*/

void display_string(int row, int col, char *str, int attr)
{
    register int i;
    char far *scrn_ptr;

    scrn_ptr = get_screen_addr();
    scrn_ptr = char_addr(scrn_ptr, row, col);
    for (i = 0; str[i]; i++) {
        *scrn_ptr++ = str[i];
        *scrn_ptr++ = attr;
    }
}   /* display_string */
```

Recall that we described the operation of a similar function from this module, **display_char()**, in Chapter 3, where we first mentioned DOS screen-management operations. **display_string()** performs the same operations as **display_char()**, except it must loop over each character in the string.

Top-down design would have us call **display_char()** in a loop to display a string; however, we don't want to invoke **display_char()** for each character that's printed. In particular, once the beginning of video memory is determined and the offset is calculated for the first character of the string, it's wasteful to repeat these calculations for subsequent characters.

As a variation on **display_string()**, consider **display_blanks()**:

```
/*
display_blanks displays a series of blanks at the
specified row and column.
*/

void display_blanks(int row, int col, int count, int attr)
{
    char far *scrn_ptr;

    scrn_ptr = get_screen_addr();
    scrn_ptr = char_addr(scrn_ptr, row, col);
    while (count-- > 0) {
         *scrn_ptr++ = BLANK;
         *scrn_ptr++ = attr;
    }
}   /* display_blanks */
```

display_blanks() is useful mainly for selective screen clearing operations. For example, you could use **display_blanks()** to clear a portion of **ed**'s top status line, in order to display printer status information during a print operation. Subsequently, you could clear the printer status information and redisplay the information that normally appears on the top status line, for example, the filename. Providing a parameter for the video attribute, enhances the utility of **display_blanks()**.

6.5 The Screen Management Module

At this point we should commit to one of the screen management strategies outlined in Chapter 2. The calls to **get_screen_addr()** in our character display module above indicate our decision. Namely, we prefer to implement *screen.c* as a closed module with limited possibility of corruption by outside agents.

screen.c contains the final two of our five external variables for the editor project; both externals are private:

```
/****  screen.c  ****  screen handling routines  ****/

#include <dos.h>
#include "scrnprnc.h"
#include "screen.h"
...
...

/*
```

```
globals:
*/

static char far *screen;                /* private ptr. to video RAM */
static char exit_screen[SCREEN_SIZE];   /* private screen buffer */
```

Specifically, the **static** modifier restricts the lexical scope of **screen** and **exit_screen** to the name space created for functions defined in *screen.c*.

The first function is **get_screen_addr()**, which provides read-only access to **screen** as discussed earlier:

```
/*
get_screen_addr() returns the start of video memory.
*/

char far *get_screen_addr(void)
{
    return screen;
}   /* get_screen_addr */
```

Strictly speaking, the **far** modifier is unnecessary for our application, since we intend to compile **ed** with the compact memory model, which uses 32-bit pointers by default. However, another application, such as a simple calculator, would typically use a small memory model; hence, the screen address should be explicitly handled as a far pointer to prevent programmer insanity in a subsequent project.

Most applications must (1) initialize **screen**, and (2) test the video mode. These operations are related; the starting address for video memory is a function of the type of video hardware. Specifically, video memory begins at the absolute address B0000000H for monochrome systems and B8000000H for color systems. (These constants are given in *scrnprnc.h*.) To enhance reusability in future projects, we should factor video operations into a number of small functions. For example, **get_video_mode()** uses a ROM-BIOS call to determine the video mode, monochrome or color:

```
/*
get_video_mode() returns the screen mode.
*/

int get_video_mode(void)
{
    union REGS r;

    r.h.ah = GET_VIDEO_MODE;
    int86(VIDEO_INT, &r, &r);
    return r.h.al;
```

```
}    /* get_video_mode */
```

(More elaborate determinations of video mode are possible, but unnecessary for many applications. For an in-depth treatment see Duntemann [1989].)

get_video_mode() is useful in **set_screen_addr()** for initializing our pointer to video memory, **screen**:

```
/*
set_screen_addr() sets the screen pointer to the
appropriate video buffer address.
*/

void set_screen_addr(void)
{
    screen = (char far *) ((get_video_mode() == MONO_MODE) ?
                                        MONO_SCREEN : COLOR_SCREEN);
}    /* set_screen_addr */
```

Often, an application needs to control the characteristics of the cursor, specifically, cursor size and shape. When this is the case, it's good etiquette to restore the user's previous cursor characteristics upon program termination. The following function, **dos_level_cursor()**, can be used to record the cursor characteristics during program initialization and restore its shape and size during program termination:

```
/*
dos_level_cursor() handles cursor operations.  It saves the current
cursor size and position in four internal static variables, or re-
stores the cursor size and position previously saved, depending on the
value of "operation."
*/

void dos_level_cursor(int op)
{
    union REGS r;
    static int row, column, start, end;

    if (op == CURSOR_RESTORE) {          /* restore the cursor */
        r.h.ah = SET_CURSOR_POS;
        r.h.dh = row;
        r.h.dl = column;
        r.h.bh = 0;
        int86(VIDEO_INT, &r, &r);
        r.h.ah = SET_CURSOR_SIZE;
        r.h.ch = start;
```

```
        r.h.cl = end;
        r.h.bh = PAGE_0;
        int86(VIDEO_INT, &r, &r);
    }
    else {                              /* save the cursor */
        r.h.ah = READ_CURSOR_POS;
        r.h.bh = PAGE_0;
        int86(VIDEO_INT, &r, &r);
        row = r.h.dh;
        column = r.h.dl;
        start = r.h.ch;
        end = r.h.cl;
    }
}   /* dos_level_cursor */
```

The constants in **dos_level_cursor()** are pretty self-explanatory. Duncan (1988) provides more information on the BIOS and hardware details associated with cursor manipulation.

Given these definitions, we can put together a function that's useful for initializing the video system for most applications:

```
/*
video_initialize() determines the screen address and saves the
screen buffer in the exit_screen array (global); it returns the
video_mode.  (restore_exit_screen() recovers the old screen.)
*/

int video_initialize(void)
{
    int i;

    set_screen_addr();
    for (i = 0; i < SCREEN_SIZE; i++)
        exit_screen[i] = screen[i];
/*  memcpy(exit_screen, screen, SCREEN_SIZE);*/
    dos_level_cursor(CURSOR_SAVE);   /* record its characteristics */
    return get_video_mode();
}   /* video_initialize */
```

video_initialize() calls **set_screen_addr()** to initialize **screen**, and then saves an image of the screen in the private variable **exit_screen**. Immediately before the application terminates, **restore_exit_screen()** should be called to restore the screen to its pre-application state:

```
/*
restore_exit_screen() restores the user's screen that existed prior to
the current program's execution.  The user's screen was saved by
video_initialize().
*/

void restore_exit_screen(void)
{
    int i;

    for (i = 0; i < SCREEN_SIZE; i++)
        screen[i] = exit_screen[i];
/*  memcpy(screen, exit_screen, SCREEN_SIZE);*/
    dos_level_cursor(CURSOR_RESTORE);    /* reset cursor size/posn. */
}   /* restore_exit_screen */
```

This strategy ensures that the user can still see any important on-screen information that existed prior to the application's invocation.

In the previous two functions we could have employed **memcpy()** for screen copying operations. (Calls to **memcpy()** have been commented out.) However, **memcpy()** is a reasonably sophisticated function, and using it here doesn't "tap its potential." We can reduce the size of the executable file by providing our own simple loop.

The last function that we mention is **cursor_rc**:

```
/*
cursor_rc positions the cursor at the specified coordinates.
*/

void cursor_rc(int row, int column)
{
    union REGS r;

    r.h.ah = SET_CURSOR_POS;
    r.h.dh = row;
    r.h.dl = column;
    r.h.bh = PAGE_0;
    int86(VIDEO_INT, &r, &r);
}   /* cursor_rc */
```

It uses a ROM-BIOS service call to set the cursor to the row and column coordinates given in **row** and **column**. For our editor application, **cursor_rc** is used primarily by the windowing routines.

Sometimes with an application that doesn't require windows, you need to display a message for the user. **display_string()** can handle this task; however, it doesn't perform any cursor manipulation. In particular, it doesn't advance the cursor to the location of the message. Cursor management would be required, for example, if the application required a response to the message. In this case, you could use **cursor_rc** in conjunction with **display_string()** for low-level interaction with the user, or to build a higher-level function. In any case, providing these services as atomic functions in their respective modules enhances extensibility.

7

Developing a General-purpose Windowing System

The screen and keyboard modules described in Chapter 6 provide the fundamental tools for building a windowing system. In this chapter we provide a reasonably complete windowing system. Although it does not provide as many windowing routines as some of the full-scale, commercial windowing packages, its facilities are adequate for most programming projects.

7.1 Background

In this book we have two goals: (1) to focus on a number of reusability issues related to C and C++, and (2) to provide a reasonably significant software product as a demonstration tool. In particular, we don't want our discussion to be dominated by DOS-related issues. In order to balance these two goals we'll implement a very simple window design that can be extended in various ways.

Our discussion in earlier chapters covering IBM PC hardware and MS-DOS characteristics provides all the background necessary for the windowing system designed in this chapter. Of course, other PC and/or DOS books, such as Duncan (1988), can be consulted for additional information on the PC video system. One book, by Schildt (1988), provides a brief introduction to DOS video basics, plus several examples of the traditional approach used by DOS programmers to develop pop-up windows, pull-down menus, and so on. Schildt (1988) also provides a number of small demonstration programs for pop-up window and pull-down menu routines. Another book, by Rochkind (1988), also covers video (display) programming.

Our window system uses the traditional PC video-addressing algorithm, given in numerous DOS books and described in Chapter 3. In our opinion, Schildt (1988) is quite representative of the way that most DOS programmers design video routines (moderate amount of abstraction); hence, it is reasonable to start with a similar design and algorithms. Specifically, we'll set up a window descriptor table for each pop-up window, and then design a family of functions that perform window operations using the values stored in a given window descriptor table

The window system given in Schildt (1988) supports basic window operations, such as would be required for a pop-up, window-based calculator or notepad; hence, it provides a good introduction to the basics of manipulating a PC's display. (If you have limited experience with PC display operations, you may want to consult Schildt [1988]). In our case, however, we need a more sophisticated window system; we must design a system that supports the horizontal and virtual scrolling operations required for full-scale editing operations. Moreover, since we are developing our software from a system of reusable modules, we must incorporate our existing screen and keyboard modules into the design.

7.2 Abstract Data Structures and Window Handles

In Chapter 5 we provided a preview of the high-level interface to the window module. Typically, each application must define as many window data structures, in array form, as necessary to meet the needs of the application:

```
window_frame wframe[MAIN_EDIT_WIN + MIN_NUM_WINS];
```

Each window is identified by its position in the array. With this approach it's convenient to define preprocessor constants with highly mnemonic names to serve as window handles, for example:

```
#define MAIN_EDIT_WIN       0       /* window array positions   */
...
...
#define FIND_WIN            3
```

An alternate approach is to design a windows package in which window handles are pointers to window data structures, instead of indexes into an array of window structures. That is, if **window_frame** is a data structure given in a header file associated with the window module, the application could define its windows as follows:

```
window_frame main_edit_win, find_win;
```

Subsequently, these windows could be passed to the appropriate window functions, either directly:

```
activate_window(&main_edit_win, "Editor 1.0", ...);
```

or, indirectly by passing a pointer to a window:

```
activate_window(main_edit_win_ptr, "Editor 1.0", ...);
```

The primary advantage of the array-based approach is that you can avoid the slightly awkward "->" syntax. For example, with pointer-based window handles, a function in the window module would reference a structure component such as **window->header**, where **window**, a function parameter, is a pointer to a **window_frame**, representing, say, **&main_edit_win**:

```
void activate_window(window_frame *window, char *hdr, ...)
    ...
    if (*hdr)
        window->header = hdr;
    ...
```

The primary disadvantage with designing a module based on arrays is that the array name must be *assumed* during the design of the window module. For example, a window function is invoked with the array index as an argument:

```
activate_window(MAIN_EDIT_WIN, "Editor 1.0", ...);
```

In this case, the function in the window module would reference a structure component by position only, using a hard-coded array name:

```
void activate_window(int n, char *hdr, ...)
    ...
    if (*hdr)
        wframe[n].header = hdr;
    ...
```

In our opinion, the trade-offs are equal for both approaches. Despite the close relationship between pointers and array references in C, it is often argued that using array references promotes a higher level of programming than using pointers. On the other hand, C programmers are known for their "love of pointers." Incidentally, with C++, as we'll investigate in the second half of the book, this issue simply disappears, because windows will be established as objects. For now, we'll use the array-based approach, as do Schildt (1988) and Rochkind (1988), two references we mentioned earlier that focus on DOS environments. One example of windowing software that uses the pointer-based approach is SunView™ (Sun Microsystems, 1988); see Chapter 17 for an example.

7.3 Abstract Data Structures and External Variables

There is no single best way to make use of abstraction. Our primary interest is in designing reusable C modules for windows, screens, and so on—reusability is an overriding concern. Note that we're discussing application-dependent modules simply to provide a concrete overview of our application-independent modules. We're primarily interested in the latter modules and how they affect the design of the former type of module.

One question is: Does the use of a global variable conflict with the use of information-hiding techniques to reduce the surface complexity of a program? We don't believe so, for the following reason. We've argued that we're concerned with software reusability at the module level, where a module is a tightly-bound collection of data, plus the procedures necessary for manipulating that data. Hence, we don't want to put anything in, say, a window module, that limits (or complicates) its reusability. For this reason, our window module will be designed to work in concert with any window described by the abstract data type **window_frame**, where the physical *definition*, or instantiation, of a window occurs outside the window module.

7.4 The Window Descriptor Table Array

First, let's describe what we need in the array elements, mentioning some of the associated functions. Afterward, we can examine the windowing functions in more detail.

Chapter 5 provided a preview of our design. Specifically, we want an array-based windowing system. The data associated with each window can be represented by the window structure, **window_frame**, given in *windowsc.h*:

```
typedef struct {
    int start_r;
    ...
    int end_c;
    ...
} window_frame;
```

(We'll fill in some of the variables in the subsequent discussion.) In other words, **window_frame** serves as a simple descriptor table for each window. At a particular point in time there could be, say, five windows, defined by the program such that two windows are currently displayed, one overlapping the other, with the cursor present in the top-most, overlapping window; see Figure 7.1.

In this case, each defined window exists as an array element. For example, in Chapter 5 we defined the array of window structures **wframe**:

```
window_frame wframe[MAIN_EDIT_WIN + MIN_NUM_WINS];
```

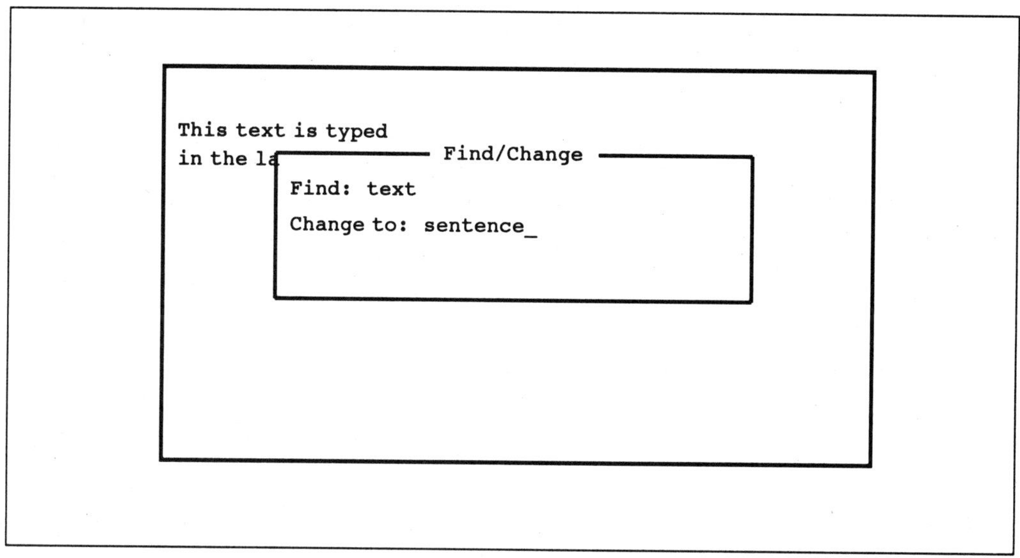

Figure 7.1 Overlapping Windows

where "MAIN_EDIT_WIN + MIN_NUM_WINS" evaluates to the number of windows (plus 1) that are required to support the editor system.

Let's consider some of the variables in the window structure. Recall from our screen module that "r" means row and "c" means column throughout our source code. Every window must have physical coordinates. Hence, we can use **start_r** to represent the starting row position, **start_c** to represent the starting column position, **end_r** to represent the ending row position, and **end_c** to represent the ending column—all coordinates are zero-based. For our purposes, it's convenient to use the outside row/column to display a window border.

What else do we need in the structure **window_frame**? In order to manage overlapping windows, we must be able to store, and then restore, part of the screen image of the currently active window—before we can activate an alternate window. That is, if a small prompt box pops up over an edit window, when the prompt box is deactivated, the previous text must be redisplayed to restore the previous on-screen image of the edit window.

To provide this capability each window structure in the array must allocate a buffer large enough to store the portion of the screen that it pops up over. Specifically, when a window is activated, the current contents of video memory that map to the on-screen location of the to-be-displayed window, both the text and attributes for each character, must be copied to this buffer. Before looking at a function that performs this task, consider the data structures that are required. First, we must add a pointer variable to **window_frame** for representing the buffer:

```
typedef struct {
    int start_r;
    ...
    int end_c;
    char *window_save_buffer;
    ...
} window_frame;
```

The buffer itself can be allocated dynamically from memory using the C library function **malloc()** at the time the window is physically created. Note that the window array merely allocates a structure, specifically, a descriptor table, for each window; each window must be instantiated by the function **make_window()** at run-time. (Recall the example of **make_window()** given in Chapter 5.) The pointer variable **window_save_buffer** can be used to reference the dynamically allocated buffer.

The function **window_save_screen_area()** performs the copy operation:

```
/*
window_save_screen_area() saves the screen area to a buffer.
*/

void window_save_screen_area(int n)
{
    register int i, j, k = 0;
    char *win_buf;
    char far *win_ptr, far *win_ptr_2;

    win_buf = wframe[n].window_save_buffer;
    win_ptr = get_screen_addr();
    for (i = wframe[n].start_c; i < wframe[n].end_c + 1; i++)
        for (j = wframe[n].start_r; j < wframe[n].end_r + 1; j++) {
            win_ptr_2 = char_addr(win_ptr, j, i);
            win_buf[k++] = *win_ptr_2;
            win_buf[k++] = *(win_ptr_2 + 1);
            *win_ptr_2 = BLANK;
        }
}   /* window_save_screen_area */
```

Another pointer variable is useful in providing a header, or title, for each window. If we provide a built-in capability for associating a title with each window, then each time a window is popped up, its title will be displayed in the center of the top border. If a header isn't required for a window, the programmer can supply a null header. Our descriptor table structure now includes:

```
typedef struct {
    int start_r;
    ...
    int end_c;
    char *window_save_buffer;
    char *header;
    ...
} window_frame;
```

Note that we don't have to allocate space for the maximum length header in the window descriptor table. By allocating a pointer only, we can take advantage of literal strings (argument passing). For example, consider **allocate_windows()** from Chapter 5:

```
int allocate_windows(void)
{
    return (make_window(MAIN_EDIT_WIN, "", 1, 0, 23, 79) == TRUE &&
            ...
            ...
            make_window(FIND_WIN,
                "Find/Change", 3, 16, 7, 16 + POPUP_WIDTH) == TRUE);
}   /* allocate_windows */
```

The second argument to **make_window()** is the window header. The find window title, "Find/Change", is allocated by the compiler; see Figure 7.1. Its starting address is passed to **make_window()**; this address can then be assigned to **header** in the descriptor table. On the other hand, the edit window does not have a header.

7.5 Window Instantiation

Now that we've previewed our application program, **ed**, and the window data structure, let's look at **make_window()**, the function that establishes, or instantiates, a window:

```
/*
make_window() establishes a window.  Each window is referenced by
number.  make_window() returns TRUE, if no errors occur; it returns
a special code, if memory can't be allocated, and it returns
FALSE otherwise.
*/

int make_window(int n, char *header, int start_r, int start_c,
                int end_r, int end_c)
{
    char *save_ptr;
```

```
    if ((start_r > 23) || (start_r < 0) ||
        (start_c > 78) || (start_c < 0))
        return FALSE;
    if ((end_r > 24) || (end_c > 79))
        return FALSE;
    if ((save_ptr =
            (char *) malloc((end_r - start_r + 1) *
                            (end_c - start_c + 1) * 2)) == NULL)
        return CANT_ALLOCATE_WIN;

    wframe[n].window_save_buffer = save_ptr;
    wframe[n].start_r = start_r;          /* window boundaries */
    wframe[n].end_r = end_r;
    wframe[n].start_c = start_c;
    wframe[n].end_c = end_c;
    wframe[n].header = header;
    wframe[n].is_active = FALSE;
    wframe[n].offset = 0;                 /* see windowsc.h */
    wframe[n].cursor_r = 0;               /* see windowsc.h */
    wframe[n].virtual_c = 0;              /* see windowsc.h */
    return TRUE;
}   /* make_window */
```

After performing some error checking, **make_window()** initializes the variables we've discussed so far. Note that in the call to **malloc()** we must multiply by two because there are two bytes for each on-screen character: text and attribute.

There are several additional variables that we must now address. The complete window structure is

```
typedef struct {
    int offset;       /* physical column = virtual column - offset */
    int cursor_r;     /* physical row for the cursor */
    int virtual_c;    /* virtual column for the cursor */
    int start_r, end_r;
    int start_c, end_c;
    char *window_save_buffer;
    char *header;
    int is_active;
} window_frame;
```

First, the variable **is_active** is used by a number of functions that must know whether or not the window is already active. **activate_window()** provides one example:

```
/*
activate_window() switches to a particular window.
*/

void activate_window(int n, char *header, int header_attr,
                             int border_attr)
{
    if (!wframe[n].is_active) {
        window_save_screen_area(n);
        wframe[n].is_active = TRUE;
        window_display_border(n, border_attr);
        window_display_header(n, header, header_attr);
    }
}   /* activate_window */
```

In the case of **activate_window()**, it doesn't make sense to activate a window if it's already active.

The three remaining variables are used for cursor manipulation. Each window must have two variables to represent the cursor's current row-column coordinates; in a simpler window system we might call these variables **cursor_r** and **cursor_c**. Note that the values of the window coordinates, **start_r**, **end_c**, and so on, are physical rows and columns. Cursor coordinates, on the other hand, are given relative to their respective window. For example, if **cursor_r** has value 1 for some window, then the cursor is on the second row of that window, regardless of the window's position on the screen.

Consider column, or horizontal, positioning. Our window system must provide horizontal cursor movement for our edit module. In order to provide horizontal scrolling, we can use a combination of two variables, **virtual_c** and **offset**, (instead of **cursor_c**) to formulate the column coordinate.

We use the term "virtual" to reflect the fact that a general window system must support a shifted image, that is, a view of the underlying window. In this case, physical window column *c*, the on-screen column, corresponds to logical column (c - a), where a is an arbitrary offset—the number of columns that the window has been shifted. For our purposes, it's sufficient to support a shift in one direction only. Specifically, the window contents can be shifted left, or, in other words, the window frame can be scrolled to the right over the underlying window contents.

In terms of our **window_frame** variables, **virtual_c** is the sum of **offset**, the current window offset, and the physical window column *c*. We only need two column variables in our structure, since any two values in this relationship can be used to derive the third value. For example, if a window is 40 columns wide, not counting the border columns, and the current values for **offset** and **virtual_c** are 10 and 49, respectively, the cursor is currently positioned in the 39th column. For this window, column 39 is the rightmost column (0 to 39); hence, a pending cursor movement to the right would require special action, namely, additional window scrolling.

The role of the cursor variables is easily demonstrated by looking at a function that manipulates the cursor; one such function is **window_go_rc()**. **window_go_rc()** is used to position the cursor at the specified coordinates; for example, "window_go_rc(1, 2, 3)" positions window number 1's cursor in row 2 and column 3 (zero-based). Consider the definition of **window_go_rc()**:

```
/*
window_go_rc() sets the coordinates within a window.
*/

int window_go_rc(int n, int r, int c)
{
    if ((r < 0) || ((r + wframe[n].start_r) >= (wframe[n].end_r - 1)))
        return FALSE;
    if ((c < 0) || ((c + wframe[n].start_c - wframe[n].offset) >=
                    (wframe[n].end_c - 1)))
        return FALSE;
    wframe[n].cursor_r = r;
    wframe[n].virtual_c = c;
    cursor_rc(wframe[n].start_r + r + 1,
                    wframe[n].start_c + c + 1 - wframe[n].offset);
    return TRUE;
}   /* window_go_rc */
```

The fourth statement of the function

```
    wframe[n].virtual_c = c;
```

updates **virtual_c** to the value passed as the third argument. This update can occur only if the value passed as **c** satisfies the *complement* of the following condition:

```
    (c < 0) || ((c + wframe[n].start_c - wframe[n].offset) >=
                    (wframe[n].end_c - 1))
```

That is, **c** must be greater than or equal to 0, and **c** - **offset** must not exceed the bounds of the window, specifically, **end_c** - **start_c** - 1.

Vertical scrolling, on the other hand, is provided by DOS. **window_scroll()** encapsulates the ROM-BIOS call and the window coordinates:

```
/*
window_scroll() scrolls a window up, or down, one line, depending
on the value of the second argument, operation.
*/
```

```
void window_scroll(int n, int operation)
{
    union REGS r;

    r.h.ah = operation;
    r.h.al = 1;
    r.h.ch = wframe[n].start_r + 1;
    r.h.cl = wframe[n].start_c + 1;
    r.h.dh = wframe[n].end_r - 1;
    r.h.dl = wframe[n].end_c - 1;
    r.h.bh = NORMAL_VIDEO;
    int86(VIDEO_INT, &r, &r);
}   /* window_scroll */
```

window_scroll() scrolls the window one line. The direction depends on the value of **operation**, either **SCROLL_UP** or **SCROLL_DOWN**. Note that only the area inside the border should be scrolled.

The next chapter provides examples of horizontal and vertical scrolling operations.

7.6 Miscellaneous Window Operations

Now that we've described our window descriptor table, we can overview several of the functions that provide basic window operations. Afterward, you can turn to Appendix A, if you're interested in the examining the remaining functions that make up the window module.

First, consider the complement of **activate_window()**, **deactivate_window()**:

```
/*
deactivate_window() clears a window, restoring the previous screen.
*/

void deactivate_window(int n)
{
    if (wframe[n].is_active) {
        wframe[n].offset = 0;
        wframe[n].cursor_r = 0;
        wframe[n].virtual_c = 0;
        wframe[n].is_active = FALSE;
        window_restore_screen_area(n);
    }
}   /* deactivate_window */
```

Each time a window is deactivated, it is necessary (with our design) to reset the cursor variables, so that when that window is reactivated, write operations will begin relative to the top-left position—other functions depend on this logic.

The call to **window_restore_screen_area**() restores the screen area occupied by the *n*th window to its previous image. It doesn't matter what previously occupied this location, for example, blanks, underlined text, normal or reverse video—any displayable text. **window_restore_screen_area**()'s definition is

```
/*
window_restore_screen_area() recovers the screen area
used by a window.
*/

void window_restore_screen_area(int n)
{
    register int i, j, k = 0;
    char *win_buf;
    char far *win_ptr, far *win_ptr_2;

    win_buf = wframe[n].window_save_buffer;
    win_ptr = get_screen_addr();
    for (i = wframe[n].start_c; i < wframe[n].end_c + 1; i++)
        for (j = wframe[n].start_r; j < wframe[n].end_r + 1; j++) {
            win_ptr_2 = char_addr(win_ptr, j, i);
            *win_ptr_2++ = win_buf[k++];
            *win_ptr_2 = win_buf[k++];
        }
}   /* window_restore_screen_area */
```

Our window system is text-, not graphics-, based. Text-based windows are preferable for applications where there's no need for displaying graphics, primarily because (with IBM-compatible PCs) text processing is considerably faster.

The window border is the only graphics-like component of our window. However, we don't need true graphics-mode processing to display a border, since a number of box-drawing characters are provided in the extended ASCII character set, which is used with IBM-compatible PCs. For example, the "ASCII code" for the vertical bar is 179 (decimal). *windowsc.h* includes definitions for the single-line, box-drawing characters:

```
/****  windowsc.h  ****  constants used by windows.c  ****/
...
...

#define VERTICAL_BAR        179     /* 186 */
#define HORIZON_BAR         196     /* 205 */
```

```
#define TOP_LEFT_CORNER      218       /* 201 */
#define BOT_LEFT_CORNER      192       /* 200 */
#define TOP_RIGHT_CORNER     191       /* 187 */
#define BOT_RIGHT_CORNER     217       /* 188 */
...
...
```

(Double-line equivalents are given in the comments.)

window_display_border() demonstrates a simple method of displaying a window border:

```
/*
window_display_border() puts a border around a window.
*/

void window_display_border(int n, int attr)
{
    register int i;

    for (i = wframe[n].start_r + 1; i < wframe[n].end_r; i++) {
        display_char(i, wframe[n].start_c, VERTICAL_BAR, attr);
        display_char(i, wframe[n].end_c, VERTICAL_BAR, attr);
    }
    for (i = wframe[n].start_c + 1; i < wframe[n].end_c; i++) {
        display_char(wframe[n].start_r, i, HORIZON_BAR, attr);
        display_char(wframe[n].end_r, i, HORIZON_BAR, attr);
    }
    display_char(wframe[n].start_r, wframe[n].start_c,
                    TOP_LEFT_CORNER, attr);
    display_char(wframe[n].start_r, wframe[n].end_c,
                    TOP_RIGHT_CORNER, attr);
    display_char(wframe[n].end_r, wframe[n].start_c,
                    BOT_LEFT_CORNER, attr);
    display_char(wframe[n].end_r, wframe[n].end_c,
                    BOT_RIGHT_CORNER, attr);
}   /* window_display_border */
```

Two **for** loops provide the vertical and horizontal borders, respectively. The first **for** loop displays, in tandem, the left-hand and right-hand vertical, line-drawing characters; the second **for** loop displays the horizontal borders. Recall that **display_char()** is defined in the character display module. After the vertical and horizontal borders are completed, **window_display_border()** calls **display_char()** to fill in the corners.

When we described the pointer variable **header** in **window_frame**, we mentioned that we wanted our windows to have the ability to display a header. **window_display_border()**

performs its task without regard for the window header. We can use a separate function to overlay the center portion of the top window border with a header, if one is provided by the programmer:

```
/*
window_display_header() displays a header, centered on the top line
of a window border.
*/

void window_display_header(int n, char *alt_header, int attr)
{
    char *hdr_ptr;
    int hdr_start, hdr_len;

    hdr_ptr = (*alt_header == EOS) ? wframe[n].header : alt_header;
    hdr_len = strlen(hdr_ptr);
    hdr_start = ((wframe[n].end_c - wframe[n].start_c - 1 - hdr_len)
                / 2) + 1 + wframe[n].start_c;
    if (hdr_start < wframe[n].start_c)
        return;
    display_string(wframe[n].start_r, hdr_start, hdr_ptr, attr);
    if (hdr_len > 0) {
        display_char(wframe[n].start_r, hdr_start - 1, BLANK, attr);
        display_char(wframe[n].start_r, hdr_start + hdr_len, BLANK,
                        attr);
    }
}   /* window_display_header */
```

The first statement in **window_display_header()** establishes a local pointer to one of two headers. Recall that **window_frame** provides one header variable, namely, **header**, a pointer to a character string. **header** serves as a place-holder for a default window header, which a programmer must provide during window instantiation with **make_window()**. (The default header can be null.)

Note from our earlier definition of **activate_window()** that each time a window is activated a header may be specified as an argument; this header overrides the default header. Specifically, **activate_window()** first calls **window_display_border()** to draw the border. Then **activate_window()** calls **window_display_header()** to center the header on the top border. If **alt_header**, the alternate header, is null, the default header is used. Lastly, if the header isn't null, a blank is displayed before and after the header for readability.

In our opinion, the provision for default and alternate headers greatly enhances the functionality of the headers—they become dynamic sources of information. For example, in **ed** a message and/or query window is used to display warning messages and prompt for information (such as a filename). We can provide a default header such as "Attention" for displaying a warning such as "** no tag has been set **" that requires no further elaboration.

However, for a warning such as "** file not found **", we can override the default header with the filename that the user specified—that is, we can use the header area for user feedback. This provision for "variable headers" is the main reason for having **window_display_header()** provide the leading and trailing space around a header, instead of forcing the programmer to insert space manually. For example, a filename variable, without modification, can be passed as an argument to **activate_window()**:

```
activate_window(ATTN_WIN, filename, NORMAL_VIDEO, NORMAL_VIDEO);
```

In subsequent chapters we make extensive use of the header area of certain windows.

7.7 Window Input and Output

For our window system we want very simple input and output routines. We've already discussed the importance of avoiding calls to high-level DOS functions, which can be interrupted by a break sequence. All communication with the user through a window can be handled by two fundamental window I/O functions, **window_putchar()** and **window_getche()**. (They are named after similar C library functions.)

First, consider **window_putchar()**, the character output function:

```
/*
window_putchar() prints a character in a window.
*/

int window_putchar(int n, char ch)
{
    register int r, c;
    char far *win_ptr;

    if (!wframe[n].is_active)
        return FALSE;
    /*
    no error checking
    */
    r = wframe[n].cursor_r + wframe[n].start_r + 1;
    c = wframe[n].virtual_c + wframe[n].start_c + 1 -
            wframe[n].offset;
    if (ch == LF) {
        wframe[n].cursor_r++;
        wframe[n].virtual_c = 0;
        wframe[n].offset = 0;
    }
    else {
        win_ptr = char_addr(get_screen_addr(), r, c);
```

```
        *win_ptr++ = ch;
        *win_ptr++ = NORMAL_VIDEO;
        wframe[n].virtual_c++;
    }
    window_go_rc(n, wframe[n].cursor_r, wframe[n].virtual_c);
    return TRUE;
}   /* window_putchar */
```

window_putchar() makes only one distinction regarding the contents of **ch**. If a linefeed character (LF) is passed to **window_putchar()**, the cursor must be repositioned at the beginning of the next row of the window. This operation requires modifications to all three cursor-control variables.

For all characters except a linefeed, **window_putchar()** attempts to print/display the character, using the same video memory update operation that we've used elsewhere. In this case, **virtual_c** is unconditionally incremented. If the cursor is already positioned in the righmost window column, the character will be displayed, and then **virtual_c** will be incremented to an out-of-bounds value. **window_putchar()** always uses normal video; you may want to modify this feature, as we'll do for our C++ modules.

Cursor management involves two complementary processes: (1) updating the window descriptor table's cursor variables, and (2) physically repositioning the cursor. For the scenario we just described, involving bumping against the right-hand border, process (1) can be performed, but **window_go_rc()** won't be able to reposition the cursor. For this reason, any function affected by an out-of-bounds cursor should check the cursor variables. In this manner, we can use one cursor variable both to record cursor position and to serve as an indicator that the cursor has been advanced to an out-of-window position.

Given **window_putchar()**, we can build high-level functions for window output, for example, **window_puts()**:

```
/*
window_puts() prints a string in a window.
*/

int window_puts(int n, char *str)
{
    if (!wframe[n].is_active)
        return FALSE;
    for ( ; *str; str++)
        window_putchar(n, *str);
    return TRUE;
}   /* window_puts */
```

Another useful function that we've included in *windows.c* is **window_puts_center()**; see Appendix A for its definition.

Now consider window input. In Chapter 6 we described *keyboard.c*, a module that provides basic keyboard processing. Our primary window input function, **window_getche()**, requires one keyboard function, namely, **get_keystroke()**. **window_getche()** can be defined as follows:

```
/*
window_getche() reads a character from a window, with echo.
*/

int window_getche(int n)
{
    union keystroke key;

    if (!wframe[n].is_active)
        return FALSE;
    window_go_rc(n, wframe[n].cursor_r, wframe[n].virtual_c);
    key.word = get_keystroke();
    if (!key.byte[0] || key.byte[0] == RETURN || key.byte[0] == BKSP
            || key.byte[0] == TAB || key.byte[0] == EOF_CHAR)
        return key.word;
    echo_char(n, key.byte[0]);
    return key.word;
}   /* window_getche */
```

One local variable, **key**, is needed to hold the user's keystroke, as returned by **get_keystroke()**. If the ASCII byte of **key** is null, a non-ASCII key has been captured; hence, **key**'s value is simply returned to the calling function—it can't be displayed. If one of several "special" ASCII characters occurs, **window_getche()** returns the entire 16-bit value as well, without further processing—let the caller decide what to do.

For most applications it's necessary to echo the keystroke typed by the user. (We won't define a no-echo version.) **echo_char()** is a simple function that uses **display_char()** for echoing the typed character; see Appendix A for its definition.

We need an analog to **window_puts()** for reading strings typed by the user. String input, however, is a little more complicated than string output. Specifically, we need to ensure that the user types valid characters. There are several legitimate conditions for screening string input; however, for many applications it's convenient to filter out all non-printable characters. We call our function **window_gets_filter()**:

```
/*
window_gets_filter() reads a string from a window, up to some maximum
limit, as long as printable ASCII characters are entered.  If <Esc> is
pressed, it returns FALSE.
*/
```

```
int window_gets_filter(int n, char *str, int limit)
/*
limit is the limit for number of characters that can be read.
*/
{
    char ch, *temp, *start;
    int i;

    temp = start = str;
    for (i = 0, limit--; i < limit; ) {
        ch = window_getche(n);      /* truncate returned value */
        switch (ch) {
            case ESC:
                *start = EOS;       /* return a null string */
                return FALSE;
            case RETURN:
                *str = EOS;
                return TRUE;
            case BKSP:
                if (str > temp) {
                    str--;
                    i--;
                    backspace_char(n);
                }
                break;
            default:
                if (!isprint(ch)) {
                    *str = EOS;
                    return TRUE;
                }
                *str = ch;
                str++;
                i++;
            }
        }
    if (i == limit)      /* reached limit, terminate string */
        *str = EOS;
    return TRUE;
}   /* window_gets_filter */
```

In our application, **window_gets_filter()** is used primarily to prompt the user for filenames. To use this function a programmer must pass a pointer that represents a location in the calling program where the accumulated input can be stored. Since characters are read in a loop, there must be some limit on the number of characters that can be read and stored.

Of course, this limit should *not* be established in **window_gets_filter()**. Therefore, the programmer must supply an argument indicating the maximum number of characters that will be accepted—otherwise, a keyboard-happy user could type characters forever! The parameter **limit** monitors the number of characters that have been accepted.

Consider the various return conditions for **window_gets_filter()**. If the user types a non-printable character, the loop is terminated and a null-terminated string is provided. If the user types too many characters, as monitored by **limit**, the loop is terminated and a truncated, null-terminated string is made available.

In addition, a distinction is made between voluntary termination of input by pressing **<Enter>** and voluntary termination by pressing **<Esc>**. In both cases a null-terminated string is provided; however, the return values are different. If the value returned from a call to **window_gets_filter()** is **FALSE**, the user pressed **<Esc>**. This distinction makes it possible for the user to abandon a string input operation, and for the programmer to take appropriate action. For example, we can cancel a file write operation when the user abandons his or her response to a request for a filename.

7.8 Access Functions

Our current design requires a publicly defined window array; see Chapter 5 for a discussion of the rationale behind this design. Specifically, the application must define a window array, which the window module can then reference. Providing this type of inter-module communication is common among C programmers. Even though the window array is public, you may want to minimize direct references to the "internal workings" of the window descriptor table.

For example, we could provide several access functions for the critical variables in **window_frame** that are required in other modules. **r_pos** is an access function that returns the current row coordinate within a window:

```
/*
r_pos() returns the current row (y-coordinate) within
a given window.
*/

int r_pos(int n)
{
    return wframe[n].cursor_r;
}   /* r_pos */
```

You could also define access functions that return the column coordinate, the rightmost column in a given window, and so on.

Taking this approach, it's possible to restrict the use of "wframe[n].<some variable>" to a limited number of modules. In the next chapter, where we begin development of the edit module, we want to reduce the chance for logic errors. Using access functions instead of "raw" external variables helps the programmer minimize the chance for unintentional modifications to critical variables.

8

A Window Interface to the Edit Module

In this chapter we discuss *editwin.c*, an interface module that couples *edit.c* and *windows.c*. The functions in *editwin.c* manipulate the window descriptor table directly, providing general-purpose text display and scrolling operations for the windows. With *editwin.c* and *edit.c*, described in the next chapter, our C implementation of **ed** will be complete.

We discuss *editwin.c* first, because it makes extensive use of several functions from the *windows.c* module, given in Chapter 7. Although *editwin.c* also uses several functions from *edit.c*, which we address subsequently, these functions are quite straightforward, and a black-box view of them is sufficient at this point.

8.1 Buffer-related Window Management

The window module, as developed in Chapter 7, is designed to read and write characters and strings. In particular, the output functions for strings, such as **window_puts()**, are *not* designed to display a string that contains newline characters. However, with many applications it's necessary to display a character buffer in the window that overflows both the horizontal and vertical dimensions. That is, there are more lines to display than there are rows in the window, and some of the lines may exceed the right-hand window border.

There are a number of ways that we could factor the remaining modules that are required to complete our editor application. So far we've built a number of reusable C modules that can be used for a variety of applications. Many PC applications require a custom user interface incorporating, for example, windows—even a simple calculator could be designed with a window interface.

At this point, however, we require more specialized modules. Many window applications, for example, a calculator, would not need support for buffer processing. Our approach involves dividing the remaining functions into two modules, both of which are editor-specific. In particular, we won't separate support for buffer processing from support for general editing operations. As an exercise, you might want to consider an alternate breakdown, as we will in later chapters.

8.2 Displaying a Buffer in a Window

Displaying (filling) a window with characters is one of the primary tasks in managing a character buffer in a window. For each newline sequence in the buffer, the cursor must be advanced to the left-hand column of the next row of the window. Vertically, the display operation is complete once the last row of the window has been filled, regardless of the number of characters remaining in the buffer. Horizontally, the display operation is complete for each row, once the last column of the window has been filled. **window_fill()** performs this task:

```
/*
window_fill() clears and then fills a window with the contents of
a buffer.  The fill operation begins with the specified window
coordinates, based on the specified offset within the buffer.
*/

int window_fill(int n, int r, int c, char *buffer, long buf_offset)
{
    register int column, last_r, last_c, win_offset;

    if (!wframe[n].is_active)
        return FALSE;
    else {
        window_go_rc(n, r, c);
        window_clr_rest(n);
        window_go_rc(n, r, c);
        for (column = 0, win_offset = window_offset(n, TEST),
                last_r = wframe[n].end_r - wframe[n].start_r - 2,
                last_c = rightmost_col(n);
                buffer[buf_offset] && (wframe[n].cursor_r <= last_r);
                buf_offset++) {
            if (buffer[buf_offset] == LF) {
```

```
                column = 0;
                wframe[n].virtual_c = win_offset;
                wframe[n].cursor_r++;
            }
            else if (column < win_offset)
                column += skip_offset(n, &buffer[buf_offset],
                                        column, win_offset);
            else if (wframe[n].virtual_c > last_c)
                ;
            else
                put_text(n, &buffer[buf_offset]);
        }
        window_go_rc(n, r, c);
        return TRUE;
    }
}   /* window_fill */
```

It's important to overwrite the previous contents of the window without leaving residual text. That is, if we display the new text without clearing the window, there could be residual characters at the end of some lines and near the bottom of the window. Specifically, if the new text for a particular row has fewer characters than the old text for that row, the old text's trailing characters must be cleared. Also, if the old text filled the entire window, whereas there isn't enough new text to fill the lower portion of the window, the bottommost rows must be cleared.

There are essentially two approaches to guaranteeing that extraneous characters do not remain after a window refresh operation. Consider the case in which the new text for a row is "shorter" than the text that previously existed on that row. We could (1) follow each row's write operation with a clear-to-end-of-line operation, or (2) clear the entire window before filling the window with new text. In general, the second approach is faster. Thus, in our case, **window_fill()** begins with a call to **window_clr_rest()** (see *windows.c*). **window_clr_rest()** clears the remainder of a window, beginning at the current cursor location. That is, if the cursor is in the middle column of the fourth row of a window, it clears the remainder of that row and all subsequent rows.

Consider **window_fill()**'s parameters. The second and third parameters specify the window coordinates where the fill operation should begin. The fourth and fifth parameters specify the character buffer that supplies text for the window refresh operation and the buffer offset of the first character to be displayed, respectively. Note that for general editing support it would be too restrictive to assume that window fill operations always begin in the top-left position of a window, or that text is always taken from the beginning of a buffer. For example, if a user of **ed** were to delete the last character on a line of text (the carriage return), near the middle row of the window, the remainder of that row and all subsequent rows must be redisplayed, beginning with the next character in the buffer.

The body of the **for** loop is quite straightforward. Note that it processes one character at a time. If a newline is encountered, the cursor variables must be updated appropriately—

the newline is not "printed." (In our editing routines, newlines are represented on-screen as blanks; **window_clr_rest()** has already cleared the entire window.)

Otherwise, that is, for any character except a newline, a displayable character must be processed; there are two conditions wherein it cannot be displayed. First, if a line of text is longer than there are columns in the window, **window_fill()** must skip over all characters in the buffer subsequent to the last character that fits on that row, down to the next newline character or the end of the buffer, whichever comes first. Second, if the window has been scrolled to the right *n* characters, the first *n* characters in the buffer after each newline must be skipped. **skip_offset()** performs the latter operation:

```
/*
skip_offset() skips over those characters in the buffer that
would be output to the left of the leftmost column, given the
currently active window offset.  If a tab advances the cursor into
the window beyond the leftmost column, the window column coordinate
(virtual_c) must be updated accordingly.
*/

int skip_offset(int n, char *buf_ptr, int current_pos, int win_offset)
{
    int offset_adjustment, padding;

    if (*buf_ptr == TAB) {
        padding = tab_fill_size(current_pos);
        offset_adjustment = current_pos + padding - win_offset;
        if (offset_adjustment > 0)
            wframe[n].virtual_c += offset_adjustment;
        return padding;
    }
    else
        return 1;
}   /* skip_offset */
```

Note that **skip_offset()** is called on a character-by-character basis; it does *not* strip out the first *n* characters, up to the size of the window offset, all at once. Using this approach simplifies the overall logic of the **for** loop in **window_fill()** and makes it easier to use existing, general functions, such as **tab_fill_size()**. (If a tab character is encountered, the cursor must be advanced to the next tab column, based on the current tab size as defined in another module, in our case, the editing module.)

Finally, if the current character falls within the displayable area of the window, **put_text()** is called to display it:

```
/*
put_text() outputs the text to the window, taking into
consideration any tab characters that are encountered.
*/

void put_text(int n, char *buf_ptr)
{

    if (*buf_ptr == TAB)
        fill_tabs(n, tab_fill_size(wframe[n].virtual_c));
    else
        window_putchar(n, *buf_ptr);
}   /* put_text */
```

If the character is not a tab, **put_text()** simply calls **window_putchar()**. Otherwise, the tab character must be expanded on-screen. **fill_tabs()** is defined in *edit.c*. It simply advances the cursor to the next tab column, where the distance in characters is determined by **tab_fill_size()**. An abstract view of these tabbing functions is adequate at present; we'll discuss their definitions subsequently.

8.3 Managing Horizontal Scroll Operations

In this module, and in *edit.c*, it is necessary to keep track of the current window offset—the amount the window has been scrolled. For example, during editing, a find operation may advance the cursor to a buffer position within a line that's beyond the window border. In this case, the window must be scrolled to display the text. The window remains in this scrolled state until an editing operation occurs that forces it to undo the scrolling—one example would be the user entering a carriage return. We use the function **window_offset()** to control the current window offset, the total number of characters that the window has been scrolled. For example, if the user continues typing without pressing a carriage return, then each time the cursor approaches the right window border the window must be scrolled by an arbitrary increment.

window_offset() can be defined as follows:

```
/*
window_offset() manages the current window offset.
*/

int window_offset(int n, int new_value)
{
    if (new_value == TEST)
        return wframe[n].offset;
    else
        return wframe[n].offset = new_value;
```

```
}   /* window_offset */
```

Specifically, it manages the window offset variable, leaving the procedural details of scrolling to other functions. **window_offset()** makes use of a technique that we use throughout our edit module. We often design functions such that one argument in a function call can be used to implement a simple message-passing scheme. Here, if the message **TEST** is passed, **window_offset()** returns the current window offset; otherwise, the argument is taken as the new value for the window offset.

Again using the editor as an example, each time the cursor approaches the rightmost window column, say, during text entry, the window must be scrolled right. **window_shift_right()** handles the procedural details of scrolling:

```
/*
window_shift_right() shifts the window to the right the specified
number of columns.  If possible, the cursor (window coordinates only)
is also shifted by the same amount.  Some routines may need to
readjust the cursor.
*/

void window_shift_right(int n, char *buffer, int num_columns)
{
    int cur_r, cur_c;

    wframe[n].offset += num_columns;
    cur_c = (wframe[n].virtual_c += num_columns);
    if (cur_c >= window_line_length(n, buffer))
        cur_c = window_line_length(n, buffer) - 1;
    cur_r = r_pos(n);
    window_go_rc(n, 0, wframe[n].offset);
    window_fill(n, 0, wframe[n].offset, buffer,
                top_left_pos(n, TEST));
    window_go_rc(n, cur_r, cur_c);
}   /* window_shift_right */
```

num_columns is an arbitrary value. (A compound test condition in the **if** statement could be used to generalize **window_shift_right()** to support a negative shift; this modification is left as an exercise.) The local variable **cur_c** (current column coordinate) is used to attempt to maintain the appropriate cursor position in the buffer. Note that the new column coordinate cannot be beyond the rightmost character on a line (the newline character); the on-screen, window line length is measured by **window_line_length()** from *edit.c*.

Shifting the window mainly involves redisplaying the window with text from the buffer. Note that **window_fill()** begins with row 0, the top of the window; the column coordinate is equal to the newly established window offset. Also, the buffer offset is the value returned by the call "top_left_pos(n, TEST)", which corresponds to the buffer character that's currently associated with the top-left window position. (See *edit.c*.)

We must be able to restore a "shifted window." **window_restore_shift()** manages this operation:

```
/*
window_restore_shift() repositions/redisplays the text
without any text offset in the window.
*/

void window_restore_shift(int n, char *buffer)
{
     if (window_offset(n, TEST) > 0) {
          window_restore_offset_and_column(n);
          window_shift_right(n, buffer, 0);
     }
}    /* window_restore_shift */
```

To do so it calls **window_restore_offset_and_column()** to reset the appropriate window descriptor table variables:

```
/*
window_restore_offset_and_column() restores/resets two window
shift-related variables without redisplaying the text.
*/

int window_restore_offset_and_column(int n)
{
     if (window_offset(n, TEST) > 0)
          wframe[n].offset = wframe[n].virtual_c = 0;
     return wframe[n].virtual_c;
}    /* window_restore_offset_and_column */
```

Once the cursor variables are reset, **window_restore_shift()** can call **window_shift_right()** with a shift argument of 0 to redisplay the window. With this method of factoring the procedural and data management details of window scrolling, **window_shift_right()**'s overall utility is enhanced; it is used quite often in *edit.c*.

9

Developing a General-purpose Edit Module

In this chapter we discuss *edit.c*, the final module needed to complete our implementation of **ed**, a simple full-screen editor. In general, we focus on design considerations, examining individual functions as necessary to outline and explain our design. After completing this chapter you may want to turn to Appendix A for a close examination of the remaining functions in *edit.c*.

9.1 Overall Design for the Edit Module

Examining the application-dependent modules in Chapter 5 provides an overview of the structure of the edit module. In general, *edit.c* includes all the facilities directly associated with editing a character buffer, depending on *windows.c* and *editwin.c* for window-related operations. *edit.c* does not provide file management or overall, cyclical management of the editing operation. That is, the application-dependent modules are responsible for calling the proper functions from *edit.c* (and elsewhere) to initialize, maintain, and terminate editing operations.

The edit module, however, does provide the application with some assistance in managing essential operations. For example, *edit.c* includes the following function, responsible for initializing all critical edit module variables:

```
/*
initialize_edit() establishes initial values for a number of critical
editor-status variables.  Each critical variable is maintained inside
its respective routine, as given below.
*/

void initialize_edit(int n)
{
    window_go_rc(n, 0, 0);
    edit_buf_len(n, RESET);
    buf_cursor_pos(n, RESET);
    top_left_pos(n, RESET);
    tag_pos(n, UNDEFINED);
    buffer_modified(n, FALSE);
    insert_mode(SET);
}   /* initialize_edit */
```

initialize_edit() begins by positioning/initializing the cursor control variables. Next, **initialize_edit()** resets a number of buffer management variables, including variables for buffer length, cursor position (in the buffer), and window position over the buffer. Ancillary variables used by support functions are initialized as well, including the tag, or mark, and the buffer-modified and insert-mode indicators.

In Chapter 5 we briefly addressed the issue of autonomy in the edit module. If *edit.c* were endowed with considerable control of editing operations, including file management operations, the (application) programmer would lose some design flexibility that could be useful with various applications. On the other hand, if the edit module shirks all responsibility for managing edit operations, each application will have a lot of editing-related work to do. The design we've chosen for *edit.c* provides one solution to the division-of-labor issue, namely, management of all critical editing variables. As mentioned, later chapters discuss a different approach.

If a character buffer is being edited in a window, a number of important variables must be maintained; these variables are critical to overall editing operations. In our edit module, the edit buffer is managed as a simple string containing displayable characters, including newline characters. The edit buffer is null-terminated with the traditional end-of-string character **'\0'**.

Treating the edit buffer as a string simplifies both editor design and implementation. Alternatively, a two-dimensional character array, or a linked list data structure, could be used to store each line of text. Although this approach offers some advantages, it has disadvantages as well. In particular, using a sophisticated data structure doesn't necessarily provide greater performance. For example, the logic required for text search operations is simpler with a string-based edit buffer—this can be important in implementing an editor in a high-level language. String-based edit buffers have been used in many commercial editors, for example, EMACS editors.

One advantage of a string-based edit buffer is that, in a pinch, you can use the string-processing libraries that accompany C compilers. For example, if you don't want to write a text search function during your initial implementation, you can use **strstr()**. Likewise, you can make use of the built-in string copy and string concatenate functions that accompany your compiler.

9.2 Management of Critical Editing Variables

Although having a supply of built-in functions is useful during initial development, in many cases you'll find the built-in string functions to be intolerably slow (depending on the compiler). Moreover, frequent use of a compute-intensive function such as **strlen()** during buffer update operations can slow your editor to a crawl. For data as central to edit operations as buffer length, it's better to have the edit module maintain current values, as opposed to calling functions to perform time-consuming calculations.

In our edit module there are several variables, such as buffer length, that are critical to ongoing editing operations. A programmer might choose to store this information in global variables. However, for the reasons outlined in Chapter 2, we prefer to maintain this type of information in dedicated functions, using local static storage. For example, **edit_buf_len()** keeps track of the current buffer length:

```
/*
edit_buf_len() is used to maintain the current edit buffer length,
avoiding unnecessary calls to the built-in function strlen(), which
can be very slow for large files.  WARNING--no error checking.
*/

long edit_buf_len(int n, long new_length)
{
    static long edit_length[MAIN_EDIT_WIN + 1];

    if (new_length == TEST)
        return edit_length[n];
    else if (new_length == INCR)
        return ++edit_length[n];
    else if (new_length == DECR)
        return --edit_length[n];
    else
        return edit_length[n] = new_length;
}   /* edit_buf_len */
```

edit_buf_len() accepts three messages as the second argument: **TEST**, **INCR**, and **DECR** for testing, incrementing, and decrementing **edit_length**'s value, respectively. Passing any other value as the second argument establishes a new edit buffer length.

During the development of a module such as *edit.c*, it's absolutely essential to include error-trapping statements—especially for functions like **edit_buf_len()** that play a critical role in program logic. However, once a module is believed to be bug-free, the error traps are sometimes removed to improve efficiency. (If there is anything that the user can do to corrupt, say, buffer length, the module needs to be redesigned.) Without development-level error checking, programmers face the problem of introducing bugs during updates to the module; hence, module development should be reasonably complete before stripping out error traps. In this case, error checking to prevent negative values for **new_length** has been removed.

Consider the local (array) variable in **edit_buf_len()**. In *edit.c* we've made the decision to support multiple edit buffers. To do so, we must maintain an array of values for each critical editing variable. Recall from Chapter 5 that various functions in *ed.c* pass window handles as arguments to subordinate editing functions. Thus, although our window system depends on an array of window descriptors, established as a public variable, there is no reason that editing variables should be made public. In fact, by maintaining editing variables locally, we enhance the generalizability of our module and reduce the possibility of errors associated with global variable usage.

Recall that in order to allocate multiple buffers, the interface file *editintc.h* must be set up properly with the constant **MAIN_EDIT_WIN** serving as a floater, separating edit windows from auxiliary windows:

```
/****  editintc.h ****  constants for the edit interface  ****/

#define MAIN_EDIT_WIN        0        /* window array positions   */
#define HELP_WIN             1
...
```

If the editor has only one edit buffer, **MAIN_EDIT_WIN** must be set to 0. In this case, the **edit_length** array in **edit_buf_len()** will contain one element, specifically, "MAIN_EDIT_WIN + 1" evaluates to 1.

How significant for overall efficiency is the burden of passing window numbers—when only one edit window is used? According to our estimates with **ed**, by passing these arguments we suffer approximately a 5 percent increase in the size of the executable file, with no noticeable performance decrease. In exchange for a slightly larger executable file, we gain a considerable amount of flexibility in how the edit module can be used, for example, in implementing multiple linear buffers or recursively allocated buffers.

The use of functions to encapsulate editing variables is also useful in associating related operations with updates to those variables. Consider **buffer_modified()**:

```
/*
buffer_modified() records whether or not the buffer has been modified,
and displays an indicator of this condition on screen, each time that
it changes.
*/

int buffer_modified(int n, int change_state)
{
    static int modified[MAIN_EDIT_WIN + 1];

    if (change_state != TEST) {
        modified[n] = change_state;
        if (modified[n])
            tag_pos(n, UNDEFINED);
        display_char(BOT_ROW, MODIFIED_COLUMN,
                (modified[n] ? 'M' : BLANK), rev_border_color);
    }
    return modified[n];
}   /* buffer_modified */
```

If the edit buffer is modified, an "M" is displayed on-screen as a reminder; see Figure 4.1. Also, each time the buffer is modified, the tag is turned off. Other functions can test the value returned by a call to **buffer_modified**(), for example, "buffer_modified(MAIN_EDIT_WIN, TEST)", to decide whether or not certain steps should be taken, for example, abandoning an editing session without saving changes to the buffer.

We've included a limited amount of flexibility for changing the position where the buffer-status indicator is displayed. The row and column coordinates are taken from the constants **BOT_ROW** and **MODIFIED_COLUMN**, which are defined in *editintc.h*.

At this point, we should consider the other constants in *editintc.h* as well:

```
/****  editintc.h ****  constants for the edit interface  ****/

#define MAIN_EDIT_WIN       0       /* window array positions   */
#define HELP_WIN            1
#define ATTN_WIN            2
#define FIND_WIN            3
#define MIN_NUM_WINS        4

#define TOP_ROW             0       /* used during display      */
#define BOT_ROW             24      /* operations only          */
#define MODIFIED_COLUMN     77
#define INSERT_MODE_COLUMN  78
```

```
#define MAX_BUF_SIZE          64000    /* "limit" constants, plus  */
#define MAX_CLIP_SIZE         64000    /* miscellany               */
#define MAX_UNDO_SIZE         5000
#define MAX_STR               45
#define POPUP_WIDTH           48       /* must be MAX_STR + 3      */
#define MIN_STR               7
#define MAX_NAME              80
#define HALF_PAGE             10
#define PAGE                  20
#define TAB_SIZE              4
#define PUNCTUATION           "()!_:;\"',.?"
```

Certainly, programmers differ in their opinions and use of **#define** constants for implementing module parameters. Our use of **#define**s is reasonably restrained. In some cases, it's necessary to use variables, instead of constants to support dynamic modifications. For example, **TAB_SIZE** is used as a default value only; run-time modifications to tab size are handled by dedicating another function for tab size management:

```
/*
tab_size manages changes to the tab size.
*/

int tab_size(int operation)
{
    static int tab_width = TAB_SIZE;
    int new_size;
    char temp_str[MIN_STR];

    if (operation != TEST) {
        activate_window(ATTN_WIN,
                    "change takes effect with next screen update",
                    rev_border_color, rev_border_color);
        window_go_rc(ATTN_WIN, 0, 1);
        window_puts_center(ATTN_WIN, "Enter tab size: ");
        if (!window_gets_filter(ATTN_WIN, temp_str, MIN_STR))
            *temp_str = EOS;
        deactivate_window(ATTN_WIN);
        if ((new_size = atoi(temp_str)) > 0)
            tab_width = new_size;
    }
    return tab_width;
}   /* tab_size */
```

tab_size() activates the attention window, a multi-purpose query window, and prompts for a new tab size. **tab_size()** illustrates the use of alternate headers during window activation to override the standard window header. This feature allows the programmer to hold down the total number of windows, while providing a limited level of customization for each use of a multi-purpose window.

During an edit session a character is displayed in the top-left position of the window, except when the buffer is empty, or when a tab character occupies that position. In our edit module we must keep track of the buffer offset that corresponds to the top-left window position. Doing so facilitates window refresh operations. For example, if a window must be scrolled, or if a page-up operation is performed, this variable is consulted (and potentially modified). Consider **top_left_pos()**:

```
/*
top_left_pos() records the current position in the edit buffer of
the character displayed in the top-left position of the screen.
WARNING--no error checking.
*/

long top_left_pos(int n, long new_position)
{
    static long top_position[MAIN_EDIT_WIN + 1];

    if (new_position != TEST)
        top_position[n] = new_position;
    return top_position[n];
}   /* top_left_pos */
```

top_left_pos() is one of the simplest of the buffer management functions; its use in window refresh operations is discussed in a later section.

Next, consider tagging (bookmark) operations. We want our edit windows to allow the user to set a tag that can be used to mark one end of a block of text. (The cursor delimits the other end of the tagged text.) **tag_pos()** manages two local static variables:

```
/*
tag_pos records the buffer position, and column on the screen,
of the current buffer tag.  WARNING--no error checking.
*/

long tag_pos(int n, long info)
{
    static long tag_position[MAIN_EDIT_WIN + 1];

    if (info != TEST)
        tag_position[n] = info;
```

```
    return tag_position[n];
}   /* tag_pos */
```

Here, **tag_position** corresponds to the buffer offset of the character where the user has set a tag. **tag_pos()**'s importance in supporting clipboard operations is illustrated in a later section.

If a programmer implements an editor with multiple buffers, it may be necessary to keep track of how may edit buffers are currently in use. For example, if only two edit buffers have been opened for editing, the user can't be allowed to switch to the fourth edit buffer; **edit_window_count()** provides this capability:

```
/*
edit_window_count() keeps track of how many edit windows have
been opened.
*/

int edit_window_count(int count)
{
    static int num_edit_windows;

    if (count == TEST)
        return num_edit_windows;
    else if (count == INCR)
        return ++num_edit_windows;
    else if (count == DECR)
        return --num_edit_windows;
    else
        return num_edit_windows = count;
}   /* edit_window_count */
```

Each time the user opens a new edit window, or closes an existing window, **edit_window_count()** must be called to update the window count.

The remaining critical variables and encapsulating functions are similar in design and are given in Appendix A.

9.3 Buffer Management Operations

The number of edit buffers is established by the editor application. For example, **edit_main()** in *ed.c* contains the expression

```
    ... ((ed_buffer = create_buffer(MAX_BUF_SIZE)) != NULL) ...
```

which allocates **ed_buffer** as a local pointer to a block of memory containing **MAX_BUF_SIZE** bytes.

create_buffer() simply calls the library function **malloc()**:

```
/*
create_buffer() allocates storage for a buffer from the heap.
*/

char *create_buffer(long buffer_size)
{
    return (char *) malloc(buffer_size);
}   /* create_buffer */
```

Although **create_buffer()**'s definition is simple, it's better to encourage the programmer to use a common buffer allocation function than to use **malloc()** directly.

The edit module takes on the responsibility for managing supplemental buffers, for example, those buffers used during cut-and-paste and undelete operations. Instead of allocating these buffers globally, they're allocated within the scope of high-level functions that provide dispatching services for buffer-related operations. Consider **cut_and_paste()**:

```
/*
cut_and_paste() manages cut and paste operations.  The clipboard
is maintained internal to this function.  Clipboard operations are
performed by calling cut_and_paste() with the proper "operation"
argument.
*/

int cut_and_paste(int n, char *buffer, int operation)
{
    static char *clipboard;

    if (operation == CUT_CLIPBOARD || operation == COPY_CLIPBOARD)
        return cut_or_copy(n, buffer, clipboard, operation);
    else if (operation == PASTE_CLIPBOARD)
        return paste(n, buffer, clipboard, MAX_BUF_SIZE);
    else if (operation == CREATE_CLIPBOARD) {
        clipboard = create_buffer(MAX_CLIP_SIZE);
        *clipboard = EOS;
        return (clipboard != NULL) ? TRUE : FALSE;
    }
    else if (operation == DESTROY) {
        free(clipboard);
        return TRUE;
    }
    else
        return FALSE;
```

```
}   /* cut_and_paste */
```

cut_and_paste() serves as a clipboard manager. Message constants are passed as the second argument to **cut_and_paste()**; the message "CREATE_CLIPBOARD" is used to create the clipboard.

According to our current design, the application is responsible for calling **cut_and_paste()** to create and to deallocate the clipboard. Alternatively, these tasks could be assumed by routines internal to the edit module. Allocation of supplemental buffers, for example, could be assumed by **initialize_edit()**. In this case, deallocation of buffers could be handled by a function that encapsulates all buffer and file clean-up operations.

Next consider the undo buffer, a small clipboard-like buffer that's used to provide simple undelete capabilities for deleted words, lines, and partial lines. Analogous to the clipboard manager, **undo_op()** manages undo operations:

```
/*
undo_op() manages a small, internal "clipboard" that is used for
del_word(), del_eol(), and del_line() operations.
*/

int undo_op(int n, char *buffer, long value, int operation)
{
    static char *un_buffer;
    static long cursor_when_cut = UNDEFINED;

    if (operation == CUT_UNDO) {
        cursor_when_cut = buf_cursor_pos(n, TEST);
        return cut_to_undo(n, buffer, un_buffer, value);
    }
    else if (operation == PASTE_UNDO) {
        return paste_from_undo(n, buffer, un_buffer, cursor_when_cut);
    }
    else if (operation == CREATE_UNDO) {
        un_buffer = create_buffer(MAX_UNDO_SIZE);
        *un_buffer = EOS;
        return (un_buffer != NULL) ? TRUE : FALSE;
    }
    else if (operation == CANCEL_UNDO) {
        cursor_when_cut = UNDEFINED;
        *un_buffer = EOS;
    }
    else if (operation == UPDATE_UNDO_OFFSET) {
        return update_undo_offset(n, un_buffer,
                        &cursor_when_cut, value);
    }
```

```
    else if (operation == UPDATE_UNDO_OFF_CUT) {
        return update_undo_offset_for_cut(n, un_buffer,
                            &cursor_when_cut, value);
    }
    else if (operation == DESTROY) {
        free(un_buffer);
        return TRUE;
    }
    else
        return FALSE;
}   /* undo_op */
```

The use of a clipboard-style undo buffer is debatable. The disadvantage of this approach is that, unless special precautions are taken, the user can delete a word and then undelete that word several times. For our edit module, we've adopted the position that this type of undo operation is perfectly acceptable. In the strictest interpretation of "undo," we've implemented simple undelete, not real undo operations. Of course, full-scale programmer's editors provide more sophisticated undo operations; in fact, level of support for undo operations is a hallmark of programmers' editors. Our support for undo is similar to that provided by simple editors and word processors.

One advantage of a clipboard-style undo buffer is the ability to share certain functions. For example, both **cut_and_paste()** and **undo_op()** share **paste()** for clipboard paste operations. Where possible, we want to share functions in order to minimize the overall size of the executable file.

The paste section of **undo_op()** is significant enough to require a separate function, because we've given **undo_op()** the responsibility of restoring the cursor to its previous location before attempting the undo:

```
/*
paste_from_undo() handles the process of repositioning the
cursor and performing the undo operation.
*/

int paste_from_undo(int n, char *buffer, char *un_buffer,
                        long cursor_when_cut)
{
    if (strlen(un_buffer) > 0) {
        if (buf_cursor_pos(n, TEST) != cursor_when_cut) {
            buf_cursor_pos(n, cursor_when_cut);
            redisplay_window(n, buffer,
                        current_column_offset(n, buffer));
        }
        return paste(n, buffer, un_buffer, MAX_BUF_SIZE);
    }
```

```
    else {
        message_query(ATTN_WIN, "", "** nothing to undo **");
        return FALSE;
    }
}   /* paste_from_undo */
```

In our opinion, it's unacceptable to make undo operations contingent on the cursor remaining on the same line where the delete operation occurred, or even worse, remaining at the exact position of the delete operation. **undo_op()** uses **cursor_when_cut** to record the buffer offset where the delete operation occurred, in order to restore the cursor and refresh the screen before undoing the deletion. Note that **cursor_when_cut** must be adjusted for each buffer modification that occurs at an offset that precedes the undo offset.

undo_op() uses a different cut function than **cut_and_paste()** because (1) cut operations are simpler with undo, and (2) the general cut-and-paste facility must support clipboard copy operations as well. The detailed operation of the cut-and-paste functions is left as an exercise to the reader; see Appendix A.

Exercise: In general, we've designed our critical buffer variables to support multiple edit buffers; however, there is one exception—we've provided only one undo marker. The current version of **ed** supports only one edit buffer, so this approach is minimally adequate. If, however, you would like to build a C version of **ed** with *n* edit buffers, you must make some provision for handling undo operations when the user is switching among edit windows. One approach would be to maintain *n* undo markers, one for each edit buffer, that is, provide an array definition in **undo_op()** similar to

```
static long cursor_when_cut[<max_num_edit_windows>];
```

The modifications to the *edit.c* implied by this definition are quite trivial and are left as an exercise to the reader. (We'll add this capability in the C++ version of **ed**.)

9.4 A General Message and Prompt Facility

Many circumstances can arise during edit operations in which the user must be issued a message. For example, if the user attempts to paste a block of text from the clipboard that would cause the edit buffer to exceed the maximum allowable size, the user must be notified. By design, our edit module depends on the existence of a general-purpose message and query window.

The pop-up windows must be allocated by the programmer in an application-dependent module, as demonstrated in Chapter 5:

```
... make_window(ATTN_WIN,
                "Attention", 11, 16, 13, 16 + POPUP_WIDTH) ...
```

Placement of the message-and-query window, that is, the *attention window* (**ATTN_WIN**), within the edit window is left up to the application.

Because this window is defined in an application module, a programmer is free to use it for other application-dependent messages. The attention window could be used directly by the application. That is, the application could activate it, use it, and then deactivate it. This approach is used by **get_alt_file_spec()** from *edfile.c*:

```
/*
get_alt_file_spec() prompts the user for a filename/file_spec.
*/

char *get_alt_file_spec(int n)
{
    static char file_spec[MAX_STR];

    activate_window(n,
        "Enter a Filename", rev_border_color, rev_border_color);
    window_go_rc(n, 0, 1);
    window_puts(n, "File: ");
    window_gets_filter(n, file_spec, MAX_STR);
    deactivate_window(n);
    return file_spec;
}   /* get_alt_file_spec */
```

Typically, however, the attention window should be accessed by way of a higher level function such as **message_query()**, which is provided by *edit.c*:

```
/*
message_query() issues a message and queries the user.
*/

int message_query(int n, char *header, char *message)
{
    char ch;

    activate_window(n, header, rev_border_color, rev_border_color);
    window_go_rc(n, 0, 1);
    window_puts_center(n, message);
    ch = window_getche(n);
    deactivate_window(n);
    return (toupper(ch) == 'Y') ? TRUE : FALSE;
}   /* message_query */
```

The exact window that will be used to host messages and queries is left up to the programmer; however, throughout the edit module, **message_query()** is hosted by the window associated with the handle **ATTN_WIN**.

Like many C functions, **message_query()** is designed to return a sometimes-useful value, in this case, the user's response to a yes-no query. Taking this approach, the programmer can use **message_query()** to display a message, using the returned value simply as an indicator that the user has read the message—that is, for a "Press any key..." type of response. For example, consider the potential error mentioned earlier, in which there is insufficient room to support a paste operation. **paste()** includes the following:

```
...
else
    message_query(ATTN_WIN, "",
            "** not enough space to paste/insert **");
...
```

Or, the programmer can use **message_query()** for user feedback, as in this function from *edfile.c*:

```
/*
ok_to_overwrite() makes sure it's OK to overwrite an existing
file.
*/

int ok_to_overwrite(char *filename)
{
    if (!file_exists(filename))
        return TRUE;
    else
        return message_query(ATTN_WIN, filename,
                        "File exists; overwrite (y/n): ");
}   /* ok_to_overwrite */
```

ok_to_overwrite() returns the result of the user's response directly to the calling function, presumably a function that writes the edit buffer to disk.

9.5 Calculating Buffer Offsets

In Chapter 3 we discussed the ramifications of a segmented memory architecture, plus the memory models supported by compiler manufacturers for operations that require pointer arithmetic. There are a number of functions in the edit module that must split the edit buffer and/or combine edit buffer segments. As an example, consider **paste()**, one of the functions called in **cut_and_paste()** and **undo_op()** above:

```
/*
paste() inserts the contents of a generic buffer at the
current cursor position in the edit buffer.  It is used
by both cut_and_paste() and undo_op().
*/

int paste(int n, char *buffer, char *from_buffer, long max_area)
{
    long cursor, from_length;

    cursor = buf_cursor_pos(n, TEST);
    from_length = strlen(from_buffer);
    if (from_length > 0 &&
            from_length <= max_area - edit_buf_len(n, TEST) - 1) {
        buffer_modified(n, TRUE);
        undo_op(n, buffer, from_length, UPDATE_UNDO_OFFSET);
        memmove(&buffer[cursor + from_length], &buffer[cursor],
                    edit_buf_len(n, TEST) - cursor + 1);
        edit_buf_len(n, edit_buf_len(n, TEST) + from_length);
        memcpy(&buffer[cursor], from_buffer, from_length);
        if (linefeed_free(from_buffer, from_length))
            redisplay_rest_of_line(n, buffer, 0);
        else
            if (window_offset(n, TEST) == 0)
                window_fill(n, r_pos(n), c_pos(n), buffer, cursor);
            else
                window_shift_right(n, buffer, 0);
        return TRUE;
    }
    else {
        if (from_length == 0)
            message_query(ATTN_WIN, "",
                    "** clipboard is empty **");
        else
            message_query(ATTN_WIN, "",
                    "** not enough space to paste/insert **");
        return FALSE;
    }
}   /* paste */
```

paste() is used to insert the contents of the clipboard into the edit buffer at the current cursor location. If the "from buffer," in this case, the clipboard, is no larger than the remaining space in **buffer**, the following memory operations occur:

```
...
memmove(&buffer[cursor + from_length], &buffer[cursor],
            edit_buf_len(n, TEST) - cursor + 1);
edit_buf_len(n, edit_buf_len(n, TEST) + from_length);
memcpy(&buffer[cursor], from_buffer, from_length);
...
```

First, **memmove()** is used to open up a space in the edit buffer. Specifically, all characters between the cursor and the end of the buffer are moved (copied) forward in the buffer, leaving a hole into which **from_buffer** can be copied. The distance that each character is moved, that is, the amount of the shift, is equal to the number of characters on the clipboard (the length of **from_buffer**).

memmove() has the call syntax:

```
memmove(<target_buffer_addr>, <source_buffer_addr>, <length>)
```

In our case, the same buffer is used as the source and destination. The first two arguments in the call to **memmove()** are offsets with the edit buffer.

With some C compilers you could write:

```
memmove(buffer + cursor + from_length, ...
```

In this case, the starting address of **buffer** would be incremented by the offsets stored in **cursor** and **from_length**. In fact, this approach will work with MS-DOS C compilers, as long as either (1) you use a small memory model, or (2) you use a large memory model and take precautions to normalize the *segment:offset* values. The first alternative isn't practical for an editor application, unless it's a special-purpose editor designed to use small buffers.

The second alternative typically leads to compiler-dependent source code. Some programmers/companies are willing to develop an entire business around the special features of one compiler. Other programmers don't want to become financially (and mentally) dependent on a particular compiler manufacturer. Harbison and Steele (1987; p. 274) also provides a reminder of the problems that can arise with pointer arithmetic and segmented address spaces.

Our approach avoids these problems by taking advantage of the basic rules of array referencing and address arithmetic provided by C, which each compiler manufacturer must support. In the case of our paste operation, we let the compiler find the proper location in memory, namely, "buffer[cursor + from_length]". Then, instead of using the value stored there, we can take its address "&buffer[cursor + from_length]".

Likewise, in calling **memcpy()** to perform the actual paste operation, we can use "&buffer[cursor]" to calculate the proper target address. We take advantage of the flexibility provided by the address-of operator and the subscript operator in a similar manner elsewhere in the edit module to avoid the previously mentioned addressing problems.

9.6 Providing Support for Search-and-replace Operations

Search-and-replace operations require memory copy operations as well. We can provide a simple search-and-replace facility within the edit module by using our now common technique of establishing a "data manager" that encapsulates static storage and associated procedural activity. We call our search-and-replace manager **find_and_change()**:

```
/*
find_and_change manages simple text find (search) and change
(replace) operations.  Previous find-and-change activity is
recorded within find_and_change() to allow the user to repeat
the command.
*/

int find_and_change(int n, char *buffer, int operation)
{
    static char find_text[MAX_STR] = "";
    static char change_text[MAX_STR] = "";
    static int last_operation = FALSE;
    long offset;

    if (operation == REPEAT_IT && !last_operation)
        return FALSE;                           /* nothing to repeat */

    if (operation != REPEAT_IT)
        if (!prompt_for_pattern(FIND_WIN, last_operation = operation,
                                find_text, change_text)) {
            deactivate_window(FIND_WIN);
            return FALSE;                       /* user pressed <Esc> */
        }
    offset = (operation == REPEAT_IT) ? 1 : 0;/* don't find it again */
    if ((offset = string_search(buffer, find_text,
            buf_cursor_pos(n, TEST) + offset)) == -1) {
        display_not_found(FIND_WIN, operation, find_text);
        return FALSE;
    }
    else {
        deactivate_window(FIND_WIN);
        buf_cursor_pos(n, offset);
        redisplay_window(n, buffer, current_column_offset(n, buffer));
        if (operation == CHANGE_IT || last_operation == CHANGE_IT)
            replace_text(n, buffer, offset, find_text, change_text);
        return TRUE;
    }
}   /* find_and_change */
```

First, **find_and_change()** checks to see if the **REPEAT_IT** message has been sent. In this case, the value of **last_operation** is used to determine the type of search-and-replace activity. Otherwise, **last_operation** is updated to the current value of **operation**, and the user is prompted for a search pattern using **prompt_for_pattern()**:

```
/*
prompt_for_pattern() prompts the user for the search pattern, and
optionally, a replacement pattern.  It activates, but does not
deactivate, the "find" window.  It returns FALSE, if <Esc> was
pressed.
*/

int prompt_for_pattern(int n, int operation, char *find_text,
                              char *change_text)
{
    char find_txt[MAX_STR], change_txt[MAX_STR];

    activate_window(n, "", rev_border_color, rev_border_color);
    window_puts(n, " Find: ");
    if (!window_gets_filter(n, find_txt, MAX_STR))
        return FALSE;
    if (operation == CHANGE_IT) {
        window_go_rc(n, 1, 0);
        window_puts(n, " Change to: ");
        if (!window_gets_filter(n, change_txt, MAX_STR))
            return FALSE;
        strcpy(change_text, change_txt);
    }
    strcpy(find_text, find_txt);
    return TRUE;
}   /* prompt_for_pattern */
```

prompt_for_pattern() uses the find window (**FIND_WIN** window handle) to host its queries—if the message/argument is **CHANGE_IT**, there will be a second prompt for the replacement pattern. Note that the find window is activated with the default header. Also, the first call to **window_gets_filter()**—to retrieve the search pattern—takes place conditionally. That is, if the user pressed **<Esc>**, the search-and-replace operation is abandoned. (Recall from Chapter 7 that **window_gets_filter()** returns **FALSE**, if the user presses **<Esc>**.)

Note that **prompt_for_pattern()** doesn't deactivate the find window. If the search pattern cannot be found, **display_not_found()** needs this window to display a message to the user:

```
/*
display_not_found() displays a "pattern not found" message for the
user, and then deactivates the "find" window.
*/

void display_not_found(int n, int operation, char *find_text)
{
    if (operation == REPEAT_IT) {
        activate_window(n, "", rev_border_color, rev_border_color);
        window_puts(n, " Find: ");
        window_puts(n, find_text);
    }
    window_cursor_bottom(n);
    window_puts(n, " Pattern not found -- press any key...");
    window_getche(n);
    deactivate_window(n);
}   /* display_not_found */
```

Text search operations are performed by **string_search()**. We mentioned earlier that, in a pinch, you could use **strstr()** to perform text searches. We don't use it here for two reasons. First, **strstr()** is too slow with most MS-DOS C compilers; for a large file, it can take several seconds (minutes) to locate the text. Second, **strstr()** returns the *address* of the search text, if it finds it, whereas we need the offset within the edit buffer. You could calculate the offset by subtracting the address where the text is found from the starting address of the buffer: "buffer - strstr(buffer, find_text)". This technique, however, may not work because of the pointer subtraction. (See Chapter 3, plus the previous section on calculating buffer offsets.)

The easiest solution is to write our own function that returns the offset, namely, **string_search()**:

```
/*
string_search() searches search_string for the first occurrence of
search_text.  If search_text is null, it returns -1, instead of
entering the search loop; otherwise, it returns the buffer offset
where search_text begins.
*/

long string_search(char *search_ptr, char *search_text,
                   register long offset)
{
    register int next;
    register long begin_match_offset = offset;

    if (*search_text)
```

```
        for (next = 0; search_ptr[offset]; offset++)
            if (search_ptr[offset] == search_text[next]) {
                begin_match_offset = offset;
                while (search_text[next] &&
                        search_ptr[offset++] == search_text[next++])
                    ;
                if (!search_text[next] &&
                        search_ptr[--offset] == search_text[--next])
                    return begin_match_offset;
                offset = begin_match_offset;
                next = 0;
            }
    return -1;
}   /* string_search */
```

string_search() takes a buffer offset as the third argument, allowing the search operation to begin at any designated offset. The outer (**for**) loop advances through the edit buffer. Each time a match is found between the current character in the edit buffer and the first character of the search text, **search_text**, the inner (**while**) is invoked to perform a character-by-character comparison of the edit buffer and the remaining characters in the search text. If a complete match is found, the offset is returned for the beginning character of the matched text from the edit buffer.

The performance of **string_search()** would be enhanced slightly, if it didn't have to increment **offset** each time the outer loop is repeated. However, this overhead is justified, because returning a buffer offset instead of an address fits well with our scheme to avoid explicit pointer arithmetic. As presently written, the search efficiency of **find_and_change()** is comparable to most commercial editors.

9.7 Insertion and Deletion with Provisions for Undo

In principle, inserting and deleting characters is similar to pasting and cutting a clipboard, respectively. In practice, character insertion is the messiest operation in the edit module. Insertion is tedious because we must provide for a number of different circumstances, including insert versus overstrike mode, an overflowing edit buffer, special processing of some characters, and so on.

Our approach to handling these special circumstances is to check for them up front with **insertion_special_conditions()**:

```
/*
insertion_special_conditions() handles a number of special condi-
tions that can occur relative to insertion of characters.
*/

int insertion_special_conditions(int n, char ch, char *buffer)
```

```
{
    if (edit_buf_len(n, TEST) + 1 >= MAX_BUF_SIZE) {
        if (ch != CR)
            window_go_rc(n, r_pos(n), c_pos(n) - 1);
        redisplay_rest_of_line(n, buffer, 1);
        message_query(ATTN_WIN, "", "** edit space is full **");
        return TRUE;
    }
    else if (!insert_mode(TEST) && ch == CR) {
        down(n, buffer);
        home(n, buffer);
        return TRUE;                    /* do "local" CR only */
    }
    else if (!insert_mode(TEST) && ch == TAB) {
        advance_cursor_to_next_tab(n, buffer);
        return TRUE;                    /* do "local" TAB only */
    }
    else
        return FALSE;
}   /* insertion_special_conditions */
```

First, we must ensure that there is room in the edit buffer for another character; if not, the previous cursor position must be recovered and the line must be redisplayed. (Unless the character is a carriage return, **window_getche()** has already echoed it.)

Practically every editor handles character insertion in overstrike mode slightly, if not very, differently. If the user enters a carriage return in overstrike mode, we simply perform a local cursor movement—the edit buffer isn't modified. Also, if the user presses **<Tab>** in overstrike mode, we simply advance the cursor according to the established "tab stops" (that is, based on the value returned by **tab_size()**).

Otherwise, we use **insert_char()** to modify the edit buffer:

```
/*
insert_char() inserts characters into the buffer and updates
the screen as necessary.  It must take into consideration the
fact that window_getche() has already updated the current
screen coordinates--for displayable characters.
*/

int insert_char(int n, char ch, char *buffer)
{
    int tab_overwrite;
    long insert_point;

    if (insertion_special_conditions(n, ch, buffer))
```

```
        return FALSE;
    else {
        buffer_modified(n, TRUE);
        if (ch == CR)
            ch = LF;
        insert_point = buf_cursor_pos(n, TEST);
        if (insert_mode(TEST) || buffer[insert_point] == LF) {
            memmove(&buffer[insert_point + 1], &buffer[insert_point],
                        edit_buf_len(n, TEST) - insert_point + 1);
            edit_buf_len(n, INCR);
            undo_op(n, buffer, 1, UPDATE_UNDO_OFFSET);
        }
        else
            if (buffer[insert_point] == EOS) {  /* in overwrite mode */
                buffer[insert_point + 1] = EOS; /* don't destroy EOS */
                edit_buf_len(n, INCR);
            }
        tab_overwrite =
            !insert_mode(TEST) && buffer[insert_point] == TAB;
        buffer[insert_point] = ch;
        if (!insert_mode(TEST) && !tab_overwrite &&
                !adjacent_to_rightmost_column(n)) /* simple over- */
            buf_cursor_pos(n, INCR);     /* write, so just increment */
        else
            insert_window_update(n, buffer, ch, insert_point);
        return TRUE;
    }
}   /* insert_char */
```

If the user enters a carriage return in insert mode, several special steps must be taken. First, we represent CR/LF pairs in the edit buffer by a linefeed (LF) only. In general, this simplifies editing operations. Thus, if the user pressed **<Enter>**, **ch** will contain **CR**, and we must replace it with **LF**. We can strip carriage returns during a file read operation and insert carriage returns during a file write operation by opening the file for text mode processing. (See *edfile.c*.)

Next, if the user is in insert mode, or in overstrike mode with the cursor positioned at the end of the line, we must open a space in the edit buffer. (Inserting a character in overstrike mode should never "wipe out" an end-of-line character.) We use the same technique that we discussed earlier for a clipboard paste operation. Note that inserting a character at the end of the buffer in overstrike mode is a special condition—we can't allow the new character to overwrite the end-of-string character. Similarly, inserting a character in overstrike mode when the cursor is positioned on a tab character requires special processing. Note that several conditions require incrementing the buffer cursor offset (**buf_cursor_pos**()) and/or the edit buffer length (**edit_buf_len**()), two of the critical editing variables managed by special functions.

Lastly, **insert_window_update**() must be called if the character insertion requires a window refresh operation:

```
/*
insert_window_update() performs the screen-related updates for
the edit window subsequent to character insertion.  Also, it
increments the buffer position.
*/

void insert_window_update(int n, char *buffer, char ch,
                            long insert_point)
{
    int cur_c;

    if (ch == LF) {
        window_clr_eol(n);
        window_restore_shift(n, buffer);
        if (window_down_line(n)) {
            buf_cursor_pos(n, INCR);
            window_fill(n, r_pos(n), 0, buffer, insert_point + 1);
        }
        else
            window_scroll_up(n, buffer, 0);
    }
    else {
        cur_c = c_pos(n);
        if (ch != TAB)              /* must back up--window_getche()*/
            window_go_rc(n, r_pos(n), --cur_c); /* incr'd. position */
        if (adjacent_to_rightmost_column(n)) {
            window_shift_right(n, buffer, tab_size(TEST) * 2);
            window_go_rc(n, r_pos(n), cur_c);
        }
        else
            redisplay_rest_of_line(n, buffer, 0);
        window_buffer_forward(n, buffer);
    }
}   /* insert_window_update */
```

If the user pressed **<Enter>**, the cursor must be positioned at the beginning of the next line. As part of this operation, the remainder of the current line must be cleared and the remainder of the window must be redisplayed. In addition, if the window has been scrolled, a shift operation must be performed. Lastly, if the cursor cannot be moved down a line within the window, as determined by **window_down_line()**, the window must be scrolled by **window_scroll_up()**.

If the newly inserted character is not a linefeed/newline, we must make allowances for insertion of a tab character, or for being near a window border. Note that **window_getche()** automatically advances the window (physical) cursor position—a generalized window system should do this. However, we must override the default cursor positioning in our edit module, since we want to make editor-specific interpretations of certain characters. Cursor positioning is handled by two special edit module functions: **window_buffer_forward()** and **window_buffer_backward()**.

Lastly, **adjacent_to_rightmost_column()** keeps watch for an "approaching window border from the right." If this situation arises, the edit window is scrolled in increments of twice the tab width. Otherwise, **redisplay_rest_of_line()** can handle the window update.

Deletion of characters is considerably easier:

```
/*
del_char() deletes a character from the buffer
and updates the screen.
*/

int del_char(int n, char *buffer)
{
    char ch;
    long cur_pos;

    if ((cur_pos = buf_cursor_pos(n, TEST)) == edit_buf_len(n, TEST))
        return FALSE;
    else {
        buffer_modified(n, TRUE);
        undo_op(n, buffer, -1, UPDATE_UNDO_OFFSET);
        ch = buffer[cur_pos];
        memmove(&buffer[cur_pos], &buffer[cur_pos + 1],
                    edit_buf_len(n, TEST) - cur_pos);
        edit_buf_len(n, DECR);
        if (ch != LF)
            redisplay_rest_of_line(n, buffer, tab_size(TEST));
        else
            if (window_offset(n, TEST) == 0)
                window_fill(n, r_pos(n), c_pos(n), buffer, cur_pos);
            else
                window_shift_right(n, buffer, 0);
        return TRUE;
    }
}   /* del_char */
```

Typically, the edit buffer is shifted by one character, overwriting the character under the cursor, and the remainder of the line is redisplayed. The buffer deletion operation is accomplished with **memmove()**; it is similar to cutting text from the buffer.

On the other hand, if the cursor is positioned at the end of a line, the window must be refreshed, allowing for the possibility that the window has been scrolled. Although we're still working with black-box abstractions of several of these functions, you can see that we have a good level of cooperation between our **redisplay_...** functions and the window scrolling functions discussed in Chapter 8.

Next consider word-deletion. Top-down design would have us delete a word by deleting characters in a loop! However, this approach is too slow and doesn't fit well with our undo strategy. Instead, **del_word()** determines the (whitespace) bounds of the current word, and then calls **undo_op()** to perform the actual deletion:

```
/*
del_word() deletes a "word," or string of characters.  Leading
blanks are also deleted.  Punctuation characters serve as
word delimiters also.  del_word() determines the location of
the to-be-deleted characters and calls undo_op() to perform
the deletion.  Deletions performed by undo_op() can be undone.
*/

int del_word(int n, char *buffer)
{
    long last;      /* the last/final character to be deleted */

    if ((last = buf_cursor_pos(n, TEST)) == edit_buf_len(n, TEST))
        return FALSE;
    else {
        if (buffer[last] == LF)
            last++;
        else if (buffer[last] == BLANK || buffer[last] == TAB)
            while (buffer[last] == BLANK || buffer[last] == TAB)
                last++;
        else {
            if (ispunc(buffer[last]))
                last++;
            while (buffer[last] && !isspace(buffer[last]) &&
                    !ispunc(buffer[last]))
                last++;
            if (buffer[last] == BLANK)
                last++;
        }
        return undo_op(n, buffer, last, CUT_UNDO);
    }
```

```
}   /* del_word */
```

The punctuation (whitespace) criteria used by **ispunc()** are stored in a string constant in *editintc.h* and can be modified for each editor application.

Deleting the remainder of a line and deleting an entire line are handled in an analogous manner by **del_eol()** and **del_line()**, respectively. Their definitions are quite short and are given in Appendix A.

A programmer achieves nirvana when a high-level operation can be accomplished by a minimum number of calls to existing functions. Deleting the word to the left of the cursor is handled by calls to **word_left()** and **del_word()**:

```
/*
del_word_left() deletes the word to the left of the cursor.
*/

int del_word_left(int n, char *buffer)
{
    if (word_left(n, buffer))
        return del_word(n, buffer);
    else
        return FALSE;
}   /* del_word_left */
```

word_left() handles the cursor movement, including the check to determine if the cursor is already at the beginning of the edit buffer.

Deleting a character to the left of the cursor is just as easy:

```
/*
backspace() moves the cursor to the left one column
and then deletes that character.
*/

int backspace(int n, char *buffer)
{
    if (cursor_left(n, buffer))
        return del_char(n, buffer);
    else
        return FALSE;
}   /* backspace */
```

The high-level cursor movement functions such as **word_left()** and **cursor_left()** are discussed in a subsequent section.

9.8 Canonical Breakdown of Cursor Movement Operations

In the next section we discuss several of the high-level cursor movement functions. Before doing so, let's consider several examples that outline the variety of high- and low-level cursor functions required to implement cursor movement. In general, cursor movement functions fall into three categories: (1) those that manipulate the edit buffer cursor (**buf_cursor_pos()**), (2) those that manipulate both the edit buffer cursor and the window cursor, and (3) those that perform window refresh and cursor movement.

Within reason, we would like to factor our cursor movement operations into functions that (1) minimize the overall size of the executable file, and (2) allow a high degree of internal reusability of functions. That is, we want to look for commonalities in cursor movement operations. In fact, if we can accomplish goal (2), goal (1) will be achieved as a by-product. In general, we cannot achieve a high degree of internal reusability of functions by writing large, sweeping cursor movement functions.

First, every programmer can think of a number of actions that require repositioning the cursor at the beginning of a line. It would be a mistake, however, to lock together buffer cursor movement and window cursor movement for an operation as basic as moving the cursor to the beginning of the line. In some cases, it's convenient to move the buffer cursor to the beginning of a line, temporarily, in order to accomplish some other objective, for example, redisplaying the edit window contents. For this reason, moving the buffer cursor to the first character in a given line should be implemented as a stand-alone operation. Consider **go_line_start()**:

```
/*
go_line_start() moves the cursor to the beginning of the current line
in the buffer; it does NOT update the cursor position in the window.
*/

long go_line_start(int n, char *buffer)
{
    register long i;

    if ((i = buf_cursor_pos(n, TEST)) == 0)
        return FALSE;
    else if (buf_line_length(n, buffer) == 1)
        return i;
    else {
        if (buffer[i] == LF)
            i--;
        for ( ; i >= 0 && buffer[i] != LF; i--)
            ;
        i++;
        return buf_cursor_pos(n, i);
    }
}   /* go_line_start */
```

The beginning of a (logical) line is found by performing two operations. First, scan backward in the edit buffer, beginning with the current buffer cursor position (offset), until a linefeed is encountered, or until the beginning of the buffer is reached (actually, one position past the beginning). Second, increment the index variable. **go_line_start()** returns the result of calling **buf_cursor_pos()** to update the current buffer offset.

As an example of a function that performs both buffer and window cursor movement, consider **window_buffer_forward()**:

```
/*
window_buffer_forward() increments both the buffer and window
positions.  It must take tabbing into consideration.  Note: this
procedure performs no error checking--it must be called in the
proper context.
*/

void window_buffer_forward(int n, char *buffer)
{
    if (buffer[buf_cursor_pos(n, TEST)] == TAB)
        window_go_rc(n, r_pos(n), next_tab_column(n));
    else
        window_go_rc(n, r_pos(n), c_pos(n) + 1);
    buf_cursor_pos(n, INCR);
}   /* window_buffer_forward */
```

window_buffer_forward() advances the cursor by one character. **buf_cursor_pos()** takes care of buffer cursor operations, while **window_go_rc()** from *windows.c* takes care of window cursor operations. Note that a tab character requires special processing for the window update (**next_tab_column()** calculates the proper column), but not for the buffer update using **buf_cursor_pos()**.

The edit window may have to be refreshed during a number of high-level cursor operations. In some cases, it's necessary to redisplay the entire window; **redisplay_window()** performs this task:

```
/*
redisplay_window() redisplays the edit buffer in the edit window
with the cursor positioned (vertically) in the middle of the window.
*/

int redisplay_window(int n, char *buffer, int current_c)
{
    int lines_moved;
    long old_buf_pos;

    old_buf_pos = go_line_start(n, buffer);
```

```
    lines_moved = move_backward_x_lines(n, buffer, HALF_PAGE);
    top_left_pos(n, buf_cursor_pos(n, TEST));
    buf_cursor_pos(n, old_buf_pos);
    window_go_rc(n, lines_moved, DUMMY);
    if (!window_adjust_cursor_position(n, buffer, current_c))
        window_shift_right(n, buffer, 0);
    return lines_moved;
}   /* redisplay_window */
```

Each text editing system must adopt a strategy for repositioning the cursor during paging operations, tag and cursor exchange operations, and so on. Our system always repositions the cursor in the middle of the screen. Some programmers like this approach; some programmers prefer one of several alternate strategies.

Because we've made a decision to position the cursor in the middle of the screen any time that it's necessary to redisplay the edit window, a single, generalized function is sufficient. **redisplay_window()** must (1) record the old buffer cursor line, (2) reposition the buffer cursor backward a half page, (3) associate a new buffer offset with the top-left window position, (4) reposition the buffer cursor to its former line, (5) advance the window cursor the proper row, and (6) synchronize the buffer and window cursor variables, based on the previous cursor column coordinate. The latter value must be passed to **redisplay_window()**, as **current_c**.

The three functions described in this section, plus the lower level functions that they're built from, provide an indication of our strategy for breaking down cursor movement into its canonical forms. The low-level functions are used repeatedly by the high-level functions, and they isolate the gory details associated with managing an approaching border, tab characters, and so on. Each of the low-level functions is given in Appendix A.

9.9 High-level Cursor Movement Operations

By and large, high-level cursor movement is performed by several small functions that orchestrate calls to the low-level functions. As an example, consider the function that moves the cursor up one line:

```
/*
up() moves the cursor up one line.  If possible, the previous
cursor column position is retained.  Scrolling may be required.
*/

int up(int n, char *buffer)
{
    if (!window_up_line(n))
        return window_scroll_down(n, buffer, c_pos(n));
    else
        return buffer_up_line(n, buffer, c_pos(n));
```

```
}   /* up */
```

window_up_line() is a function from *windows.c* that physically repositions the window cursor, if possible. If the cursor is already on the top line, **window_scroll_down()** is called to scroll the window by one line. If the window cursor can be repositioned without scrolling, **buffer_up_line()** is called to update the buffer cursor.

window_scroll_down()'s definition is reasonably simple as well, since it takes advantage of existing low-level functions:

```
/*
window_scroll_down() is used to move the cursor up one line (closer to
the BEGINNING of the buffer) and redisplay the buffer.  It is a secon-
dary function, and is called by, for example, up(), when the cursor is
already on the top line.
*/

int window_scroll_down(int n, char *buffer, int current_c)
{
    if (top_left_pos(n, TEST) > 0) {
        buf_cursor_pos(n, top_left_pos(n, TEST) - 1);
        top_left_pos(n, go_line_start(n, buffer));
        if (!window_adjust_cursor_position(n, buffer, current_c)) {
            window_scroll(n, SCROLL_DOWN);      /* didn't have  */
            go_line_start(n, buffer);           /* to redisplay */
            window_go_rc(n, r_pos(n), 0);       /* just scroll  */
            redisplay_rest_of_line(n, buffer, 0);
            window_adjust_cursor_position(n, buffer, current_c);
        }
        return TRUE;
    }
    else
        return FALSE;
}   /* window_scroll_down */
```

It's traditional for C programmers to design functions that return results that can be either used or discarded. We've employed this technique quite frequently. Even if you're designing a function for which no existing function would use a returned value, it may be reasonable to return a value anyway, especially if doing so is quite natural, given the purpose of the function.

Most of our functions use the returned values of the functions they call, at least on some occasions. Consider the calls to **go_line_start()** in **window_scroll_down()**. On one occasion the returned value is used; in the other situation the returned value is of no interest.

In Chapter 2 we discussed the proliferation of local variables. Unnecessary local variables can (1) increase the complexity of a function, (2) negatively impact the size of executable files, and (3) slow down a program. Note that **window_scroll_down()** combines 11 function calls in ten lines of source code—without using any local variables. Long function names enhance the readability and self-documentation of the function definition.

cursor_left() provides an example of one of our more lengthy high-level functions:

```
/*
cursor_left() moves left one column.  If necessary, the cursor wraps
around to the end of the previous line--at the top of the screen
this operation requires scrolling.
*/

int cursor_left(int n, char *buffer)
{
    int cur_c;

    if (buf_cursor_pos(n, TEST) == 0)
        return FALSE;
    else {
        if (adjacent_to_leftmost_column(n, buffer))
            if ((cur_c = c_pos(n)) > 0) {
                home(n, buffer);
                window_adjust_cursor_position(n, buffer, cur_c - 1);
            }
            else {
                up(n, buffer);
                if (!go_right_as_far_as_possible(n, buffer))
                    endd(n, buffer);
            }
        else
            window_buffer_backward(n, buffer);
        return TRUE;
    }
}   /* cursor_left */
```

Moving the cursor one character toward the left can give rise to several special circumstances. In the simplest case, a call to **window_buffer_backward()** is sufficient.

We use **adjacent_to_leftmost_column()** to detect the need for special processing; it initiates calls to other internally reusable functions. If the edit window has been scrolled, **home()** takes over. Subsequently, **window_adjust_cursor_position()** is called to synchronize the window and buffer cursors at the proper locations. Lastly, if the window has not been scrolled (and the cursor is at the left border), a combination of **up()**, **go_right_as_far_as_possible()**, and **endd()** are used to move the cursor to the end of the previous line. (**home()** and **endd()** move the cursor to the beginning and end of a line, respectively, with some special conditions; see below.)

Earlier we discussed **delete_word()**, which handles word extraction internally for maximum efficiency. For our word-oriented cursor movement functions, it's sufficient to "farm out" basic cursor movement to existing functions. For example, **word_right()** uses **cursor_right()**:

```
/*
word_right() advances the cursor to the beginning of the next
"word," that is, to the beginning of the next "run" of characters.
Punctuation characters serve as word delimiters also.
*/

int word_right(int n, char *buffer)
{
    long i;

    for (i = buf_cursor_pos(n, TEST);
            buffer[i] && !isspace(buffer[i]) &&
            !ispunc(buffer[i]); i++)
        cursor_right(n, buffer);
    for (i = buf_cursor_pos(n, TEST);
            buffer[i] && (isspace(buffer[i])); i++)
        cursor_right(n, buffer);
    if (ispunc(buffer[i++])) {
        cursor_right(n, buffer);
        for ( ; buffer[i] && isspace(buffer[i]); i++)
            cursor_right(n, buffer);
    }
    return TRUE;
}   /* word_right */
```

Again, the punctuation criteria can be controlled by changes to the string constant **PUNCTUATION** in *editintc.h*.

Our **home()** and **endd()** functions are reasonably sophisticated. Let's consider **endd()**'s operations before presenting the function. In the most common situation, **endd()** moves the cursor to the end of the current line. However, if the cursor is already at the end of the line, we want **endd()** to provide a service as well—not just do nothing. In this case, **endd()** advances the cursor to the end of the *next* line. Thus, the **<End>** operation is convenient for creeping down the right-hand side of the edit window.

endd() provides special handling for horizontal scrolling. If the current line extends past the edge of the window, the first execution of **endd()** positions the cursor on the rightmost character in the window, allowing for tabs. A subsequent execution of **endd()** shifts the window and positions the cursor at the end of the line. Here's **endd()**:

```
/*
endd() moves the cursor:
    to the end of the current line,
    to the rightmost position in the window, or
    down one line, plus another endd() operation,
depending on the cursor's current position.  It must accommodate
tabs and "null" columns at the rightmost window position.
*/

int endd(int n, char *buffer)
{
    if (buffer[buf_cursor_pos(n, TEST)] == LF)
        down(n, buffer);
    else if (adjacent_to_rightmost_column(n))
        window_shift_right(n, buffer,
                    window_line_length(n, buffer) - c_pos(n) - 1);
    else
        ;   /* cursor is within the window */
    return go_right_as_far_as_possible(n, buffer);
}   /* endd */
```

endd() performs, that is, manages, a considerable amount of work in eight lines of code. Note that **endd()** accomplishes these tasks without allocating local variables and without requiring dedicated functions. Every function call involves either a high- or low-level function that's used elsewhere.

The last function that we discuss is **top_of_buffer()**:

```
/*
top_of_buffer() moves the cursor to the beginning
of the file/buffer.
*/

int top_of_buffer(int n, char *buffer)
{
    if (buf_cursor_pos(n, TEST) == 0)
        return FALSE;
    else {
        buf_cursor_pos(n, RESET);
        top_left_pos(n, RESET);
        window_offset(n, RESET);
        window_fill(n, 0, 0, buffer, 0);
        return TRUE;
    }
}   /* top_of_buffer */
```

It is representative of several high-level functions: **page_up()**, **page_down()**, **bottom_of_buffer()**, **top_of_window()**, and so on, all of which either minimize or avoid local variables altogether, while maximizing the use of existing functions.

Because the edit module achieves a high-level of internal reusability of its functions, the space requirements for the editing-related operations are quite small in comparison to, say, basic window management operations. We, for example, have a commercial, multi-window editor that is only (approximately) 12K larger than its installation program (44K versus 32K)! Both the editor and the installation program use identical window, screen, and keyboard modules. The primary differences between the two programs are the edit module and a reasonably large file-related module for the editor.

At this point, we've completed the development of several reusable modules, culminating in an editor application that provides medium-level editing capabilities. You may want to examine the remaining functions in detail, or just use them as black-box abstractions. In the next chapter, we investigate several features of C++. In subsequent chapters we demonstrate the power of C++ by using it to develop similar modules. Despite certain similarities, you'll find that C++'s tools support a new approach to programming.

10

Overview of C++

This book assumes from the beginning that you are familiar with C. However, because C++ is a recent extension to C, many C programmers have had less exposure to C++. With this in mind, this chapter provides a brief overview of C++. Obviously, a one-chapter overview cannot substitute for a C++ book, such as Stroustrup (1986), Lippman (1989), or Wiener and Pinson (1988).

On the other hand, in this chapter it is possible to outline those features of C++ that will be used in the remaining chapters. If you are familiar with C++, you may want to skip this chapter entirely. We should reiterate that this overview does not include a complete description of C++'s features.

10.1 Background

C++ was developed by Bjarne Stroustrup at AT&T Bell Laboratories, originally to support large-scale, event-driven simulation projects. Many of the existing C++ compilers are language translators that produce C as the target code—preprocessors. Recently, C++ software development environments have become available that either (1) hide the translation-via-C characteristic, or (2) compile C++ programs directly to object code.

There are advantages and disadvantages to both C++ translators that output C and "true" C++ compilers. The former can be designed to make use of an already existing, debugged

C compiler, possibly a compiler of the programmer's own choosing. If the programmer can choose the C compiler, he or she can make use of existing compiler-specific source code libraries. On the other hand, with some of the earlier-developed, non-fully integrated environments the C++ preprocessing activity may be quite noticeable, even to the point of hampering source-level debugging strategies.

True C++ compilers are sometimes faster, especially when the number of compilation passes is minimized. Their disadvantage is that (for compiler developers) it can be more costly to debug and update compilers than translators. Consequently, it may take developers longer to deliver a compiler upgrade than a translator upgrade.

C++ is an ideal language for developing system software for at least two reasons. First, it retains all of C's features, including C's concise syntax, C's rich set of operators, and so on. Second, C++ implements all of the critical OOP features (except for garbage collection, which some OO programmers believe is critically important). Specifically, C++ provides three important tools that are necessary to support large-scale, ongoing programming projects, that is, encapsulation, hierarchical class decomposition, and dynamic binding. Some OO-like languages do not implement one or more of these capabilities.

10.2 Syntactic Components of C++

In this section we highlight several of C++'s syntactic extensions to C.

10.2.1 Comments

A double-slash signals that the remainder of the line should be ignored by the compiler. For example:

```
printer dos_prn;                    // allocate the printer here
```

The convenience afforded by this small enhancement to C's commenting rules is easily underestimated. In particular, you can comment your functions with "//" internally, and then "comment out" an entire function with "/* ... */", avoiding the nested-comments error which can plague C programmers. (This feature alone should attract C programmers to C++!)

10.2.2 Flexibility in the Placement of Variable Definitions

One of the most often cited features of C++ is the ability to locate variable definitions near their point of usage, for example:

```
for (int i = 10; i > 0; i--)
```

In our opinion, this feature offers mixed blessings. It's true that it allows you to allocate storage for **i** at the top of the loop governed by **i**. However, if you use this feature, you will have no convenient "legend" of variables at the top of each function—you must study the entire function to determine its usage of variables. On the other hand, if you write small functions, scattered variable definitions may not be a problem.

10.2.3 enum, class, struct, and union Qualifiers

With C++, user-defined types are treated just like built-in data types during variable declarations and definitions. For example, a variable of type union can be defined without the **union** qualifier. Consider the keystroke union described earlier:

```
union keystroke {                       /* represents a key's   */
    unsigned char byte[2];              /* data and scan code   */
    int word;
};
```

In a subsequent definition of a **keystroke** variable, either of the following is legitimate:

```
    ...
    union keystroke key;            // traditional C, with qualifier
    keystroke key;                  // C++, without qualifier
    ...
```

The same syntactic rules apply for **enum**, **struct**, and **class** data structures. **class** is discussed in a subsequent section.

10.2.4 The Scope Resolution Operator

C++ provides the operator **::** (double colons) for resolution of scope conflicts between global and local variables. By prepending a variable name with "::", a function can reference a global variable with the same name as a local variable. The following program illustrates this feature:

```
#include <stdio.h>

static int x = 4;

int main()
{
    int x = 8;

    printf("Local x = %d, Global x = %d\n", x, ::x);
}
```

The scope resolution operator is also used in class definitions, as discussed later.

10.2.5 The const Specifier

C++ provides lexical-level, as opposed to C's preprocessor-level, support for constants. By attaching the **const** type specifier to a variable definition you can guard against accidental changes to an identifier's value:

```
    const float pi = 3.14159;
```

In Chapter 2 we discussed the advantages of call-by-value parameters, coupled with use of a **return** statement, for communicating function output, as opposed to using call-by-reference parameters. With C, however, string processing must be done by passing and returning pointers, opening the door for inadvertent modifications of character arrays. Using C++'s **const** qualifier you can prevent inadvertent modification of string arguments and subsequent access to private data returned by a function, for example:

```
const char *get_ssn(char *ssn)
{
    return ssn;
}
```

In this case, **get_ssn()** wraps the social security number in a protective layer. If a programmer accesses **ssn** by way of the (access) function **get_ssn()**, there is no chance for inadvertent, or intentional, modification of **ssn**.

10.2.6 Type Conversion

With C++, a value can be converted to an alternate type, either user-defined or built-in, using a function-call-like syntax. Consider the following program:

```
#include <stdio.h>

int main()
{
    int x = 3;
    long y, z;

    y = (long)x;              // C's cast
    z = long(x);              // C++'s function-call style
    printf("x = %d y = %ld z = %ld\n", x, y, z);
}
```

You may prefer this syntax to the old-style cast.

10.2.7 Reference Parameters

In C, you must explicitly pass an address to achieve call-by-reference parameter passing. For example, consider the familiar function **swap()**, given in many introductory C books:

```
void swap(int *ptr_x, int *ptr_y)
{
    ...
}
```

swap() is called as follows:

```
    swap(&a, &b);
```

With C++, you can avoid the cumbersome use of pointers and address operators:

```
#include <stdio.h>

void swap(int &, int &);

int main()
{
    int x = 10, y = 20;

    printf("x = %d, y = %d\n", x, y);
    printf("Now swap them...\n");
    swap(x, y);
    printf("x = %d, y = %d\n", x, y);
}

void swap(int & x, int & y)
{
    int temp;

    temp = x;
    x = y;
    y = temp;
}
```

The reference parameter operator **&** (ampersand) signals the compiler to use call-by-reference parameters. Where appropriate, reference parameters are a welcomed relief. Also, reference parameters are commonly used in passing structure instances among procedures—to avoid call-by-value copy operations. Even though reference parameters make call-by-reference easy to use, call by value is still the preferred approach for communicating scalar values among procedures—the functional style leads to less errors.

10.2.8 Default and Unspecified Parameters

You can use the ellipsis, **...**, in C++ to suppress type checking and permit an unspecified number of arguments; it's analogous to the **vararg** facilities that are available with C systems that support ANSI C.

When possible, a variable number of arguments is, perhaps, more cleanly implemented by using C++'s facility for default parameters, that is, default argument values. The following program illustrates default parameters:

```
#include <stdio.h>

void countdown(int i = 10);          // default parameter value of 10
                                     // in the function prototype

int main()
{
    countdown(5);                    // override the default
    countdown();                     // accept the default
}

void countdown(int i)
{
    while (i > -1)
        printf("%d ", i--);
    printf("...B-L-A-S-T-O-F-F...\n");
}
```

Although a variable number of arguments is used in **main()** in the calls to **countdown()**, the usage of variable parameters is strictly controlled—with compile-time checking of argument/parameter passing. In Chapter 17 we provide "real" examples of where **...** is quite useful.

10.2.9 Overloaded Function Definitions

C++ allows you to define multiple functions with the same name, as long as the parameter lists differ in type and/or number of parameters. For example, consider the following program:

```
#include <stdio.h>

overload print_ssn;        // signal the overloading of print_ssn
void print_ssn(long);      // prototypes for the overloaded function
void print_ssn(char *);
int main()
{
    long int_ssn = 123456789;
```

```
    static char str_ssn[] = "123-45-6789";

    print_ssn(int_ssn);
    print_ssn(str_ssn);
}

void print_ssn(long ssn)
{
    printf("Social security number:  %ld\n", ssn);
}

void print_ssn(char *ssn)
{
    printf("Social security number:  %s\n", ssn);
}
```

With early versions of C++ the keyword **overload** was used to signal the compiler to expect multiple definitions of a function, distinguished by their parameter lists, as given in the function prototypes. (Unique names had to be generated behind the scenes, in order to eliminate confusion during compilation and linking.) In this case, the compiler takes on the responsibility of matching function calls and functions, based on the number and/or type of arguments in each function call.

With C++ 2.0, the keyword **overload** is optional and used primarily to inform/signal the reader that overloaded functions are being used. In order to provide type-safe linkage across compiled modules (one of the principal enhancements provided by C++ 2.0), every function is encoded with a unique identifier. For this reason, **overload** is no longer necessary for distinguishing among multiple definitions of a function.

10.2.10 Language Support for Memory Management

C compilers provide support for dynamic memory management through library functions, for example, **malloc()**. In contrast, C++ provides two *language primitives* that support basic, dynamic allocation and deallocation of storage from the heap. **new** and **delete** are illustrated by the following program:

```
#include <stdio.h>

int main()
{
    int num_ltrs;

    printf("How many letters (characters) in your first name?  ");
    scanf("%d", &num_ltrs);
    getchar(); // absorb the newline
```

```
    char *first_name = new char[num_ltrs + 1];
    printf("Enter your first name:   ");
    gets(first_name); // just hope the user doesn't type too many!
    printf("Hello, %s.\n", first_name);
    delete first_name;
}
```

In this example, we declare the type and define storage for **first_name** at the point where we need it. We use **new** to allocate "num_ltrs + 1" bytes (characters) from the heap. Before the program terminates, **delete** is used to free the memory held by **first_name**.

10.2.11 cin and cout

Like C, the C++ language does not provide built-in support for input or output. However, the C++ **class** construct, which we begin discussing in the next section, makes it easy to define input and output streams. Normally, C++ implementations define input and output classes following the convention established in Stroustrup (1986). These classes are used to define several streams, including **cin** and **cout**; they are typically found in *stream.h*, or *stream.hpp*.

Although **cin**, **cout**, and their associated operators are not C++ syntactic constructs, it's convenient to discuss them briefly at this point—so that we can go ahead and use them. A simple example illustrates their most common usage:

```
#include <stream.hpp>
#include <ctype.h>

int main()
{
    int age;
    char yes_no;

    cout << "Do you have a dog (y/n)?  ";
    cin >> yes_no;
    if (toupper(yes_no) == 'Y') {
        cout << "How old is your dog?  ";
        cin >> age;
        cout << "In human terms, your dog is approximately "
             << age * 7 << ".\n";
    }
}
```

cout is an output stream to which you can send data: integers, reals, characters, strings, and so on. Each item sent to **cout** is identified/separated by the operator **<<**. **cin** is an input stream from which you can receive data; each input variable is separated by the operator **>>**.

With C, it can be difficult to interleave simple I/O for some applications, because whitespace characters are left in the input stream. (See the call to **getchar()** in the previous section—the "name" program.) **cin** and **cout** eliminate some of these problems. Consider the following example:

```
#include <stream.hpp>

int main()
{
    int num_ltrs;

    cout << "How many letters (characters) in your first name?  ";
    cin >> num_ltrs;
    char *first_name = new char[num_ltrs + 1];
    cout << "Enter each letter of your first name...\n";
    first_name[num_ltrs--] = '\0';
    while (num_ltrs > -1) {
        cout << "Next letter:  ";
        cin >> first_name[num_ltrs--];
    }
    cout << "Backwards, your name is:  " << first_name;
    delete first_name;
}
```

Using **printf()** and **scanf()** to implement this program is awkward.

These examples illustrate all the functionality that we need in our subsequent examples. Stroustrup (1986) provides reference coverage of the C++ I/O system and Berry (1988) provides an excellent tutorial discussion of C++ I/O.

10.2.12 The class Specifier

The **class** specifier, along with other C++ features, provides the capability for object-oriented programming. In this section, we're concerned primarily with introducing the syntax associated with **class**, and not with object-oriented programming. A more complete discussion of object-oriented programming follows in subsequent chapters.

A class (**class**) is a structure (**struct**) that typically "contains" both data and procedures; either type of component may be declared as private or public. With C, if a structure itself is accessible, all elements within the structure are accessible. In addition, all communication with a structure takes place using externally defined functions. With C++, on the other hand, a class provides a template that can be used to encapsulate a body of data and a set of operations against that data, such that component-level data access is strictly controlled.

As an example, consider the class **rectangle**:

```
class rectangle {
private:
    int length, width;
public:
    rectangle(int l = 0, int w = 0)
    {
        length = l;
        width = w;
    }
    void print_stats();
    void put_length(int);
    void put_width(int);
};
```

rectangle is a composite data type (a structure) that contains a private and a public section. As written, the private components of **rectangle**, namely, **length** and **width**, can be accessed by **rectangle**'s own functions, but not by any other function. In this case, **print_stats()**, **put_length()**, and **put_width()** have unlimited access to **length** and **width**. (The *function* **rectangle()** is discussed shortly.)

The definitions for these three functions can be given within the class definition. Typically, however, especially with long definitions, a function definition is given separately. For example:

```
void rectangle::print_stats()
{
    cout << "\nLength = " << length;
    cout << "\nWidth = " << width;
    cout << "\nArea = " << length * width << "\n";
}
```

The class name and the scope resolution operator are prepended to the function name to qualify **print_stats()**; otherwise, the compiler would not assume any relationship between **print_stats()** and **rectangle**. Within the definition of **print_stats()**, the private variables **length** and **width** can be accessed without special qualification.

Access functions can be defined as necessary to retrieve and/or modify the variables within **rectangle**. For example, **put_length()** modifies the length variable:

```
void rectangle::put_length(int length)
{
   if (length > 0)
       rectangle::length = length;
}
```

Also, **put_width()** modifies the width variable:

```
void rectangle::put_width(int width)
{
    if (width > 0)
        rectangle::width = width;
}
```

Lastly, consider the function **rectangle()**, defined within the class definition of **rectangle**. Functions within a class that are given the class name are called *constructors*. They are executed automatically each time an instance of that class is created, for example:

```
rectangle r;
```

Constructors can be designed to accept arguments, and default values can be provided. In our example, if a **rectangle** is defined without arguments, default values of 0 are assigned to **length** and **width**. On the other hand, the following definition:

```
rectangle r(4, 5);
```

assigns the values 4 and 5 to **r.length** and **r.width**, respectively.

With C, structure components are accessed by using the syntax: "<structure name>.<structure component>". With C++, a class's components (public or private) can be accessed by member functions by specifying the component name alone, as demonstrated in the previous function definitions. Non-member functions can access the *public* components of a class by using the "dot-qualifier" syntax, for example:

```
...
rectangle r(4, 5);
r.print_stats();
...
```

The following program provides a more complete demonstration of the syntax necessary to manipulate an instance of a class:

```
int main()
{
    cout << "\n\nBeginning the rectangle demonstration:";
    rectangle rect1(2, 3), rect2;
    cout << "\nRectangles created...";
    rect2.put_width(3);
    rect2.put_length(4);
    cout << "\nRectangle 2's width and length set...";
    cout << "\nRectangle 1:";
    rect1.print_stats();
    cout << "\nRectangle 2:";
```

```
    rect2.print_stats();
    exit(0);
}
```

10.3 Elements of Object-oriented Programming

When we make the following definition in a program:

```
    int x;
```

we don't normally think of **x** as an *object*, at least not in traditional programming. In this case, **x** is viewed as a static data structure—it just lies there helplessly, waiting to be stepped on by a procedure, built-in or user-defined.

Object-oriented programming, on the other hand, brings a totally new view to the data-procedure relationship. With an object-oriented approach to programming, the data-procedure relationship is emphasized by encapsulating data and the legitimate operations against that data in one composite data structure. *Encapsulation* involves much more than just declaring the data and procedures "together." In particular, *encapsulation* provides a mechanism for establishing strict control over access to data.

When you and I think of, say, an animal, we think of more than just the physical cell structure of that animal. Every dog has a number of inseparable static characteristics, such as its hair color, its breed, and so on. More importantly, however, dogs are distinguished by their actions/behaviors. The Newfoundland breed is well known for its personality, especially as manifested in its *actions* around children. "Newfoundland" is an *abstraction* for a *type* of dog with certain characteristics, both static and dynamic. Almost without exception, each instance of "Newfoundland" is an *object* that inherits all of the characteristics of its "class."

Likewise, object-oriented programming provides a mechanism for building abstractions about objects, living and non-living. Every rectangle, for example, has a length and width. Depending on the intended application, we may want to associate a set of actions with rectangles, such as printing its characteristics, modifying its length, and so on. In some cases, we may want to associate additional static attributes with a rectangle, say, color.

We can also depend on class *derivation* to establish specificity. For example, we could define a panel class that inherits all the characteristics of a rectangle, plus others, such as color, physical location, and so on. Based on our earlier definition of **rectangle**, consider **panel**:

```
enum panel_color {red, blue, green};

class panel : public rectangle {
private:
    panel_color color;
public:
    panel(panel_color color = red)       // complete definition
```

```
    {
        panel::color = color;
    }
    panel_color get_color()                // complete definition
    {
        return color;
    }
    void print_panel_color();              // prototype only
    void print_stats();                    // prototype only
};
```

The syntax: "class <derived-class> : public <base-class> {...};" establishes a new class of objects, **<derived-class>**, based on an existing class, **<base-class>**, that inherits the private and public *members* from the base class. C++ programmers refer to the components of a class as *members* of that class. For example, **color**, **width**, and **length** are members of class **panel**. Also, **print_panel_color()** is sometimes referred to as a *member function* of **panel**. In most object-oriented languages these member functions are typically called *methods*. In this book, we use the latter term for functions that belong to a class, reserving the term *function* for stand-alone procedures. Lastly, note that by including the keyword **public** we're indicating that public members of the base class should retain their public status in the derived class.

Every panel inherits all of the characteristics of a rectangle. Also, according to its current definition, **panel** has five additional members: **color**, **panel()** (the constructor), the access method **get_color()**, and two methods that provide printing facilities:

```
void panel::print_panel_color()
{
    switch (color) {
        case red:
            cout << "It's a red panel.\n";
            break;
        case blue:
            cout << "It's a blue panel.\n";
            break;
        case green:
            cout << "It's a green panel.\n";
            break;
    }
}
void panel::print_stats()
{
    rectangle::print_stats();
    print_panel_color();
}
```

The second print method, **print_stats()**, has the same name as a method in its parent. Printing the characteristics of a panel involves printing the inherited rectangle characteristics (using the inherited method **print_stats()**), and then using **print_panel_color()** to print those characteristics that are specific to panels. The scope resolution operator allows the development of a hierarchy of classes in which each subsequently derived class can inherit, and then enhance, a common method, in this case **print_stats()**.

Programmers can elicit roughly the same actions from parent objects and derived objects by sending a "common message" to each. Contrast this object-oriented form of overloading method names with the use of **overload** in Section 10.2.9. Because the differences among classes in a hierarchy are hidden within each class, and controlled by defining new variations of a common method, changes to data structures tend to have localized, not sweeping, impacts on the source code.

The term *data hiding* refers to the practice of isolating the characteristics of an object at the class level, with strict control over external access to data using access methods, plus dedicated methods for internal access. The practice whereby a common message, for example, "<object>->print_stats()", can invoke similar actions in a hierarchy of class objects, depending on the type of **<object>**, is called *polymorphism*.

main() provides a simple demonstration of how these classes can be used:

```
int main()
{
    rectangle rect1(2, 3), rect2;
    panel pan;
    rect2.put_width(3);
    rect2.put_length(4);
    pan.put_width(4);
    pan.put_length(5);
    cout << "\nRectangle 1:";
    rect1.print_stats();
    cout << "\nRectangle 2:";
    rect2.print_stats();
    cout << "\nPanel:";
    pan.print_stats();
    exit(0);
}
```

panel demonstrates a powerful programming concept provided by object-oriented languages: *programming by difference*. The implications for reusability are obvious. We can design debugged, closed classes (data and associated operations) and later *reuse* those classes in new applications—as is, or by deriving new classes that account for the variations inherent in each new application.

So what, C++ provides a fancy type of **struct** called a **class**. What's the big deal? In fact, many of the syntactic contributions outlined previously have nothing to do with object-oriented programming—C++ serves as a convenient vehicle for delivering updates to C. It's easy to underestimate the contributions of the class concept to programming. When combined with the file-level, module development facilities from traditional C, the syntactic construct **class** offers tremendous potential for constructing source-level libraries of reusable software components.

11

Designing C++ Interface and Implementation Files

The C++ **class** construct facilitates the development of self-contained, source-level modules that can be referenced by other modules during compilation. In this chapter we discuss several topics related to the division of C++ source code across files, including simple hierarchical partitioning of classes. A more sophisticated treatment of hierarchical class development is presented in subsequent chapters where we outline the development of a hierarchy of window classes, some of which support various levels of text editing.

11.1 Designing the rectangle Class

In the previous chapter we used a simple rectangle example to introduce the C++ **class** construct. In terms of physical setting, we made no distinction between the class definition and its method definitions—that is, all of **rectangle**'s components, and **main()**, could have been placed in the same source file. How should **rectangle** be declared/defined to promote its reuse by other modules?

In our C implementation of **ed** we set aside an external declaration file for each module of C functions, for example, *edit.c* is accompanied by *edit.h*. C++ programmers have adopted a similar practice, based on the separation of method definitions from class/variable definitions that's inherent in the **class** construct. The C++ analog of an external declaration file in C is called the class *interface* file, or module; it contains the class definition with the public-private breakdown of variables and methods. In the class interface, most methods have declarations, not definitions; hence, the interface file serves as a header file that can be included in all source-level modules using that class. Consider the interface for **rectangle**:

```
////     rectangl.hpp     ////     interface for class:   rectangle


#include <stream.hpp>


class rectangle {
private:
    int length, width;
public:
    rectangle(int l = 0, int w = 0)
    {
        length = l;
        width = w;
    }
    int get_length();
    int get_width();
    void put_length(int);
    void put_width(int);
    void print_stats();
};
```

Depending on the C++ system, the source file suffixes could be: *.h*, *.hpp*, *.hxx*, *.c*, *.cpp*, *.cxx*, or any other convention established by a particular compiler vendor. All of the examples in this book were compiled with the Zortech C++ compiler (Zortech, 1989), which follows the *.hpp* and *.cpp* naming convention. Thus, *rectangl.hpp* contains the interface for **rectangle**.

The public and private keywords are used to control access to a class's components; both variables and methods can appear in either the public or private section. Typically, only methods are public, while all variables, and possibly some methods, are private. The constructor **rectangle()** is public, implying that it is acceptable for other modules to define **rectangle** objects—that is, **rectangle** is a concrete class. (Chapter 13 discusses abstract classes.) It's not uncommon for a class to have multiple constructors—the constructor is overloaded—allowing various forms of initialization.

In the current definition of **rectangle** there are six methods; a constructor is defined and five other methods are declared, four of which are typically called access methods. That is, **get_length()**, **get_width()**, **put_length()**, and **put_width()** are public methods that *access* the private components of **rectangle**. The "get_" and "put_" naming convention isn't necessary, but it's common with other object-oriented languages. The primary purpose of an access method is to provide a form of strictly controlled access to an otherwise protected component of a data structure. In this case, **put_length()** allows an external agent to modify **length**, as long as the value is greater than zero.

When method definitions are given within a class definition, those methods are said to be *inline* methods. During compilation each call to an inline method is expanded, much like a macro expansion. The expansion mechanism, unlike that for **#define** macros in C, guarantees procedure-like behavior; that is, the resulting program will behave as if a true function call had been used. Inline methods can be useful for reducing function-call overhead. However, since C/C++ function-call overhead is minimal, the use of inline methods should be restricted to very small methods. If a method is "called" many times throughout a program, and if the method body contains more than one or two statements, an inline definition can negatively impact the size of the resulting executable file. Rafter (1989a, b) discusses various issues related to the performance of inline versus standard methods.

Note that even though *rectangl.hpp* doesn't use the C++ I/O streams, *stream.hpp* is **#include**d anyway. Specifically, *rectangl.hpp* provides the file inclusion needed by *rectangl.cpp*. This practice is common among C++ programmers, because it saves keystrokes later. Every module that uses **rectangle**s will have to include *stream.hpp* somewhere, due to the use of **cin** and **cout** in *rectangl.cpp*; thus, providing the inclusion in *rectangl.hpp* "automates things."

Typically, the methods for a class are defined in a separate file, called the *implementation* file. The implementation of **rectangle** is given in *rectangl.cpp*:

```
////    rectangl.cpp    ////    implementation of class:  rectangle


#include "rectangl.hpp"


int rectangle::get_length()
{
    return length;
}

int rectangle::get_width()
{
    return width;
}

void rectangle::put_length(int length)
{
    if (length > 0)
        rectangle::length = length;
```

```
}

void rectangle::put_width(int width)
{
    if (width > 0)
        rectangle::width = width;
}

void rectangle::print_stats()
{
    cout << "\nLength = " << length;
    cout << "\nWidth = " << width;
    cout << "\nArea = " << length * width << "\n";
}
```

As in our earlier example, the method names are prefaced with "rectangle::" to signal their relationship with the method declarations given in the class definition of **rectangle**. Note that *rectangl.cpp* requires only one file inclusion, namely, *rectangl.hpp*.

11.2 Designing Class Hierarchies

Programming by difference is the practice of building classes to meet new requirements by defining the new classes as variations of existing classes. For example, suppose we need to add the concept of color to **rectangle** for a new "class" of applications. In this case, we can set up another interface file, defining the new class, **panel**:

```
////    panel.hpp    ////    interface for class:  panel


#include "rectangl.hpp"


enum panel_color {red, blue, green};


class panel : public rectangle {
private:
    panel_color color;
public:
    panel(int, int, panel_color color = red);
    panel_color get_color();
    void print_panel_color();
    void print_stats();
};
```

In particular, we don't have to "touch" *rectangl.hpp*—at this point it represents a closed module.

As mentioned in the previous chapter, the **public** keyword indicates that the public components of the base class will be public components of the derived class as well, that is, an external agent could define an instance of **rectangle** (a **rectangle** object):

```
rectangle rect1(10, 12);
```

and then send it a message to change its length:

```
rect1.put_length(4);
```

Likewise, because of the **public** qualifier in the class definition for **panel**, an instance of panel can respond to a similar message:

```
...
panel pan1(10, 12);
...
pan1.put_length(4);
...
```

Next, consider the default value used during initialization of instances of **panel**, when a color value is not provided, for example:

```
panel pan1(3, 4);
```

and the defaults used during initialization of **rectangle** instances, when length and width are not provided, for example:

```
rectangle rect2;
```

Given our current definitions for **rectangle** and **panel**, the following isn't legal:

```
panel pan;            // illegal
```

Even though a panel is a rectangle, the (sole) constructor declaration for **panel**:

```
panel(int, int, panel_color color = red);
```

provides default values for **color** only. Hence, multiple constructors are necessary to support a variety of initialization defaults for **rectangle** and/or **panel**.

Constructors, like other methods, can be defined in the implementation section of a class module. For example, *panel.hpp* provides only a declaration for its constructor, relegating the definition to *panel.cpp*:

```
////    panel.cpp    ////    implementation of class:  panel


#include "panel.hpp"


panel::panel(int l, int w, panel_color color) : (l, w)
{
    panel::color = color;
}

panel_color panel::get_color()
{
    return color;
}

void panel::print_panel_color()
{
    switch (color) {
        case red:
            cout << "It's a red panel.\n";
            break;
        case blue:
            cout << "It's a blue panel.\n";
            break;
        case green:
            cout << "It's a green panel.\n";
            break;
    }
}

void panel::print_stats()
{
    rectangle::print_stats();
    print_panel_color();
}
```

There must be a mechanism whereby a constructor for a derived class instance can pass along initialization information to the base class constructor. With C++, when an instance of a class is created, a constructor is automatically executed. If that instance is created from a derived class, both the base and derived class constructors will be executed. The class hierarchy determines the order in which the constructors are executed; the base class constructor is called before the derived class constructor.

The syntactic mechanism for communicating information to parent class constructors can be seen in the definition of **panel()**:

```
panel::panel(int l, int w, panel_color color) : (l, w)
{
    panel::color = color;
}
```

The "parameter-like list" following the colon indicates the subset of arguments given in a call to the constructor that should be passed on to the parent constructor. In this case, the values for the first two arguments, represented by **l** and **w**, are passed on to the constructor for **rectangle**.

11.3 Controlled Access to Class Components

Given our current definitions of **rectangle** and **panel**, an instance of either class can receive a message to modify its length. In fact, every public method of **rectangle** is available for sending messages to instances of **panel**, due to the **public** qualifier in the definition of the class **panel**. There are several mechanisms for providing selective inheritance of access to public and private components of an instance. C++ books consider these mechanisms in detail; in this section we discuss several aspects of controlled access to class components that are relevant to our interests.

We can quite easily illustrate one technique for controlling access to class members. Consider *altpanel.hpp*:

```
////    altpanel.hpp    ////    interface for class:  alt_panel


#include "panel.hpp"
#include <string.h>

class alt_panel : panel {
private:
    int area;
    char *panel_name;
public:
    alt_panel(int l, int w, char *name, panel_color color = red) :
                (l, w, color)
    {
        panel_name = new char[strlen(name) + 1];
        strcpy(panel_name, name);
        area = l * w;
    }
    ~alt_panel()
```

```
    {
        delete panel_name;
    }
    void calculate_area();
    void print_alt_stats();
};
```

Parenthetically, **alt_panel** adds the capability of associating a name with an object. We did this simply to illustrate a destructor. (A destructor has the same name as a class, except its name is prepended with a tilde, "~", for example, **~alt_panel()**.) Destructors are called as a definition goes out of scope. In this case, the destructor is called to deallocate the space on the heap occupied by **panel_name**.

Getting back to our main concern, **alt_panel** provides an alternative definition for panels in which there is no automatic access to the ancestor class methods inherited from **rectangle** and **panel**—the **public** qualifier is omitted during the definition of **alt_panel**.

The effect of the omission of **public** is that external agents that define *instances* of **alt_panel** cannot send messages to, for example, **put_length()**, to change the value of the length attribute. In other words, **alt_panel** has adopted all responsibility for controlling modifications to these variables. There are any number of reasons for needing this level of control over class members.

To illustrate this point, **alt_panel** adds the private member **area** to the collection of attributes that make up a panel. **area**'s value is a direct function of two existing attributes, **length** and **width**. **area** represents the general situation in which some variable is provided to hold a frequently calculated intermediate result. The problem is that an instance of **alt_panel** can become *inconsistent* if a change is made to either **length** or **width** without automatic recalculation of **area**'s value.

By removing the **public** qualifier, external agents are prohibited from introducing this type of inconsistency; however, the implementation of **altpanel** must accept the burden of maintaining consistent attribute values:

```
////    altpanel.cpp    ////    implementation of class:  alt_panel


#include "altpanel.hpp"


void alt_panel::calculate_area()
{
    area = rectangle::get_length() * rectangle::get_width();
}

void alt_panel::print_alt_stats()
{
    cout << "\nPanel name = " << panel_name;
```

```
    cout << "\nArea = " << area << "\n";
}
```

We don't need to provide detailed examples of how *altpanel.cpp* could manage its attributes. We should point out, however, that **altpanel**'s methods have no direct access to **length** and **width**, since these variable are private members of **rectangle**. Thus, the following method won't compile:

```
void alt_panel::calculate_area()
{
    area = length * width;
}
```

Access methods, such as **get_length()** and **get_width()**, provide one mechanism whereby base classes, such as **rectangle**, can ensure read-only access to private members for all subsequent derived classes. **calculate_area()** demonstrates how these access methods can be used in a derived class:

```
void alt_panel::calculate_area()
{
    area = rectangle::get_length() * rectangle::get_width();
}
```

Note that in this case the access methods must be prefaced with "rectangle::", even though they are public methods. (You may want to consult a C++ book for a perspective on why this "syntactic sugar" is necessary.)

The problem with access methods, in some cases, is that they also grant any external agent read-only access to private members. From a data-hiding point of view, this level of access may be unacceptable—if a function can access a private variable, it is in one sense dependent on any future changes to that variable. As one alternative to access methods, C++ provides the **protected** keyword, yielding three levels of access to a class's members:

- private — accessible only by methods of the same class
- protected — accessible to methods of derived classes as well
- public — freely accessible ("anything goes")

The **friend** construct provides another alternative to the access-method approach for granting access to private members. In the following class declaration:

```
class rectangle {
    friend class panel;      // panel is forever granted access
                             // to rectangle's innermost secrets
private:
    int length, width;
public:
    rectangle(int l = 0, int w = 0)
```

...

the statement "friend class panel;" provides unlimited access to the private members of **rectangle** for all the methods of class **panel**. From a reusability standpoint, the problem with this facility is that the base classes (modules) *can't be closed*. Each time a new class is derived, the existing parent-grandparent hierarchy must be modified to grant "friendship status." (The more general problem with **friend** is that it defeats the built-in protections provided by data encapsulation.)

What significance does any of this have for our editor application? In our case, we must define a hierarchy of window classes such that each derived window class has access to the variable members of its ancestor classes. We can make the edit-module variables protected members of their respective classes; this allows the derived classes access without fear of corruption by external agents.

We end this section with a simple program that illustrates each of the classes defined in this chapter:

```
////    pandemo.cpp    ////    a simple rectangle and panel demo


#include <stdlib.h>
#include "altpanel.hpp"


int main()
{
    rectangle rect1(2, 3), rect2;
    panel pan1(3, 4);
    alt_panel pan2(6, 8, "Penelope");
    rect2.put_width(3);
    rect2.put_length(4);
    cout << "\nRectangle 1:";
    rect1.print_stats();
    cout << "\nRectangle 2:";
    rect2.print_stats();
    cout << "\nPanel 1:";
    pan1.print_stats();
    cout << "\nPanel 2:";
    pan2.print_alt_stats();
    exit(0);
}
```

11.4 Nested/Hierarchical Inclusion of Interface Files

The previous sections outlined a scheme whereby each module that uses, say, the **panel** class, must **#include** *panel.hpp*, the interface to **panel**. With a simple hierarchical development of classes, such as **rectangle**, **panel**, and **alt_panel**, this approach presents no problems. However, most class hierarchies aren't this simple. For example, if an editor module includes the interfaces for two different window modules, say, *window-a.hpp* and *window-b.hpp*, each of which includes the base window interface, *windows.hpp*, the compiler will balk at the multiple definitions generated by each inclusion of *windows.hpp*. Note that this type of clashing of class interfaces only occurs at the source code level. Once modules are compiled and moved into libraries, these problems disappear.

The most common solution to source level management/inclusion of interfaces is to surround each interface with conditional preprocessor statements that detect whether or not that class interface has already been included during the current compilation process. Given the previous definition of **rectangle**, all that's necessary is to surround the contents of *rectangl.hpp* with an **#ifndef-#endif** block, plus a unique preprocessor constant:

```
////    rectangl.hpp    ////    interface for class:  rectangle


#ifndef RECTANGLHPP
#define RECTANGLHPP 1
#include <stream.hpp>


class rectangle {
private:
    int length, width;
public:
    rectangle(int l = 0, int w = 0)
    {
        length = l;
        width = w;
    }
    int get_length();
    int get_width();
    void put_length(int);
    void put_width(int);
    void print_stats();
};

#endif
```

Using the characters from the filename in the **#define** constant guarantees that *rectangl.hpp*'s contents won't be defined twice.

This type of combination of conditional preprocessor directives and preprocessor identifiers is appropriate for small- and medium-scale projects. For larger projects, especially when libraries of classes are shared among programmers in a multi-user environment, a more sophisticated approach is necessary. In particular, programming-support software with version management and make-like capabilities would be helpful; these tools are just beginning to appear for commercial C++ systems.

It's possible to design your own scheme for tracking dependencies among C++ library modules. Coggins and Bollella (1989a) describe a C++ library management scheme that uses the standard preprocessor facilities, but in a more sophisticated way than we've outlined with the **rectangle-panel** hierarchy. They take advantage of the file system's hierarchical directory structure to organize a three-level hierarchy of C++ modules, based on the hierarchy in the classes. Coggins and Bollella's system makes use of *dependency files* for each class, in conjunction with a *prelude file* for each library.

One of the goals of any system that automates C++ library management is screening out classes that aren't needed for a particular application. That is, when compiling from source-code libraries, it's important that unused classes don't get compiled into the object modules that will be linked together to form the executable software. This problem can be significant with a large, complex class hierarchy that's developed over time to satisfy the needs of a variety of programming projects.

Coggins and Bollella (1989a) address this problem by using a separate source code file for each method. Although the per-method, average compilation times can be significant with this approach, professional programmers are generally more concerned with *recompilation* times, and with the quality of the final result. With their approach, a programmer never has to recompile a source file of 50 methods in which only one method has been changed. Nevertheless, there may be some situations in which creation of a separate file for each method would be unfeasible. Coggins and Bollella (1989b) discusses this scheme for source-level class management as well.

12

Basic MS-DOS Software Components in C++

In this chapter we discuss the C++ versions of the keyboard and screen modules. Our module organization is somewhat different from that for the C version of **ed**. The keyboard module is analogous to the keyboard module from Chapter 6. However, in this chapter the display and screen modules from Chapter 6 are combined into one screen module.

In the first half of this book we described in detail many of the functions in the application and support modules. In general, the same tasks are taken on by the modules in this and subsequent chapters. Consequently, we'll be devoting less discussion to the statement-by-statement details of the methods in each class, focusing on the bigger picture, as dictated by our use of C++.

12.1 The Keyboard Module

Using a design similar to that described in Chapter 11, we can separate our keyboard-related source code into interface and implementation sections. First, consider the keyboard interface:

```
//// keyboard.hpp //// interface for class: keyboard ////


#ifndef KEYBOARDHPP
#define KEYBOARDHPP 1
#include <dos.h>
#include "spkdos.h"


/*
a data structure for keystrokes
*/

union keystroke {                   // represents a key's
    unsigned char byte[2];          // data and scan code
    int word;
};


class keyboard {
    int break_status;
public:
    keyboard();
    ~keyboard();
    int get_keystroke();
    int alt_key_depressed();
};

#endif
```

To avoid redundant inclusions during compilation, we always surround the body of the interface file with conditional preprocessor statements, as described in Chapter 11. Also, the **keystroke** data type is defined here for convenience.

First, we should mention our "*.h" header files. *spkdos.h* is a header file, analogous to the C header file *scrnprnc.h*; it contains screen, printer, and keyboard constants for DOS operations. We no longer need to make a distinction between header files that contain constants and header files that contain external declarations. The C++ interface files are analogous to the C header files that were used for external declarations. Henceforth, "*.h" files contain constants and "*.hpp" files contain class interfaces.

keyboard has one private variable, **break_status**; it's used to record the PC break status at the time the application is initialized. (If a section of a class definition is not preceded by **public** or **protected**, its members are private.) Next, four public methods are declared, all of which are defined in the implementation file, *keyboard.cpp*:

```
////  keyboard.cpp  ////  implementation of class:  keyboard  ////


#include "keyboard.hpp"
    ...
    ...
```

Again, all header file inclusion is handled by *keyboard.hpp*, so that *keyboard.cpp* can simply include its interface.

One constructor is defined:

```
/*
keyboard stores the current status of the break flag, and
then turns keyboard break off.
*/

keyboard::keyboard()
{
    REGS r;

    r.h.ah = 0x33;              // control break function
    r.h.al = 0;                 // get status function
    int86(0x21, &r, &r);
    break_status = r.h.dl;
    r.h.ah = 0x33;
    r.h.al = 1;                 // set status function
    r.h.dl = OFF;
    int86(0x21, &r, &r);
}   /* keyboard */
```

The constructor takes care of recording the current break status, and then turns off **<Ctrl>-<Break>** detection. Note that the qualifier **union** is not necessary for the **REGS** data structure, as discussed in Chapter 10.

One destructor is defined:

```
/*
~keyboard restores the break status.
*/

keyboard::~keyboard()
{
    REGS r;

    r.h.ah = 0x33;
```

```
    r.h.al = 1;                  // set status function
    r.h.dl = break_status;
    int86(0x21, &r, &r);
}   /* ~keyboard */
```

Its only duty is to restore the break status stored in **break_status**.

Let's mention one other method, namely, **get_keystroke()**:

```
/*
get_keystroke() reads and returns the 16-bit scan code of a key.
*/

int keyboard::get_keystroke()
{
    REGS r;

    r.h.ah = KEYBOARD_READ;
    int86(KEYBOARD_INT, &r, &r);
    return r.x.ax;
}   /* get_keystroke */
```

Its definition is analogous to **get_keystroke()** from *keyboard.c.*

Note that all three method names are prefaced with "keyboard::", since their definition must be related back to the declarations given in the interface.

In an application, a keyboard object could be allocated by a statement such as:

```
    keyboard dos_keybd;
```

The constructor would be executed automatically, saving the break status. Typically, the destructor would be executed when **dos_keybd** goes out of scope.

The keyboard module is obviously similar to its C cousin. The same is true for the screen module, which is described next. However, most of the other modules that are described in subsequent chapters have very different organizations from their C counterparts.

12.2 The Screen Module

For the C++ version, the screen module handles screen-management operations *and* character display operations. Consider *screen.hpp*:

```
////  screen.hpp  ////  interface for class:  screen  ////


#ifndef SCREENHPP
```

```
#define SCREENHPP   1

#include <dos.h>
#include "colors.h"
#include "spkdos.h"          // assorted DOS-related constants


class screen {
    int video_mode;
    int row, column, start, end;
    int attr;                           // background attribute
    char far *screen_ptr;
    char exit_screen[SCREEN_SIZE];      // a "screen buffer"

    char far *char_addr(char far *base, int r, int c) {
        return base + (r * 160) + (c * 2);
    }
public:
    screen(int = BACK_ATTR);
    ~screen();
    int get_video_mode();
    char far *get_screen_addr();
    void save_dos_level_cursor();
    void restore_dos_level_cursor();
    void clrscn(int = BACK_ATTR);
    void restore_exit_screen();
    void cursor_rc(int, int);
    void display_string(int, int, char*, int = BACK_ATTR);
    void display_blanks(int, int, int, int = BACK_ATTR);
    void display_char(int, int, char, int = BACK_ATTR);
};

#endif
```

All member variables and one member function have been given private status. We don't anticipate the development of derived screen classes that would require access to these private members. If derived classes are a possibility, you could give these members protected status.

The private method **char_addr()** takes the place of the macro by the same name in *display.c*. Because **char_addr()** is defined inside the class definition, it will be compiled as an inline method.

Next consider default arguments. We set up **screen** so that the constructor and several of the public methods provide a default value for the screen's background attribute. This default value is stored in **BACK_ATTR**. Thus, a programmer has header-level control over the screen's (default) background color, plus function-level control as well. In particular, this scheme allows compile-time substitution of other color constants when a screen object is initialized, or run-time color modification by passing values to the individual methods. The main point is that C++'s default argument facilities make it very easy to provide rather fine-grained control, even with closed modules.

At this point we can consider several of the methods given in the implementation section. (See Appendix B for the complete module.) First, consider the constructor:

```
/*
screen() determines the screen address and saves the screen
buffer in the exit_screen array.  Also, it set the video_mode.
*/

screen::screen(int attr)
{
    screen::attr = attr;
    video_mode = get_video_mode();
    screen_ptr = (char far *) ((video_mode == MONO_MODE) ?
                                 MONO_SCREEN : COLOR_SCREEN);
    for (register int i = 0; i < SCREEN_SIZE; i++)
        exit_screen[i] = screen_ptr[i];
    save_dos_level_cursor();     // record its characteristics
}   /* screen */
```

Note that C++ makes it convenient to use the same name for the constructor parameter and the class member, **attr**—the scope resolution operator takes care of the name conflict.

At present, our destructor is null:

```
/*
~screen() does nothing but clean-up at present.  In some cases, a
call to restore_exit_screen() would be appropriate here.
*/

int screen::~screen()
{
}   /* ~screen */
```

One operation that you might like to add to the destructor is restoring the previous DOS screen upon exit from the application. However, we prefer to do the restore operation manually. Having manual control makes it particularly easy to (1) restore the exit screen, and (2) issue an error message before our program terminates.

The screen module provides an access function for direct video display operations:

```
/*
get_screen_addr() returns the physical screen address.
*/

char far *screen::get_screen_addr()
{
    return screen_ptr;
}   /* get_screen_addr */
```

get_screen_addr() returns the starting address of video RAM. We've used the **const** specifier to qualify how it can be used. Note, however, that although this usage of **const** prevents some forms of accidental modifications to the returned pointer, C++ pointers are inherently low-level data structures.

With pointers, we can always copy the address into another pointer variable and then proceed to modify the data that's stored at that address. In fact, you may recall that our display operations use this technique:

```
/*
display_char() displays a character with the specified
attribute at a particular coordinate on the screen.
*/

void screen::display_char(int row, int col, char ch, int attr)
{
    char far *scrn_ptr = screen_ptr;
    scrn_ptr = char_addr(scrn_ptr, row, col);
    *scrn_ptr++ = ch;
    *scrn_ptr = attr;
}   /* display_char */
```

display_char(), as a method in the screen module, has access to private members, in this case, **screen_ptr**. The screen module depends on **screen_ptr**'s value remaining constant; a number of methods perform operations that begin at the start of video memory, for example, **restore_exit_screen()**:

```
/*
restore_exit_screen() restore the DOS (exit) screen and cursor.
*/

void screen::restore_exit_screen()
{
    for (register int i = 0; i < SCREEN_SIZE; i++)
        screen_ptr[i] = exit_screen[i];
    restore_dos_level_cursor();     // reset cursor size/position
```

```
}    /* restore_exit_screen */
```

Because of the low-level nature of pointer operations, C/C++ programmers have adopted the policy of making a copy of a pointer variable, and then manipulating the copy, not the original, as in:

```
    char far *scrn_ptr = screen_ptr;
```

from the first line of **display_char()**.

As an alternative, you might consider using the **const** specifier in the following manner:

```
    char far *const screen_ptr = <initial_value>;
```

which prevents the modification of **screen_ptr**'s value. In this case, **<initial_value>** could be calculated by an inline method. (This usage of **const** prevents modifications to the value held in **screen_ptr**, as opposed to preventing modifications to the data that it *references*.)

Consider the role that (variable) members play in providing a repository for information. Recall **dos_level_cursor()** from *screen.c*. It uses static local storage to record the cursor coordinates and characteristics. With **dos_level_cursor()**, the programmer must send one of two messages, either **CURSOR_SAVE** or **CURSOR_RESTORE**, to save or restore the user's cursor. The **class** construct allows us to store cursor information in the object itself, as members. (Normally, a screen object will be allocated during initialization of an application, and deallocated at its termination.)

With an object-oriented approach, the cursor management function no longer has to serve as a repository of cursor information. Thus, we can split the function into two components, one that is responsible for saving cursor information in the private area of the screen object, and one that is responsible for restoring the cursor. **save_dos_level_cursor()** performs the former task:

```
/*
save_dos_level_cursor() saves the current cursor size and position.
*/

void screen::save_dos_level_cursor()
{
    REGS r;

    r.h.ah = READ_CURSOR_POS;
    r.h.bh = PAGE_0;
    int86(VIDEO_INT, &r, &r);
    row = r.h.dh;
    column = r.h.dl;
    start = r.h.ch;
    end = r.h.cl;
```

```
}    /* save_dos_level_cursor */
```

This approach allows us to get rid of our message constants. As a result, the statement:

```
dos_level_cursor(CURSOR_SAVE);
```

in **video_initialize()**, in the module *screen.c*, can be replaced by the statement:

```
save_dos_level_cursor();
```

in the constructor for **screen** in *screen.cpp*. As a rule, object-oriented programmers strive to minimize the number of parameters for a method. In this case, no parameters are required. Optimally, message passing should be encoded in a method's name, as opposed to in a method's argument values.

Both **save_dos_level_cursor()** and **restore_dos_level_cursor()** (see the earlier definition of **restore_exit_screen()**) are invoked by methods from their own class; hence, an "<object>." qualifier isn't necessary. It would be possible to design our screen-management class so that both of these methods were invoked manually. In that case, the following statements might appear in **main()**, or elsewhere:

```
...
screen dos_screen;
...
dos_screen.save_dos_level_cursor();
...
dos_screen.restore_dos_level_cursor();
...
```

That is, **dos_screen** is the name of the screen object; consequently, "dos_screen.save_dos_level_cursor()" sends **dos_screen** a directive to initiate the actions that are required to save the cursor characteristics.

13

Designing a Window Class Hierarchy

This chapter introduces a hierarchy of window classes that's useful for various applications. One subset of the hierarchy, namely, windows that do not require buffering activity, is described in this chapter. Window classes with text-editing capabilities are discussed in Chapter 14.

The rationale behind hierarchical class development and the use of abstract classes is introduced in this chapter. After we've completed the design of our window hierarchy in Chapter 14, we'll look back at some of our decisions. References are provided so you can find more formal discussions of the rules for designing class hierarchies.

13.1 Advantages of Class Hierarchies

In the first half of this book we designed a series of "cooperating" modules that could support windowing and editing operations: *windows.c*, *edit.c*, and *editwin.c*. The breakdown of functions and data structures across these three modules, although somewhat arbitrary, serves its purpose. That is, if you need basic windowing capabilities for an application, you can include *windows.c* in your application. If, on the other hand, you need full-scale editing, all three modules are required.

From a design perspective, the most noteworthy characteristic of our C modules is the size of *edit.c*. It's been our experience that many C programmers tend to build modules that differ greatly in size. That is, programmers factor functions into modules based on their use of common data structures—if there are a lot of related functions, the resulting module will be quite large. In our case, *display.c* is very small and *edit.c* is very large.

We've witnessed a tendency to build large modules any time that a programmer anticipates an inconvenience if a module is further divided. For example, if you're building an application with editing capabilities, it's more "convenient" to manipulate two or three modules than to keep track of 20 edit-related modules. Object-code libraries can help with file management problems, once a module is closed, but until then, programmers often prefer to work with source-code files.

Unfortunately, the development time for large modules/projects may be several weeks, or even months. In addition to the inconveniences associated with arbitrarily split modules, it takes a lot of up-front, disciplined program design to produce reusable modules. C's lack of any *formal* mechanism for classifying variables and their associated functions tends to compound these source-level design problems.

C++, on the other hand, provides the **class** construct to assist the programmer in factoring data structures and procedures over any number of modules. To take advantage of the power afforded by **class**, you must be willing to spend a significant amount of time developing class hierarchies, before jumping into development of an application. In many cases, after developing a large class hierarchy you will have to allocate more development time for follow-up refinement (iterative improvement) of the hierarchy.

Although C++ provides language-level support for factoring programs into small modules, many C++ programming environments do not provide any form of automated support for the development and refinement of class hierarchies, other than traditional make facilities. For example, the Smalltalk (Goldberg and Robson, 1983) and C_talk™ (CNS, 1987) programming environments provide on-screen creation, deletion, viewing, and modification of class hierarchies.

This type of support for C++ programming is just beginning to appear, for example, ObjectWorks™ a C++ programming environment from ParcPlace™ Systems (1989) for Sun workstations. In the next few years this type of programming environment should become commonplace, encouraging the programmer to develop small classes and sophisticated class hierarchies.

For many programmers, it's these design-related aspects of object-oriented programming that are the most difficult—the object-oriented language syntax is trivial by comparison. For this reason, many experts suggest that you take some time to study a "pure" object-oriented language, such as Smalltalk, before becoming too set in your ways with C++. It's been our experience that the advantages offered by hierarchical class design more than offset the up-front development time.

13.2 Abstract Classes

An *abstract class* is one that is created solely for its contribution to the overall design process, and not for the direct creation of instances. That is, abstract classes have no instances, while *concrete classes* do. In particular, an abstract class can serve as a starting point for *programming by difference*—it serves as a class-building template. Other abstract and/or concrete classes can be derived from an abstract class, such that a class (or class hierarchy) can be tailored to the particular needs of one or more applications.

From this perspective, it's inappropriate to introduce variable and/or methods in an abstract class that inhibit future derivations; that is, the opportunity for tailoring derived classes should be maximized. Johnson and Foote (1988) suggest that an abstract class should have as few variables as possible, and that its methods should be incomplete. That is, abstract class methods should serve as place-holders for tailored, derived-class methods.

How incomplete should method definitions be in an abstract class? In our opinion, there is no universally appropriate answer to this question. In many cases, it may be appropriate to provide one or more null method definitions in the abstract class. Suppose, however, that every class that's derived from a particular base class requires a minimal amount of common functionality. In this case, it may be appropriate to provide that functionality in a base class method.

Specifically, C++ provides two mechanisms that assist the programmer in tailoring the methods of each class to specific circumstances. First, a programmer can provide a minimal method definition in an abstract class, and then supplement (enhance) that definition in a derived class. For example, an abstract class named **window** could be endowed with the method **deactivate()**, providing a basic form of window deactivation. Default activities would include restoring the previous text to the screen area occupied by the window, and resetting an indicator variable that records whether or not the window is currently active.

A derived window class, depending on its needs, could supplement the base class definition:

```
int <derived_window_class>::deativate()
{
    window::deactivate();        // execute the inherited deactivate()
    <reset some additional variables>
}   /* deactivate */
```

For example, a window object for the derived class might need to reset the cursor variables—when a window is activated, the cursor is placed in the top-left position. Note that this type of enhancement of default methods can be resolved during compilation.

Virtual methods (or virtual functions), C++'s facility for dynamic binding, provides the second mechanism for tailoring methods in derived classes. A virtual method is a method for which the compiler will generate code to select the proper derived class method at run-time. A programmer signals the need for dynamic binding of objects to methods in the following manner:

```
class window {
    <variables>
public:
    ...
```

```
virtual int deactivate() = 0;
...
```

With a virtual method, the programmer can provide a "pure" declaration in the abstract class, requiring each derived class to provide its own complete definition, or the programmer can provide a minimal definition in the abstract class and supplement that definition in the derived classes, as we did with the non-virtual example of **deactivate()**.

The simple "method-enhancing" mechanism and the virtual method mechanism differ with respect to when the method selection/substitution takes place: during compilation or during execution. With the latter approach, given the following statement:

```
<object_ptr>-><message>;
```

the compiler must generate the executable code plus the data structures required to (1) evaluate the type (class) of the object pointed to by **<object_ptr>**, (2) perform a table look-up to choose the method that implements **<message>** for the referenced object, and (3) execute the code (send the message to the object).

The virtual method facility is very important. It adds dynamic binding capabilities to a language that, in all other respects, performs its binding during compilation. Although C++'s dynamic binding is quite efficient in comparison to many object-oriented languages, the price for dynamic binding can be significant.

The real question is: Does the application require dynamic binding? The employee-manager database application is the classic example of a situation in which dynamic binding can be very useful. For example, consider an employee class and a manager class, where the latter is derived from the former. With the virtual method capability you can build, say, a *heterogeneous* linked list of pointers to employee and manager objects, and traverse this list issuing the same message to both types of objects:

```
...
<generic_employee_pointer>->print_paycheck();   // in a loop
...
```

The run-time code that's generated for dynamic binding must perform the table look-up operation required to associate each employee object (regular or manager) with the proper version of **print_paycheck()**. When a generic (base class) pointer is used in this manner with objects of specialized type, method selection can't take place during compilation—method selection depends on the type of the object, not the type of pointer. However, the compiler can use information implicit in the class hierarchies to maximize the efficiency of method selection.

Virtual methods and pointers to objects go hand in hand. However, are there other situations in which virtual methods can be useful? Consider their potential importance in developing a reusable class hierarchy. If a method is defined as "virtual" in an abstract class interface, then a derived, concrete class can provide a replacement method, modifying that portion of the class implementation as necessary—a substitute method. In this case, no source-level changes are required for the base class.

On the other hand, virtual methods aren't always necessary. Suppose you're developing an editor with various types of windows, each supporting a different level of text editing. If it's feasible to bind window objects to their methods during compilation, there may be no justification for using dynamic binding. It should be clear from the example using **deactivate()** that it's possible to build reusable classes with default methods that can be overridden or enhanced during compilation. We'll address these issues again after we complete our window hierarchy in Chapter 14.

Typically, a programmer will choose a mixture of compile- and run-time method selection that's appropriate for a particular application, or compiled module. It's possible to provide dynamic binding for objects—while minimizing the number of virtual methods. Chapter 17 demonstrates how to provide support for dynamic binding of (pointers to) window objects and window methods. In particular, we'll demonstrate how to allow a programmer to augment a compiled module with heterogeneous window objects, where these objects are under control of the compiled module.

The class hierarchies developed by C++ programmers often have more breadth than depth with minimal usage of abstract classes. Johnson (1989) attributes this lack of depth in class hierarchies to lack of experience with object-oriented programming—C++ programmers fail to understand the importance of abstract classes in class hierarchies.

We agree with this view with some qualifications. It's important to consider the application. For example, consider the Smalltalk programming environment. The entire Smalltalk system is object-oriented—developed from deep class hierarchies that employ many abstract classes. In order to maximize the programmer's potential for extending the environment, it's absolutely necessary to provide a carefully constructed class hierarchy with many abstract classes. However, for a finite, and somewhat restricted, class hierarchy, it's appropriate to relax some of the rules related to the use of abstract classes, for example, the rules related to the minimization of variables in abstract classes, and so on.

Our goal here is to provide a reasonably deep class hierarchy that uses abstract classes, but without the level of class abstraction that would be required to generalize our design to quite different applications. In particular, our design will be useful for character-based windows and character-based editing only.

13.3 A Window Hierarchy for Prompting and Editing

Our hierarchy of window classes will be designed to provide general-purpose windowing and editing services. Although our window hierarchy will not meet the needs of all applications, we've found that it provides reasonably complete services without introducing unnecessary complications and without imposing too many burdens on a program that doesn't need the full range of services.

This section summarizes the nodes in our window hierarchy. Subsequent sections, plus Chapter 14, address the various classes in detail. Chapter 16 demonstrates the use of components of this hierarchy to build a separate editor class.

Figure 13.1 outlines our system of window classes. At the root of the hierarchy is **window**, an abstract class. Abstract classes are incomplete classes in the sense that they are missing either variables, or methods, or both that are necessary to create and manage a (useful) window object.

Immediately subordinate to **window** are two classes, **msg_window** and **buf_window**. The former class provides a branching point for classes that don't need buffering services, but that do need basic character and string processing, plus cursor movement. Two examples are **query_box** and **num_box**. **query_box** provides simple prompting capabilities, including the capability of reading a yes-no response to a prompt. **num_box** is similar, except that it reads a numeric response to a prompt.

Additional classes can be derived from either abstract or concrete base classes. For example, **msg_window** is a concrete class. It has all of the variables and methods necessary to support the creation of **msg_window** objects. Instances of **msg_window** provide read and write support for characters and strings. Its derived classes are concrete as well.

buf_window, on the other hand, is abstract. It has a number of methods associated with it for managing the display of a character buffer in a window; however, any window with buffer support will require additional methods and/or variables.

Two classes are derived from **buf_window**, one abstract and one concrete. **text_window** is an abstract class that enhances **buf_window** with additional methods and variables, as necessary to support simple text editing. Some of its members include: **tag_pos()**, **set_tag_pos()**, **cursor_left()**, and so on.

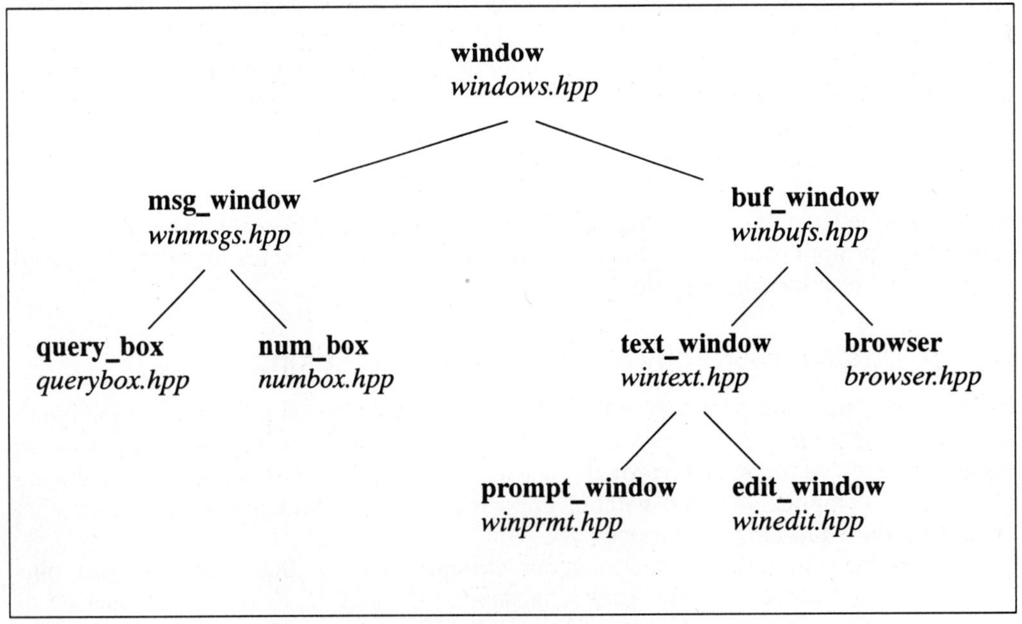

Figure 13.1 A Prompt and Edit Window Hierarchy

browser, a concrete derivation of **buf_window**, provides the necessary methods for supporting a window that allows the user to page, or browse, through a text buffer. It has a window redisplay facility that always keeps the cursor in the top-left window position. By definition, its operations provide read-only access to a character buffer.

Two concrete classes are derived from **text_window**. **edit_window** supports full-scale editing of a buffer. By association with another class, **buffer**, it provides cut-and-paste operations. Further breakdown of **edit_window** is left as an exercise to the reader.

The other class that's derived from **text_window**, **prompt_window**, is a special-purpose edit window that provides prompting services, designed for a one-line window. It supports full-scale editing (except for cut and paste operations) of the string that has been collected as the user's response to the prompt. For example, the window automatically scrolls to the right if the user's response is too long for the prompt window. Also, the cursor movement commands operate consistently with those of **edit_window**—both are derived from **text_window**.

Note that our current design gives the programmer some opportunity to pick and choose among classes, in order to match the application (whereas *edit.c* is an all-or-nothing module). For example, **query_box** and **num_box** provide low-overhead prompting, while **prompt_window** provides much more sophisticated management of the user's response, along with the requisite overhead.

13.4 window: The Root Window Class

window, as the basis for the other window classes, defines variables for representing a window's physical dimensions, plus other variables that are required in all window classes. In this section, we describe **window**, and use it to motivate discussion of several issues that arise in the development of class hierarchies.

13.4.1 The Interface to window

First, let's consider *windows.hpp*, the interface file for **window**:

```
////  windows.hpp  ////  interface for class:  window  ////


#ifndef WINDOWSHPP
#define WINDOWSHPP  1

#include <stdio.h>
#include <dos.h>
#include <stdlib.h>
#include <string.h>
#include <ctype.h>
#include "spkdos.h"
#include "windows.h"
#include "keyboard.hpp"
```

```
#include "screen.hpp"


extern screen dos_screen;
extern keyboard dos_keybd;


/*
In window, a physical row coordinate is adequate for vertical
cursor movement.  However, in order to provide horizontal scrolling
within a window, the column position is virtualized.  In this case,
the physical column is a function of the current offset within the
window and the virtual column coordinate.
*/

class window {
protected:
    int error_state;
    int win_no;          // for external, nominal usage
    int offset;          // physical column = virtual column - offset
    int cursor_r;        // physical row for the cursor
    int virtual_c;       // virtual column for the cursor
    int start_r, end_r;
    int start_c, end_c;
    char *window_save_buffer;
    char *header;
    int is_active;
    int attr;            // background attribute
    char far *char_addr(char far *base, int r, int c) {
        return base + (r * 160) + (c * 2);
    }
public:
    window(int, char *, int, int, int, int, int);
    ~window();
    int get_error_state() {
        return error_state;
    }
    int get_win_no() {
        return win_no;
    }
    void set_background_attr(int color) {
        window::attr = color;
    }
    int activate(char *, int = REV_BORDER_COLOR,
```

```
                        int = REV_BORDER_COLOR);
    int deactivate();
    void display_header(char *, int);
    void display_border(int);
    int wputchar(char);
    int wgetche();
    void echo_char(char);
    void clr_rest();
    void clr_eol();
    int up_line();
    int down_line();
    void cursor_bottom();
    void scroll(int);
    int go_rc(int, int);
    int rightmost_col();
    int bottommost_row();
    void save_screen_area();
    void restore_screen_area();
};

#endif
```

To provide a feel for the design of our interface files, we've listed the entire contents of *windows.hpp*. For most of the classes defined later, we won't show file inclusions, and so on.

On occasion, an interface includes more than just the class definition. Since it serves as a root for a window hierarchy, *windows.hpp* automatically provides for some of the needs of subsequent window classes. In particular, the **#include** directives for library routines won't need to be duplicated in subsequent window interfaces, since, for example, *winbufs.hpp* will include *windows.hpp* to obtain the class definition for **window**. Note that the window attributes are specified as **protected**, allowing access by derived class methods. The **extern** declarations for **dos_screen** and **dos_keybd** are discussed in the next section.

13.4.2 Supporting Objects: Allocated Globally or Passed by Pointer?

Beyond the class definition, an interface file may include related information as well. For example, the keyboard and screen objects must be allocated somewhere. Let's consider two broad approaches to handling basic devices, such as a keyboard or a display. Typically, devices are shared objects. Therefore, it may not be appropriate to have every class that performs output to the screen allocate its own **screen** object, complete with temporary buffers. We'll use the keyboard as an example, because it's a simple object. However, it should be clear that the allocation of shared objects is an important issue for a variety of situations/applications. For example, consider a (serial) communications class that must coordinate activities with a serial port object, an editor class that must support multiple command sets, and so on.

First, **window** could be designed to use a hard-coded keyboard object, defined either globally or as a variable member of the class. In the latter case, a local definition of a device within **window** would be useful primarily if no other non-**window**-derived class intended to use it, or if it makes sense to pass it among classes in some manner. Unfortunately, it's hard to anticipate (1) the types of derivations that will occur over time in a class hierarchy, and (2) the interactions among a class hierarchy and related classes. Normally, we prefer local definitions; however, for certain shared objects, global definitions may be more appropriate.

If a device is allocated globally, it's straightforward to allow other modules (classes) to reference it. (Convenience of access is a frequent motivation for using global variables.) Beyond the normal disadvantages to using global variables, one disadvantage of this approach is that the device name and interface must be communicated to each potential user of the class.

Are there other alternatives? A common alternative is to have each object that requires a particular device define a pointer that functions as a place-holder for that device. In this case, the burden is shifted to the user of the high-level object (the window) to perform the storage allocation for the device (the keyboard), before allocating the high-level object. Typically, a pointer to the device would be passed to the constructor of the high-level object. In many cases, placing this burden on the class user is perfectly acceptable. In fact, with this approach, the class user may gain some flexibility.

We should note that this approach makes use of an object-oriented principle called *composition* (Goldstein, 1989). Our window hierarchy is a product of class *derivation*—the specialization of a class by adding additional, or distinguishing, features. All classes that have variable members make use of composition in the narrow sense. Typically, we use the term composition to refer to the process of composing classes from other classes. For example, in Chapter 16 we use composition to build an editor class from the window hierarchy, a help class, and so on.

Goldstein (1989) discusses the use of pointers as place-holders—*pluggable pointers*. An example is given for a sophisticated editor that supports multiple command sets, where the editor class defines a pointer to the class **CommandSet**. In this case, composition via a pluggable pointer is used to improve the editor's functionality.

There are at least three reasonably minor disadvantages to using pointers as place-holders. First, the user of the high-level class must accept the burden of allocating the low-level object in conjunction with allocation of the high-level object. Second, these objects must be allocated in the proper order.

Third, if the high-level class is abstract, its constructors will be hidden. (We discuss this issue in subsequent sections and chapters.) Hence, each derived class constructor must shoulder the burden of communicating the address of the low-level object to the high-level object, so that the latter can be properly initialized. (The syntax for the latter operation is discussed subsequently.) Moreover, with shared objects the address of the low-level object must be passed to each constructor of each high-level object that participates in the sharing.

Having addressed the pros and cons of both approaches (sharing object definitions versus passing object addresses), we should stop short of making sweeping generalizations. Ultimately, we must respect individual programming preferences and recognize that different situations give rise to different solutions.

In our opinion, allocating pointers as place-holders is justified in a sophisticated class in which the burden of managing interdependent object allocations (editor and command set objects) is more than offset by the gain in class generalizability. On the other hand, for our window class we believe that it's perfectly acceptable to allocate simple, shared objects globally—and inform the class user of their existence as necessary. Overall, our use of global objects is very restricted.

Given our commitment to global allocation of shared objects, where should we put them? We've made the decision to define them in *windows.cpp*, since, by our design, every window will require keyboard and window management. Because these data structures are defined in *windows.cpp*, we need external declarations for them in *windows.hpp*:

```
extern screen dos_screen;
extern keyboard dos_keybd;
```

13.4.3 Protecting against Direct Invocation of window()

In our earlier summary of the window class hierarchy, we designated certain classes as abstract classes and others as concrete classes. There is, however, no formal mechanism for making such a designation—abstract classes are merely those for which the class definition is too incomplete to support object instantiation. You can, however, prevent the "unauthorized" instantiation of objects from an abstract class such as **window** by giving the constructor(s) **protected** status. In this book, we're presenting our class hierarchies, as if they are still under development. In many cases, it's better to postpone the movement of a constructor declaration to the **protected** section of the class definition until after all debugging operations are complete.

13.4.4 Defining window's Attributes

Have we violated the rule stated earlier regarding minimizing the number of members in an abstract class, since **window** defines several variables and methods? Ultimately, decisions regarding the location of variables in a hierarchy depend on the characteristics of the existing and potential class derivations. We've made the commitment to window classes that each require (are based on) the physical and logical characteristics implicit in **window**'s variables. For example, the physical definition of all subsequently derived window objects will be determined by their values for **start_r**, **end_r**, and so on. Logically, cursor movement in derived window objects will be based on **cursor_r**, **virtual_c**, and so on, plus their associated methods, for example, **cursor_bottom()**.

Consider a variable such as **has_border** that could record whether or not a window has a (visible) border. Should it be included as a member of **window**? In this case, the decision is less debatable. If you anticipate windows with and without borders, you should design your classes such that borders can be added by simple derivation, or possibly, by multiple inheritance. In the first case, a derived class would be defined as a refinement of an existing class—programming by difference: a new characteristic is added to the derived class. In the second case, a new class is derived from two existing classes, say, with one class providing basic functionality and another class providing more ephemeral features, such as borders, color modifications, and so on. (The pros and cons of using multiple inheritance to add functionality to a class are discussed in Chapter 14.)

What about headers? In our opinion, it's more convenient for the programmer to control the presence or absence of a header dynamically, during window initialization and activation—as with our C implementation, headers are supplied as arguments. Note that **activate()** (declared in *windows.hpp*) is supplied with default header and border attributes.

By our design, all window objects are assumed to need provisions for displaying a border, clearing the remainder of the window, moving the cursor up one line, and so on. In addition, we've made provisions for all window objects to read and display characters. Alternatively, you could design a hierarchy in which this capability is added by a derived class. On the other hand, we've made no provisions for reading and displaying strings; **msg_window** will provide this capability.

window provides two facilities for "secondary support," that is, they aren't strictly necessary in order for the window system to be operational. First, each window object can be assigned a window number. The overhead for this feature is minimal: one variable, **win_no**, and one access function, **get_win_no()**, plus a parameter in the constructor. A window number provides the programmer with an additional mechanism for keeping track of windows; this can be useful when you have a large number of windows, or any time you don't want to refer to them by their memory addresses (pointers). For example, a multiple buffer editor could display a window number on-screen to remind the user which window is currently active.

Second, **window** has a limited facility for reporting "internal" errors. **error_state** is an object-wide error flag that can be set to indicate that an error has occurred. Each window object must set aside enough memory to save the screen area that it will overwrite. This memory area, referenced by **window_save_buffer**, is allocated dynamically; consequently, there must be a mechanism to ensure that both the window and its heap-based buffer have been properly allocated. **get_error_state()** can be used by the programmer to interrogate window allocation.

13.4.5 An Overview of window's Methods

Initialization of **error_state** is provided by the constructor in *windows.cpp*. Before addressing the constructor, consider the first few lines from *windows.cpp*:

```
////  windows.cpp  //// implementation of class:  window  ////
////
////  classes used:  screen and keyboard


#include "windows.hpp"
```

```
    ...
    ...

/*
globals:
*/

screen dos_screen(BACK_ATTR);     // used by almost any module
keyboard dos_keybd;               // that uses windows

    ...
    ...
```

As mentioned earlier, a screen object is allocated with a default background attribute that's suitable for windowing applications (typically, normal video). Also, a keyboard object is provided for interpreting keystrokes. Of course, additional screen objects could be defined elsewhere, as dictated by an application. Note that both of these objects are public, so that they can be used by other modules as well.

The constructor is designed to require initialization values for seven window attributes:

```
/*
window() initializes the window and sets up a buffer where the
existing screen area can be saved during the window's activation.
*/

window::window(int win_no, char *header, int start_r, int start_c,
                int end_r, int end_c, int attr)
{
    error_state = FALSE;
    if ((start_r > 23) || (start_r < 0) ||
            (start_c > 78) || (start_c < 0))
        error_state = TRUE;
    if ((end_r > 24) || (end_c > 79))
        error_state = TRUE;
    char *save_ptr = new char[(end_r - start_r + 1) *
                                (end_c - start_c + 1) * 2];
    if (save_ptr == NULL)
        error_state = TRUE;

    window_save_buffer = save_ptr;
    window::win_no = win_no;
    window::header = header;
    window::start_r = start_r;                // window boundaries
```

```
    window::end_r = end_r;
    window::start_c = start_c;
    window::end_c = end_c;
    window::attr = attr;
    is_active = FALSE;
    offset = 0;                 // see windows.hpp for an explanation
    cursor_r = 0;               // see windows.hpp for an explanation
    virtual_c = 0;              // see windows.hpp for an explanation
}   /* window */
```

That is, no default attributes have been supplied. You can easily modify the initialization requirements by making changes to the constructor's declaration in *windows.hpp*. Regardless of whether or not you choose to supply a default background attribute, it's useful to be able to set the background attribute dynamically; *windows.hpp* provides this capability with the inline method **set_background_attr()**:

```
    void set_background_attr(int color) {
        window::attr = color;
    }
```

error_state is reset initially. It can be set by either invalid window coordinates or a memory allocation error. Although **error_state** doesn't distinguish between these two types of errors, the former is a programmer error that must be corrected during program development, while the latter is (in some cases) a run-time error.

A destructor is necessary to release the heap storage:

```
/*
~window releases the screen save area for each window.
*/

window::~window()
{
    delete window_save_buffer;
}   /* ~window */
```

A window object will be released automatically with a definition such as:

```
    <derived_window_type> edwinna(1, "edwinna",
                                  10, 5, 20, 70, SOME_COLOR);
```

when the object goes out of scope. Or, if the window object were allocated dynamically with **new**, **delete** would be used to release the window's storage. (In later chapters, our editor applications will provide examples of both approaches.)

We noted **activate()**'s provision for default border and header values in our discussion of *windows.hpp*. Either the default or the supplied attributes are passed along by **activate()** to their respective methods, **display_border()** and **display_header()**:

```
/*
activate() makes the window active.
*/

int window::activate(char *header, int header_attr, int border_attr)
{
    if (!is_active) {
        save_screen_area();
        is_active = TRUE;
        display_border(border_attr);
        display_header(header, header_attr);
        return TRUE;
    }
    return FALSE;
}   /* activate */
```

You may want to review the illustration of default values given with the rectangle and panel examples in Chapter 11.

Next, **deactivate()**'s task is simple—just reset the activity flag and restore the screen area:

```
/*
deactivate() clears the window, restoring the previous screen.
*/

int window::deactivate()
{
    if (is_active) {
        is_active = FALSE;
        restore_screen_area();
        return TRUE;
    }
    else
        return FALSE;
}   /* deactivate */
```

In the next section, we'll consider **deactivate()** again.

Lastly, **display_header()** illustrates the use of the screen object **dos_screen** by a **window** method to display the header:

```
/*
display_header() displays a header, centered on the top line of
the window border.
*/

void window::display_header(char *alt_header, int h_attr)
{
    char *hdr_ptr = (*alt_header == EOS) ? header : alt_header;
    int hdr_len = strlen(hdr_ptr);
    int hdr_start =
            ((end_c - start_c - 1 - hdr_len) / 2) + 1 + start_c;
    if (hdr_start < start_c)
        return;
    dos_screen.display_string(start_r, hdr_start, hdr_ptr, h_attr);
    if (hdr_len > 0) {
        dos_screen.display_char(start_r, hdr_start - 1,
                                BLANK, h_attr);
        dos_screen.display_char(start_r, hdr_start + hdr_len,
                                BLANK, h_attr);
    }
}   /* display_header */
```

Although **dos_screen** is *allocated* in *window.cpp*, it is not a window. Hence, messages sent by **window** objects to display a character must be sent to the appropriate **screen** object, in this case, **dos_screen**: "dos_screen.display_char()".

13.5 msg_window: A Class for Managing Messages

msg_window is a concrete class that adds just enough capability to the abstract class **window** to support reading and displaying strings. Its interface is:

```
////  winmsgs.hpp  ////  interface for class:  msg_window  ////


#ifndef WINMSGSHPP
#define WINMSGSHPP  1

#include "windows.hpp"


class msg_window : public window {
public:
    msg_window(int, char *, int, int, int, int, int = BACK_ATTR);
    int deactivate();
```

```
    int wputs(char *);
    int wputs_center(char *);
    int wgets_filter(char *, int);
    void backspace_char();
};

#endif
```

For this class, no additional variables are needed; however, four methods, **wputs()**, **wputs_center()**, **wgets_filter()**, and **backspace_char()**, are necessary to support string I/O. (Their definitions are similar to their C equivalents; see *winmsgs.cpp* in Appendix B.)

First, consider the constructor:

```
/*
msg_window() initializes the window and sets up a buffer where the
existing screen area can be saved during the window's activation.
*/

msg_window::msg_window(int win_no, char *header, int start_r,
        int start_c, int end_r, int end_c, int attr) :
        (win_no, header, start_r, start_c, end_r, end_c, attr)
{
}   /* msg_window */
```

Although its body is null, it performs a useful function. Specifically, it parcels out the initialization information required by the derived class constructor and the parent constructor, using the syntax: "<constructor_name>(<total_parm_list>) : (<args_for_parent_constructor>) {...};". (Parent class constructors are executed before derived class constructors.) In this case, "everything" is passed on to the parent constructor, **window::window()**.

Note that the constructor declaration in *winmsgs.hpp* provides a default value for the last initialization argument, namely, the window background attribute. If, for example, you wanted to set up a text search window with a reverse video background, you could provide the following override:

```
msg_window search_win(0, "search", 3, 16, 7, 40, REVERSE_VIDEO);
```

Parenthetically, note that **search_win** is a "real" window object—it is an instance of a concrete class. In the previous section, we had to use **<derived_window_type>** in our example:

```
<derived_window_type> edwinna(1, "edwinna",
                                10, 5, 20, 70, SOME_COLOR);
```

because **window** is an abstract class.

The last **msg_window** method that we mention is **deactivate()**:

```
/*
deactivate() calls the related parent function to restore the
previous screen text, and, in addition, resets the cursor
position.
*/

int msg_window::deactivate()
{
    if (window::deactivate()) {
        cursor_r = virtual_c = offset = 0;
        return TRUE;
    }
    else
        return FALSE;
}   /* deactivate */
```

deactivate() provides our first example of combining an ancestor method with a similarly named method in a derived class, where the latter either modifies or enhances the functionality of the ancestor method. In general, object-oriented programmers favor the use of common names for methods that perform similar tasks in an inheritance hierarchy.

The use of common method names where appropriate is one component of the process of developing *standard protocols* for classes. Standardizing the message-passing schemes for related classes can greatly increase the readability and reusability of those classes. The syntactic restrictions inherent in traditional languages, such as C and Pascal, discourage the use of common names for similar procedures.

As mentioned earlier, on occasion it's appropriate for methods to take advantage of, that is, build upon, the default functionality of ancestor methods without resorting to dynamic binding. **msg_window::deactivate()** illustrates this situation. In this case, dynamic binding simply doesn't enter the picture; it doesn't matter how **msg_window** objects are manipulated, with pointers, or otherwise. The implication here is that all **msg_window** objects should reset the cursor to the top-left window position. (Messages aren't retained from one activation of the window to the next.)

In contrast, when base class pointers are used to manipulate a derived class object, dynamic binding may be required. Our earlier example with employees and managers provides one illustration. A similar situation arises with windows, when a generic window pointer must be used to manipulate various types of windows, say, read-only browsers and full-scale edit windows. In these cases, standard protocols are important as well.

The term *polymorphism* is used to characterize the latter type of of behavior—when dynamic binding is required to establish which object should receive the message. Polymorphism is a characteristic of a class hierarchy whereby objects belonging to each derived class in the hierarchy are designed to respond to the same message, for example, "<each_window>->deactivate()", but with slightly different behavior, as implemented in their respective class methods. Use of a consistent set of messages across classes for similar operations enhances the readability of the source code at each level in the hierarchy. Thus, even though window deactivation may require different actions depending on the type (class) of window, it's important not to have numerous deactivation methods, each with a different name.

13.6 query_box: A Simple Yes-no Prompt Box

The following definition illustrates the power of C++'s **class** construct:

```
query_box attn_win("Attention", 11, 16, 50, <any_color>);
```

That is, with a one-line definition we can set up a window that handles simple queries. Then, with a one-line statement we can issue messages that require a "Press any key..." response:

```
attn_win.message("", "** already at end of line **");
```

or, messages that require a yes-no response:

```
answer = attn_win.message(filename,
                  "Can't write file; try again (y/n): ");
```

Given our existing class hierarchy with **window** at the root and **msg_window** derived from **window**, **query_box** can be defined as follows:

```
////  querybox.hpp  ////  interface for class:  query_box  ////


#ifndef QUERYBOXHPP
#define QUERYBOXHPP 1

#include "winmsgs.hpp"


class query_box : public msg_window {
    int user_response;
public:
    query_box(char *, int, int, int, int = BACK_ATTR);
    get_user_response() {
        return user_response;
    }
    int message(char *, char *, int = REV_BORDER_COLOR,
                    int = REV_BORDER_COLOR);
```

```
};

#endif
```

One private variable, **user_response**, has been added to the members inherited from **msg_window**, along with an access function for retrieving its value.

Also, a constructor must be provided; its implementation is given in *querybox.cpp*:

```
/*
query_box() constructs the query window.  Since it is a one-line
window, it must fill two additional initialization values needed
by the window constructor.
*/

query_box::query_box(char *hdr, int start_r, int start_c,
                     int end_c, int attr) : (DUMMY, hdr,
                     start_r, start_c, start_r + 2, end_c, attr)
{
}   /* query_box */
```

In the current implementation, we've made a decision not to trouble the programmer with window numbers for simple prompt boxes. The first initialization argument for **query_box** is the window header; this header is passed to the parent constructor as the second argument, with **DUMMY** as the first argument. If you prefer to support numbered prompt boxes, you could add the required initialization parameter to **query_box()**.

The method **message()** displays the prompt/message and returns a yes-no response that can be discarded:

```
/*
message() issues a message and queries the user.
*/

int query_box::message(char *hdr, char *msg, int hdr_attr,
                         int bdr_attr)
{
    activate(hdr, hdr_attr, bdr_attr);
    go_rc(0, 1);
    wputs_center(msg);
    char ch = wgetche();
    deactivate();
    return (user_response = (toupper(ch) == 'Y') ? TRUE : FALSE);
}   /* message */
```

Note that it uses methods inherited from both **msg_window** and **window**.

Strictly speaking, since **message()** returns the Boolean result of its yes-no query, **user_response** isn't necessary. In some cases, however, storing the Boolean value in **user_response** makes the use of **message()** more convenient. In particular, the programmer can issue a prompt in one statement, and then use **get_user_response()** in a later statement to test the stored value, facilitating the use of **message()** in conditional expressions.

13.7 num_box: A Prompt Box for Numeric Responses

Analogous to **query_box, num_box** accommodates numeric responses. Its class definition, given in *numbox.hpp*, is:

```
class num_box : public msg_window {
    long user_response;
public:
    num_box(char *, int, int, int, int = BACK_ATTR);
    long get_user_response() {
        return user_response;
    }
    long message(char *, char *, int = REV_BORDER_COLOR,
                    int = REV_BORDER_COLOR);
};
```

message() differs slightly:

```
/*
message() issues a request for a numeric quantity.
*/

long num_box::message(char *hdr, char *msg, int hdr_attr,
                        int bdr_attr)
{
    char temp_str[15];

    activate(hdr, hdr_attr, bdr_attr);
    go_rc(0, 1);
    wputs_center(msg);
    wgets_filter(temp_str, 14);
    user_response = atol(temp_str);
    deactivate();
    return user_response;
}   /* message */
```

In this case, **atol()** is used to convert the string response to a long integer. Note that control over the number of digits that can be read in is provided by the second argument to **wgets_filter()**. As with **query_box**, the user's response is stored in **user_response** so that the programmer can access it as many times as necessary, without having to set up a local variable.

14

A Window Hierarchy with Editing Facilities

There are many applications for which it's necessary to provide some form of text editing in a window. In this chapter we discuss several classes that complete the window hierarchy outlined in Chapter 13, providing windows with various levels of editing capabilities. For convenience, we extend the term "edit" to include read-only operations, for example, browsing, in addition to full-scale, read-write operations.

14.1 buf_window: Adding Buffer Support to window

Editing operations require a character buffer. **buf_window** is an abstract class that supplements **window** with the variables and methods required for minimal window-based, buffer support. The interface file *winbufs.hpp* includes the following class definition:

```
class buf_window : public window {
protected:
    char *buffer;
    long buf_length, buf_cursor_pos, top_left_pos, max_buf_size;
    int tab_width, page_size;
```

```
public:
    buf_window(int, char *, int, int, int, int, long, int);
    ~buf_window() {
        delete buffer;
    }
    long get_max_size() {
        return max_buf_size;
    }
    long set_buf_length(long);
    long get_buf_length();
    long get_cursor_pos();
    int change_tab_width();
    int move_forward_x_lines(int);
    int move_backward_x_lines(int);
    long go_line_start();
    long go_line_end();
    char last_char_on_line();
    int linefeed_free(char *, register long);
    int buf_line_length();
    int window_line_length();
    int previous_column();
    int next_tab_column();
    int tab_fill_size(int);
    int fill_tabs(int);
    int strlen_with_tabs(char *, register int);
    int current_column_offset();
    int window_fill(int, int, long);
    int skip_offset(char *, int);
    void put_text(char *);
    void window_shift_right(int);
    void window_restore_shift();
    int window_restore_offset_and_column();
    long read_from_disk(char *);
    int write_to_disk(char *, long = 0, long = 0);
    long line_count();
    long line_count(long, long);
};
```

Seven protected variables are added for use by derived classes, plus a number of methods. Primarily, the methods in **buf_window** provide basic buffer and screen management for a text window that supports tabbing and horizontal scrolling; many of these methods have C counterparts in *edit.c* and *editwin.c*. Although this may seem like a considerable number of methods for an abstract class, it isn't unusual, given the sophistication of the window hierarchy. Johnson and Foote (1988) suggest that a class with 50 to 100 methods is suspiciously large. With 31 methods, **buf_window** is the second-largest class in our window hierarchy.

One of the benefits of a hierarchical breakdown is that it's reasonably straightforward to split an abstract class without negatively impacting its derived classes. For example, you could partition **buf_window** into two classes, giving the parent class a new name, making **buf_window** one of its derived classes. As long as **buf_window**'s derived classes can inherit the necessary members from **buf_window** or its ancestors, there is no impact on a derived class, such as **edit_window**.

Let's consider several of the methods from *winbufs.cpp*, including the constructor **buf_window()**:

```
/*
buf_window() establishes initial values for a number of
critical window and buffer variables.
*/

buf_window::buf_window(int win_no, char *hdr, int start_r,
        int start_c, int end_r, int end_c, long buf_size, int attr) :
        (win_no, hdr, start_r, start_c, end_r, end_c, attr)
{
    buffer = new char[buf_size];
    max_buf_size = buf_size;
    if (buf_size <= 0)
        error_state = FALSE;
    else if (buffer == NULL)
        error_state = TRUE;
    else {
        error_state = FALSE;
        buffer[0] = EOS;
    }
    if (attn_win.get_error_state())
        error_state = TRUE;
    buf_length = RESET;
    buf_cursor_pos = top_left_pos = RESET;
    tab_width = TAB_SIZE;
    page_size = end_r - start_r - 1;      // no page overlap
    go_rc(0, 0);                          // with this setting
}   /* buf_window */
```

buf_window() passes seven of the eight initialization arguments to the parent constructor **window()**.

One argument, represented by **buf_size**, is used with **new** to allocate storage from the heap. If the programmer passes a non-positive argument for the buffer size, or if the requested storage isn't available, **buffer** will be null and **error_state** will be set. If the attention window can't be allocated, **error_state** will be set as well. (Note that only the memory-allocation conditions have run-time significance.) Otherwise, the buffer has been allocated, requiring that several buffer-related variables be initialized.

error_state, and its access method **get_error_state()**, are inherited from **window**. In particular, there is no requirement to redefine them in **buf_window**. If, however, you needed to distinguish between a memory error related to allocating **window::window_save_buffer** and a similar error related to allocating **buf_window::buffer**, you could add additional error-detecting logic.

One of **buf_window**'s methods, **change_tab_width()**, illustrates a local definition of a window from elsewhere in the window hierarchy:

```
/*
change_tab_width() manages changes to the tab size.
*/

int buf_window::change_tab_width()
{
    num_box get_tab("", 11, 16, 16 + POPUP_WIDTH, BACK_ATTR);
    int new_width;

    get_tab.message("change takes effect with next screen update",
                    "Enter tab size: ");
    if ((new_width = int(get_tab.get_user_response())) > 0 &&
            new_width <= MAX_TAB)
        tab_width = new_width;
    return tab_width;
}   /* change_tab_width */
```

We could have used the value returned by **message()** directly; however, given the length of the string arguments to **message()**, using **get_user_response()** is less awkward.

buf_window includes two methods for disk I/O operations. First, **read_from_disk()** can be used to load the buffer with text:

```
/*
read_from_disk() loads a buffer from a disk file.
*/

long buf_window::read_from_disk(char *filename)
{
    FILE *buf_file;

    if ((buf_file = fopen(filename, "rt")) == NULL)
        return CANT_READ;
    else {
```

```
        for (register long len = 0; (len < max_buf_size) &&
                ((buffer[len] = fgetc(buf_file)) != EOF); len++)
            ;
        if (len == max_buf_size) {          // file is too large
            fclose(buf_file);
            return TOO_LARGE;
        }
        else {                              // OK to process it
            buffer[len] = EOS;
            fclose(buf_file);
            return len;
        }
    }
}   /* read_from_disk */
```

read_from_disk() used traditional (C) I/O functions. The stream facilities included with most C++ systems provide basic I/O, as required here. However, at the time of this writing the stream methods provided with some C++ implementations are less efficient than their C library counterparts. This situation will chance, of course, as C++ implementations mature. If you prefer using methods from the C++ stream library, the substitution is trivial. (See Berry [1988] for an excellent coverage of C++'s stream facilities.)

Second, **write_to_disk()** provides buffer-to-disk operations:

```
/*
write_to_disk() writes a buffer to disk and returns TRUE, if no
errors occur.
*/

int buf_window::write_to_disk(char *filename, long start,
                              long num_chars)
{
    FILE *buf_file;
    register int write_ok = TRUE;
    register long i;

    if ((buf_file = fopen(filename, "wt")) == NULL)
        return CANT_WRITE;
    else {
        if (num_chars != DUMMY)
            for (i = start; buffer[i] && write_ok == TRUE
                                && num_chars--; i++)
                write_ok = (fputc(buffer[i], buf_file) != EOF);
        else
            for (i = 0; buffer[i] && write_ok == TRUE; i++)
```

```
            write_ok = (fputc(buffer[i], buf_file) != EOF);
        if (write_ok == TRUE)
            write_ok = (fputc(EOF_CHAR, buf_file) != EOF);
        fclose(buf_file);
        return write_ok;
    }
}   /* write_to_disk */
```

As with our C version of **ed**, disk I/O operations are performed in text mode to simplify CR/LF processing. (Using text mode reduces the window hierarchy's dependency on OS idiosyncrasies.)

Our buffers are simple character arrays with no built-in capability for line-based operations. Sometimes it's useful to know how many newlines occur in a buffer. For example, in order to calculate whether or not a buffer will fit in the remaining space on a (DOS) disk, you must know both the buffer length and the number of newline sequences—with text mode I/O each **\n** will be replaced by **\r\n**.

There are two common situations that must be accommodated: (1) counting **LF**s in the entire buffer, and (2) counting **LF**s in a buffer segment. The second situation occurs when it's necessary to count newlines in a buffer segment of arbitrary length. For example, consider an editor application in which the user has marked a block of text and wants to write it to a disk file. (Counting newlines in the *tail-end* of a buffer is a trivial variation of the first situation).

It's possible to accommodate situations (1) and (2) with one method. However, for a small penalty in space efficiency, we can increase the run-time efficiency by handling each situation in a separate method. (Although we've been down-playing efficiency considerations, I/O performance shouldn't be unnecessarily slow.) For example, saving the entire buffer to disk is a common editor operation; hence, it should be as efficient as possible. **line_count()** handles situation (1):

```
/*
line_count() counts the number of lines in a buffer.
*/

long buf_window::line_count()
{
    register long i, num_lines;

    for (i = 0, num_lines = 0; buffer[i]; i++)
        if (buffer[i] == LF)
            num_lines++;
    return num_lines;
}   /* line_count */
```

Note that using "*buffer++" as the test condition won't work with the large memory models of some DOS compilers for the reasons outlined in Chapter 3—"buffer[i]" is more portable.

Because of C++'s facility for overloading methods, we can accommodate situation (2) with a method of the same name:

```
/*
line_count() counts the number of lines in a buffer segment.
*/

long buf_window::line_count(long start, long num_chars)
{
    register long i, num_lines;

    for (i = start, num_lines = 0; buffer[i] && num_chars--; i++)
        if (buffer[i] == LF)
            num_lines++;
    return num_lines;
}   /* line_count */
```

These two methods are distinguished by their implied messages (call sequences); the latter method will be used, if a buffer offset and segment length are provided as arguments.

14.2 browser: A Read-only Window with Restricted Cursor Movement

browser is a concrete class that supplements **buf_window** with the minimum tools necessary for paging through a character buffer that's displayed in a window. In addition, **browser** is designed to endow an object with "self-control." **browser** has the following class definition:

```
class browser : public buf_window {
public:
    browser(int, char *, int, int, int, int, long, int = BACK_ATTR);
    int dispatcher();
    int process_cmd(union keystroke);
    int page_up();
    int page_down();
    int top_of_buffer();
    int bottom_of_buffer();
    int redisplay_window();
};
```

In addition to the constructor, **browser** contains four cursor movement methods, its own method for redisplaying a window, and two methods for dispatching commands.

First, consider **browser()**:

```
/*
browser() passes initialization values to the parent constructor.
*/

browser::browser(int win_no, char *hdr, int start_r, int start_c,
          int end_r, int end_c, long buf_size, int attr) :
          (win_no, hdr, start_r, start_c, end_r, end_c,
             buf_size, attr)
{
}   /* browser */
```

browser doesn't require any initialization procedures that can't be handled by ancestor constructors; hence, its body is null.

Next, consider cursor movement operations. According to our design, **browser** will support only four operations, as implied by the following keystrokes: **<Ctrl>-<PgUp>**, **<Ctrl>-<PgDn>**, **<PgUp>**, and **<PgDn>**. Given these restrictions, it's convenient to maintain the cursor in the leftmost column. **browser**'s **top_of_buffer()** supports the first operation:

```
/*
top_of_buffer() moves the cursor to the beginning of the file/buffer.
*/

int browser::top_of_buffer()
{
    if (buf_cursor_pos == 0)
        return FALSE;
    else {
        buf_cursor_pos = top_left_pos = RESET;
        offset = RESET;
        window_fill(0, 0, 0);
        return TRUE;
    }
}   /* top_of_buffer */
```

bottom_of_buffer() implements the second operation:

```
/*
bottom_of_buffer() moves the cursor to the last displayable
line in the file/buffer.
*/
```

```
int browser::bottom_of_buffer()
{
    if (buf_cursor_pos == buf_length)
        return FALSE;
    else {
        buf_cursor_pos = buf_length;
        go_line_start();
        redisplay_window();
        return TRUE;
    }
}   /* bottom_of_buffer */
```

bottom_of_buffer() uses its own method for redisplaying a window:

```
/*
redisplay_window() redisplays the buffer in the window.
*/


int browser::redisplay_window()
{
    top_left_pos = buf_cursor_pos;
    go_rc(0, 0);
    window_shift_right(0);
}   /* redisplay_window */
```

This version of **redisplay_window()** is simpler than that required for normal text editing.

The **<PgUp>** operation uses **browser::redisplay_window()** as well:

```
/*
page_up() moves up one page.  The cursor remains
in the top-left corner.
*/

int browser::page_up()
{
    if (buf_cursor_pos == 0)
        return FALSE;
    else {
        move_backward_x_lines(page_size);
        redisplay_window();
        return TRUE;
    }
}   /* page_up */
```

In particular, since **redisplay_window()** hasn't been declared virtual, and it hasn't been provided in an ancestor class, the compiler (linker) has no choice but to demand its definition by **browser**.

The last cursor movement operation is provided by **page_down()**:

```
/*
page_down() moves down one page.  The cursor remains
in the top-left corner.
*/

int browser::page_down()
{
    if (buf_cursor_pos == buf_length)
        return FALSE;
    else {
        move_forward_x_lines(page_size);
        redisplay_window();
        return TRUE;
    }
}   /* page_down */
```

Its operation is complementary to **page_up()**.

Now let's consider management of these operations. Recall that *edit.c* supplies functions for text editing, but puts all of the burden for knowing and invoking those functions on the C application (that is, on the application programmer). In our C++ modules we want to do things differently. In particular, we want to build into **browser** a capability for sending messages to its own methods.

Although this capability can be provided by one method, we can offer the programmer more variability by having two methods share the responsibility. First, the most basic operation, processing a single keystroke command, can be handled by a separate method:

```
/*
process_cmd() processes keystroke commands.  It returns FALSE
if it can't do anything with a command.
*/

int browser::process_cmd(keystroke key)
{
    if (key.byte[0])            // ASCII character, so just return
        return FALSE;
    switch (key.byte[1]) {
        case PGUP:
            page_up();
            break;
```

```
        case PGDN:
            page_down();
            break;
        case CTRL_PGUP:
            top_of_buffer();
            break;
        case CTRL_PGDN:
            bottom_of_buffer();
            break;
        default:
            return FALSE;               // can't process command
    }
    return key.word;
}   /* process_cmd */
```

With this method, the programmer can set up a browser and then send a message to process a keystroke, as often as necessary:

```
    ...
    browser b(1, "Browser", 2, 0, 22, 79, BROWSER_SIZE);
    ...
    if (b.process_cmd(key))
        // command was processed OK
    else
    ...
```

With **process_cmd()** alone, the burden is still on the programmer to read keystrokes, and if necessary, to process them repetitively. We can add repetition to **browser** by providing another method that dispatches keystrokes to **process_cmd()**:

```
/*
dispatcher() dispatches keystroke commands to process_cmd(),
as long as process_cmd() can continue to process them.
*/

int browser::dispatcher()
{
    keystroke key;

    if (buf_cursor_pos != 0)
        top_of_buffer();
    else
        window_fill(0, 0, 0);
    do
```

```
        key.word = wgetche();
    while (process_cmd(key));
    return key.word;
}   /* dispatcher */
```

With **dispatcher()**, the programmer can send a message to a browser to "do its thing," as long the proper keystrokes are received. Normally, it makes sense to stop short of adding any additional logic. In general, the programmer is the best judge of what to do if the user presses a key that can't be processed.

browser is our first example of putting the control loop for processing an object within the object itself. In some of our more sophisticated window classes, which support many editing operations, this capability will prove to be quite important. Chapter 17 will illustrate additional advantages to using this approach.

14.3 text_window: Adding Text Editing Support

buf_window provides basic buffer management in a window, but has no capability for text editing. In this section we discuss **text_window**, an abstract class derived from **buf_window** with enhancements for (1) cursor movement, (2) tag operations, and (3) character insertion and deletion. Its interface includes:

```
class text_window : public buf_window {
protected:
    long tag_pos;
    int insert_mode;
public:
    text_window(int, char *, int, int, int, int, long, int);
    int process_cmd(keystroke);
    int get_insert_mode();
    long set_tag_pos();
    long set_tag_pos(int);
    long get_tag_pos();
    int insert_char(char);
    int insertion_special_conditions(char);
    void advance_cursor_to_next_tab();
    void insert_window_update(char, long);
    int del_char();
    int backspace();
    int up();
    int down();
    int cursor_left();
    int cursor_right();
    int word_left();
    int word_right();
```

```
        int home();
        int endd();
        int page_up();
        int page_down();
        int top_of_buffer_redisplay();
        int top_of_buffer();
        int bottom_of_buffer();
        int top_of_window();
        int bottom_of_window();
        void exch_tag_cursor_redisplay();
        long exch_tag_cursor();
        int get_tag_column();
        int redisplay_window(int);
        void redisplay_rest_of_line(int);
        int window_scroll_up(int);
        int window_scroll_down(int);
        int buffer_up_line(int);
        int buffer_down_line(int);
        int window_adjust_cursor_position(int);
        void adjust_onscreen_position(int);
        int adjacent_to_leftmost_column();
        int adjacent_to_rightmost_column();
        void window_buffer_forward();
        void window_buffer_backward();
        int go_right_as_far_as_possible();
        int ispunc(char);
};
```

text_window adds two additional variables, one for tag management and one for insertion-related operations. Although it meets the somewhat arbitrary "less than 50 methods" rule, with 44 methods **text_window** is the largest class in our hierarchy.

text_window is an abstract class; it stops short of providing several capabilities required in most text editors, for example, cut-and-paste operations, undo support, and so on. While **text_window**'s capabilities are basic to most editors, editors tend to vary in their support for high-level editing operations. Thus, it's better to omit high-level operations from the abstract class, so that each derived class can implement the functionality that it needs.

The tag-related variables are initialized by the constructor (defined in *wintext.cpp*):

```
/*
text_window() establishes initial values for a number of
critical editor variables.
*/


text_window::text_window(int win_no, char *hdr, int start_r,
```

```
    int start_c, int end_r, int end_c, long buf_size, int attr) :
    (win_no, hdr, start_r, start_c, end_r, end_c, buf_size, attr)
{
    set_tag_pos(UNDEFINED);
}   /* text_window */
```

All of **text_window()**'s initialization arguments are passed to ancestor constructors where error detection is handled.

Like the concrete class **browser**, **text_window** provided a method for processing keystrokes, namely, **process_cmd()**:

```
/*
process_cmd() processes keystroke commands.  It returns FALSE if it
can't do anything with a command.
*/

int text_window::process_cmd(keystroke key)
{
    if (key.byte[0])
        return FALSE;           // can't process read-write commands
    switch (key.byte[1]) {
        case LEFT:
            cursor_left();
            break;
        case RIGHT:
            cursor_right();
            break;
        ...
        ...
        case CTRL_END:
            bottom_of_window();
            break;
        case TAG:
            set_tag_pos();
            break;
        case UNTAG:
            set_tag_pos(UNDEFINED);
            break;
        case TAG_CURSOR:
            exch_tag_cursor_redisplay();
            break;
        case SET_TABS:
            change_tab_width();
            break;
```

```
        default:
            return FALSE;           // can't process command
    }
    return key.word;
}   /* process_cmd */
```

Testing the value of **insert_mode** is a common operation; hence, it can be provided in **text_window**:

```
/*
get_insert_mode() determines the insert/overwrite state.
*/

int text_window::get_insert_mode()
{
    return insert_mode;
}   /* get_insert_mode */
```

On the other hand, modifying **insert_mode** is best left to derived classes, so that they can tailor this operation to their specific needs, for example, updating an on-screen indicator of insert mode status.

With C++ we can take advantage of method overloading in several situations. For example, we don't have to pass message constants as arguments to functions that perform various operations against critical editor variables, as we did in our C edit module. Instead, we can overload a common method name. Consider tag management. We can define a method named **set_tag_pos()** that requires no arguments to set the tag at the current cursor position:

```
/*
set_tag_pos() sets a tag; it uses buf_cursor_pos to
set the tag position.
*/

long text_window::set_tag_pos()
{
    return (tag_pos = buf_cursor_pos);
}   /* set_tag_pos */
```

We can define a separate method for undoing a tag:

```
/*
set_tag_pos() allows a tag to be turned off.
*/
```

```
long text_window::set_tag_pos(int new_pos)
{
    if (new_pos == UNDEFINED)
        tag_pos = UNDEFINED;
    return tag_pos;
}   /* set_tag_pos */
```

If **UNDEFINED** is passed as an argument, the tag is turned off; otherwise, it does nothing but return the current tag position. (Alternatively, you could provide methods with two different names, one for setting the tag and one for undoing the tag.)

Lastly, recall that **buf_window** does not supply a method for redisplaying a window after changes are made to the on-screen text. **browser**, for example, requires its own **redisplay_window()**, one that keeps the cursor in the top-left corner of the window. **redisplay_window()** was omitted from **buf_window** for another reason: a sophisticated version of **redisplay_window()**, with arguments that provide suggestions for cursor adjustment, requires the cursor management methods of **text_window**, in particular, **window_adjust_cursor_position()**:

```
/*
redisplay_window() redisplays the buffer in the text window with
the cursor positioned (vertically) in the middle of the window.  It
assumes that the cursor is positioned at the beginning of the line
(in the buffer).
*/

int text_window::redisplay_window(int current_c)
{
    long old_buf_pos = go_line_start();
    int lines_moved = move_backward_x_lines(page_size / 2);
    top_left_pos = buf_cursor_pos;
    buf_cursor_pos = old_buf_pos;
    go_rc(lines_moved, DUMMY);
    if (!window_adjust_cursor_position(current_c))
        window_shift_right(0);
    return lines_moved;
}   /* redisplay_window */
```

window_adjust_cursor_position() in turn must call other methods defined by **text_window**. The details of these support methods (given in Appendix B) are left as an exercise.

14.4 edit_window: A Concrete Class for Full-scale Text Editing

edit_window is a concrete class, derived from **text_window**, that adds one variable for recording whether or not the buffer has been modified, plus a number of methods that make

edit_window comparable in function to our C edit module, *edit.c*. **edit_window** has the following class definition:

```
class edit_window : public text_window {
protected:
    int buf_mod_state;
public:
    edit_window(int, char *, int, int, int, int, long,
                    int = BACK_ATTR);
    int dispatcher();
    int process_cmd(keystroke);
    int buffer_modified(int);
    int buffer_modified();
    int set_insert_mode(int);
    int insert_char(char);       // variation of parent method
    int del_char();              // variation of parent method
    int backspace();             // variation of parent method
    int del_word();
    int del_word_left();
    int del_eol();
    int del_line();
    int paste(char *);
    int paste_from_buffer(char_buffer &);
    int copy_to_clipboard();
    int cut_to_clipboard();
    int cut_to_undo(long);
    int paste_from_undo();
    int find_and_change(int);
    int prompt_for_pattern(int, char *, char *);
    int replace_text(char *, char *, long);
    void display_not_found(int, char *);
    long string_search(char *, char *, register long);
    int update_undo_dependent_offset(long);
    int update_undo_dependent_offset_for_cut(long);
};
```

Consider the constructor **edit_window()**:

```
/*
edit_window() establishes initial values for a number of
critical window variables.
*/


edit_window::edit_window(int win_no, char *hdr, int start_r,
```

```
    int start_c, int end_r, int end_c, long buf_size, int attr) :
    (win_no, hdr, start_r, start_c, end_r, end_c, buf_size, attr)
{
    buffer_modified(FALSE);
    set_insert_mode(SET);
    if (find_win.get_error_state() || clip_bd.get_error_state() ||
            undo_buf.get_error_state())
        error_state = TRUE;      // can't use the editor w/o these
}   /* edit_window */
```

edit_window() initializes two of its members, plus **error_state**, which is inherited from **window**, the root window class. Note that if any memory allocation errors occur in allocating **find_win**, **clip_bd**, **undo_buf**, or any of the heap variables inherited by **edit_window**, **error_state** will be set. Note also that since constructors for global objects are executed during program initialization, it will be important to allocate **edit_window** objects as local variables. Doing so will ensure that **find_win**'s **error_state** is initialized before **edit_window**'s **error_state**. **get_error_state()** can be interrogated by the application to ensure that memory allocation has taken place normally.

edit_window objects should be able to manage the execution of **edit_window** tasks. Recall that **text_window** provides a version of **process_cmd()** for associating keystrokes with editing tasks. Likewise, **edit_window** provides a **process_cmd()** method to handle its enhancements to **text_window**:

```
/*
process_cmd() processes keystroke commands.
*/

int edit_window::process_cmd(keystroke key)
{
    if (key.byte[0])
        switch (key.byte[0]) {
            case EOF_CHAR:              // don't allow the user to
                break;                  // enter an EOF character
            case BKSP:
                backspace();
                break;
            default:
                insert_char(key.byte[0]);
                break;
        }
    else
        switch (key.byte[1]) {
            case DEL:
                del_char();
```

```
                break;
            case DWORD:
                del_word();
                break;
            case DWORD_LEFT:
                del_word_left();
                break;
            case DEOL:
                del_eol();
                break;
            case DLINE:
                del_line();
                break;
            case CUT:
                cut_to_clipboard();
                break;
            case COPY:
                copy_to_clipboard();
                break;
            case PASTE:
                paste_from_buffer(clip_bd);
                break;
            case FIND_TEXT:
                find_and_change(FIND_IT);
                break;
            case CHANGE_TEXT:
                find_and_change(CHANGE_IT);
                break;
            case REPEAT_FC:
                find_and_change(REPEAT_IT);
                break;
            case UNDO:
                paste_from_undo();
                break;
            case INS:
                set_insert_mode(get_insert_mode() ? RESET : SET);
                break;
            default:
                return text_window::process_cmd(key);    // submit to
        }                                                 // a higher authority
    return key.word;
}   /* process_cmd */
```

If **process_cmd()** encounters a keystroke that it can't handle, it submits it to **text_editor::process_cmd()**. If neither method can process the keystroke, **FALSE** is returned; otherwise, the associated method is executed and the keystroke is returned. Note that compile-time binding is sufficient for choosing the proper **process_cmd()** method.

Since **edit_window** is a concrete class, it's a good idea to provide the programmer with a method that can manage multiple keystrokes; **dispatcher()** provides this service:

```
/*
dispatcher() dispatches keystroke commands to process_cmd(),
as long as process_cmd() can continue to process them.
*/

int edit_window::dispatcher()
{
    keystroke key;

    do {
        key.word = wgetche();
    } while (process_cmd(key));
    return key.word;
}   /* dispatcher */
```

dispatcher() makes an **edit_window()** object quite autonomous; in particular, an application can allocate and manage an **edit_window** object with minimal source code.

text_window provided methods for generic insertion and deletion of characters. These methods are adequate for **edit_window**'s insertion and deletion operations, except that **edit_window** objects must manage a variable and update an on-screen indicator related to the buffer's modification status. **edit_window::insert_char()** calls **buffer_modified()** to perform these services after calling **text_window::insert_char()**:

```
/*
insert_char() inserts characters into the buffer and updates
the screen as necessary.  It must take into consideration the
fact that window::wgetche() has already updated the current
screen coordinates--for displayable characters.
*/

int edit_window::insert_char(char ch)
{
    text_window::insert_char(ch);
    if (insert_mode)
        update_undo_dependent_offset(1);
    buffer_modified(TRUE);
}   /* insert_char */
```

del_char() and **backspace()** operate in a similar manner; **del_char()**'s definition is:

```
/*
del_char() deletes a character from the buffer
and updates the screen.
*/

int edit_window::del_char()
{
    if (text_window::del_char())
        update_undo_dependent_offset(-1);
    buffer_modified(TRUE);
}   /* del_char */
```

On the other hand, methods such as **del_eol()** are too specialized to be implemented by **text_window**. At present, high-level deletion operations are provided by **edit_window** objects, for example, **del_eol()**:

```
/*
del_eol() deletes all characters between the cursor and the end of
the line by first determining the respective buffer offsets, and
then calling cut_to_undo().  As with del_word(), this operation can
be undone.
*/

int edit_window::del_eol()
{
    long last_pos;        // the last/final character to be deleted

    if (buffer[last_pos = buf_cursor_pos] == LF ||
            buffer[last_pos] == EOS) {
        attn_win.message("", "** already at end of line **");
        return FALSE;
    }
    else {
        while (buffer[last_pos] && buffer[last_pos] != LF)
            last_pos++;
        return cut_to_undo(last_pos);
    }
}   /* del_eol */
```

One alternative would be to add another abstract class between **text_window** and **edit_window** that could provide more editor functionality than **text_window**. By increasing the depth of the hierarchy, the intermediate classes would be smaller, hence, more easily tailored to a variety of applications.

14.5 edit_window's Friends: A Buffer Hierarchy

edit_window requires buffers for cut-and-paste and undo operations; in our current implementation, they are allocated as private objects in the **edit_window** implementation module. (See Section 14.7 for more information.) In this section, we discuss a small hierarchy that provides these special buffering services. The interface for the entire hierarchy is given in *buffers.hpp*.

char_buffer is the root class. It automates the allocation and deallocation of character buffers:

```
class char_buffer {
    int error_state;
protected:
    long max_buf_size;
    char *buffer;
public:
    char_buffer(long);
    ~char_buffer() {
        delete buffer;
    }
    int get_error_state() {
        return error_state;
    }
    long get_max_size() {
        return max_buf_size;
    }
    char *get_buffer() {
        return buffer;
    }
    long read_from_disk(char *);
    int write_to_disk(char *, long = 0, long = 0);
    long line_count();
    long line_count(long, long);
};
```

The last four methods are used for buffer I/O; they are equivalent in function to four methods from *winbufs.cpp* that we've already discussed.

In general, the root class in a hierarchy should be abstract. Are there circumstances that justify violating this rule? In our opinion, it's important to recognize that C++ is fundamentally different from pure object-oriented languages, such as Smalltalk. Smalltalk, for example, is a true supporter of latent typing and dynamic binding. (Actually, with a pure object-oriented language like Smalltalk, traditional latent typing is subsumed by dynamic binding—every object is capable of responding to a prescribed set of messages.) C++, on the other hand, is primarily a strongly typed language, with some provision for dynamic binding via virtual methods.

Regardless of the level of data abstraction promoted by a particular class hierarchy, a C++ programmer will always need strongly typed objects, for example, an integer object that provides loop control. Likewise, a character buffer is a basic component of many C++ applications. Moreover, transferring a character buffer between disk and memory is a basic operation for many C++ applications. For these reasons, it is quite legitimate to set up a concrete class for character buffers—one that automates the allocation and deallocation of storage from the heap, with methods for disk I/O.

char_buffer() takes care of the messy details of allocating and initializing a buffer from the heap:

```
/*
char_buffer() allocates and initializes a character buffer.
*/

char_buffer::char_buffer(long buf_size) {
    max_buf_size = buf_size;
    buffer = new char[buf_size];
    if (buffer == NULL)
        error_state = TRUE;
    else {
        error_state = FALSE;
        buffer[0] = EOS;
    }
}   /* char_buffer */
```

With this definition, we can allocate a buffer, use it, and destroy it in short order:

```
    ...
    char_buffer *default_path = new char_buffer(500);
    if (!default_path.get_error_state()) {
        default_path.read_from_disk("\\<program path>\\config.dat");
        strcat(default_path, filename);
        ...
        ...
        delete default_path;
    }
    else
        // error--can't do it
    ...
```

Although **char_buffer** could be useful for a variety of applications, it's included here for two reasons. First, it serves as a vehicle for transferring files between memory and disk, for example, editor support operations such as merging an existing file with the current edit buffer. Second, it serves as a base class for two classes needed by **edit_window**, namely, **clipboard** and **undo_buffer**. **clipboard** is a simple derivation of **char_buffer**:

```
class clipboard : public char_buffer {
    friend class edit_window;
public:
    clipboard(long buf_size) : (buf_size) {
    }
};
```

undo_buffer's derivation is equally simple:

```
class undo_buffer : public char_buffer {
    friend class edit_window;
private:
    long cursor_when_cut[MAX_WINDOWS + 1];
public:
    undo_buffer(long buf_size) : (buf_size) {
        for (int i = 0; i <= MAX_WINDOWS; i++)
            cursor_when_cut[i] = UNDEFINED;
    }
};
```

We (personally) don't like to use the **friend** facility in C++, primarily because it leads to a hard-coded relationship between two different modules that inhibits closing the "friendly" module. That is, each class that uses either a clipboard or an undo buffer must modify *buffers.hpp*. We did, however, want to have one example of **friend**, and its usage here is typical. One alternative is to define the latter two classes as structures (**structs**), or explicitly make all of their members public.

There are other ramifications of the simple buffer hierarchy, as we've designed it here. In particular, it allows us to set up a single paste method in **edit_window** that can accept either a clipboard or an undo buffer as an argument using reference parameters. For example, *winedit.cpp* includes the following definition:

```
/*
paste_from_buffer() provides a mechanism for performing a top-level
paste operation, hiding the details of the necessary call to paste(),
where the proper buffer must be given as an argument.
*/

int edit_window::paste_from_buffer(char_buffer &gen_buf)
```

```
{
    update_undo_dependent_offset(strlen(gen_buf.get_buffer()));
    return paste(gen_buf.get_buffer());
}   /* paste_from_buffer */
```

C++ allows an implicit pointer assignment of a derived class object to a base class pointer. Similarly, a derived class object can be passed by reference to a method that's designed to accept a base class object. In this case, **gen_buf** is a reference parameter that can be assigned to either a **clipboard** or an **undo_buffer** object, since both are derived from **char buffer**.

In this situation, there is no need for any form of dynamic binding. In particular, we aren't binding objects and methods as with virtual methods: "<object_ptr>-><message>". **gen_buf** is bound to the proper object (clipboard or undo buffer) based on method-to-method activity within the class **edit_window**. That is, **paste_from_buffer()** is always invoked with an argument whose type is known by the compiler—**undo_buf** and **clip_bd** aren't involved in any implicit pointer assignments. Here, **paste_from_buffer()** extracts the buffer from the buffer object and passes it to **paste()**, a generic paste method from **edit_window**. The latter method takes a memory address as an argument and, beginning at that address, pastes characters into the **edit_window** object.

Lastly, why did we define redundant methods for memory-to-disk buffer operations in *winbufs.cpp* and *buffers.cpp*? We did it because **buf_window** and **char_buffer** are very different classes. That is, having four operations in common does not justify imposing an arbitrary relationship between two otherwise distinct classes. As one alternative, we could have nested **char_buffer** within **buf_window**. That is, we could have defined a **char_buffer** object as a member of each **buf_window** object—instead of establishing a simple buffer as a top-level member of **buf_window**.

With this approach to class nesting, **char_buffer**'s I/O methods would have been sufficient. In fact, we used this approach in earlier versions of our buffer and window hierarchies. One disadvantage of this approach is the syntax incurred by having **buffer** nested within a **char_buffer** object—**buffer** is the most commonly accessed member of the window classes. When **buffer** is nested within a **char_buffer** object, the syntax in the window class methods for accessing the buffer is just too cumbersome—for example, the array references (**buffer[i]**), the buffer arguments to functions like **memcpy()**, and so on.

14.6 prompt_window: A Prompt Box Class with Editing Capabilities

Both **query_box** and **num_box** allow the programmer to prompt the user and record the user's response. They are designed as low-overhead prompt boxes. As such, they lack editing capabilities other than **<Backspace>**. Moreover, the user's response is not "remembered" and redisplayed each time a prompt box is reactivated.

Using **text_window** it's straightforward to derive a window class with editing capabilities, plus the capability of retaining the edited text from one activation of the window to the next. Typically, with **edit_window** the method **write_to_disk()** would be used to record the edited text on disk. However, with a prompt box class it's important to provide the programmer with the capability of retrieving the edited text for subsequent use by the application. **prompt_window** provides these services:

```
class prompt_window : public text_window {
public:
    prompt_window(int, char *, int, int, int, int, long,
                    int = BACK_ATTR);
    int dispatcher(int = BREAK_PROMPT);
    int dispatcher();
    int process_cmd(keystroke);
    char *get_line(char *put_to, int len) {
        strncpy(put_to, buffer, len);
        return put_to;
    }
    int set_insert_mode(int);
    int del_rest_of_line();
};
```

prompt_window defines the inline method **get_line()** for transferring the contents of the window's buffer to the application. Specifically, the programmer can allocate a buffer of a fixed size, for example,

```
    char prompt_data[MAX_PROMPT_INPUT];
```

where **MAX_PROMPT_INPUT** is a parameter defined in a header file, such as *windows.h* or *editintc.h*.

Subsequently, the user's response in the prompt box can be retrieved with a statement such as:

```
    get_line(prompt_data, MAX_PROMPT_INPUT);
```

By forcing the programmer to specify a maximum string/buffer length, it's less likely that a (verbose) user will be given the opportunity to overwrite the application's buffer. For convenience, **get_line()** copies the buffer to the address represented by the first parameter, **put_to**, *and* returns a pointer to this area, as do many of the traditional string functions such as **strncpy()**.

prompt_window's constructor must set the insert mode status, as required by methods such as **insert_char()**:

```
/*
prompt_window() passes window initialization values to the
parent constructor.
*/
```

```
prompt_window::prompt_window(int win_no, char *hdr, int start_r,
        int start_c, int end_r, int end_c, long buf_size, int attr) :
        (win_no, hdr, start_r, start_c, end_r, end_c, buf_size, attr)
{
    set_insert_mode(SET);
}   /* prompt_window */
```

Consistent with **browser** and **edit_window**, **prompt_window** defines a dispatching method(s):

```
/*
dispatcher() dispatches keystroke commands.  A programmer-defined
"break key" can be used to abandon the prompt box, in addition to
the <Enter> and <Esc> keys.
*/

int prompt_window::dispatcher(int break_prompt)
{
    keystroke key;

    top_of_buffer_redisplay();
    do {
        key.word = wgetche();
        process_cmd(key);
    } while (!((!key.byte[0] && key.byte[1] == break_prompt) ||
                key.byte[0] == CR || key.byte[0] == ESC));
    return key.word;
}   /* dispatcher */
```

By using the dispatcher, the programmer is relieved of low-level duties, such as ensuring that the cursor is positioned at the beginning of the text each time the prompt box is activated.

dispatcher() deactivates the prompt box when any one of three keystrokes is received: **<Enter>**, **<Esc>**, or the value represented by **break_prompt**, which is passed as an argument to **dispatcher()**. In the interface for **prompt_window**, the key bound to **BREAK_PROMPT** is used as the default break key. Of course, the programmer can dedicate any available key as a break command, overriding the default. (A second dispatcher with no parameters is provided as well; see Appendix B. Its utility will be addressed in Chapter 17.)

process_cmd() takes care of binding commands to methods:

```
/*
process_cmd() processes keystroke commands.
*/
```

```
int prompt_window::process_cmd(keystroke key)
{
    if (key.byte[0])
        switch (key.byte[0]) {
            case ESC:                   // terminate the prompt editing
            case CR:
                return key.word;
            case EOF_CHAR:              // don't allow the user to
                break;                  // enter an EOF character
            case BKSP:
                backspace();
                break;
            default:
                insert_char(key.byte[0]);
                break;
        }
    else
        switch (key.byte[1]) {
            case DEL:
                del_char();
                break;
            case DEOL:
                    del_rest_of_line();
                break;
            case INS:
                set_insert_mode(get_insert_mode() ? RESET : SET);
                break;
            default:
                return text_window::process_cmd(key);   // submit to
        }                                               // a higher authority
    return key.word;
}   /* process_cmd */
```

prompt_window's cursor movement commands are consistent with those of **edit_window**—both classes inherit **text_window::process_cmd()**. **prompt_window** inherits **insert_char()**, **del_char()**, and **backspace()** as well. However, it does not provide undo capabilities or a family of high-level deletion methods like those available with **edit_window**, which are tied to an undo buffer.

It does provide one method, **del_rest_of_line()**, for minimal, high-level deletion operations:

```
/*
del_rest_of_line() deletes the remaining characters on
a line without the possibility of undelete.
*/

int prompt_window::del_rest_of_line()
{
    if (buffer[buf_cursor_pos] == LF ||
            buffer[buf_cursor_pos] == EOS)
        return FALSE;
    else {
        long start = buf_cursor_pos;
        long end = go_line_end();
        memmove(&buffer[start], &buffer[end], buf_length - end + 1);
        buf_length -= end - start;
        buf_cursor_pos = start;
        redisplay_rest_of_line(UNDEFINED);
        return TRUE;
    }
}   /* del_rest_of_line */
```

Lastly, **prompt_window** provides a simple version of **set_insert_mode**():

```
/*
set_insert_mode() sets insert/overwrite mode and displays
an indicator of the current state.
*/

int prompt_window::set_insert_mode(int change_state)
{
    return (insert_mode = change_state);
}   /* set_insert_mode */
```

Unlike **edit_window**, it doesn't need to update an on-screen indicator of insert mode's status.

14.7 Global Constructors

Every **edit_window** object requires secondary windows, for example, a search-and-replace window, plus supporting data structures such as a clipboard. If these structures were defined local to **edit_window**, that is, as class members, they would be allocated for each **edit_window** object. Actually, you can override the allocation of a distinct data structure for each object of a class, by making a class member static—a *class variable*. A class variable is shared by all objects of that class and must be initialized outside the class definition.

In some cases, however, it's more appropriate to allocate an object globally than to create it as a nested component of another class; in our opinion, this is true for the clipboard and for the support windows in our application. For this reason, each structure is declared as a private, global object in the implementation file for **edit_window**, *winedit.cpp*. Their definitions are:

```
static msg_window find_win(0, "Find/Change", 3, 16, 7,
                           16 + POPUP_WIDTH, BACK_ATTR);
static clipboard clip_bd(MAX_BUF_SIZE);
static undo_buffer undo_buf(MAX_UNDO_SIZE);
```

As with our C version of **ed**, several editing parameters, such as **MAX_BUF_SIZE**, are maintained in *editintc.h* for fine-tuning each application.

What are the implications of the definition of global objects? A primary concern is that if there are run-time, initialization dependencies among various global objects, you must be careful about the order in which the objects are created, that is, the order in which global constructors are executed. Specifically, *within* a given file, C++ guarantees that global constructors are executed based on the lexical order of object definitions in the source file. There are, however, no guarantees about the order of execution of global constructors *across* object modules.

Schwarz (1989) discusses a technique whereby global objects are "wrapped" in a dedicated class to control the execution of constructors. Schwarz describes how supplemental class members can be used to keep track of, or control, the number of times a constructor has been executed. In a similar manner, it's possible to use a dedicated class (class object) to control the order of execution of various constructors.

For our application, there are no conflicts. The three global objects described in this section are private to *winedit.cpp*. These objects are used by **edit_window** objects, which are allocated as automatic local variables during program execution, that is, subsequent to the execution of **main()**.

14.8 Critique of Our Class Hierarchies

Naturally, there are a number of theories about how to design abstract classes and where to use them. For example, as a general rule, the top of a class hierarchy should be abstract (Johnson and Foote, 1988). Also, as we mentioned earlier, some programmers believe that it's important to minimize the number of variables in an abstract class. Some object-oriented programmers suggest that it's important to control access to the variable members of a class by forcing methods to send them messages. That is, an object should access its own variables by using access methods. This approach minimizes the dependency of the class methods on one particular data representation.

In our window hierarchy, we haven't honored the latter rule. In particular, we've used **protected** sections in order to provide derived classes with direct access to base class variables. This technique is widespread in the C++ community, because of the importance of run-time efficiency in many applications.

Given the goals and recognized limitations of our design, we have minimized the proliferation of variables in our abstract classes. For example, to gain some simplicity in our overall design, we accept the limitation that our windows will always be defined by row-column coordinates, so that we can include these variables as part of the abstract class from which other window classes will be derived.

Our window hierarchy does not employ *multiple inheritance*; that is, there is no class that inherits attributes from two or more classes simultaneously. In our opinion, multiple inheritance should be reserved for situation in which there's a compelling reason for using it, and should never be used for quick-and-dirty, patchwork class building. Often, it's tempting to design a small class(es) that functions in a supporting role, say, a class that contains color and/or size attributes. These "minor" classes can be inherited during a more significant class derivation, as in Figure 14.1.

In general, employing single (class) inheritance for class *specialization* is preferable to employing multiple (class) inheritance for class *composition*, because it leads to fewer syntactic and conceptual problems during low-level class reuse, that is, during subsequent derivations. Perhaps the least significant, but most often discussed, problem that can arise is name clashes. For example, if two classes both contain the variable **x**, and if both classes are inherited during the creation of a new class, there will be two versions of **x**. Languages such as C++ provide mechanisms for solving this type of syntactic problem.

In many cases, it's more appropriate to nest classes than to employ multiple inheritance. With the example in Figure 14.1, it would be more appropriate to instantiate **color_class** as a variable member of **window_class**. Some experts (see Meyer [1988a]) use the "is-a" link criterion (popularized in early AI research) in deciding whether or not to derive a new class from multiple parents. In our example, **window_class_with_colors** "is a" **window_class**, but **window_class** "is not a" **color_class**. In subsequent chapters, we use class nesting in deriving a help class that employs a **browser** object to build a help system, and in deriving

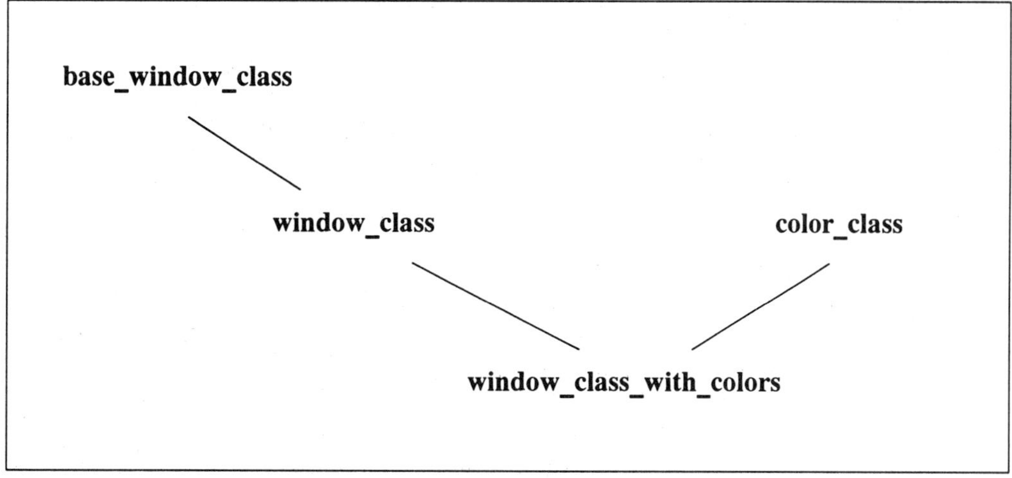

Figure 14.1 Multiple Inheritance of Classes

an **editor** class from components of our window hierarchy.

We should reiterate that our window hierarchy is designed for tutorial purposes and that it supports specific windowing operations, whereas the windowing system that accompanies Smalltalk is designed to support the entire Smalltalk programming environment.

To some extent, C++ can accommodate Smalltalk-like programming. By this we mean that it can support the development of deep hierarchies with many abstract classes where the abstract classes serve as "type-less shells." The practice of loading the abstract classes with numerous (null) virtual method definitions is typical of this approach. In this case, classes are given their "true type," or functionality, during subsequent derivation activities as variables and methods are added. In many situations this approach to designing a class hierarchy is appropriate; in others it is not.

In particular, it is not necessary to take this approach, in order to accommodate dynamic binding of, say, **buf_window** pointers to **browser**, **prompt_window**, and/or **edit_window** object. In our opinion, the use of dynamic binding should be restricted to situations in which it is truly required, especially if run-time performance is critical. Moreover, where possible, classes should have high-level methods that serve as interfaces to low-level methods. Lastly, small, concrete hierarchies are legitimate in many circumstances, for example, **char_buffer**.

For a more formal treatment of the pros and cons of class design, we refer you to the *Journal of Object-oriented Programming* and to *The C++ Report*. In particular, Johnson and Foote (1988) provide an excellent discussion of the use of abstract classes in a Smalltalk programming environment—much of their discussion is applicable to C++ applications. Johnson (1989) discusses the importance of abstract classes in C++. Chapter 17 of this book provides more discussion of virtual methods and dynamic binding. In particular, Chapter 17 demonstrates how to virtualize the high-level methods that govern an object, in order to avoid the proliferation of numerous low-level virtual methods.

15

ed: Using Recursion to Implement Nested Edit Windows

This chapter builds a simple editor to demonstrate the window hierarchy that we designed in the previous chapters. We emphasize the generalizability of our classes and the importance of minimizing global variables by using recursive functions to provide a secondary edit window that's subordinate to the primary edit window.

To illustrate the **browser** class, this version of **ed** uses a disk-based help system, in contrast to the C implementation of **ed** in which the help text was stored within the executable file.

Lastly, to illustrate the class **prompt_window**, **ed** provides support for a DOS-shell prompt box that "remembers" its content from one invocation of the shell to the next.

15.1 Application Modules that Support main()

In this chapter we discuss several of the most important functions required in the implementation of **ed**. These functions are spread over three modules: *edhelp.cpp*, *ed.cpp*, and *edfile.cpp*. Unlike our class hierarchy files, which contain class interfaces and class implementations in *.hpp* and *.cpp* files, respectively, two of the application modules for **ed** use traditional functions, not methods, that is, these modules do not define classes with member functions.

This approach emphasizes that a hybrid language such as C++ allows the programmer to mix traditional and object-oriented programming freely. For the class-free modules, *ed.cpp* and *edfile.cpp* contain function definitions and *ed.hpp* and *edfile.hpp* contain external declarations.

15.2 help: ed's Help System

Before considering the functions that are split between *ed.cpp* and *edfile.cpp*, we must develop a help system for **ed**. In our C version of **ed** the help text was stored as an array of pointers to pages of text. Hard-coding the help text into the executable file is feasible only when the help text is relatively small. In the current version of **ed** we can use the **browser** class to display the help text, taken from an ordinary text file.

Although too simplistic for large software products, this type of help system is fine for products such as **ed**—the commands have a linear, as opposed to hierarchical, logical organization. This type of help system is easy to set up because a programmer can enter text into the help file with an editor (**ed**). The following class definition is from *edhelp.hpp*:

```
class help {
    int error_state;
    browser help_win;
public:
    help(int, char *, int, int, int, int, int);
    get_error_state() {
        return error_state;
    }
    void present_help_screens();
};
```

help illustrates nesting one class within another class. In this case, **help_win**, a **browser** object, is a member of **help**.

help() sets up a **help** object:

```
/*
help() sets up a read-only edit buffer (browser) for the help system.
*/

help::help(int win_no, char *hdr, int start_r, int start_c, int end_r,
    int end_c, int buf_size) :
    help_win(win_no, hdr, start_r, start_c, end_r, end_c, buf_size)
{
    long buf_len = help_win.read_from_disk(HELP_SPEC);
    help_win.set_buf_length(buf_len);
```

```
    error_state = help_win.get_error_state();
}   /* help */
```

If the ancestor constructors are unsuccessful in initializing the window object, **help::error_state** will be set to **TRUE**. **help** provides an inline access method, **get_error_state()**, for testing the result of the window allocation operations.

The constructor uses the **read_from_disk()** method, inherited from **buf_window**, to load the help text from disk. The location of the help text is a program parameter that can be set in *editintc.h* by changing the value of **HELP_SPEC**. Note that we're using the constructor to load the help system during program initialization, as opposed to loading the help system from disk each time the user presses **HELP** (the help key).

Next, consider the tasks required each time the user activates the help system; **present_help_screens()** manages this operation:

```
/*
present_help_screens() displays help information in a window.
*/

void help::present_help_screens()
{
    keystroke key;

    if (help_win.get_buf_length() <= 0) {
        attn_win.message(HELP_SPEC, "** can't read help file **");
        return;
    }
    help_win.activate("");
    if (help_win.get_cursor_pos() != 0)
        help_win.top_of_buffer();
    else
        help_win.window_fill(0, 0, 0);
    do
        key.word = help_win.wgetche();
    while (help_win.process_cmd(key));
    help_win.deactivate();
}   /* present_help_screens */
```

First, if the help file can't be found during program initialization, the buffer's length will be non-positive. In this case, the attention window is used to display a message; in particular, the editor shouldn't fail just because the help file can't be loaded. (**attn_win** is a public object allocated in *winbufs.cpp*.)

If the help buffer has been loaded with text, pressing the help key activates the help window and initiates keystroke processing. Recall that for maximum flexibility **browser** objects provide a two-stage form of autonomous operation. In the current version of **ed**,

present_help_screens() illustrates the low-level method **process_cmd()**. To use this method properly, the programmer must take on the responsibility of repeatedly processing the user's keystrokes.

Also, the programmer must understand the behavior of **window_fill()** and **top_of_buffer()**. That is, if the previous keystroke left the cursor at the beginning of the help text, **window_fill()** is called to fill the screen; otherwise, the cursor is moved to the beginning of the buffer before displaying any text. In some cases, this level of control might be appropriate; however, most of the time it would be more appropriate to call **dispatcher()**, as we'll illustrate in the next chapter. Note that if you prefer, you can control access to lower-level methods by making them private, or protected.

15.3 ed: Some Assembly Required

In this section we address several aspects of the modules *ed.cpp* and *edfile.cpp*, which are given in Appendix B.

Overall, *ed.cpp* is similar to *ed.c*, which implemented the C version of **ed**. In particular, it has a similar breakdown into functions: **issue_error_messages()**, **edit_main()**, **edit_text()**, and so on. *ed.cpp* uses two public pointers to demonstrate that objects can be manipulated with pointers, just like traditional C data structures. One pointer references the help system; the other is used to support a DOS-command prompt box:

```
help *ed_help;
prompt_window *dos_cmd;
```

Pointers to objects are useful when it's necessary to share objects among modules but inappropriate to pass them as arguments.

In the current application, **main()** defines the help and DOS windows as local variables, ensuring that each allocation occurs without complications:

```
/*
main() sets up a pointer variable for the incoming file
specification, performs some screen handling, and invokes
a file specification routine, check_args().
*/

int main(int argc, char *argv[])
{
    char *file_spec;
    ...
    ...
    // initialize the help system and a line-edit prompt box //

    ed_help = new help(DUMMY, "ed 1.0 - Help", 2, 1, 22, 78,
                       int(file_size(HELP_SPEC)));
```

```
    dos_cmd = new prompt_window(DUMMY, "", 20, 10, 22,
                              10 + PROMPT_STR + 3, MAX_PROMPT_INPUT);

    // check buffer allocations (OK to continue if help file error) //

    if (dos_cmd->get_error_state() || ed_help->get_error_state()) {
        issue_error_messages(CANT_ALLOCATE_BUFS, file_spec);
        exit(1);
    }

    dos_screen.clrscn();
    display_edit_info();
    int edit_status = edit_main(1, file_spec);

    delete ed_help;
    delete dos_cmd;
    dos_screen.restore_exit_screen();
    if (edit_status == QUIT || edit_status == EXIT)
        exit(0);
    else {
        issue_error_messages(edit_status, file_spec);
        exit(1);
    }
}   /* main */
```

At present, Zortech C++ is the dominant C++ implementation. Given its widespread usage, we've included some Zortech-specific code in *ed.cpp* and *edfile.cpp* that demonstrates checking for floppy disk errors. The Zortech-related code is quite isolated; you can strip it out if you prefer, as we've done with the **...**s in **main**(); see Appendix B.

In addition to allocating and deallocating the help and DOS windows, **main**() clears the screen, displays the editor borders, initiates an edit session with **edit_main**(), and issues error messages during program termination. In the call to **edit_main**(), **main**() provides a window number, the argument 1 indicates that this is the first edit session.

Consider **edit_main**():

```
/*
edit_main() processes the active edit buffer.  In addition, it
reports/returns error codes for a number of file errors that can
occur during editor initialization.
*/

int edit_main(int win_no, char *filename)
{
    int edit_status;
```

```
    edit_window edwin(win_no, "", 1, 0, 23, 79, MAX_BUF_SIZE);

    if (edwin.get_error_state())
        return CANT_ALLOCATE_BUFS;
    long file_length = edwin.read_from_disk(filename);
    if (file_length == TOO_LARGE)
        edit_status = TOO_LARGE;
    else {
        edwin.activate("", NOR_BORDER_COLOR, NOR_BORDER_COLOR);
        if (file_length == CANT_READ)                // a new file
            edwin.set_buf_length(0);
        else
            edwin.set_buf_length(file_length);
        display_filename(win_no, strupr(filename));
        edit_status = edit_text(edwin, filename);
        if (edit_status == EXIT)
            write_from_buffer(edwin, filename);
        edwin.deactivate();
    }
    return edit_status;
}   /* edit_main */
```

edit_main() defines an **edit_window** object named **edwin**, using the value passed as **win_no** from **main()**. **edit_main()** is responsible for two fairly low-level operations: (1) checking error conditions using **get_error_state()**, and (2) loading the edit buffer using **read_from_disk()**.

The former operation, in some form, is hard to get around. Note that C++ constructors don't return values like, say, **malloc()**. Thus, for a complex object such as **edit_window**, having to test the value returned by **get_error_state()** (or something similar) isn't unreasonable. In the definition of **edwin**, the constructor provides for storage allocation much like the compiler does with built-in types: "int i;". In this case, we want to design **edit_main()** so that it can be called multiple times, that is, recursively. To allow graceful termination from recursive functions, it's necessary to test for proper storage allocation, and return if there is insufficient space on the heap.

The second operation, loading the buffer with text from a file, could be handled elsewhere with more autonomy, say, by the constructor. Again, it depends on whether or not you want the window classes to serve as black boxes. During development, it's convenient to design a class hierarchy to be rather open-ended. As the hierarchy is refined and becomes stable, you can gradually hide the details of its operation—that is, move from a white-box to a black-box design.

Next, consider the editing process per se, as implemented by **edit_text()**. Like **help**, **ed**'s help class, **edit_text()** takes on the responsibility of managing the user's keystrokes:

```
/*
edit_text() analyzes incoming characters and calls the
appropriate routines.
*/

int edit_text(edit_window &edwin, char *filename)
{
    keystroke key;

    edwin.window_fill(0, 0, 0);
    do {
        do {
            key.word = edwin.wgetche();
            if (!edwin.process_cmd(key))
                dispatch_extended_code(edwin, key.byte[1], filename);
        } while (key.byte[0] || !(key.byte[1] == QUIT ||
                                  key.byte[1] == EXIT));
    } while (key.byte[1] == QUIT &&
            edwin.buffer_modified() &&
            !attn_win.message("", "Abandon changed text (y/n): "));
    return key.byte[1];
}   /* edit_text */
```

edit_text() is called with two arguments, the edit window and the filename of the text that should be displayed in the window. Note that, for efficiency, the edit window object is passed by reference.

Even though **edit_text()** is small in size, the programmer must understand something about the inner workings of an **edit_window** object; that is, you must fill the window first and then process keystrokes in a loop. Here, the inner loop governs the repetitive processing of keystrokes by calling **process_cmd()**; if a keystroke can't be processed, **dispatch_extended_code()** is called:

```
/*
dispatch_extended_code() processes commands by calling the
appropriate routines.
*/

void dispatch_extended_code(edit_window &edwin,
                            unsigned char command, char *filename)
{
    switch (command) {          // 8-bit command codes ==> unsigned
        case HELP:
            ed_help->present_help_screens();
            break;
```

```
        case SAVE_FILE:
            if (write_from_buffer(edwin, filename))
                edwin.buffer_modified(FALSE);
            break;
        case WRITE_FILE:
            write_alt_file(edwin, get_alt_file_spec());
            break;
        case INSERT_FILE:
            insert_file(edwin, get_alt_file_spec());
            break;
        case SECOND_WIN:
            if (alt_edit_window()) {
                display_filename(1, filename);
                edwin.buffer_modified(edwin.buffer_modified());
                edwin.set_insert_mode(edwin.get_insert_mode());
            }
            break;
        case DOS_CMD:
            execute_dos_command();
            break;
        default:
            break;
    }
}   /* dispatch_extended_code */
```

dispatch_extended_code() handles a number of file operations that aren't (shouldn't be) provided by **edit_window**, for example, saving an edit buffer as a disk file. The outer loop implements this application's method for terminating an edit session.

With **dispatch_extended_code**() the edit window object is passed by reference, in turn, to subordinate functions from *edfile.cpp*. You may want to examine how they operate; in general, they pass messages to **edwin** requesting it to write all or part of the buffer to disk, to invoke its insert-mode handler, and so on.

In contrast to **edwin**, which is declared local to **edit_main**() and then passed to subordinate functions, the help object can be sent messages by using the global pointer **ed_help**. In **dispatch_extended_code**() the statement

```
ed_help->present_help_screens();
```

requests that **ed_help** present its help screens. The usage of "->" with objects is analogous to its usage with structures in C.

In general, we agree with the opinion that using reference parameters leads to fewer errors than using pointers, since you're working at a higher level of abstraction (Carroll, 1989). However, we wanted to provide at least one example of pointers to objects. As an exercise, you may want to consider other locations (functions) where the help system could be declared as a local object and then passed by reference, if necessary, as we did with **edwin**.

15.4 Nested Edit Sessions Using Recursion

SECOND_WIN is one of the keystrokes handled by **dispatch_extended_code()**; it is bound to the function **alt_edit_window()** from *edfile.cpp*. **alt_edit_window()** illustrates the use of nested edit sessions.

Because we've minimized global variables in our application, a nested edit session is easily implemented using recursion. In particular, since **edit_main()** allocates **edwin** locally and passes it to subordinate functions, we can initiate a nested edit session by calling **edit_main()** recursively from a function that's subordinate to **edit_main()**, in this case, **alt_edit_window()**:

```
/*
alt_edit_window() is used to open an additional, alternative
edit window.
*/

int alt_edit_window()
{
    if (alt_edit_active) {
        attn_win.message("Alternate Edit Window",
                         "** can't open more edit windows **");
        return FALSE;
    }
    char *file_spec = get_alt_file_spec();
    if (*file_spec == EOS)
        return FALSE;

    alt_edit_active = TRUE;
    int edit_status = edit_main(2, file_spec);
    if (edit_status == CANT_ALLOCATE_BUFS)
        attn_win.message("Alternate Edit Window",
                         "** can't allocate memory **");
    else if (edit_status == TOO_LARGE)
        attn_win.message(file_spec, "** file is too large **");
    else
        edit_status = TRUE;
    attn_win.message("Alternate Edit Window",
                     "** returning to primary edit window **");
    alt_edit_active = FALSE;
    return edit_status;
}   /* alt_edit_window */
```

alt_edit_window() handles several secondary tasks, such as prompting for a filename and checking for errors, in addition to performing its primary task, calling **edit_main()**:

```
    int edit_status = edit_main(2, file_spec);
```

In this case, **2** is bound to **win_no** in **edit_main()**. As mentioned, having a window number assists the programmer in keeping track of window operations, even basic operations like displaying a window number, as handled by **display_filename()** from *ed.cpp*:

```
/*
display_filename() shows the filename along the top line,
along with the number of the current edit buffer.
*/

void display_filename(int win_no, char *filename)
{
    char temp_str[MIN_STR];

    dos_screen.display_blanks(TOP_ROW, 0, 71, REV_BORDER_COLOR);
    dos_screen.display_string(TOP_ROW, 3, "File: ",
                              REV_BORDER_COLOR);
    dos_screen.display_string(TOP_ROW, 9, filename,
                              REV_BORDER_COLOR);
    itoa(win_no, temp_str, 10);
    dos_screen.display_char(TOP_ROW, 1, temp_str[0],
                              REV_BORDER_COLOR);
}   /* display_filename */
```

The window number is displayed in column 1 of the top status line; see Figure 4.1.

In this application we wanted to illustrate how easy it is to incorporate recursion into our window applications. In its present form, **alt_edit_window()** has been set up to allow only one nested edit window. This limitation is implemented by making the following private definition in *edfile.cpp*:

```
static int alt_edit_active = FALSE;
```

If **alt_edit_active** has been set, **alt_edit_window()** issues a message and returns:

```
    ...
    if (alt_edit_active) {
        attn_win.message("Alternate Edit Window",
                         "** can't open more edit windows **");
        return FALSE;
    }
```

```
...
```

Otherwise, it sets **alt_edit_active** and continues:

```
...
alt_edit_active = TRUE;
int edit_status = edit_main(2, file_spec);
...
```

Although there is nothing in our design that prohibits further nesting of edit windows, in most cases, three or more edit windows should be handled by a non-nested design. (See the next chapter.)

15.5 dos_cmd: A DOS-command Prompt Box

Given our current arsenal of screen, keyboard, and window classes, it's quite easy to set up an editable, pop-up window for processing DOS command from within **ed**, or for exiting to a DOS shell. **dispatch_extended_code()** binds the keystroke represented by **DOS_CMD** to the function **execute_dos_command()**.

```
...
case DOS_CMD:
    execute_dos_command();
    break;
...
```

Suppose the user wants to use **ed** to (1) edit a source file, (2) execute a compiler, (3) edit the source file again, and so on. Minimally, the command for invoking the compiler, plus its arguments, should be retained from one compilation to the next. The process of storing the previous DOS command can be handled by setting up a window with editing capabilities. Clearly, using an **edit_window** object (with cut-and-paste capabilities) would be overkill. **prompt_window**, on the other hand, is ideal for providing storage for small text items, such as a DOS command. In addition, it allows the user to modify the DOS command, for example, compiler options for a compilation.

Before executing a DOS command, several steps should be taken to prepare for a clean interface to the DOS command processor. First, the current screen should be saved—the entire screen: the top and bottom status lines plus the edit window itself. Also, when the temporary DOS shell terminates, the previous screen should be redisplayed.

To increase its functionality, **execute_dos_command()** should allow the user to execute the current DOS command, the one displayed in the window, *or* exit directly to a DOS shell. With the former operation, the user's DOS command is passed to the DOS command processor, but once the command is executed, control is returned to the application. In the latter case, the contents of the prompt box are not passed to DOS. Instead, **execute_dos_command()** sets up a DOS shell, providing the user with a DOS prompt where any number of DOS commands can be executed. In this case, the user returns to **ed** by typing "exit", the DOS command for terminating the current shell.

Third, it's important to provide some level of error handling. For example, if **system()**, the function that manages the DOS shell, incurs an error, it returns an error code. In our case, we want to indicate this type of error in our attention window.

There are many subtle variations on setting up a DOS shell; **execute_dos_command()** illustrates one approach:

```
/*
execute_dos_command() temporarily suspends execution of the current
program and executes the DOS command given in the pop-up window.
*/

void execute_dos_command()
{
    char cmd_spec[MAX_PROMPT_INPUT], *temp_screen;
    char far *dos_scrn = dos_screen.get_screen_addr();
    keystroke key;
    int dos_error = FALSE, go_dos = FALSE;

    dos_cmd->activate("<Alt-D> invokes a DOS shell",
                              NOR_BORDER_COLOR, NOR_BORDER_COLOR);
    dos_cmd->top_of_buffer_redisplay();
    do {
        key.word = dos_cmd->wgetche();
        dos_cmd->process_cmd(key);
    } while (!((!key.byte[0] && key.byte[1] == DOS_CMD) ||
              key.byte[0] == CR || key.byte[0] == ESC));
    dos_cmd->deactivate();
    if (key.byte[0] == ESC)              // abandon the prompt box
        return;
    if ((temp_screen = new char[SCREEN_SIZE]) == NULL) {
        attn_win.message("DOS",
                         "** can't allocate necessary memory **");
        return;
    }
    if (!key.byte[0] && key.byte[1] == DOS_CMD) // second Alt-D, so
        go_dos = TRUE;                          // go out to DOS
    else
        go_dos = FALSE;
    memcpy(temp_screen, dos_scrn, SCREEN_SIZE);
    dos_screen.clrscn(NORMAL_VIDEO);
    dos_screen.cursor_rc(0, 0);
    if (go_dos || dos_cmd->get_buf_length() == 0) {
```

```
        dos_screen.display_string(0, 0,
            "Type \"exit\" to return to ed", NORMAL_VIDEO);
        dos_error = system("command");
    }
    else
        dos_error =
            system(dos_cmd->get_line(cmd_spec, MAX_PROMPT_INPUT));
    dos_screen.display_string(24, 64, "Press any key...",
                              REVERSE_VIDEO);
    dos_keybd.get_keystroke();
    memcpy(dos_scrn, temp_screen, SCREEN_SIZE);
    delete temp_screen;
    if (dos_error)
        attn_win.message("DOS",
                   "** unknown error; can't invoke command **");
}   /* execute_dos_command */
```

Both for illustration and to test our implementation of **prompt_window**, this version of **execute_dos_command**() does not use **dispatcher**(). In a later example we'll illustrate and test **dispatcher**().

Consider what takes place after the prompt window is deactivated. First, if the user pressed **<Esc>**, the edit session is reactivated. Otherwise, **execute_dos_command**() attempts to allocate a buffer from the heap to hold the current screen image. If this operation fails, a memory-allocation error message is displayed before returning to the edit session. Otherwise, the current screen image is copied to the buffer that begins at **temp_screen**, the screen is cleared, and the cursor is positioned in the top-left corner of the screen.

The user can exit directly to a DOS shell by pressing **DOS_CMD** a second time; thus, this condition must be tested for and recorded in the indicator variable **go_dos**. If either (1) the user presses a second **DOS_CMD**, or (2) the prompt box buffer is empty, the DOS shell is invoked by passing the argument "command" to **system**(). Otherwise, **get_line**() is used to extract the DOS command from the buffer, which is then passed to **system**(). In either case, **dos_error** records whether or not **system**() encounters any errors.

Lastly, the screen-related operations are performed before returning the user to the edit session.

15.6 Wildcard File Processing—an Exercise for the Reader

ed, as described in this chapter, is easily extended in a number of ways. For example, we've demonstrated how recursion can be used to implement nested windows. Our favorite extension involves modifying the call to **edit_main**() in **main**() so that a function named, say, **process_file_specification**(), is called instead; it in turn calls **edit_main**(), that is, you can wedge a call to **process_file_specification**() between **main**() and **edit_main**().

process_file_specification() would be responsible for building a list of all files that match a particular wildcard file specification, for example:

```
C>ed *.h
```

and processing each file in turn. Also, you could have **alt_edit_window()** call **process_file_specification()**, so that a set of files can be edited in the secondary window as well.

We've become so accustomed to our commercial editor **ie**, which has these extensions, that we can't develop a project without it. Quite often, a professional programmer can have a project that spans 40 or 50 "*.c" and "*.h" files. With that many files, it's easy to overlook one or more files while performing routine source code maintenance. Examples include cleaning up comment sections in various files and making changes to a constant that appears in numerous files (for example, changing **MAX_STR** to **MAX_STR_LEN**).

Overlooked, subtle changes can lead to a software product that blows up at the worst possible moment for the user. By adding **process_file_specification()**, a function that calls the DOS compiler's **findfirst()** and **findnext()** library functions to retrieve each matching file, you can guarantee that no files are overlooked. Moreover, because the clipboard is maintained as a private object, and because operations such as find-and-change make use of static storage, text is "remembered" from one edit session to the next.

Consequently, with the addition of **process_file_specification()** to the current implementation of **ed**, you can call up one file in the primary edit window, cut part of its contents to the clipboard, and then edit a series of files in the secondary edit window, inserting the clipboard text in each file.

Lastly, if you choose to add this capability, you should set up **process_file_specification()** so that it honors a break command, such as **<Alt>-B**. Otherwise, you'll have to press **QUIT** continually, in order to skip the remaining files in a wildcard specification that don't require editing.

16

Designing a Reusable Editor Class

browser, **edit_window**, and **prompt_window** each provide a two-level interface to their services via **dispatcher()** and **process_cmd()**. It's reasonable to lobby for the internalization of the latter method. That is, **dispatcher()**, or a similar method, could be set up as the sole mechanism for activating an object of one of these classes.

For our window hierarchy, it's easy to provide this level of privacy by making the appropriate methods protected—all except a carefully chosen set of methods, such as **dispatcher()**, **get_insert_mode()**, **get_buf_length()**, and so on. As an alternative, however, we could build an editor class that encapsulates several of the window classes, hiding many of the details that are otherwise left up to the programmer. Of course, you may want to add privacy to the window hierarchy to enhance the black-box characteristics of its classes, in addition to providing higher level classes.

This chapter demonstrates the steps required to build a high-level editor class from our existing window hierarchy with self-contained support for a help system and a DOS shell facility. In addition, in order to make our demonstration more interesting, we'll design a new user-interface with support for *n* overlapping edit windows.

16.1 editor: A Self-contained Multi-window Editor

Although our window hierarchy provides significant windowing and editing capabilities, building a stand-alone editor still requires a considerable amount of work on the programmer's part. More importantly, the programmer must be quite familiar with the window hierarchy, in order to pass the appropriate messages for loading the edit buffer, testing for memory allocation errors, and so on.

To automate the use of our window hierarchy for editing services, we can set up an "umbrella" class that brings together the help system, the DOS prompt box, and the edit window(s). Consider **editor** (from *editor.hpp*), a class that provides an arbitrary number of edit windows based on the program parameter **MAX_WINDOWS** (from *editintc.h*):

```
class editor {
    int error_state;
    int cur_win;    // the current editor window--an array position
    help *ed_help;
    prompt_window *dos_box;
    edit_window *ed[MAX_WINDOWS];    // array of ptrs. to edit_windows
    char filename[MAX_WINDOWS][MAX_STR];
public:
    editor();
    ~editor();
    int dispatcher(char *);
    int init_edit(char *);
    int edit_file();
    int close_current_window();
    int close_active_windows();
    int file_active();
    int file_spec_ok(char *);
    void alt_edit_window(int);
    void switch_edit_window(int);
    void execute_dos_command();
    void display_edit_info();
};
```

(Appendix C contains complete source code for *editor.hpp* and *editor.cpp*, plus replacements for the modules from Appendix B, as necessary, to provide a complete implementation of **ed**. For example, given *editor.cpp*, *ed.cpp* is reduced to just three functions.)

First, let's consider the user interface. **editor** uses a top and bottom status line just like our previous versions of **ed**; these lines are displayed when **ed** is started. (**ed** is an editor built from **editor**.) If a filename is not specified on the command line, an edit window is not opened. Once an edit window has been opened, the screen is identical to the one that's pictured in Figure 4.1.

An **editor** application can manage up to **MAX_WINDOWS** edit windows; for our purposes, assume that the maximum is five. When activated, each edit window is displayed in the same screen location, specifically, between the top and bottom status lines—**editor** uses overlapping edit windows. A user can switch to an arbitrary edit window, numbered 1 through 5, by pressing the appropriate key; this operation is initiated by **alt_edit_window**(), which calls **switch_edit_window**(). The commands for switching edit windows are: **FIRST_WIN**, **SECOND_WIN**, ..., **FIFTH_WIN**, respectively. (Currently these commands are bound to: **<Alt>-1**, **<Alt>-2**, ... **<Alt>-5**), respectively, in *keys.h*.) Note that this approach allows direct, as opposed to sequential, access to each edit window. (The Zortech editor, **zed**, that accompanies the Zortech C++ compiler [Zortech, 1989] uses a similar approach for switching windows.)

Once an edit window is chosen, for example, using the command **THIRD_WIN** to choose window 3, an edit session is initiated by the command **EDIT_FILE** (currently bound to **<Alt>-E**). Once a file is associated with an edit window, **editor** maintains that association. That is, if a file is loaded into window 3, the user can switch to another window and later come back to window 3—the previous editing state is maintained. Thus, a user can initiate edit sessions in any window, in any order, and then toggle among the windows with or without saving current changes to each window.

With our current class definition, **editor** defines the help system and the DOS prompt box facility as private members. In addition, it defines an array of pointers to **edit_window** objects, based on the parameter **MAX_WINDOWS**. **error_state** is used to record memory-allocation errors on a window-by-window basis. A private variable, **cur_win**, is used as an index into the array of edit windows. In particular, **cur_win** is used to keep track of the current edit window. Lastly, an array of strings, **filename**, is used to associate filenames with edit windows.

The constructor **editor**() sets up **ed_help** and **dos_box**; these two objects are shared by all edit windows:

```
/*
editor() initializes the data structures needed
for the editor system.
*/

editor::editor()
{
    ed_help = new help(0, "ed 1.0 - Help", 2, 1, 22, 78,
                        int(file_size(HELP_SPEC)));
    dos_box = new prompt_window(0, "", 20, 10, 22,
                    10 + PROMPT_STR + 3, MAX_PROMPT_INPUT,
                    BACK_ATTR);
    if (dos_box->get_error_state() || ed_help->get_error_state())
        error_state = TRUE;
    else {
        error_state = FALSE;
        display_edit_info();
        cur_win = 0;
```

```
        for (int i = 0; i < MAX_WINDOWS; i++)
            ed[i] = NULL;
    }
}   /* editor */
```

The edit window array, **ed**, is zero-based as usual. **editor()** initializes the editor system by setting each edit window pointer to **NULL**. Also, **ed[0]** is the current window—**cur_win** is used to index the array.

editor's destructor releases the storage occupied by the help and DOS windows:

```
/*
~editor() must delete the help and prompt box systems.
*/

editor::~editor()
{
    delete ed_help;
    delete dos_box;
}   /* ~editor */
```

16.2 dispatcher(): Scheduling and Overseeing Editor Operations

editor provides its own dispatcher for dispatching commands to the appropriate methods, for example, **EDIT_FILE** is bound to the method **edit_file()**. **editor::dispatcher()** uses a **switch** to implement its dispatch table:

```
/*
dispatcher() dispatches keystrokes to the appropriate routines.
First, keystrokes are handed over to the edit_window's own dis-
patcher.  If the edit_window dispatcher can't process a keystroke,
it simply returns and the editor dispatcher takes over.
*/

int editor::dispatcher(char *file_spec)
{
    int terminate_edit;
    keystroke key;

    if (error_state)
        return CANT_ALLOCATE_BUFS;
    strcpy(filename[0], file_spec);
    if ((terminate_edit = init_edit(filename[0])) < 0) // use the
        return terminate_edit;                       // "passed" file
    else                                             // spec., if possible
```

```
    terminate_edit = FALSE;
do {
    dos_screen.cursor_rc(1, 0);        // an arbitrary location
    if (ed[cur_win] != NULL)
        key.word = ed[cur_win]->dispatcher();
    else
        key.word = dos_keybd.get_keystroke();
    switch (key.byte[1]) {
        case FIRST_WIN:
        case SECOND_WIN:
        case THIRD_WIN:
        case FOURTH_WIN:
        case FIFTH_WIN:
            alt_edit_window(key.byte[1] - FIRST_WIN);
            break;
        case EDIT_FILE:
            edit_file();
            break;
        case SAVE_FILE:
            if (file_active())
                if (write_from_buffer(ed[cur_win],
                        filename[cur_win]))
                    ed[cur_win]->buffer_modified(FALSE);
            break;
        case WRITE_FILE:
            if (file_active())
                write_alt_file(ed[cur_win], get_alt_file_spec());
            break;
        case INSERT_FILE:
            if (file_active())
                insert_file(ed[cur_win], get_alt_file_spec());
            break;
        case HELP:
            ed_help->present_help_screens();
            break;
        case DOS_CMD:
            execute_dos_command();
            break;
        case EXIT:
            if (file_active())
                if (write_from_buffer(ed[cur_win],
                        filename[cur_win]))
                    ed[cur_win]->buffer_modified(FALSE);
            close_current_window();
```

```
                break;
            case QUIT:
                close_current_window();
                break;
            case ALT_EXIT:
                terminate_edit = close_active_windows();
                break;
            default:
            break;
        }
    } while (!terminate_edit);
    return key.byte[1];
}   /* dispatcher */
```

In contrast to the dispatchers for the window classes, **editor::dispatcher()** must oversee a heterogeneous environment. That is, under the appropriate conditions, **editor::dispatcher()** must be prepared to relinquish control to an **edit_window** object, to the help object, or to the DOS shell object, and to process commands such as **INSERT_FILE**, **EXIT**, **QUIT**, and so on.

The latter set of operations includes switching to a new/different edit window; this window can be either null or active. If this window is active, the edit window dispatcher can assume control of command processing. However, if a switch is made to a "null" window (only the top and bottom status lines are displayed), there is no edit window dispatcher. In this case, a message is passed directly to **dos_keybd** to read a keystroke:

```
if (ed[cur_win] != NULL)
    key.word = ed[cur_win]->dispatcher();
else
    key.word = dos_keybd.get_keystroke();
```

Also, if the edit window dispatcher can't process a command, it will be returned in **key.word**. Thus, **key.word** always contains the most recently received command.

In effect, the set of all possible keystrokes is partitioned into edit window commands and non-edit window commands. As long as the user types commands recognized by the (active) edit window, its dispatcher maintains control. Otherwise, **editor::dispatcher()** assumes responsibility for interpreting the contents of **key.word**. Because of the ordering of events within the **do-while** loop, if the user switches to an active window, or initiates an edit session in a window, the edit window dispatcher is given control first.

Giving the edit window top priority is important for efficient processing of editing operations. For example, if the number of non-edit window commands is increased by, say, 40, there will be no effect on the performance of the edit window dispatcher, that is, the number of commands that the edit window dispatcher must oversee remains constant. Primarily, we've argued that providing window objects with their own dispatchers is important because it allows us to control access to an object—to migrate toward black-box classes as the window hierarchy matures. In this case, however, our design reduces the programmer's work (recall *ed.c*) *and* assists in scheduling/prioritizing the operations performed by various objects within the application.

16.3 Methods for Managing Multiple Windows

editor provides direct access to each edit window. A user can switch to a different edit window using one of the commands: **FIRST_WIN**, ..., **FIFTH_WIN**. **alt_edit_win()** oversees this process:

```
/*
alt_edit_win() deactivates the current window and switches
to the specified window (makes it active).
*/

void editor::alt_edit_window(int cur_win)
{
    if (ed[editor::cur_win] != NULL)
        ed[editor::cur_win]->deactivate();
    switch_edit_window(cur_win);
}   /* alt_edit_window */
```

Because edit windows overlap on-screen, **alt_edit_window()** must deactivate the current window (in the physical window-frame sense), if it contains an active edit session, before switching to the new window.

switch_edit_window() activates the edit session in the new window, if a session exists:

```
/*
switch_edit_window() activates the specified window, performing
related operations, such as displaying the filename.
*/

void editor::switch_edit_window(int cur_win)
{
    if (ed[cur_win] != NULL) {
        display_filename(cur_win + 1, filename[cur_win]);
        ed[cur_win]->buffer_modified(ed[cur_win]->buffer_modified());
        ed[cur_win]->set_insert_mode(
                        ed[editor::cur_win]->get_insert_mode());
        ed[cur_win]->activate("", NOR_BORDER_COLOR, NOR_BORDER_COLOR);
        ed[cur_win]->redisplay_window(
                        ed[cur_win]->current_column_offset());
    }
    else {
```

```
        display_edit_info();
        display_filename(cur_win + 1, "");
    }
    editor::cur_win = cur_win;
}   /* switch_edit_window */
```

Switching windows involves (1) updating the top and bottom status lines, (2) redisplaying the contents of the edit window, and (3) updating the window index variable, **cur_win**. Note that, once initialized by **init_edit()**, each **edit_window** object retains its "internal state" until it is destroyed by **close_current_window()**. Thus, if the user switches to a *non-null* edit window, each **edit_window** variable will already have the proper value. In particular, the statement

```
    ed[cur_win]->buffer_modified(ed[cur_win]->buffer_modified());
```

is executed solely for the purpose of redisplaying the on-screen status indicator of whether or not the current edit window has unsaved modifications.

Consider the process that's involved in initiating an edit session. If, at some point, the user presses **EDIT_FILE**, **edit_file()** oversees the process of initializing an edit session in the current window:

```
/*
edit_file() prompts for a filename and then begins an edit session
in the current window.  If the edit window is already active, it is
closed first.
*/

int editor::edit_file()
{
    if (close_current_window()) {
        strcpy(filename[cur_win], get_alt_file_spec());
        return init_edit(filename[cur_win]);
    }
    else
        return FALSE;
}   /* edit_file */
```

First, if the user requests a new edit session in a window that is currently active, **close_current_window()** must be called to perform an orderly shutdown before starting the new session:

```
/*
close_current_window() closes the current edit window, if it
is active.  The user is given an opportunity to abandon the
close operation, if the window contains unsaved changes.
*/

int editor::close_current_window()
{
    if (ed[cur_win] != NULL) {
        if (ed[cur_win]->buffer_modified())
            if (!attn_win.message("", "Abandon changed text (y/n): "))
                return FALSE;
        ed[cur_win]->deactivate();
        delete ed[cur_win];
        ed[cur_win] = NULL;
        display_filename(cur_win + 1, "");
    }
    return TRUE;
}   /* close_current_window */
```

Edit sessions are initiated by **init_edit()**, using **new** to allocate an **edit_window** object:

```
/*
init_edit() checks for a number of errors.  If possible, it creates
an edit_window object and assigns it to the array set up to hold
pointers to edit_window objects.  Next, init_edit() loads the edit
window's buffer.
*/

int editor::init_edit(char *filename)
{
    if (*filename == EOS || !file_spec_ok(filename)) {
        display_filename(cur_win + 1, "");
        return FALSE;
    }
    ed[cur_win] = new edit_window(cur_win + 1, "", 1, 0, 23, 79,
                                   MAX_BUF_SIZE, BACK_ATTR);
    if (ed[cur_win]->get_error_state()) {
        close_current_window();
        attn_win.message("", "** can't allocate memory **");
        return CANT_ALLOCATE_BUFS;
    }
    long file_length = ed[cur_win]->read_from_disk(filename);
    if (file_length == TOO_LARGE) {
```

```
        close_current_window();
        attn_win.message(filename, "** file is too large **");
        return TOO_LARGE;
    }
    ed[cur_win]->activate("", NOR_BORDER_COLOR, NOR_BORDER_COLOR);
    if (file_length == CANT_READ)                // a new file
        ed[cur_win]->set_buf_length(0);
    else
        ed[cur_win]->set_buf_length(file_length);
    display_filename(cur_win + 1, strupr(filename));
    ed[cur_win]->window_fill(0, 0, 0);
    return TRUE;
}   /* init_edit */
```

If the filename passed to **init_edit()** is either null or invalid, the window number is displayed without a filename and an edit session is not started. The former condition arises when the user invokes the editor application without specifying a filename. The latter condition arises when the user types an illegal filename.

16.4 Providing for Graceful Program Termination

The command **EXIT** is used to save the contents of the current window to disk and terminate *that* edit session. To terminate the editor, that is, to return to the DOS prompt, a user can manually switch to each edit window and execute either **EXIT** or **QUIT**, before exiting with **ALT_EXIT**. However, with a multi-file editor it's easy for a user to forget which windows contain modified edit buffers and which do not. Hence, **ALT_EXIT** should protect against inadvertent loss of changes during program termination.

If a user presses **ALT_EXIT**, **close_active_windows()** is invoked to scan each window for unsaved changes:

```
/*
close_active_windows() scans all windows.  It attempts to close each
active window.  If the buffer has unsaved changes, the user can
abandon that close operation.  In this case, close operations are
abandoned on all remaining active buffers.
*/

int editor::close_active_windows()
{
    if (!close_current_window())
        return FALSE;
    for (int i = 0; i < MAX_WINDOWS; i++)
        if (ed[i] != NULL)
            if (ed[i]->buffer_modified()) {
```

```
                switch_edit_window(i);
                if (!close_current_window())
                    return FALSE;
            }
            else
                close_current_window();
    return TRUE;
}   /* close_active_windows */
```

For each active edit session with unsaved changes, its window is reactivated so that the user can see the text and make a decision to save or abandon the text.

16.5 Use dispatcher(), not process_cmd()

In Chapter 15 we demonstrated how the programmer can take control of low-level command dispatching by using **process_cmd()**. In most cases, it's preferable to use **dispatcher()** instead. Whether or not **process_cmd()** (plus other methods) should remain in the **public** section or be moved to a **protected** section depends on a number of issues, including the programming audience for the class hierarchy and the maturity of the current implementation.

The increase in convenience for the programmer in using **dispatcher()** instead of **process_cmd()** can be seen in our current version of **execute_dos_command()**:

```
/*
execute_dos_command() temporarily suspends execution of the current
program and executes the DOS command given in the pop-up window.
The pop-up window can be edited.
*/

void editor::execute_dos_command()
{
    keystroke key;
    char cmd_spec[MAX_PROMPT_INPUT], *temp_screen;

    char far *dos_scrn = dos_screen.get_screen_addr();
    int dos_error = FALSE, go_dos = FALSE;
    dos_box->activate("<Alt-D> invokes a DOS shell",
                        NOR_BORDER_COLOR, NOR_BORDER_COLOR);
    key.word = dos_box->dispatcher(DOS_CMD);
    dos_box->deactivate();
    if (key.byte[0] == ESC)             // abandon the prompt box
        return;
    ...
    ...
```

```
    // same as before
    ...
    ...
}   /* execute_dos_command */
```

That is, the single statement:

```
    key.word = dos_box->dispatcher(DOS_CMD);
```

is sufficient to provide command processing and to register the terminating command (the break prompt) for subsequent processing.

Should window activation/deactivation be moved to the dispatcher as well? Although this approach could be useful in some cases, overall, it's better to keep these operations separate. Keeping dispatching operations separate from window activation/deactivation gives the programmer more control over how and when the window object is used.

For example, consider the situation in which a user accidentally presses a key such as **<F12>**, which isn't mapped to any command. With the current implementation of **editor**, (1) **ed[i]->dispatcher()** would terminate, (2) the returned command (in **key.word**) would be unrecognized by **editor::dispatcher()**, consequently, (3) **ed[i]->dispatcher()** would be invoked again. Having **ed[i]->dispatcher()** activate and deactivate the window would produce a disturbing screen flash (flicker with a fast CPU).

In the previous chapter, we promised to rectify our dependency on **process_cmd()** in the help system implementation (*edhelp.cpp*). *edhelp.cpp* in Appendix C contains the following version of **present_help_screens()**:

```
/*
present_help_screens() displays help information in a window.
*/

void help::present_help_screens()
{
    keystroke key;

    if (help_win.get_buf_length() <= 0) {
        attn_win.message(HELP_SPEC, "** can't read help file **");
        return;
    }
    help_win.activate("");
    help_win.dispatcher();
    help_win.deactivate();
}   /* present_help_screens */
```

This implementation of **help** demonstrates that C++ provides the tools to hide the details of an implementation, when doing so is appropriate. From the programmer's point of view, a simple help system can be built by wrapping an existing class, **browser**, in a new class, accompanied by a constructor, a destructor, an error-testing method, and a method for help-system activation:

```
class help {
    int error_state;
    browser help_win;
public:
    help(int, char *, int, int, int, int, int);
    get_error_state() {
        return error_state;
    }
    void present_help_screens();
};
```

The procedure abstraction provided by **browser**'s methods enables the programmer to construct a new abstract data structure, the class **help**, which can be used to create, manage, and destroy a help system in a total of six statements:

```
    ed_help = new help(0, "ed 1.0 - Help", 2, 1, 22, 78,
                        int(file_size(HELP_SPEC)));
    ...
    case HELP:
        ed_help->present_help_screens();
        break;
    ...
    delete ed_help;
```

Once this system is built, the programmer can provide any application with simple help screens by linking in *edhelp.cpp* and providing new help text in the file named by **HELP_SPEC**.

16.6 Using editor

As with **help**, **editor** is straightforward to use. **ed**, our stand-alone editor, can be assembled from the three functions given in *ed.cpp*: **main()**, **check_args()**, and **issue_error_messages()**. The latter two functions are straightforward. **main()**'s definition is

```
/*
main() sets up a pointer variable for the incoming file specification,
performs some screen handling, and invokes a file specification routine,
check_args().
*/
```

```
int main(int argc, char *argv[])
{
    char *file_spec;

    ...
    // interrupt handler for floppy-disk errors
    ...

    if ((file_spec = check_args(argc, argv)) == NULL)
        exit(1);
    dos_screen.clrscn();
    editor ed;
    int edit_status = ed.dispatcher(file_spec);
    dos_screen.restore_exit_screen();
    if (issue_error_messages(edit_status, file_spec))
        exit(1);
    else
        exit(0);
}   /* main */
```

editor::dispatcher() takes care of testing for proper memory allocation. If **ed** fails, **ed.dispatcher()** returns an error status, which can be examined before continuing with the remainder of the program; in this case, **ed** calls **issue_error_messages()** before terminating.

By modifying the interface to **editor** in *editintc.h*, it's quite easy to add secondary editing facilities to several classes of applications, for example, a language translator environment, a database package, and so on.

edfile.cpp, as with our previous implementations, contains the major file-processing functions; see Appendix C.

17

A Registration System for Objects and Functions

So far we've investigated three levels of support for window-based editing, as provided by *edit.c*, *winedit.cpp*, and *editor.cpp*. *edit.c* places a considerable burden on the developer, whereas *editor.cpp* removes much of this burden by presenting the developer with a self-contained editor class. With the latter class, the developer can incorporate edit windows into an application with very little effort.

A logical question at this point would be: Can we do even more to enhance reusability? This chapter addresses this issue in two ways. First, we provide a brief overview of one manufacturer's support for software development in a window-based programming environment. Second, we demonstrate how an object and function registration mechanism can be used to further enhance the reusability of a C++ class hierarchy. For continuity, our demonstration builds on our existing tools, specifically, the class **editor**.

17.1 The Notifier Concept in Object-oriented Windowing Environments

Sun Microsystems® provides a family of UNIX-based workstations to address the computing needs of a variety of users. One of the hallmarks of their workstation family is SunView™, a user interface toolkit for window-based software development. Although Sun Microsystems now offers an X Windows replacement for SunView, we'll use the older product in our example because of its historical significance.

SunView (Sun Microsystems, 1988) provides the developer with an entire system of high-level windows that supports the development of graphics-based applications. SunView supports drawing, text editing, and window-based menu operations via buttons, panels, scroll bars, and so on. However, SunView is much more than a library of window routines. SunView, as a user-interface toolkit, provides the programmer with high-level mechanisms for controlling the underlying OS, that is, menu- and window-based support for multi-processing applications.

The operations required to support sophisticated applications in a multi-process (and multi-user) operating environment are considerable. How does SunView ease the burden on the developer associated with initializing, managing, and terminating an application that uses numerous computing resources? SunView's window system takes on the responsibility of managing each application through its *notification-based* control system (Sun Microsystems, 1988).

Specifically, a *notifier* is established for each window-based application. A notifier is a general-purpose process management facility that mediates the requests for resources by clients within a process—an application. In the simplest sense, the notifier manages input, that is, events (such as clicking a mouse button), and dispatches them to the appropriate event handler. Thus, the notifier relieves the programmer from many duties that recur in application after application.

In particular, we're interested in the mechanism whereby an application can *catalog*, or *register*, (special) events with the notifier. That is, suppose a programmer must create a text editor in a window as part of a larger application. In this case, the programmer can register various application-specific tasks with the notifier, say, a pop-up help system activated by a button.

SunView provides a convenient mechanism whereby tasks are paired with events. For example, the developer can (1) have SunView provide a button in a window panel for some application-specific task, such as invoking a help system, and (2) register an associated *callback procedure* with the notifier. In this manner, if the notifier, which is responsible for detecting each event, encounters a mouse click on the help button, it *calls back* to the application's help procedure—the help procedure is paired with the help button.

17.2 A SunView Example

We can illustrate the basic operation of a notification-based system with a window-based version of the common **hello** program. When activated, **hello** will display a simple window on the screen with the label "Hello", along with a mouse button labeled "Good-bye". Figure

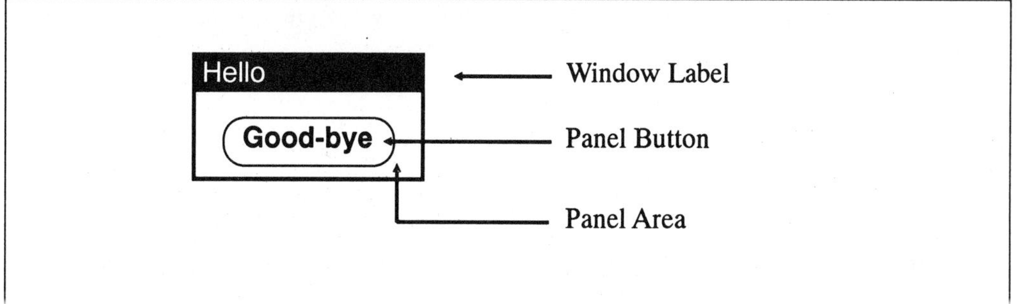

Figure 17.1 A Simulated SunView Window

17.1 provides a simulation of the window-based hello program. Pressing the mouse button will deactivate the window, that is, terminate **hello**.

SunView windows are composed of a frame "object," plus an assortment of other "objects" such as a (control) panel, canvas, text window, and so on. ("Object" is used in the generic sense; actually, C structures are used to represent each window entity.) The frame object unifies, or manages, the various objects that compose a window. For example, to create a simple on-screen frame that contains a panel with one button, we must first define two data structures (objects):

```
...
Frame hello_frame;
Panel hello_panel;
...
```

Then, we must instantiate each object:

```
...
hello_frame = window_create(NULL, FRAME,
                            FRAME_LABEL, "Hello", 0);
hello_panel = window_create(hello_frame, PANEL, 0);
...
```

(Panels must have a "home" frame.) In essence, the message **FRAME** is provided as the second argument to **window_create()** to signal the creation of a frame, based on (optional) frame-related information; in this case, the frame is created with the label "Hello". (**window_create()** takes an unspecified number of arguments; hence, the argument list must be zero-terminated.)

Likewise, **window_create()** is used to create a panel within the frame; the first argument is used to specify the appropriate frame for the panel. (Buttons are displayed in panels.) Because we've specified no optional information, we get an (essentially) invisible panel inside the frame. That is, the panel is not visibly set off within the frame—we want a very simple example.

Next, we can add a button to the panel and register a callback procedure using **panel_create_item()**:

```
    ...
    panel_create_item(
        hello_panel, PANEL_BUTTON,
        PANEL_LABEL_IMAGE, panel_button_image(hello_panel,
                                    "Good-bye", 0, 0),
        PANEL_NOTIFY_PROC, quit_proc, 0);
    ...
```

You can see the implicit association between the panel button and the application-supplied procedure **quit_proc()**. The previous statement creates a **PANEL_BUTTON** for the panel **hello_panel** labeled "Good-bye". If the user clicks the mouse over this button the notifier will execute the **PANEL_NOTIFY_PROC** named **quit_proc()**.

quit_proc()'s definition is:

```
static void quit_proc()
{
    window_set(hello_frame, FRAME_NO_CONFIRM, TRUE, 0);
    window_destroy(hello_frame);
}   /* quit_proc */
```

window_set() is called to disable any confirmation of the quit operation by the user. **window_destroy()** then performs clean-up operations.

The entire **hello** program is:

```
/****    sunex.c    ****/

#include <suntool/sunview.h>
#include <suntool/panel.h>

static void quit_proc();

Frame hello_frame;
Panel hello_panel;

main()
{
    hello_frame = window_create(NULL, FRAME,
                            FRAME_LABEL, "Hello", 0);
    hello_panel = window_create(hello_frame, PANEL, 0);
```

```
    panel_create_item(
        hello_panel, PANEL_BUTTON,
        PANEL_LABEL_IMAGE, panel_button_image(hello_panel,
                                            "Good-bye", 0, 0),
        PANEL_NOTIFY_PROC, quit_proc, 0);
    window_fit(hello_panel);     /* minimize panel around button */
    window_fit(hello_frame);     /* minimize frame around panel */
    window_main_loop(hello_frame);
    exit(0);
}   /*main */

static void quit_proc()
{
    window_set(hello_frame, FRAME_NO_CONFIRM, TRUE, 0);
    window_destroy(hello_frame);
}   /* quit_proc */
```

Although we "haven't done justice" to the incredible power of SunView, our simple example illustrates the mechanism whereby callback procedures are registered with the notifier. With only a slight increase in the amount of code, you can create a significantly more powerful program using additional SunView facilities.

Once the callback procedures are registered with the notifier, **window_main_loop()** is called to turn control over to the notifier. In other words, the application is *not* responsible for basic flow of control—**main()** relinquishes all control over the application, except for the execution of registered callback procedures. In our example, the window structures and functions are terminated by the notifier after executing the callback procedure **quit_proc()**.

At this point, you should see a resemblance between the function **window_main_loop()** and the dispatchers in both our window hierarchy and our **editor** class. Our dispatchers, and our window operations in general, are quite simple in comparison to the notifier as it exists in the SunView system. On the other hand, our editor system is quite useful; **editor**, as a class, provides a considerable amount of abstraction, as evidenced by the small size of *ed.cpp* in Chapter 16.

Parenthetically, it's interesting to note the steps taken in SunView to provide an structure-based programming environment that exhibits some of the characteristics of an object-oriented programming environment. For example, SunView incorporates its own form of standard protocols; in our example, the function **window_create()** is used to create both frames and panels—only the arguments differ. The SunView system provides consistent function names for numerous operations that can occur against different data structures; another example is **window_fit()**. The standard protocols for window operations that are common across various types of window components (panels, canvases, TTY windows, and so on) greatly enhances the SunView toolkit.

The disadvantage, in our opinion, of the structure-based approach as provided by the C-based toolkit, in comparison to a true object-oriented approach, is an increased surface-level complexity for the application, especially for a large application, primarily because the "object handles" must be passed from function to function. In some cases, the number of arguments to functions in the application can be reduced by using global data structures; however, we've argued against the widespread proliferation of global variables. See Section 17.5.

17.3 Implementing a Callback Mechanism for Objects

Now that we've seen a demonstration of SunView's notification-based windowing environment, let's consider how to implement a callback mechanism with C++. Given our interest in object-oriented programming, in this section we'll consider how to implement callback *objects*. In doing so, we'll also illustrate (1) virtual methods, and (2) C++'s facility for handling a variable, or unspecified, number of arguments.

We can illustrate a registration and callback mechanism by enhancing the class **editor** from Chapter 16. Except for the enhancements and modifications provided in this section, *editor.hpp* and *editor.cpp* are identical to the versions given in Appendix C.

editor manages a system of windows, including five edit windows, a help window, and various pop-up windows. All of these windows are managed by **editor::dispatcher()**. Suppose, however, that you would like to provide the developer with a facility whereby he or she could extend/enhance the functionality of the class **editor**—without having to modify the editor module. That is, given the hierarchy of window classes that **editor** is built from, let's give the developer a mechanism for augmenting an application with additional objects from the window hierarchy *such that these objects remain under* **editor::dispatcher()***'s control.*

17.3.1 Callback Object Tables

To provide this capability, we can build two tables within the editor class: (1) a callback object table, and (2) a callback command table, where there's a pair-wise correspondence between elements of the two tables. That is, the first element in the callback command table is the (keyboard) command required to execute the callback object referenced by the first element of the callback object table; see Figure 17.2.

Our two tables have the following definitions:

```
...
buf_window *callback_object[MAX_CALLBACK];
int callback_command[MAX_CALLBACK];
...
```

where **MAX_CALLBACK** is an arbitrary constant defined in *editor.hpp*. Specifically, **callback_command** stores the integer equivalents of the keystroke scan codes that we've used throughout our window classes and earlier applications. The array **callback_object** stores pointers to objects of type/class **buf_window**. Recall that **buf_window** is the abstract class; hence, a pointer to a **buf_window** object can be made to point to any object of a class that's derived from **buf_window**. At present, these classes include **browser, prompt_window**, and **edit_window**.

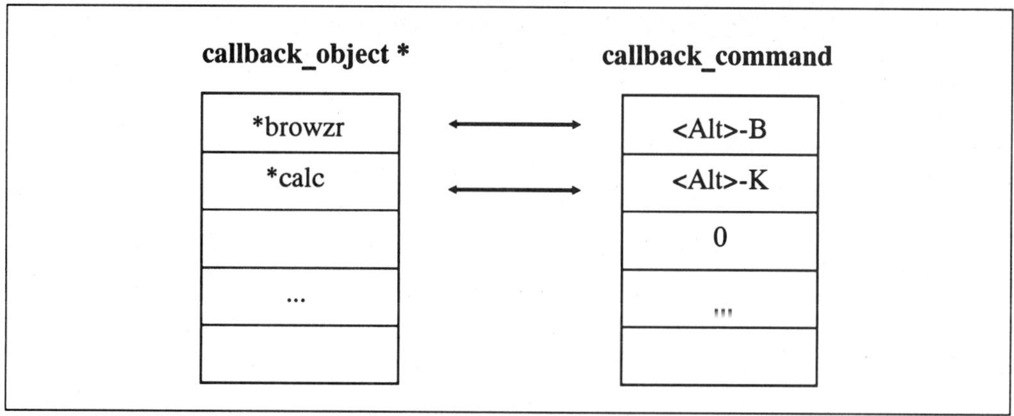

Figure 17.2 Tables for Callback Object Registration

17.3.2 Callback Object Methods

Next, we must provide methods to manage these tables. First, we need a method that allows the user to register callback objects, named **register_callback_objects()**. It will implicitly provide the pair-wise association between elements of the two callback tables. Second, we need a method, **check_with_callback_objects()**, that can look up commands in the table and execute the associated object's dispatcher, if it finds a match.

The interface, as given in *editor.hpp*, is:

```
////  editor.hpp  ////  interface for class:  editor  ////


#ifndef EDITORHPP
#define EDITORHPP   1
#include <stdarg.h>        // note the spelling--singular for Zortech C++
#include "edhelp.hpp"
#include "edfile.hpp"
#include "editintc.h"


#define MAX_CALLBACK    10          // table size


class editor {
    ...
    // same as before
    ...
```

```
    buf_window *callback_object[MAX_CALLBACK];   // new table
    int callback_command[MAX_CALLBACK];          // new table
public:
    ...
    // same as before
    ...
    int register_callback_objects(int ...);      // new method
    int check_with_callback_objects(int);        // new method
    int set_up_buf_window(int);                  // new method
    ...
    // same as before
    ...
};
```

First, consider **register_callback_objects()**. We want the programmer to be able to register an arbitrary number of callback objects and their associated commands; the ellipsis, **...**, signals a method with an unspecified number of arguments. For example, consider the following usage of **register_callback_objects()**:

```
    ...
    browser *browzr;
    calculator *calc;
    ...
    editor ed;
    ed.register_callback_objects(2, ALT_B, browzr,
                                    ALT_K, calc);
    ...
```

We could (1) design the argument list to be null-terminated, as with SunView, or, since the C++ **vararg** facility requires one fixed parameter in the method, (2) we could use the first argument to specify the number of command-object pairs. Since SunView uses the former approach, we'll use the latter approach. (If you're not familiar with how to program for an unspecified number of arguments, you may need to consult a book on either the C or C++ language; however, we'll provide a minimally adequate explanation in our example.)

The implication of the previous object definitions is that the programmer can extend the facilities of an **editor** object to accommodate callbacks to the dispatchers of, for example, a **browser** and a **calculator** object, if **editor::dispatcher()** detects either **ALT_B** or **ALT_K**. Subsequently, we'll demonstrate how to add one of these objects, a read-only browser, to the editor; first, we must consider the required methods.

register_callback_objects() processes the variable length argument list and loads the callback tables:

```
/*
register_callback_objects() uses C++'s variable number of arguments
```

```
facility (va_list(), va_start(), and va_arg()) to extract pairs of
arguments in the form: "...<command_arg>, <object_arg>...", storing
them in their respective tables, callback_command[] and call-
back_object[].  See the related method check_with_callback_objects().
*/

int editor::register_callback_objects(int pair_count ...)
{
    va_list cbo;
    va_start(cbo, pair_count);
    for (int i = 0; i < MAX_CALLBACK && i < pair_count; i++) {
        callback_command[i] = va_arg(cbo, int);
        callback_object[i] = va_arg(cbo, buf_window *);
    }
    callback_command[i] = 0;     // mark the end of the table
    va_end(cbo);
}   /* register_callback_objects */
```

C++ provides four language constructs for accommodating a variable number of arguments: **va_list**, **va_start()**, **va_arg()**, and **va_end()**. **va_list** establishes a reference name for the argument list, in this case, **cbo** (callback objects).

va_start() must be invoked to perform the overhead associated with extracting the arguments, that is, traversing the argument list. Its arguments are the name of the argument list and the last fixed parameter in the method with an unspecified number of arguments/parameters. Here, the arguments to **va_start()** are **cbo** and **pair_count**, the parameter representing the argument that specifies the number of command-object pairs to be registered with the editor object. The parameter **pair_count** is used to control loop operations, in order to traverse the list and make a fixed number of extractions.

For each cycle in the **for** loop we first extract the command and then (the pointer to) the object; **va_arg()** performs the extraction. **var_arg()**'s first argument is the name of the argument list; its second argument is the type of the argument. For the first call to **va_arg()** the argument type is **int**; for the second call, the argument type is **buf_window ***. Each argument is assigned to its respective table position. After all of the arguments have been extracted, we assign **0** to the next element, in effect, null-terminating the table. The latter operation is done to simplify table look-up operations.

va_end() must be called to signal that argument traversal has been completed for the variable length argument list.

The complementary method **check_with_callback_objects()** is used by **editor::dispatcher()** to determine if an otherwise-unknown command can be processed:

```
/*
check_with_callback_objects() can be invoked to determine if
a keystroke command is associated with a particular object from
the callback table.
```

```
*/

int editor::check_with_callback_objects(int command)
{
    for (int i = 0;
            i < MAX_CALLBACK && callback_command[i] != 0;
            i++) {
        if (command == callback_command[i]) {
            if (set_up_buf_window(i) > 0) {     // errors return value < 0
                callback_object[i]->activate("", NORMAL_VIDEO,
                                                NORMAL_VIDEO);
                callback_object[i]->dispatcher();
                callback_object[i]->deactivate();
            }
        }
    }
}   /* check_with_callback_objects */
```

check_with_callback_objects() is quite simple. It scans the callback command table in search of a match. If it finds a match, it calls **set_up_buf_window**() to load the buffer and check for errors, before turning control over to the callback object's dispatcher: "callback_object[i]->dispatcher()".

set_up_buf_window()'s definition is straightforward, requiring no special explanation:

```
/*
set_up_buf_window() loads the buffer for the window and sets the
buffer length, returning the value returned by read_from_disk().
*/

int editor::set_up_buf_window(int i)
{
    char *filename = get_alt_file_spec();
    long len = callback_object[i]->read_from_disk(filename);
    if (len == CANT_READ)
        attn_win.message(filename, "** file not found **");
    else if (len == TOO_LARGE)
        attn_win.message(filename, "** file is too large **");
    else
        callback_object[i]->set_buf_length(len);
    return len;
}   /* set_up_buf_window */
```

17.3.3 Standard Protocols

In **check_with_callback_objects()** the callback object, **callback_object[i]**, can be of any type that's derived from **buf_window**, based on the rules of C++. Note that regardless of **callback_object[i]**'s type the main task is to call its dispatcher. Recall that **browser** and **prompt_window** objects automatically handle window refresh operations in their respective dispatchers. With **edit_window** objects, however, we left the window refresh operation out of the dispatcher. Doing so violates our rule that similarly named methods in a class hierarchy (such as **dispatcher()** in our window class hierarchy) should handle their respective tasks with the same message-passing protocol, even if the underlying operations are somewhat different.

Specifically, with **edit_window** objects we made the window refresh operation manual (using **window_fill()**). We did so as a concession to performance considerations and aesthetics. In many cases, an edit window should give the appearance that any command that it can't process is "shipped out for processing." Actually, however, within **editor::dispatcher()**, **edit_window::dispatcher()** terminates and is given control again after the "foreign" command is processed. (Recall the control loop for the dispatchers in **editor::dispatcher()** in Chapter 16 that implicitly factored commands among various dispatchers.)

In our case, within **editor::dispatcher()** we want the absolute minimal baggage in **edit_window::dispatcher()**, in order to maximize keystroke processing, yet in **check_with_callback_objects()** we want the same dispatcher protocol for objects of classes **browser**, **prompt_window**, and **edit_window**. As an exercise, you should consider providing (the quite trivial) modifications to the various dispatchers to handle this situation, in a manner that suits your preferences. For example, you could either (1) overload the dispatcher definitions, or (2) provide multiple dispatchers in certain classes.

We prefer the latter technique. That is, in our existing implementation of **edit_window** (*winedit.cpp*) we can rename the dispatcher that we've used so far to, say, **minimal_dispatcher()**:

```
/*
minimal_dispatcher() dispatches keystroke commands to process_cmd(),
as long as process_cmd() can continue to process them.
*/

int edit_window::minimal_dispatcher()
{
    keystroke key;

    do {
        key.word = wgetche();
    } while (process_cmd(key));
    return key.word;
}   /* minimal_dispatcher */
```

Then, we can add **dispatcher()** for name compliance across classes:

```
/*
dispatcher() fills the window before calling miminal_dispatcher().
*/

int edit_window::dispatcher()
{
    keystroke key;

    window_fill(0, 0, 0);
    return minimal_dispatcher();
}   /* dispatcher */
```

Thus, in each class **dispatcher()** performs a "standard" task, namely, "editor" command dispatching in a newly refreshed window. In particular, the same message can be used to activate the appropriate dispatching actions for whatever type of object that **check_with_callback_objects()** is currently executing.

17.3.4 Other Modifications and Enhancements to editor

In addition to the changes and additions described so far, there are three other modifications that must be made to **editor**. First, the constructor **editor()** should be modified to initialize (null-terminate) the callback command table:

```
editor::editor()
{
    ... // same as before
    ...
        callback_command[0] = 0;            // new initialization
    }
}   /* editor */
```

With this initialization, if the programmer doesn't register any callback objects, **check_with_callback_objects()** will terminate as soon as it's called.

Also, two modifications must be made to **editor::dispatcher()**. First, there is the name change in the call to the edit window dispatcher:

```
    ...
    if (ed[cur_win] != NULL)
        key.word = ed[cur_win]->minimal_dispatcher();  // the simple
    else                                                // dispatcher
        key.word = dos_keybd.get_keystroke();
    ...
```

As mentioned, calling the low-overhead dispatcher improves edit window performance.

Second, a call to **check_with_callback_objects()** is inserted as a catch-all, or last-resort, attempt to process a so-far-unrecognized command:

```
int editor::dispatcher(char *file_spec)
{
    ...
    // same as before
    ...
    default:
        check_with_callback_objects(key.byte[1]);    // new
        break;
    ...
    // same as before
    ...
    }
}   /* dispatcher */
```

That is, we simply use the **default**, or "otherwise," clause in the **switch** to signal the callback table, look-up operation.

17.3.5 Polymorphism and the Role of Virtual Methods

Up to this point we haven't needed virtual methods. Consider the definition of an edit window object by **editor::init_edit**:

```
ed[cur_win] = new edit_window(cur_win + 1, "", 1, 0, 23, 79,
                              MAX_BUF_SIZE, BACK_ATTR);
```

where **ed** is a data structure from **editor**:

```
edit_window *ed[MAX_WINDOWS];    // array of ptrs. to edit_windows
```

Even though we're operating with pointers to objects, the compiler can determine from the previous definition that all objects are **edit_window** objects.

With our enhancement to support callback objects, we want **editor**, more specifically, **register_callback_objects()** and **check_with_callback_objects()**, to accommodate *any* type of **buf_window**-derived object: **browser**, **prompt_window**, or **edit_window**. Thus, the callback object table has a generic definition:

```
buf_window *callback_object[MAX_CALLBACK];
```

The effect of this generic table definition is that the compiler can't use traditional static binding to bind the proper objects and messages, for example:

```
...
callback_object[i]->activate("", NORMAL_VIDEO,
                              NORMAL_VIDEO);
callback_object[i]->dispatcher();
callback_object[i]->deactivate();
...
```

Because pointers to objects of a generic type/class are involved, where pointer assignments can (and will) be made dynamically, their type won't be known until the editor module is linked with an application, say, *ed.cpp*,

As we mentioned in Chapter 14, virtual methods solve this problem. Using the **virtual** specifier with a function/method declaration instructs the compiler to generate the run-time code that's necessary to determine the object's type before invoking the method. In this case, the object pointed to by **callback_object[i]** must be bound dynamically to either **browser::dispatcher()**, **prompt_window::dispatcher()**, or **edit_window::dispatcher()**, depending on the object's class.

Consider the implications. If the application registers an object of class **browser**, then four commands must be accommodated: **browser's top_of_buffer()**, **bottom_of_buffer()**, **page_up()**, and **page_down()**. If the application registers an object of class **edit_window**, numerous commands must be accommodated—**edit_window**'s versions of these same four commands, plus additional commands such as **del_line()**, **insert_char()**, and so on.

What modifications are required to our window class hierarchy to support this level of dynamic binding? Because we've factored commands among classes, and because we've placed each class's commands under control of its own dispatcher, the modification(s) to our class hierarchy are extremely trivial. Specifically, all that's necessary is to add a virtualized dispatcher in the governing class, in this case, **buf_window**, that is, one declaration is added to *winbufs.hpp*:

```
////  winbufs.hpp  ////  interface for class:  buf_window  ////


  ...
  // same as before
  ...
  virtual int dispatcher() = 0;
  ...
  // same as before
  ...
```

We tend to put all of our virtual declarations together in one location, right after the constructors and destructors (if the latter are public); however, in this case, we have only one.

buf_window is an abstract class; we don't expect to create instantiations of **buf_window**, except as place-holders for objects from derived classes. Thus, **buf_window::dis-**

patcher() is "null"—the "= 0" in the declaration indicates that the implementation for this class will not supply a definition for this virtual method. By specifying that a virtual method such as **dispatcher()** is undefined for **buf_window**, we're *implicitly* defining **buf_window** as an abstract class.

This type of "null" virtual method is said to be *pure*. At run-time, the proper (concrete) class dispatcher will be bound to the object pointed to by **callback_object[i]**, by the C++ virtual method mechanism. This mechanism consists primarily of the run-time code required to perform object-method look-up operations in a virtual method table, or *vtbl*. (Koenig [1989] provides a simple example of virtual methods. Books on the C++ language, such as Stroustrup [1986] and Lippman (1989), demonstrate virtual methods as well.)

Once again, we've reaped additional benefits from our use of a dispatcher to oversee the operations implemented by each class. In addition to presenting the programmer with a *small interface* to, say, **browser** and **edit_window**, we've localized any changes required in adding new capabilities to our window hierarchy, such as dynamic binding. More importantly, the virtual method mechanism (its overhead) is applied to the dispatcher only, as opposed to the many methods under a dispatcher's control; each **dispatcher()** is bound to its respective methods, for example, **page_up()**, during compilation, avoiding virtual table overhead that otherwise would be required for low-level methods, such as **page_up()**.

17.3.6 An Example: Adding a Pop-up, Read-only Browser

At this point, it's a trivial exercise for the developer of an application that requires an editor to supplement the editor with, say, a read-only browser that pops up over the normal edit window. Using *ed.cpp* from Chapter 16 as an example, the following modification are required in **main()**; the other two functions in *ed.cpp* require no changes.

First, we must define a keystroke to represent the command for invoking the browser:

```
#define ALT_B   48            // PC keystroke for the browser command
```

Next, a **browser** object and a pointer to that browser, **browzr**, must be defined:

```
browser *browzr = new browser(DUMMY, "Read-Only File Browser",
                    5, 5, 19, 74, 10000, NORMAL_VIDEO);
```

(Similarly, you could define **browzr** as a browser object, as opposed to a pointer to a browser object, and then take its address.)

Lastly, contingent on proper storage allocation for the browser, we can allocate an editor, register the browser as a callback object, and call the editor's dispatcher:

```
if (!(edit_status = browzr->get_error_state())) {
    editor ed;
    ed.register_callback_objects(1, ALT_B, browzr);
    edit_status = ed.dispatcher(file_spec);
}
```

The message "register_callback_objects(1, ALT_B, browzr)" signals **ed** that one callback object, **browzr**, should be invoked if the user presses the browser command **ALT_B**. When **browzr.dispatcher()** relinquishes control, **ed.dispatcher()** again assumes control of command dispatching.

The entire function **main()** for allocating an editor with a pop-up, read-only browser is:

```
int main(int argc, char *argv[])
{
    char *file_spec;
    int edit_status;

    ...
    // floppy-disk error detection
    ...

    if ((file_spec = check_args(argc, argv)) == NULL)
        exit(1);
    dos_screen.clrscn();
    browser *browzr = new browser(DUMMY, "Read-Only File Browser",
                        5, 5, 19, 74, 10000, NORMAL_VIDEO);
    if (!(edit_status = browzr->get_error_state())) {
        editor ed;
        ed.register_callback_objects(1, ALT_B, browzr);
        edit_status = ed.dispatcher(file_spec);
    }
    delete browzr;
    dos_screen.restore_exit_screen();
    if (issue_error_messages(edit_status, file_spec))
        exit(1);
    else
        exit(0);
}   /* main */
```

This type of callback mechanism, or something similar, has obvious utility for enhancing the reusability of existing classes. In general, however, using a registration system to associate functions and data structures is inferior to using object-oriented programming techniques to encapsulate data and procedures.

17.4 Implementing a Callback Mechanism for Functions

Suppose we would like to provide an object with a facility whereby the programmer can register stand-alone callback functions, as in the earlier example using SunView. This section demonstrates how to so with C++, again using **editor** as an example. Too keep the example simple, we'll enhance **editor** with a facility for consulting and executing an arbitrary number of *exit* functions during termination of the editor object. Similarly, the callback function mechanism can be used to support general callbacks to functions for any object.

17.4.1 A Callback Function Table

In the previous section, we used **buf_window** to serve as a place-holder for the real object, as registered by the application—a **browser**, **prompt_window**, or **edit_window** object. In order to allow the application to register functions, we need a generic type of function to serve as a place-holder for a real function. ANSI C and C++ provide functions of type **void** for this purpose.

For our purposes we need a simple callback function table that can accommodate pointers to functions of type **void**. The following additions are required in the interface file, *editor.hpp*, in addition to those from the previous section:

```
////  editor.hpp  ////  interface for class:  editor  ////

...
// same as before
...
#define MAX_EXIT        5            // table size


typedef void (*ptr_void_proc)();    // type: pointer to void procedure


class editor {
    ...
    // same as before
    ...
    ptr_void_proc exit_function[MAX_EXIT];  // table of exit functions
public:
    ...
    // same as before
    ...
    void register_exit_functions(int ...);  // new method
    void check_with_exit_functions();       // new method
    ...
    // same as before
    ...
};
```

First, we define a type that represents a pointer to a void function/procedure:

```
typedef void (*ptr_void_proc)();
```

Alternatively, you could skip the **typedef**, expressing the type of the table elements directly during the table's definition. In most cases, however, formally creating the type **ptr_void_proc** leads to more readable source code.

Subsequently, we can define a table of **ptr_void_procs**:

```
ptr_void_proc exit_function[MAX_EXIT];  // table of exit functions
```

17.4.2 Callback Function Methods

We need two methods for table management analogous to those for callback objects. First, **register_exit_functions()** allows the application to register an arbitrary number of exit functions:

```
/*
register_exit_functions() registers each exit function passed
by the application in a table of void functions.  See the
related method check_with_exit_functions().
*/

void editor::register_exit_functions(int arg_count ...)
{
    va_list ep;
    va_start(ep, arg_count);
    for (int i = 0; i < MAX_EXIT && i < arg_count; i++) {
        exit_function[i] = va_arg(ep, ptr_void_proc);
    }
    exit_function[i] = NULL;    // mark the end of the table
    va_end(ep);
}   /* register_exit_functions */
```

register_exit_functions() is a little simpler than **register_callback_objects()**, since there are no keystrokes to pair with the functions—all registered functions will be executed automatically upon editor termination.

Execution of registered exit functions is handled in two locations in *editor.cpp*. First, **check_with_exit_functions()** scans the array and executes whatever it finds:

```
/*
check_with_exit_functions() is called by the editor destructor
to perform the exit operations specified by the application.
*/

void editor::check_with_exit_functions()
```

```
{
    for (int i = 0;
            i < MAX_EXIT && exit_function[i] != NULL;
            i++)
        (*exit_function[i])();  // execute each function in the table
}   /* check_with_exit_functions */
```

The syntax "(*exit_function[i])()" is used to signify that we want the entity referenced by the pointer, not the pointer itself, that is, we want to execute the function at that address.

Second, the destructor for an editor object must initiate this scan and execute operation:

```
editor::~editor()
{
    delete ed_help;
    delete dos_box;
    check_with_exit_functions(); // do the application's clean-up
}   /* ~editor */
```

Note also that the constructor should initialize the exit function table, in the event that no exit functions are registered:

```
editor::editor()
{
    ...
    // same as before
    ...
        exit_function[0] = NULL;        // initialize the table
    }
}   /* editor */
```

17.4.3 An Example: Having the Object Perform Clean-up Operations

We can simulate the notification-based system provide with SunView by providing the editor object with termination functions. ("Simulate" is the operative word here; again, SunView is much more sophisticated than our simple system.)

First, to simplify the example we'll design our callback exit functions so that they require no arguments; to do so three variables must be made external:

```
/*
globals:  used to simplify the demonstration
*/


char *file_spec;
```

```
int edit_status;
browser *browzr;
```

In **main()**, we register our callback exit functions by sending the following message to **register_exit_functions()**:

```
    ...
    ed.register_exit_functions(2,
                               clean_heap,
                               send_message_and_terminate);
    ...
```

The definition for **clean_heap()** is:

```
void clean_heap()
{
    delete browzr;
}   /* clean_heap */
```

It simulates the type of heap clean-up operations that would be required in a larger application.

The second function, **send_message_and_terminate()**, restores the exit screen and issues messages:

```
/*
send_message_and_terminate() clears the screen and issues a message,
if necessary, before terminating.
*/

void send_message_and_terminate()
{
    dos_screen.restore_exit_screen();
    if (issue_error_messages(edit_status, file_spec))
        exit(1);
    else
        exit(0);
}   /* send_message_and_terminate */
```

This function demonstrates that any callback function registered with the "governing" object is free to call as many other functions as necessary—the latter functions need not be registered.

main()'s definition is:

```
int main(int argc, char *argv[])
{
    ...
    ...
    if ((file_spec = check_args(argc, argv)) == NULL)
        exit(1);
    dos_screen.clrscn();
    browzr = new browser(DUMMY, "Read-Only File Browser",
                    5, 5, 19, 74, 10000, NORMAL_VIDEO);
    if (!(edit_status = browzr->get_error_state())) {
        editor ed;
        ed.register_callback_objects(1, ALT_B, browzr);
        ed.register_exit_functions( 2,
                                    clean_heap,
                                    send_message_and_terminate);
        edit_status = ed.dispatcher(file_spec);
    }
}   /* main */
```

Similar to the SunView system, the editor's dispatcher *does* return to the main program.

17.4.4 An Exercise

The callback function facility has obvious implications for reusability as well. For example, an application could register callback functions that supplement the editor's file processing capabilities. In order to supplement file processing, the application might require access to some of the edit window data structures; this access should be provided indirectly via access methods.

As a rule, the interface to a class should be kept small—data hiding is enhanced through encapsulation. For this reason, providing additional access to a class should not be taken lightly; poorly designed access methods can compromise and complicate a class interface. As an exercise, consider adding general support for callback functions to **editor**.

17.5 Object-Oriented Programming and Registration Systems

The C++ editor project emphasizes the power of encapsulation. With a C-based implementation of a project in which there is a large, omnipresent data structure, such as a window frame, it's quite common to use a global definition of the data structure and then pass a pointer (or array index) to various functions that must manipulate the structure.

In contrast, with an object-oriented approach the association between each object and its methods is "automatic." In general, an object-oriented approach greatly enhances the design of reusable modules. For example, the task of composing the high-level class **editor** from various lower level classes is simplified because the critical editor variables necessary to manage each edit session are hidden within each **edit_window** object. On average, an **editor** method requires very few local variables (often none)—a context switch between edit sessions is handled largely by procedural action (message passing).

In our case, it would be inappropriate to devise some form of registration system to associate each dispatcher with the operations that it governs. Registration systems are more appropriate in a design where it's necessary to accommodate call backs to fairly independent events/objects. In particular, if registrants and their host must pass several data structures back and forth to each other, or perform side-effect operations on global data structures, an alternative design should be considered.

In this chapter, our registration system for objects is *used* more appropriately than our registration system for functions—our contrasting designs were intentional. One of our main objectives in this chapter has been to illustrate the syntax and mechanics necessary to support object and function registration. It's equally important, however, to point out the assistance that object-oriented programming provides in designing clean interfaces.

In retrospect, it's quite easy for an application programmer to register an object with the editor: first, the **browser** and **editor** objects are defined, then the former is registered with the latter. The interface between the two is quite small, because a **browser** object is a self-contained package. Moreover, the interaction between the two objects is prescribed by the definition of **editor**—planned in advance.

On the other hand, with a function registration system it is less convenient to provide this type of encapsulation and inter-entity coordination. Often, it's necessary to have the host *initiate* operations against data defined by the application, a situation that we simulated in the second part of this chapter by registering editor clean-up operations with the editor object. Since functions are registered by name only, subsequent to the design of the host, the application may need to define part of its data globally; see Section 17.4.3.

Is it legitimate for registrants and their host to share data? In our opinion, function registration should be restricted to situations where it supports operations that are independent of the host's data structures, unless the data sharing is minimal and can be handled in a straightforward manner using access methods.

To contrast the participants, it's perfectly acceptable for a host object to provide a function registration system, so that its dispatcher can initiate actions associated with self-contained, external events, as cataloged by the application. In this case, however, the burden is on the application not to abuse the registration mechanism.

Consider the C-based SunView toolkit described in Sections 17.1 and 17.2. For programmers who prefer to work with a traditional language, SunView provides an extremely elegant solution to the problem of managing a multitude of activities. However, a true object-oriented toolkit would go a long way toward reducing the complexity of a large application.

17.6 Class Refinement

We've suggested that there is a natural developmental process that occurs in designing a hierarchy of classes. Over time, the programmer develops a feeling for those class methods that should remain public and those methods that should be given their privacy—the class hierarchy matures after an iterative process: use class...modify class...use class... Eventually, a class/module can be closed.

In our modules we've simulated this developmental process by having methods retain their public status. Many of these methods should now become private or protected, so that applications are forced to access each class through its dispatcher. Minimally, the constructors for the abstract classes should be given **protected** status.

Our editor and window classes provide only simple examples of the power that C++ provides for object-oriented programming. C++'s power is in its syntactic support for refinement of abstract structures over time. The fact that we could retrofit virtual edit windows to our class hierarchy by adding a one-line virtual method declaration to *winbufs.hpp* exemplifies the power offered by the C++ **class** construct.

18

Informal Guidelines for Enhancing Software Reusability

In this chapter we summarize some of our suggestions for promoting software reusability. We should emphasize that our comments provide informal guidelines, not hard-and-fast rules; as such, they are applicable in many, but not all, circumstances. Where appropriate, we provide references to related material from earlier chapters using the format: "[*chapter #.section #*, ...]", for example, [1.1, 18.1].

18.1 Use Encapsulation To Hide Details

Although the techniques differ somewhat, both traditional and object-oriented languages provide tools for encapsulating data structures and related procedures.

18.1.1 Traditional Languages

With traditional languages such as C, the two most common language features for packaging data and procedures are: (1) procedure-level static scope, and (2) file-level static scope.

In many cases, local static variables can provide good protection against certain kinds of ripple effects generated by changes to data structures. For example, the function

tag_pos() provides a high-level interface to the information and operations necessary to keep track of tags in multiple edit buffers:

```
long tag_pos(int n, long info)
{
    static long tag_position[MAIN_EDIT_WIN + 1];

    if (info != TEST)
        tag_position[n] = info;
    return tag_position[n];
}   /* tag_pos */
```

Changing the number of edit buffers has no impact on the interface to **tag_pos()**, since buffer number is incorporated as a parameter. Moreover, if the nature of the data structure changes, say, from a one- to a two-dimensional edit buffer, the interface remains constant: "tag_pos(buf_no, some_value)". Even if, say, an array of pointers to strings is used to represent each edit buffer (one string per line in the buffer), **info** is adequate for passing "line-position" information. In this case, global variable references are avoided by using uniform procedural interfaces. Although small performance penalties are incurred for the function overhead, the payoff is an increase in overall program robustness against changes to *small-scale* data structures. [2.6, 9.2]

Parenthetically, text editors have traditionally been highly implementation-dependent and lacking in abstract data structures; the desire for efficiency has justified designs in which high-level functions directly manipulate the central data structures (edit buffers). In practice, it is quite difficult to build a *highly efficient* editor using a character-based edit buffer that can be re-programmed to use a line-based edit buffer without rewriting a major portion of the editor. The abstraction issues that arise in designing an editor are fundamentally different from those involved in stack-and-queue programming with abstract data types. The previous paragraph does not imply that making this sort of change in large-scale data structures would be trivial.

File-level static variables, on the other hand, can be used to provide a mechanism for controlling access to more significant data structures. If, for whatever reason, it is unreasonable to encapsulate a data structure in a function, access to that data structure can be strictly controlled by isolating it in a separate (small) module, along with the functions that manipulate it.

No matter how you rationalize it, a file-level static variable is still a global variable. In particular, a programmer cannot be 100 percent sure of how such a variable is employed, unless he or she examines the entire source file. For DOS environments, our screen module is a good example of a situation in which a private variable may be justified. The screen (the pointer to the screen) is the central data structure; it is used by most functions in the module.

In this case, (1) the operations against the global variable are clear-cut—**screen** is the starting point for iterative operations against the screen buffer, and (2) the module is reasonably small. Generally speaking, numerous private variables cannot be justified, especially when they are accessed by many functions in reasonably complex ways, for example, our edit buffer offset variables (tag position). In almost all cases, if a programmer has used numerous private variables per module, the module should be redesigned. As a general rule, functions should be used to control access to data, and private variables should be used only in special circumstances. [2.8, 6.5]

18.1.2 Object-oriented Languages

With object-oriented languages such as C++, instance variables, that is, variables inherited by each object, provide a mechanism for sharing information among methods. Some programmers have argued that object-oriented languages promote global variable usage—instance variables are essentially global variables in disguise. In defense of instance variables, we offer the following points.

In general, there are, perhaps, two major arguments against global variables: (1) they severely impact the readability of source code, leading to inadvertent programming errors when modules are "tweaked" before reuse, and (2) they don't allow for changes to data structures, as is often required in generalizing a program, say, generalizing an editor from one edit buffer to multiple edit buffers.

Consider the readability issue. First, the scope of a private or protected instance variable, unlike a traditional global variable, is restricted. An instance variable is a member of a class that (typically) occurs within a hierarchy of classes; this type of lexical structure enhances the readability of the source code. Second, with object-oriented languages, the methods that operate on instance variables have restricted scope as well. Thus, as a class hierarchy matures, methods can be elevated to protected or private status, further controlling the level of access to instance variables. This type of lexical control is simply not available with traditional languages. [11.1, 11.2, 11.3, 12.2]

Consider the issue of generalization of data structures. With traditional languages, global variables exist external to the functions that operate on them. Hence, major revisions involving global structures, say, modifying an editor to support multiple edit buffers, require widespread modifications to the call structure of many functions. On the other hand, the encapsulation of instance variables and methods within an object avoids this problem altogether. Once again, the object-oriented language provides the lexical support for this type of program generalization—a programmer simply allocates additional objects, providing additional source code to govern their high-level usage. [15.3, 15.4, 16.1, 17.3]

The main point, however, is that an argument against global variable usage is not an argument against object-oriented programming. With an OO language, a programmer still has the opportunity to use method-level lexical scope to control the amount of access to data structures. Overall, the object-oriented approach provides better control(s) for central variables than does C's file-level scope.

18.2 Use Access Methods for Inter-module Communication

For those situations in which inter-module communication is required, access functions/methods are preferable to global variables. With C, the constant specifier **const** can be used to protect information from inadvertent modification. For example, with the following access function:

```
const char *get_name(char *name)
{
    return name;
}
```

the value stored at the location addressed by **name** is given constant status. Also, it's possible to make the pointer constant. (See Stroustrup [1986] for syntax-related issues.)

A variable, or object, that has constant status via one pointer can have variable status when accessed by an alternate pointer. Although widespread application of multiple levels of access to variables can make a module hard to read, and consequently, hard to maintain, this technique is quite useful for granting read-write access to "friendly" procedures (within the same module) and read-only access to "outsiders." [2.8, 10.2.5, 12.2]

With C++, as a class hierarchy matures (and further debugging is not anticipated), it's a good idea to make many of the public methods either private or protected—that is, to reduce the size of the interface. Methods such as **go_line_start()** in the class **buf_window** should not be used by external functions, or by methods of other objects. As a general rule, the constructors for abstract classes should be given **protected** status. [14.8, 16.5, 17.5]

With C++, changing the access status of a method can be accomplished by regrouping declarations in its interface file:

```
    ...
protected:
    ...                                                     // protected variables
    ...                                                     // protected methods
    buf_window(int, char *, int, int, int, int, long, int);
    ~buf_window() {
        delete buffer;
    }
    ...
    int move_forward_x_lines(int);
    int move_backward_x_lines(int);
    long go_line_start();
    ...
public:
    long get_max_size() {
        return max_buf_size;
    }
    ...
```

Note that making methods private, as opposed to protected, may inhibit the derivation of new classes.

18.3 Use Message-passing for Inter-object Communication

If modules and classes are properly designed, much of the communication among objects will occur by sending messages between objects. First, consider communication between two objects of different classes. Strictly speaking, the operations of, say, a **screen** object, are controlled (performed) by its own methods. Typically, however, objects from different classes must work together; hence, an object's public methods provide controlled access to internal information, as well as provisions for impacting that object's behavior. For example, **get_video_mode()** allows outside agents to interrogate a screen object regarding one of its characteristics, whereas **restore_exit_screen()** permits external agents to exercise some measure of control over a screen object's behavior. [12.2]

In our opinion, it's difficult to make sweeping generalizations about the merits of allowing one object to control various operations of another object, even when the latter object's constructor(s) and/or destructor could be enlisted to perform those activities. Obviously, every **screen** object should be responsible for detecting, recording, and making available the monitor's video mode—this type of automation enhances the reusability of modules. On the other hand, allowing external objects to orchestrate certain activities, for example, those performed by **restore_exit_screen()**, increases overall flexibility, enhancing reusability in a different way.

Next, consider communication between two objects of the same class. Typically, each instance of a class has its own data. In the event that two "like" objects need to share information, you can use C++'s mechanism for creating class variables, as opposed to setting up a global variable. For example, suppose you're building an editor with multiple edit windows, however, for some reason related to the design of the application, it isn't feasible to encapsulate the edit windows inside an editor class, as we did with **editor**. [16.1] Further, suppose that you need to maintain a indicator of the currently active edit window. Although this information could be maintained in a global variable, a better alternative is to add a static variable to the class **edit_window**:

```
class edit_window : public text_window {
private:
    static edit_window *active_window;      // class variable
protected:
    int buf_mod_state;
public:
    edit_window(int, char *, int, int, int, int, long,
                    int = BACK_ATTR);
    int dispatcher();
    int process_cmd(keystroke);
    ...
```

(Of course, this type of class variable could be added at a different location in the window hierarchy.)

In this case, each **edit_window** object will be allocated (its own) data for every non-static member. However, only one copy of the pointer **active_window** will be allocated. Using this technique, methods could be defined for very strict manipulation of **active_window**. Typically, this approach would be superior to using a global variable to keep track of the active edit window.

18.4 Take Advantage of Built-in Support for Array Indexing

Traditionally, C programmers take pride in the practice of reducing each operation to its most concise lexical form:

```
...
while (*s1++ = *s2++) ;
...
```

If, however, you use this type of pointer manipulation in I/O methods for buffer classes, or in class methods that implement buffer operations in a window, their respective classes may not be reusable across compiler/hardware environments. Because of the less-than-ideal support for segmented architecture with some compiler-hardware-operating system combinations, explicit array indexing may be preferable:

```
...
for ( ; s1[i] = s2[i]; i++) ;
...
```

For similar reasons, it may be prudent to calculate buffer offsets using array indexing in conjunction with the address operator:

```
... &buffer[current_pos + increment] ...
```

We reiterate that with some machines/compilers there are never any problems with the former type of pointer arithmetic. (Harbison and Steele [1987], p. 274, mention this problem also.) [3.4, 3.5, 9.5]

18.5 Provide Multiple Constructors for the Appropriate Classes

In order to minimize confusion in the initial design of our window hierarchy, we provided only one constructor for each class. Clearly, the ultimate goal is to close each of the window modules—we're not there yet. To be reusable, however, classes must have some minimal level of flexibility. Often, it's possible to make the use of classes more convenient, or postpone the need for defining derived classes, by providing several constructors. As an example, consider the simple class **query_box**. [13.6] For one application it might be preferable to initialize **query_box** objects with explicit window numbers; for other applications, having to provide a window number argument to the constructor when it's not needed would be viewed as an inconvenience.

One solution is to overload the constructor:

```
class query_box : public msg_window {
    int user_response;
public:
    query_box(char *, int, int, int, int = BACK_ATTR);
    query_box(int, char *, int, int, int, int = BACK_ATTR);
    get_user_response() {
        return user_response;
    }
    ...
```

Providing multiple constructors enhances the reusability of the class in a small, but significant, way.

It's possible, however, to overdo the use of multiple constructors. If a particular constructor from a set of several constructors is used 90 percent of the time, are the other constructors justified? This question is often hard to answer; in some cases, there may be justification for minimizing the amount of source code associated with a particular class. It may be preferable, for example, to provide a base class with one constructor, and then define a separate derived class, which provides for the alternative initialization. The latter class could be supplied in a separate compiled module.

18.6 Identify Abstract and Concrete Classes

It's impossible to establish hard rules regarding the balance between abstract and concrete classes. In some situations, it may be appropriate to establish a stand-alone concrete class, for example, an I/O class or a class designed to support special numeric operations, say, a rational number class (Wiener and Pinson, 1988).

A few situations may warrant the design of a small class hierarchy in which all classes are concrete. Our buffer class hierarchy, for example, contains a generic root class for simple buffer operations, plus two derived classes, **clipboard** and **undo_buffer**. In this case, the root class **char_buffer** is useful for character-based data transfer between memory and disk. Generally speaking, however, any class hierarchy dominated by concrete classes should be small, and designed to serve some special purpose. [13.1, 13.2, 14.5]

In all reasonably large programming projects, it's important to look for naturally occurring hierarchies that simplify the design and reuse of individual classes. In this type of situation, the process of ferreting out common data structures, and related operations, should take precedence over identifying concrete (directly usable) classes.

Focusing on abstract structures and operations facilitates the development of reasonably deep hierarchies. In general, concrete classes can be derived on demand, as required by new applications. If a class hierarchy has sufficient depth, it will be reasonably easy to pick a good starting point for class derivations that may be required to service a particular application.

In an environment in which several programmers are involved in defining a class hierarchy, it's important not to lose control of "class derivation at the extremities." In particular, there must be a certain amount of coordination among programmers, in order to fine-tune classes that are genuinely reusable. [13.1, 13.2, 14.8]

18.7 Hierarchies Require Fine-tuning

Class hierarchies should not be reduced to binary form too hastily. The development of a good balance between abstract and concrete classes requires time, plus feedback from the programmers who use the hierarchy. With almost all significant class hierarchies, a considerable amount of iterative refinement will be required before development can be considered complete. Typically, the overall relationship among the classes will undergo refinement, as well as the interfaces of the individual classes.

18.8 Hide Low-level Classes within High-level Classes

In many cases, it's difficult for the developer of a hierarchy to balance the need for fine-tuning against the pressure from users of the hierarchy to get the product out. Ultimately, each class interface should be as small as possible, that is, a method should have its public access revoked, where appropriate. The designer of a hierarchy should't be too generous with class methods, because generosity may inhibit future refinements.

The practice of encapsulating (nesting) low-level objects within a high-level object, say, an instance of **editor**, can buy the developer some time for continued class refinement. In general, you should encourage programmers to use a high-level class, as opposed to becoming dependent on low-level classes. [16.1]

In some cases, the generalizability of a class can be enhanced by nesting a low-level object within a high-level object via a pointer to the low-level object. [13.4.2]

18.9 Put the Flow of Control in the Objects

One of our principal objectives has been to demonstrate the importance of endowing the appropriate classes with dispatching capabilities. By comparing the various versions of **ed**, it's easy to see the significance of the **dispatcher**() methods for reusability. For most applications requiring an edit window, the convenience afforded by the dispatchers would be an important consideration. [5.3, 15.3, 16.2]

However, from the point of view of class design, dispatchers provide a mechanism for grouping together operations that are common across classes. As we've shown, the use of standard protocols can enhance the reusability of classes by (1) defining standard operations for each class, and thus, (2) supporting polymorphism. The latter capability is particularly important for reusability, since it provides a mechanism for enhancing application-level extensibility, in comparison to extension by class derivation.

From the standpoint of efficiency, the run-time efficiency of the resulting applications can be enhanced if polymorphic, "class governing" methods are used to provide a small number of high-level virtual methods instead of numerous low-level virtual methods. Also, by partitioning operations into classes, each with its own dispatcher, operations that commonly occur together are grouped under the control of a single dispatch table, minimizing the number of table entries. [16.2, 17.3.5]

18.10 Use Virtual Methods Where Necessary

With C++, virtual methods are quite efficient. However, with many applications it still makes sense to avoid having an unnecessarily large number of virtual methods. As we've mentioned, you can sometimes reduce the number of virtual methods by grouping methods together under control of a higher level method, one for each class. In this manner, the high-level methods can handle the run-time binding, with each high-level method using compile-time binding to invoke subordinate methods.

There are, of course, situations in which it's inappropriate to depend on high-level control of low-level methods, as we've done with the window class hierarchy. In some cases, it may be advantageous to provide numerous pure virtual methods in each abstract class. In some circumstances, the use of pure virtual methods as place-holders can significantly enhance the reusability of a class or a class hierarchy. [14.8]

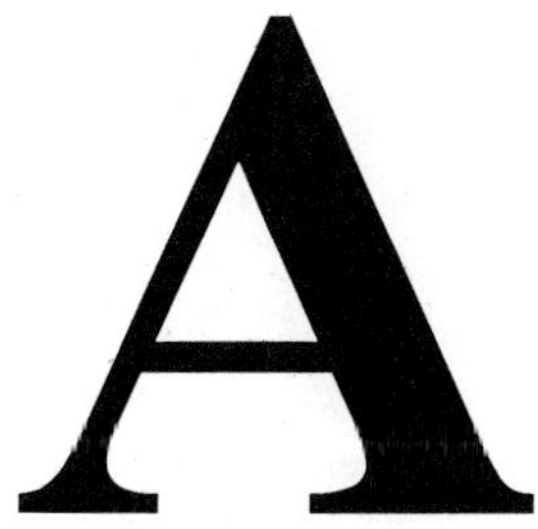

The C Version of ed

This version of **ed** has been tested with Microsoft C (Microsoft, 1988), Turbo C (Borland, 1988), and Zortech C (Zortech, 1989). It should be compiled with the compact memory model option. With Microsoft C, the compiler will generate numerous warnings for the conversions between integers and longs, as dictated by the function prototypes. If you don't like being informed of these integer conversions, you can eliminate the warning messages with a compiler option.

The source code for **ed** is listed in alphabetical order, header files first, using the module names from the various chapters. The help text is listed last. The source code begins immediately after this sentence:

```
/****  display.h  ****  external declarations for display.c  ****/

extern void display_string(int, int, char *, int);
extern void display_blanks(int, int, int, int);
extern void display_char(int, int, char, int);


/****  ed.h  ****  external declarations for ed.c  ****/
```

```
/*
wframe is the window data structure required by windows.c.
See windowsc.h.
*/

extern window_frame wframe[];


extern void main(int, char **);
extern char *check_args(int, char **);
extern int allocate_support_buffers(void);
extern int allocate_windows(void);
extern void issue_error_messages(int, char *);
extern int edit_main(int, char *);
extern int edit_text(int, char *, char *);
extern void dispatch_extended_code(int, unsigned char,
                                        char *, char *);
extern void display_edit_info(void);
extern void display_filename(int, char *);


/****  edc.h  ****  constants critical to ed  ****/

/*
This file contains header information for ed.c, the
primary source file for ed.
*/

/*
keyboard- and function-related constants appear next.  Note that
a function is represented by its keyboard extended code.  That is,
the (decimal) extended byte code for F1 is 59, which is used to
represent the HELP function.
*/

#define HELP        59              /* F1       */
#define TAG         60              /* F2       */
#define CUT         61              /* F3       */
#define PASTE       62              /* F4       */
#define DWORD       63              /* F5       */
#define DEOL        64              /* F6       */
#define DLINE       65              /* F7       */
#define UNDO        66              /* F8       */
#define QUIT        67              /* F9       */
```

```
#define EXIT         68                 /* F10       */
#define TAG_CURSOR   105                /* Alt-F2    */
#define COPY         106                /* Alt-F3    */
#define DWORD_LEFT   108                /* Alt-F5    */
#define UNTAG        111                /* Alt-F8    */
#define CHANGE_TEXT  46                 /* Alt-C     */
#define FIND_TEXT    33                 /* Alt-F     */
#define INSERT_FILE  23                 /* Alt-I     */
#define REPEAT_FC    19                 /* Alt-R     */
#define SAVE_FILE    31                 /* Alt-S     */
#define SET_TABS     20                 /* Alt-T     */
#define WRITE_FILE   17                 /* Alt-W     */
#define INS          82
#define DEL          83
#define UP           72
#define DOWN         80
#define LEFT         75
#define RIGHT        77
#define PGUP         73
#define PGDN         81
#define HOME         71                 /* beginning of line     */
#define END          79                 /* end of line           */
#define CTRL_HOME    119                /* top of screen         */
#define CTRL_END     117                /* bottom of screen      */
#define CTRL_PGUP    132                /* top of file           */
#define CTRL_PGDN    118                /* end of file           */
#define CTRL_LEFT    115                /* left one word         */
#define CTRL_RIGHT   116                /* right one word        */


#define NO_MATCH            -1          /* arbitrary error constants */
#define CANT_READ           -2
#define CANT_WRITE          -3
#define TOO_LARGE           -4
#define CANT_ALLOCATE_BUFS  -99


/****  edfile.h  ****  external declarations for edfile.c  ****/

extern void insert_file(int, char *, char *);
extern void write_alt_file(int, char *, char *);
extern char *get_alt_file_spec(int);
extern long read_from_disk(register char *, char *);
extern int write_from_buffer(int, char *, long, char *);
```

```
extern int write_to_disk(int, register char *, long, char *);
extern int file_exists(char *);
extern long file_size(char *);
extern int ok_to_overwrite(char *);


/****  edhelp.h  ****  external declarations for edhelp.c  ****/

extern void present_help_screens(int);
extern void display_help_screen(int, char *, char *);


/****  edit.h  ****  external declarations for edit.c  ****/

/*
window border colors:
*/

extern int nor_border_color;
extern int rev_border_color;


extern void initialize_edit(int);
extern void release_edit_buffers();
extern int buffer_modified(int, int);
extern int insert_mode(int);
extern int tab_size(int);
extern int edit_window_count(int);
extern long edit_buf_len(int, long);
extern long buf_cursor_pos(int, long);
extern long top_left_pos(int, long);
extern long tag_pos(int, long);
extern char *create_buffer(long);
extern int ispunc(char);
extern int message_query(int, char *, char *);
extern int insert_char(int, char, char *);
extern int insertion_special_conditions(int, char, char *);
extern void advance_cursor_to_next_tab(int, char *);
extern void insert_window_update(int, char *, char, long);
extern int del_char(int, char *);
extern int del_word(int, char *);
extern int del_word_left(int, char *);
extern int del_eol(int, char *);
extern int del_line(int, char *);
```

```
extern int backspace(int, char *);
extern int up(int, char *);
extern int down(int, char *);
extern int cursor_left(int, char *);
extern int cursor_right(int, char *);
extern int word_left(int, char *);
extern int word_right(int, char *);
extern int home(int, char *);
extern int endd(int, char *);
extern int page_up(int, char *);
extern int page_down(int, char *);
extern int top_of_buffer(int, char *);
extern int bottom_of_buffer(int, char *);
extern int top_of_window(int, char *);
extern int bottom_of_window(int, char *);
extern int cut_and_paste(int, char *, int);
extern int cut_or_copy(int, char *, char *, int);
extern int paste(int, char *, char *, long);
extern int undo_op(int, char *, long, int);
extern int paste_from_undo(int, char *, char *, long);
extern int cut_to_undo(int, char *, char *, long);
extern int update_undo_offset(int, char *, long *, long);
extern int update_undo_offset_for_cut(int, char *, long *, long);
extern void exch_tag_cursor_redisplay(int, char *);
extern long exch_tag_cursor(int);
extern int get_tag_column(int, char *);
extern int find_and_change(int, char *, int);
extern int prompt_for_pattern(int, int, char *, char *);
extern void display_not_found(int, int, char *);
extern long string_search(char *, char *, register long);
extern void replace_text(int, char *, long, char *, char *);
extern int redisplay_window(int, char *, int);
extern void redisplay_rest_of_line(int, char *, int);
extern int window_scroll_up(int, char *, int);
extern int window_scroll_down(int, char *, int);
extern int buffer_up_line(int, char *, int);
extern int buffer_down_line(int, char *, int);
extern int window_adjust_cursor_position(int, char *, int);
extern void adjust_onscreen_position(int, char *, int);
extern int adjacent_to_leftmost_column(int, char *);
extern int adjacent_to_rightmost_column(int);
extern void window_buffer_forward(int, char *);
extern void window_buffer_backward(int, char *);
extern int go_right_as_far_as_possible(int, char *);
```

```
extern int move_forward_x_lines(int, char *, int);
extern int move_backward_x_lines(int, char *, int);
extern long go_line_start(int, char *);
extern long go_line_end(int, char *);
extern char last_char_on_line(int, char *);
extern int linefeed_free(char *, register long);
extern int buf_line_length(int, char *);
extern int window_line_length(int, char *);
extern int previous_tab_column(int);
extern int previous_column(int, char *);
extern int next_tab_column(int);
extern int tab_fill_size(int);
extern int fill_tabs(int, int);
extern int strlen_with_tabs(char *, register int);
extern int current_column_offset(int, char *);


/****  editc.h  ****  constants for edit.c  ****/

#define TRUE                  1       /* logical constants */
#define FALSE                 0
#define SET                   1
#define RESET                 0

#define DUMMY                 0       /* constants denoting some      */
#define TEST                  -1      /* action, or error condition-- */
#define CREATE_CLIPBOARD      -2      /* specific value is arbitrary  */
#define CUT_CLIPBOARD         -3
#define COPY_CLIPBOARD        -4
#define PASTE_CLIPBOARD       -5
#define CREATE_UNDO           -6
#define CANCEL_UNDO           -7
#define CUT_UNDO              -8
#define PASTE_UNDO            -9
#define UPDATE_UNDO_OFFSET    -10
#define UPDATE_UNDO_OFF_CUT   -11
#define DESTROY               -12
#define INCR                  -13
#define DECR                  -14
#define COLUMN                -15
#define UNDEFINED             -16
#define FIND_IT               -17
#define CHANGE_IT             -18
#define REPEAT_IT             -19
```

```
#define CR                  '\r'    /* common character constants */
#define LF                  '\n'
#define TAB                 '\t'
#define FORMFEED            '\f'
#define EOS                 '\0'
#define BLANK               ' '
#define EOF_CHAR            26


#define NOR_BORDER_COLOR    NOR_CYAN_LOW    /* see vidconc.h */
#define REV_BORDER_COLOR    REV_CYAN_LOW
#define REV_SPECIAL_COLOR   REV_CYAN_LOW


/****  editintc.h ****  constants for the edit interface  ****/

#define MAIN_EDIT_WIN       0       /* window array positions   */
#define HELP_WIN            1
#define ATTN_WIN            2
#define FIND_WIN            3
#define MIN_NUM_WINS        4

#define TOP_ROW             0       /* used during display      */
#define BOT_ROW             24      /* operations only          */
#define MODIFIED_COLUMN     77
#define INSERT_MODE_COLUMN  78


#define MAX_BUF_SIZE        64000   /* "limit" constants, plus  */
#define MAX_CLIP_SIZE       64000   /* miscellany               */
#define MAX_UNDO_SIZE       5000
#define MAX_STR             45
#define POPUP_WIDTH         48      /* must be MAX_STR + 3      */
#define MIN_STR             7
#define MAX_NAME            80
#define HALF_PAGE           10
#define PAGE                20
#define TAB_SIZE            4
#define PUNCTUATION         "()!_:;\"',.?"


/****  editwin.h  ****  external declarations for editwin.c  ****/
```

```
extern int window_fill(int, int, int, char *, long);
extern int skip_offset(int, char *, int, int);
extern void put_text(int, char *);
extern int window_offset(int, int);
extern void window_shift_right(int, char *, int);
extern void window_restore_shift(int, char *);
extern int window_restore_offset_and_column(int);


/****  keyboard.h  ****  external declarations for keyboard.c  ****/

extern int get_keystroke(void);
extern int keyboard_alt_depressed(void);
extern void set_cntl_break(int);


/****  screen.h  ****  external declarations for screen.c  ****/

extern void clrscn(void);
extern void dos_level_cursor(int);
extern int video_initialize(void);
extern char far *get_screen_addr(void);
extern void set_screen_addr(void);
extern int get_video_mode(void);
extern void restore_exit_screen(void);
extern void cursor_rc(int, int);


/**  scrnprnc.h  **  used by screen, printer, and keyboard routines  **/

#define VIDEO_INT           0x10    /* interrupts */
#define KEYBOARD_INT        0x16
#define DOS_FUNCTION        0x21
#define CONTROL_BREAK_FUNC  0x33

#define KEYBOARD_READ   0           /* interrupt parameters */
#define KEYBOARD_STATUS 1
#define PAGE_0          0
#define SET_CURSOR_SIZE 0x01        /* Int 10 function 1    */
#define SET_CURSOR_POS  0x02        /* Int 10 function 2    */
#define READ_CURSOR_POS 0x03        /* Int 10 function 3    */
#define SCROLL_UP       6           /* Int 10 function 6    */
#define SCROLL_DOWN     7           /* Int 10 function 7    */
#define READ_CHAR       8           /* Int 10 function 8    */
```

```
#define WRITE_CHAR      9            /* Int 10 function 9    */
#define GET_VIDEO_MODE  0x0f         /* Int 10 function F    */

#define NORMAL_VIDEO    0x07         /* white on black            */
#define SCREEN_SIZE     4000         /* screen size @ 4000 bytes */
#define MONO_MODE       7            /* monochrome video mode #  */
#define MONO_SCREEN     0xb0000000   /* address of mono screen   */
#define COLOR_SCREEN    0xb8000000   /* address of color screen  */
#define CURSOR_SAVE     0            /* cursor save operation    */
#define CURSOR_RESTORE  1            /* cursor restore operation */
#define ON              1
#define OFF             0


/*
a data structure for keystrokes
*/

union keystroke {                    /* represents a key's    */
    unsigned char byte[2];           /* data and scan code    */
    int word;
};


/****   vidconc.h  ****  some video attribute constants  ****/

#define NOR_WHITE_HIGH       0x07 /* normal video -- white on black  */
#define REV_WHITE_HIGH       0x70 /* reverse video -- black on white */
#define REV_BLUE_BLINK_HIGH  0x9f /* blue background, blink, & high  */
#define REV_RED_BLINK_HIGH   0xcf /* red background, blink, & high   */
#define REV_BLUE_BLINK_LOW   0x97 /* blue background, blink, & low   */
#define REV_RED_BLINK_LOW    0xc7 /* red background, blink, & low    */
#define REV_BLUE_HIGH        0x1f /* blue background, high intensity */
#define REV_RED_HIGH         0x4f /* red background, high intensity  */
#define REV_BLUE_LOW         0x17 /* blue background, low intensity  */
#define REV_RED_LOW          0x47 /* red background, low intensity   */
#define REV_RED_BLACK_HIGH   0x48
#define REV_RED_BLACK_LOW    0x40
#define NOR_BLUE_HIGH        0x09 /* blue foreground, high intensity */
#define NOR_RED_HIGH         0x0c /* red foreground, high intensity  */
#define NOR_BLUE_LOW         0x01 /* blue foreground, low intensity  */
#define NOR_RED_LOW          0x04 /* red foreground, low intensity   */

#define NOR_CYAN_LOW         0x03
```

```
#define REV_CYAN_LOW        0x30

#define NOR_YEL_LOW         0x0e

#ifndef NORMAL_VIDEO
    #define NORMAL_VIDEO NOR_WHITE_HIGH
#endif

#ifndef REVERSE_VIDEO
    #define REVERSE_VIDEO REV_WHITE_HIGH
#endif


/****  windows.h  ****  external declarations for windows.c  ****/


extern window_frame wframe[];   /* frame must be supplied by    */
                                /* the application program      */


extern int make_window(int, char *, int, int, int, int);
extern void activate_window(int, char *, int, int);
extern void deactivate_window(int);
extern void window_display_header(int, char *, int);
extern void window_display_border(int, int);
extern int window_puts(int, char *);
extern int window_puts_center(int, char *);
extern int window_putchar(int, char);
extern int window_go_rc(int, int, int);
extern int window_gets_filter(int, char *, int);
extern void backspace_char(int);
extern int window_getche(int);
extern void echo_char(int, char);
extern void window_clr_rest(int);
extern void window_clr_eol(int);
extern int window_up_line(int);
extern int window_down_line(int);
extern void window_cursor_bottom(int);
extern void window_scroll(int, int);
extern int r_pos(int);
extern int c_pos(int);
extern int rightmost_col(int);
extern void window_save_screen_area(int);
extern void window_restore_screen_area(int);
```

```
/****  windowsc.h  ****  constants used by windows.c  ****/

#define TRUE                1          /* logical constants */
#define FALSE               0
#define CHECK_BKSP          1
#define CANT_ALLOCATE_WIN   -99

#define EOS                 '\0'       /* special characters */
#define RETURN              '\r'
#define LF                  '\n'
#define TAB                 '\t'
#define BKSP                '\b'
#define BLANK               ' '
#define EOF_CHAR            26
#define ESC                 27

#define VERTICAL_BAR        179     /* 186 */
#define HORIZON_BAR         196     /* 205 */
#define TOP_LEFT_CORNER     218     /* 201 */
#define BOT_LEFT_CORNER     192     /* 200 */
#define TOP_RIGHT_CORNER    191     /* 187 */
#define BOT_RIGHT_CORNER    217     /* 188 */

#ifndef REVERSE_VIDEO
    #define REVERSE_VIDEO   0x70    /* default attributes */
#endif
#ifndef NORMAL_VIDEO
    #define NORMAL_VIDEO    0x07
#endif

#define SCREEN_SIZE     4000        /* screen size @ 4000 bytes */


#define char_addr(base, r, c) ((base) + ((r) * 160) + ((c) * 2))


/*
In window_frame, a physical row coordinate is adequate for verti-
cal cursor movement.  However, in order to provide horizontal
scrolling within a window, the column position is "virtualized."
In this case, the physical column is a function of the current
offset within the window and the virtual column coordinate.
```

```
*/


typedef struct {
    int offset;      /* physical column = virtual column - offset */
    int cursor_r;    /* physical row for the cursor */
    int virtual_c;   /* virtual column for the cursor */
    int start_r, end_r;
    int start_c, end_c;
    char *window_save_buffer;
    char *header;
    int is_active;
} window_frame;


/****  display.c  ****  direct video display routines  ****/

#include "screen.h"
#include "display.h"


#define BLANK        ' '

#define char_addr(base, r, c) ((base) + ((r) * 160) + ((c) * 2))


/*
display_string() displays a string on the screen with the
specified attribute.
*/

void display_string(int row, int col, char *str, int attr)
{
    register int i;
    char far *scrn_ptr;

    scrn_ptr = get_screen_addr();
    scrn_ptr = char_addr(scrn_ptr, row, col);
    for (i = 0; str[i]; i++) {
        *scrn_ptr++ = str[i];
        *scrn_ptr++ = attr;
    }


/*
```

```
display_blanks displays a series of blanks at the
specified row and column.
*/

void display_blanks(int row, int col, int count, int attr)
{
    char far *scrn_ptr;

    scrn_ptr = get_screen_addr();
    scrn_ptr = char_addr(scrn_ptr, row, col);
    while (count-- > 0) {
        *scrn_ptr++ = BLANK;
        *scrn_ptr++ = attr;
    }
}   /* display_blanks */


/*
display_char() displays a character with the specified
attribute at a particular coordinate on the screen.
*/

void display_char(int row, int col, char ch, int attr)
{
    char far *scrn_ptr;

    scrn_ptr = get_screen_addr();
    scrn_ptr = char_addr(scrn_ptr, row, col);
    *scrn_ptr++ = ch;
    *scrn_ptr = attr;
}   /* display_char */


/****  ed.c  ****  contains primary routines for ed ****/

/*
    Programmer:      J. Smith
    Date:            1/20/89

    Copyright (c) 1989 Iris Computing Laboratories
*/

/*
ed is a simple, full-screen editor.  It provides the
```

```
following basic features:

     - cursor movement from the numeric keypad;
     - simple deletion of a character, word, line, or
       all characters to end-of-line;
     - simple undo (undelete) capabilities;
     - cut and paste;
     - find and/or change next occurrence of specified text;
     - processing of files of arbitrary size, based on a
       program constant.
*/


#include <stdio.h>
#include <dos.h>
#include <string.h>
#include <stdlib.h>

#include "edc.h"              /* constant and type declarations */
#include "editintc.h"
#include "editc.h"
#include "windowsc.h"
#include "scrnprnc.h"
#include "vidconc.h"

#include "ed.h"               /* external declaration header files */
#include "edfile.h"
#include "edhelp.h"
#include "edit.h"
#include "editwin.h"
#include "windows.h"
#include "screen.h"
#include "keyboard.h"
#include "display.h"


/*
globals:
*/

/*
wframe is a pop-up window frame array, required by windows.c.
*/
```

```
window_frame wframe[MAIN_EDIT_WIN + MIN_NUM_WINS];


/*
main() sets up a pointer variable for the incoming file specification,
performs some screen handling, initializes the windows, and invokes a
file specification routine, check_args().
*/

void main(int argc, char *argv[])
{
    char *file_spec;
    int edit_status;

    if ((file_spec = check_args(argc, argv)) == NULL)
        exit(1);
    if (!allocate_support_buffers()) {
        issue_error_messages(CANT_ALLOCATE_BUFS, DUMMY);
        exit(1);
    }
    if (!allocate_windows()) {
        issue_error_messages(CANT_ALLOCATE_BUFS, DUMMY);
        exit(1);
    }

    if (video_initialize() == MONO_MODE)
        rev_border_color = REVERSE_VIDEO;
    display_edit_info();
    edit_window_count(1);
    edit_status = edit_main(MAIN_EDIT_WIN, file_spec);
    release_edit_buffers();
    restore_exit_screen();
    if (edit_status == QUIT || edit_status == EXIT)
        exit(0);
    else {
        issue_error_messages(edit_status, file_spec);
        exit(1);
    }
}   /* main */


/*
check_args() checks to make sure that the proper number of arguments
is present.  It returns NULL for an error, or a character pointer
```

```
to the file spec if the argument list is OK.
*/

char *check_args(int arg_count, char *arg_vector[])
{
    if (arg_count != 2) {                    /* file_spec present? */
        puts("Usage: ED <file_spec>");
        return NULL;
    }
    if (!file_exists(arg_vector[1])) {      /* check its validity */
        if (write_to_disk(TEST, "", DUMMY, arg_vector[1]) ==
                CANT_WRITE) {
            puts("Couldn't create file:");
            puts(arg_vector[1]);
            return NULL;
        }
        else
            remove(arg_vector[1]);          /* just testing */
    }
    return arg_vector[1];
}   /* check_args */


/*
allocate_support_buffers() handles memory allocation for
all non-edit buffers.
*/

int allocate_support_buffers(void)
{
    return (cut_and_paste(DUMMY, DUMMY, CREATE_CLIPBOARD) &&
            undo_op(DUMMY, DUMMY, DUMMY, CREATE_UNDO));
}   /* allocate_support_buffers */


/*
allocate_windows() handles allocation of all windows.
*/

int allocate_windows(void)
{
    return (make_window(MAIN_EDIT_WIN, "", 1, 0, 23, 79) == TRUE &&
            make_window(HELP_WIN,
                "ed 1.0 - Help", 2, 1, 22, 78) == TRUE &&
```

```
            make_window(ATTN_WIN,
                "Attention", 11, 16, 13, 16 + POPUP_WIDTH) == TRUE &&
            make_window(FIND_WIN,
                "Find/Change", 3, 16, 7, 16 + POPUP_WIDTH) == TRUE);
}   /* allocate_windows */


/*
issue_error_messages() issues messages for a number of errors
that can occur during file initialization.
*/

void issue_error_messages(int edit_status, char *file_spec)
{
    switch (edit_status) {
        case NO_MATCH:
            puts("Couldn't find any files:");
            puts(file_spec);
            break;
        case CANT_WRITE:
            puts("Couldn't write file:");
            puts(file_spec);
            break;
        case CANT_ALLOCATE_BUFS:
            puts("Couldn't allocate memory for editing space.");
            break;
        case TOO_LARGE:
            puts("File is too large (64K max) OR can't be opened:");
            puts(file_spec);
            break;
        default:
            break;
    }
}   /* issue_error_messages */


/*
edit_main() maintains a pointer to the active edit buffer.  In
addition, it reports/returns error codes for a number of file
errors that can occur during editor initialization.
*/

int edit_main(int n, char *filename)
{
```

```
    char *ed_buffer;
    int edit_status;
    long file_length;

    activate_window(n, "", nor_border_color, nor_border_color);
    initialize_edit(n);
    if ((ed_buffer = create_buffer(MAX_BUF_SIZE)) != NULL) {
        file_length = read_from_disk(ed_buffer, filename);
        if (file_length == TOO_LARGE)
            edit_status = TOO_LARGE;
        else {
            if (file_length == CANT_READ) {      /* a new file */
                edit_buf_len(n, 0);
                strupr(filename);
            }
            else
                edit_buf_len(n, file_length);
            display_filename(n, filename);
            edit_status = edit_text(n, ed_buffer, filename);
            if (edit_status == EXIT)
                write_from_buffer(n, ed_buffer, DUMMY, filename);
        }
        free(ed_buffer);
    }
    else
        edit_status = CANT_ALLOCATE_BUFS;
    deactivate_window(n);
    return edit_status;
}   /* edit_main */


/*
edit_text() analyzes incoming characters and calls the
appropriate routines.
*/

int edit_text(int n, char *buffer, char *filename)
{
    union keystroke key;

    window_fill(n, 0, 0, buffer, 0);
    do {
        do {
            key.word = window_getche(n);
```

```
            if (key.byte[0])
                switch (key.byte[0]) {
                    case BKSP:
                        backspace(n, buffer);
                        break;
                    case EOF_CHAR:
                        break;
                    default:
                        insert_char(n, key.byte[0], buffer);
                        break;
                }
            else
                dispatch_extended_code(n, key.byte[1], buffer,
                                        filename);
        } while (key.byte[0] || !(key.byte[1] == QUIT ||
                                    key.byte[1] == EXIT));
    } while (key.byte[1] == QUIT && buffer_modified(n, TEST) &&
                !message_query(ATTN_WIN, "",
                                    "Abandon changed text (y/n): "));
    return key.byte[1];
}   /* edit_text */


/*
dispatch_extended_code() processes commands by calling the
appropriate routines.
*/

void dispatch_extended_code(int n, unsigned char command,
                            char *buffer, char *filename)
{
    switch (command) {      /* 8-bit command codes ==> unsigned */
        case DEL:
            del_char(n, buffer);
            break;
        case LEFT:
            cursor_left(n, buffer);
            break;
        case RIGHT:
            cursor_right(n, buffer);
            break;
        case UP:
            up(n, buffer);
            break;
```

```
        case DOWN:
            down(n, buffer);
            break;
        case CTRL_LEFT:
            word_left(n, buffer);
            break;
        case CTRL_RIGHT:
            word_right(n, buffer);
            break;
        case HOME:
            home(n, buffer);
            break;
        case END:
            endd(n, buffer);
            break;
        case PGUP:
            page_up(n, buffer);
            break;
        case PGDN:
            page_down(n, buffer);
            break;
        case CTRL_PGUP:
            top_of_buffer(n, buffer);
            break;
        case CTRL_PGDN:
            bottom_of_buffer(n, buffer);
            break;
        case CTRL_HOME:
            top_of_window(n, buffer);
            break;
        case CTRL_END:
            bottom_of_window(n, buffer);
            break;
        case TAG:
            tag_pos(n, buf_cursor_pos(n, TEST));
            break;
        case UNTAG:
            tag_pos(n, UNDEFINED);
            break;
        case TAG_CURSOR:
            exch_tag_cursor_redisplay(n, buffer);
            break;
        case DWORD:
            del_word(n, buffer);
```

```
        break;
    case DWORD_LEFT:
        del_word_left(n, buffer);
        break;
    case DEOL:
        del_eol(n, buffer);
        break;
    case DLINE:
        del_line(n, buffer);
        break;
    case CUT:
        cut_and_paste(n, buffer, CUT_CLIPBOARD);
        break;
    case COPY:
        cut_and_paste(n, buffer, COPY_CLIPBOARD);
        break;
    case PASTE:
        cut_and_paste(n, buffer, PASTE_CLIPBOARD);
        break;
    case FIND_TEXT:
        find_and_change(n, buffer, FIND_IT);
        break;
    case CHANGE_TEXT:
        find_and_change(n, buffer, CHANGE_IT);
        break;
    case REPEAT_FC:
        find_and_change(n, buffer, REPEAT_IT);
        break;
    case UNDO:
        undo_op(n, buffer, DUMMY, PASTE_UNDO);
        break;
    case HELP:
        present_help_screens(HELP_WIN);
        break;
    case INS:
        insert_mode((insert_mode(TEST)) ? RESET : SET);
        break;
    case SAVE_FILE:
        if (write_from_buffer(n, buffer, DUMMY, filename))
            buffer_modified(n, FALSE);
        break;
    case WRITE_FILE:
        write_alt_file(n, buffer, get_alt_file_spec(ATTN_WIN));
        break;
```

```
        case INSERT_FILE:
            insert_file(n, buffer, get_alt_file_spec(ATTN_WIN));
            break;
        case SET_TABS:
            tab_size(SET);
            break;
        default:
            break;
    }
}   /* dispatch_extended_code */


/*
display_edit_info() displays miscellaneous, editor-related
information on the screen.
*/

void display_edit_info(void)
{
    display_blanks(TOP_ROW, 0, 80, rev_border_color);
    display_string(BOT_ROW, 0,
" F1-Help F2-Tag F3-Cut F4-Paste F5-DW F6-DEOL F7-DL F8-Undo F9-Quit \
F10-End     ", rev_border_color);
    display_string(TOP_ROW, 71, "ed - 1.0", rev_border_color);
}   /* display_edit_info */


/*
display_filename() shows the filename along the top line, along with
the number of the current edit buffer.
*/

void display_filename(int n, char *filename)
{
    char temp_str[MIN_STR];

    display_blanks(TOP_ROW, 0, 71, rev_border_color);
    display_string(TOP_ROW, 3, "File: ", rev_border_color);
    display_string(TOP_ROW, 9, filename, rev_border_color);
    itoa(MAIN_EDIT_WIN - n + 1, temp_str, 10);
    display_char(TOP_ROW, 1, temp_str[0], rev_border_color);
}   /* display_filename */
```

```
/****  edfile.c  ****  file-related activities for ed.c  ****/

#include <stdio.h>
#include <dos.h>
#include <stdlib.h>
#include <string.h>
#include <ctype.h>
#include "editintc.h"
#include "editc.h"
#include "windowsc.h"
#include "scrnprnc.h"
#include "edc.h"
#include "ed.h"
#include "edfile.h"
#include "edit.h"
#include "screen.h"
#include "keyboard.h"
#include "windows.h"
#include "display.h"


#ifdef __TURBOC__
#include <dir.h>
#else
#include <direct.h>
#endif


/*
insert_file() manages the insertion of the contents of an alter-
native file in the edit area at the current cursor location.
insert_file() allocates a separate buffer, in order to take
advantage of the existing function, paste().
*/

void insert_file(int n, char *buffer, char *filename)
{
    char *insert_buffer;
    long read_status;    /* read_from_disk() and file_size() */
                         /* return the file length here      */

    if (*filename == EOS)
        return;
    if ((read_status = file_size(filename)) == -1) {
```

```
        message_query(ATTN_WIN, filename, "** file not found **");
        return;
    }
    if ((insert_buffer = create_buffer(read_status + 1)) != NULL) {
        if ((read_status = read_from_disk(insert_buffer, filename))
                == CANT_READ)
            message_query(ATTN_WIN, filename,
                            "** unknown error; can't read file **");
        else if (read_status == TOO_LARGE)
            message_query(ATTN_WIN,
                            filename, "** file is too large **");
        else
            if (read_status > 0)
                paste(n, buffer, insert_buffer, MAX_BUF_SIZE);
        free(insert_buffer);
    }
    else
        message_query(ATTN_WIN, "Insert", "** not enough memory **");
}   /* insert_file */


/*
write_alt_file() writes the edit buffer to the specified file.
*/

void write_alt_file(int n, char *buffer, char *filename)
{
    long len, tag;

    if (*filename == EOS)
        return;
    if (ok_to_overwrite(filename)) {
        if ((tag = tag_pos(n, TEST)) == UNDEFINED)
            write_from_buffer(n, buffer, DUMMY, filename);
        else {
            if ((len = buf_cursor_pos(n, TEST) - tag) == 0)
                message_query(ATTN_WIN, "", "** nothing to write **");
            else {
                if (len < 0) {
                    exch_tag_cursor(n);
                    len = -len;
                }
                write_from_buffer(n, &buffer[tag], len, filename);
            }
```

```
        }
    }
}   /* write_alt_file */


/*
get_alt_file_spec() prompts the user for a filename/file_spec.
*/

char *get_alt_file_spec(int n)
{
    static char file_spec[MAX_STR];

    activate_window(n,
        "Enter a Filename", rev_border_color, rev_border_color);
    window_go_rc(n, 0, 1);
    window_puts(n, "File: ");
    window_gets_filter(n, file_spec, MAX_STR);
    deactivate_window(n);
    return file_spec;
}   /* get_alt_file_spec */


/*
read_from_disk() loads a buffer from a disk file.
*/

long read_from_disk(register char *buffer, char *filename)
{
    FILE *ed_file;
    register long len;

    if ((ed_file = fopen(filename, "rt")) == NULL) {
        *buffer = EOS;
        return CANT_READ;
    }
    else {
        for (len = 0; (len < MAX_BUF_SIZE) &&
                ((buffer[len] = fgetc(ed_file)) != EOF); len++)
            ;
        if (len == MAX_BUF_SIZE) {      /* file is too large */
            fclose(ed_file);
            return TOO_LARGE;
        }
```

```
        else {                          /* OK to process it */
            buffer[len] = EOS;
            fclose(ed_file);
            return len;
        }
    }
}   /* read_from_disk */


/*
write_from_buffer() stores a buffer as a disk file. It does not
check for the existence of the file.  Another routine can be used
to perform the latter check.
*/

int write_from_buffer(int n, char *buffer, long num_chars,
                        char *filename)
{
    int write_status;

    if ((write_status = write_to_disk(n, buffer, num_chars, filename))
            == TRUE)
        return TRUE;
    else if (write_status == CANT_WRITE)
        while (message_query(ATTN_WIN, filename,
                "Can't write file; try again (y/n): ") &&
                !write_status)
            write_status = write_to_disk(n, buffer, num_chars,
                                get_alt_file_spec(ATTN_WIN));
    else {
        write_status = FALSE;
        message_query(ATTN_WIN, filename, "** write abandoned **");
    }
    return write_status;
}   /* write_from_buffer */


/*
write_to_disk() writes a buffer to disk and returns TRUE, if no
errors occur.  Since newline sequences are represented internal to
the editor by a single character, a line count is necessary to
determine the number of carriage returns that will be added.
*/
```

```
int write_to_disk(int n, register char *buffer,
                    long num_chars, char *filename)
{
    FILE *ed_file;
    register int i, write_ok = TRUE;

    if (*filename == EOS)
        return FALSE;
    if ((ed_file = fopen(filename, "wt")) == NULL)
        write_ok = CANT_WRITE;

    if (num_chars != DUMMY)
        for (i = 0; buffer[i] && write_ok == TRUE && num_chars--; i++)
            write_ok = (fputc(buffer[i], ed_file) != EOF);
    else
        for (i = 0; buffer[i] && write_ok == TRUE; i++)
            write_ok = (fputc(buffer[i], ed_file) != EOF);
    if (write_ok == TRUE)
        write_ok = (fputc(EOF_CHAR, ed_file) != EOF);
    fclose(ed_file);
    return write_ok;
}   /* write_to_disk */


/*
file_exists() determines whether or not a file exists.
*/

int file_exists(char *file_spec)
{
    if (file_size(file_spec) != -1)
        return TRUE;
    else
        return FALSE;
}   /* file_exists */


/*
file_size() determines the size of a file.  It returns -1, if
the file doesn't exist.
*/

long file_size(char *file_spec)
{
```

```
#ifdef __TURBOC__
    struct ffblk fb;

    if (findfirst(file_spec, &fb, 0) == 0)
        return fb.ff_fsize;
#else
  #ifdef __ZTC__
    struct FIND *file_ptr;

    if ((file_ptr = findfirst(file_spec, 0)) != NULL)
        return file_ptr->size;
  #else
    struct find_t fb;

    if (_dos_findfirst(file_spec, _A_NORMAL, &fb) == 0) /* MSC */
        return fb.size;
  #endif
#endif
    else
        return -1;
}   /* file_size */


/*
ok_to_overwrite() makes sure it's OK to overwrite an existing
file.
*/

int ok_to_overwrite(char *filename)
{
    if (!file_exists(filename))
        return TRUE;
    else
        return message_query(ATTN_WIN, filename,
                             "File exists; overwrite (y/n): ");
}   /* ok_to_overwrite */


/****  edhelp.c  ****  help routines for ed.c  ****/

#include <stdio.h>
#include "edc.h"
#include "windowsc.h"
#include "scrnprnc.h"
```

```
#include "ed.h"
#include "edhelp.h"
#include "edit.h"
#include "windows.h"
#include "display.h"


/*
also "included" below:  edhelp.hlp
*/


/*
globals:    extern int nor_border_color; see ed.c
            extern int rev_border_color;
            extern int rev_special_color;
*/


/*
present_help_screens() displays help information in a window.  Each
help screen is composed of two consecutive strings from the help
array (in the file edhelp.hlp).
*/

void present_help_screens(int n)
{
#include "edhelp.hlp"       /* help screens in a static array */

    union keystroke key;
    int command, half_page_no;

    activate_window(n, "", rev_border_color, rev_border_color);
    half_page_no = 2;       /* each page is split into two parts */
    command = PGUP;
    do {
        switch (command) {
            case PGUP:
                if (half_page_no > 0)
                    half_page_no -= 2;
                display_help_screen(n, help[half_page_no],
                                        help[half_page_no + 1]);
                break;
            case PGDN:
```

```
                if (half_page_no < MAX_HELP - 2)
                    half_page_no += 2;
                display_help_screen(n, help[half_page_no],
                                        help[half_page_no + 1]);
                break;
            default:
                break;
        }
        key.word = window_getche(n);
        command = key.byte[1];
    } while (!key.byte[0] &&
            (key.byte[1] == PGUP || key.byte[1] == PGDN));
    deactivate_window(n);
}   /* present_help_screens */


/*
display_help_screens() displays text for process_help_screens().
*/

void display_help_screen(int n, char *help1, char *help2)
{
    window_go_rc(n, 0, 0);
    window_clr_rest(n);
    window_puts(n, help1);
    window_puts(n, help2);
    window_cursor_bottom(n);
    window_go_rc(n, r_pos(n), 34);
    window_puts(n,
        "*** <PgUp>, <PgDn>, or any other key *** ");
}   /* display_help */


/****  edit.c  ****  routines for a window-based editor  ****/

#include <stdio.h>
#include <string.h>
#include <stdlib.h>
#include <ctype.h>
#include "editintc.h"
#include "editc.h"
#include "windowsc.h"
#include "scrnprnc.h"
#include "vidconc.h"
```

```
#include "edit.h"
#include "editwin.h"
#include "windows.h"
#include "display.h"


/*
globals:
*/

int nor_border_color = NOR_BORDER_COLOR;     /* window border colors */
int rev_border_color = REV_BORDER_COLOR;


/*
initialize_edit() establishes initial values for a number of critical
editor-status variables.  Each critical variable is maintained inside
its respective routine, as given below.
*/

void initialize_edit(int n)
{
    window_go_rc(n, 0, 0);
    edit_buf_len(n, RESET);
    buf_cursor_pos(n, RESET);
    top_left_pos(n, RESET);
    tag_pos(n, UNDEFINED);
    buffer_modified(n, FALSE);
    insert_mode(SET);
}   /* initialize_edit */


/*
release_edit_buffers() releases the data structures used
by the edit module.
*/

void release_edit_buffers()
{
    cut_and_paste(DUMMY, DUMMY, DESTROY);
    undo_op(DUMMY, DUMMY, DUMMY, DESTROY);
}   /* release_edit_buffers */
```

```
/*
buffer_modified() records whether or not the buffer has been modified,
and displays an indicator of this condition on screen, each time that
it changes.
*/

int buffer_modified(int n, int change_state)
{
    static int modified[MAIN_EDIT_WIN + 1];

    if (change_state != TEST) {
        modified[n] = change_state;
        if (modified[n])
            tag_pos(n, UNDEFINED);
        display_char(BOT_ROW, MODIFIED_COLUMN,
                (modified[n] ? 'M' : BLANK), rev_border_color);
    }
    return modified[n];
}   /* buffer_modified */


/*
insert_mode() toggles insert/overwrite mode and displays
an indicator of the current state.
*/

int insert_mode(int change_state)
{
    static int insert_state;

    if (change_state == TEST)
        return insert_state;
    else {
        insert_state = change_state;
        display_char(BOT_ROW, INSERT_MODE_COLUMN,
                (insert_state ? 'I' : 'O'), rev_border_color);
        return insert_state;
    }
}   /* insert_mode */


/*
tab_size manages changes to the tab size.
*/
```

```
int tab_size(int operation)
{
    static int tab_width = TAB_SIZE;
    int new_size;
    char temp_str[MIN_STR];

    if (operation != TEST) {
        activate_window(ATTN_WIN,
                    "change takes effect with next screen update",
                    rev_border_color, rev_border_color);
        window_go_rc(ATTN_WIN, 0, 1);
        window_puts_center(ATTN_WIN, "Enter tab size: ");
        if (!window_gets_filter(ATTN_WIN, temp_str, MIN_STR))
            *temp_str = EOS;
        deactivate_window(ATTN_WIN);
        if ((new_size = atoi(temp_str)) > 0)
            tab_width = new_size;
    }
    return tab_width;
}   /* tab_size */


/*
edit_window_count() keeps track of how many edit windows have
been opened.
*/

int edit_window_count(int count)
{
    static int num_edit_windows;

    if (count == TEST)
        return num_edit_windows;
    else if (count == INCR)
        return ++num_edit_windows;
    else if (count == DECR)
        return --num_edit_windows;
    else
        return num_edit_windows = count;
}   /* edit_window_count */


/*
```

```
edit_buf_len() is used to maintain the current edit buffer length,
avoiding unnecessary calls to the built-in function strlen(), which
can be very slow for large files.  WARNING--no error checking.
*/

long edit_buf_len(int n, long new_length)
{
    static long edit_length[MAIN_EDIT_WIN + 1];

    if (new_length == TEST)
        return edit_length[n];
    else if (new_length == INCR)
        return ++edit_length[n];
    else if (new_length == DECR)
        return --edit_length[n];
    else
        return edit_length[n] = new_length;
}   /* edit_buf_len */


/*
buf_cursor_pos() records the current edit buffer position.
WARNING--no error checking.
*/

long buf_cursor_pos(int n, long new_position)
{
    static long cursor_position[MAIN_EDIT_WIN + 1];

    if (new_position == TEST)
        return cursor_position[n];
    else if (new_position == INCR)
        return ++cursor_position[n];
    else if (new_position == DECR)
        return --cursor_position[n];
    else
        return cursor_position[n] = new_position;
}   /* buf_cursor_pos */


/*
top_left_pos() records the current position in the edit buffer of
the character displayed in the top-left position of the screen.
WARNING--no error checking.
```

```
*/

long top_left_pos(int n, long new_position)
{
    static long top_position[MAIN_EDIT_WIN + 1];

    if (new_position != TEST)
        top_position[n] = new_position;
    return top_position[n];
}   /* top_left_pos */


/*
tag_pos records the buffer position, and column on the screen,
of the current buffer tag.  WARNING--no error checking.
*/

long tag_pos(int n, long info)
{
    static long tag_position[MAIN_EDIT_WIN + 1];

    if (info != TEST)
        tag_position[n] = info;
    return tag_position[n];
}   /* tag_pos */


/*
create_buffer() allocates storage for a buffer from the heap.
*/

char *create_buffer(long buffer_size)
{
    return (char *) malloc(buffer_size);
}   /* create_buffer */


/*
ispunc determines if a character qualifies as a punctuation
character, according to the string constant PUNCTUATION.
ispunc() is called by, for example, del_word().
*/

int ispunc(char ch)
```

```
{
    return (strchr(PUNCTUATION, ch) != NULL) ? TRUE : FALSE;
}   /* ispunc */


/*
message_query() issues a message and queries the user.
*/

int message_query(int n, char *header, char *message)
{
    char ch;

    activate_window(n, header, rev_border_color, rev_border_color);
    window_go_rc(n, 0, 1);
    window_puts_center(n, message);
    ch = window_getche(n);
    deactivate_window(n);
    return (toupper(ch) == 'Y') ? TRUE : FALSE;
}   /* message_query */


/*
insert_char() inserts characters into the buffer and updates
the screen as necessary.  It must take into consideration the
fact that window_getche() has already updated the current
screen coordinates--for displayable characters.
*/

int insert_char(int n, char ch, char *buffer)
{
    int tab_overwrite;
    long insert_point;

    if (insertion_special_conditions(n, ch, buffer))
        return FALSE;
    else {
        buffer_modified(n, TRUE);
        if (ch == CR)
            ch = LF;
        insert_point = buf_cursor_pos(n, TEST);
        if (insert_mode(TEST) || buffer[insert_point] == LF) {
            memmove(&buffer[insert_point + 1], &buffer[insert_point],
                        edit_buf_len(n, TEST) - insert_point + 1);
```

```
            edit_buf_len(n, INCR);
            undo_op(n, buffer, 1, UPDATE_UNDO_OFFSET);
        }
        else
            if (buffer[insert_point] == EOS) {  /* in overwrite mode */
                buffer[insert_point + 1] = EOS; /* don't destroy EOS */
                edit_buf_len(n, INCR);
            }
        tab_overwrite =
            !insert_mode(TEST) && buffer[insert_point] == TAB;
        buffer[insert_point] = ch;
        if (!insert_mode(TEST) && !tab_overwrite &&
                !adjacent_to_rightmost_column(n)) /* simple over- */
            buf_cursor_pos(n, INCR);    /* write, so just increment */
        else
            insert_window_update(n, buffer, ch, insert_point);
        return TRUE;
    }
}   /* insert_char */


/*
insertion_special_conditions() handles a number of special condi-
tions that can occur relative to insertion of characters.
*/

int insertion_special_conditions(int n, char ch, char *buffer)
{
    if (edit_buf_len(n, TEST) + 1 >= MAX_BUF_SIZE) {
        if (ch != CR)
            window_go_rc(n, r_pos(n), c_pos(n) - 1);
        redisplay_rest_of_line(n, buffer, 1);
        message_query(ATTN_WIN, "", "** edit space is full **");
        return TRUE;
    }
    else if (!insert_mode(TEST) && ch == CR) {
        down(n, buffer);
        home(n, buffer);
        return TRUE;                        /* do "local" CR only */
    }
    else if (!insert_mode(TEST) && ch == TAB) {
        advance_cursor_to_next_tab(n, buffer);
        return TRUE;                        /* do "local" TAB only */
    }
```

```
    else
        return FALSE;
}   /* insertion_special_conditions */


/*
advance_cursor_to_next_tab() moves the cursor to the next tab stop.
*/

void advance_cursor_to_next_tab(int n, char *buffer)
{
    int tab_stop;
    long i;

    for (i = buf_cursor_pos(n, TEST), tab_stop = next_tab_column(n);
            buffer[i] && buffer[i] != LF && c_pos(n) < tab_stop; i++)
        cursor_right(n, buffer);
}   /* advance_cursor_to_next_tab */


/*
insert_window_update() performs the screen-related updates for
the edit window subsequent to character insertion.  Also, it
increments the buffer position.
*/

void insert_window_update(int n, char *buffer, char ch,
                            long insert_point)
{
    int cur_c;

    if (ch == LF) {
        window_clr_eol(n);
        window_restore_shift(n, buffer);
        if (window_down_line(n)) {
            buf_cursor_pos(n, INCR);
            window_fill(n, r_pos(n), 0, buffer, insert_point + 1);
        }
        else
            window_scroll_up(n, buffer, 0);
    }
    else {
        cur_c = c_pos(n);
        if (ch != TAB)              /* must back up--window_getche()*/
```

```
            window_go_rc(n, r_pos(n), --cur_c); /* incr'd. position */
        if (adjacent_to_rightmost_column(n)) {
            window_shift_right(n, buffer, tab_size(TEST) * 2);
            window_go_rc(n, r_pos(n), cur_c);
        }
        else
            redisplay_rest_of_line(n, buffer, 0);
        window_buffer_forward(n, buffer);
    }
}   /* insert window update */


/*
del_char() deletes a character from the buffer
and updates the screen.
*/

int del_char(int n, char *buffer)
{
    char ch;
    long cur_pos;

    if ((cur_pos = buf_cursor_pos(n, TEST)) == edit_buf_len(n, TEST))
        return FALSE;
    else {
        buffer_modified(n, TRUE);
        undo_op(n, buffer, -1, UPDATE_UNDO_OFFSET);
        ch = buffer[cur_pos];
        memmove(&buffer[cur_pos], &buffer[cur_pos + 1],
                    edit_buf_len(n, TEST) - cur_pos);
        edit_buf_len(n, DECR);
        if (ch != LF)
            redisplay_rest_of_line(n, buffer, tab_size(TEST));
        else
            if (window_offset(n, TEST) == 0)
                window_fill(n, r_pos(n), c_pos(n), buffer, cur_pos);
            else
                window_shift_right(n, buffer, 0);
        return TRUE;
    }
}   /* del_char */


/*
```

```
del_word() deletes a "word," or string of characters.  Leading
blanks are also deleted.  Punctuation characters serve as
word delimiters also.  del_word() determines the location of
the to-be-deleted characters and calls undo_op() to perform
the deletion.  Deletions performed by undo_op() can be undone.
*/

int del_word(int n, char *buffer)
{
    long last;      /* the last/final character to be deleted */

    if ((last = buf_cursor_pos(n, TEST)) == edit_buf_len(n, TEST))
        return FALSE;
    else {
        if (buffer[last] == LF)
            last++;
        else if (buffer[last] == BLANK || buffer[last] == TAB)
            while (buffer[last] == BLANK || buffer[last] == TAB)
                last++;
        else {
            if (ispunc(buffer[last]))
                last++;
            while (buffer[last] && !isspace(buffer[last]) &&
                    !ispunc(buffer[last]))
                last++;
            if (buffer[last] == BLANK)
                last++;
        }
        return undo_op(n, buffer, last, CUT_UNDO);
    }
}   /* del_word */


/*
del_word_left() deletes the word to the left of the cursor.
*/

int del_word_left(int n, char *buffer)
{
    if (word_left(n, buffer))
        return del_word(n, buffer);
    else
        return FALSE;
}   /* del_word_left */
```

```
/*
del_eol() deletes all characters between the cursor and the end of the
line by first determining the respective buffer offsets, and then
calling undo_op().  As with del_word(), this operation can be undone.
*/

int del_eol(int n, char *buffer)
{
    long last;      /* the last/final character to be deleted */

    if (buffer[last = buf_cursor_pos(n, TEST)] == LF ||
            buffer[last] == EOS) {
        message_query(ATTN_WIN, "",
            "** already at end of line **");
        return FALSE;
    }
    else {
        while (buffer[last] && buffer[last] != LF)
            last++;
        return undo_op(n, buffer, last, CUT_UNDO);
    }
}   /* del_eol */


/*
del_line() deletes an entire line using undo_op(); hence, this
operation can be undone.
*/

int del_line(int n, char *buffer)
{
    long last;      /* the last/final character to be deleted */

    go_line_start(n, buffer);
    window_restore_shift(n, buffer);
    window_go_rc(n, r_pos(n), 0);
    last = buf_cursor_pos(n, TEST);
    while (buffer[last] && buffer[last] != LF)
        last++;
    if (buffer[last])       /* don't delete EOS character */
        last++;
    return undo_op(n, buffer, last, CUT_UNDO);
```

```
}    /* del_line */


/*
backspace() moves the cursor to the left one column
and then deletes that character.
*/

int backspace(int n, char *buffer)
{
    if (cursor_left(n, buffer))
        return del_char(n, buffer);
    else
        return FALSE;
}    /* backspace */


/*
up() moves the cursor up one line.  If possible, the previous
cursor column position is retained.  Scrolling may be required.
*/

int up(int n, char *buffer)
{
    if (!window_up_line(n))
        return window_scroll_down(n, buffer, c_pos(n));
    else
        return buffer_up_line(n, buffer, c_pos(n));
}    /* up */


/*
down() moves the cursor down one line.  If possible, the previous
cursor column position is retained.  Scrolling may be required.
*/

int down(int n, char *buffer)
{
    if (last_char_on_line(n, buffer) == EOS)
        return FALSE;
    else
        if (!window_down_line(n))
            return window_scroll_up(n, buffer, c_pos(n));
        else
```

```
            return buffer_down_line(n, buffer, c_pos(n));
}   /* down */


/*
cursor_left() moves left one column.  If necessary, the cursor wraps
around to the end of the previous line--at the top of the screen
this operation requires scrolling.
*/

int cursor_left(int n, char *buffer)
{
    int cur_c;

    if (buf_cursor_pos(n, TEST) == 0)
        return FALSE;
    else {
        if (adjacent_to_leftmost_column(n, buffer))
            if ((cur_c = c_pos(n)) > 0) {
                home(n, buffer);
                window_adjust_cursor_position(n, buffer, cur_c - 1);
            }
            else {
                up(n, buffer);
                if (!go_right_as_far_as_possible(n, buffer))
                    endd(n, buffer);
            }
        else
            window_buffer_backward(n, buffer);
        return TRUE;
    }
}   /* cursor_left */


/*
cursor_right() advances one column.  If necessary, the cursor wraps
around to the next line--at the bottom of the screen this operation
requires scrolling.
*/

int cursor_right(int n, char *buffer)
{
    int cur_c;
    long pos;
```

```
    if ((pos = buf_cursor_pos(n, TEST)) == edit_buf_len(n, TEST))
        return FALSE;
    else if (buffer[pos] != LF && adjacent_to_rightmost_column(n)) {
        cur_c = c_pos(n);
        window_shift_right(n, buffer, tab_size(TEST) * 2);
        window_go_rc(n, r_pos(n), cur_c);
        window_buffer_forward(n, buffer);
        return TRUE;
    }
    else {
        if (buffer[pos] == LF) {
            window_restore_shift(n, buffer);
            if (window_down_line(n))
                window_go_rc(n, r_pos(n), 0);
            else
                window_scroll_up(n, buffer, 0);
            buf_cursor_pos(n, INCR);
        }
        else
            window_buffer_forward(n, buffer);
        return TRUE;
    }
}   /* cursor_right */


/*
word_left() moves the cursor left to the beginning of the previous
"word," that is, to the beginning of the previous "run" of characters.
Punctuation characters serve as word delimiters also.
*/

int word_left(int n, char *buffer)
{
    long i;

    if ((i = buf_cursor_pos(n, TEST)) == 0)
        return FALSE;
    else {
        if (isspace(buffer[i - 1]) || ispunc(buffer[i - 1])) {
            cursor_left(n, buffer);
            i = buf_cursor_pos(n, TEST);
        }
        for ( ; isspace(buffer[i]); i--)
```

```
            cursor_left(n, buffer);
        for (i = buf_cursor_pos(n, TEST);
                i > 0 && !isspace(buffer[i - 1]) &&
                !ispunc(buffer[i - 1]);
                i--)
            cursor_left(n, buffer);
        if (ispunc(buffer[i - 1]))
            cursor_left(n, buffer);
        return TRUE;
    }
}   /* word_left */


/*
word_right() advances the cursor to the beginning of the next
"word," that is, to the beginning of the next "run" of characters.
Punctuation characters serve as word delimiters also.
*/

int word_right(int n, char *buffer)
{
    long i;

    for (i = buf_cursor_pos(n, TEST);
            buffer[i] && !isspace(buffer[i]) &&
            !ispunc(buffer[i]); i++)
        cursor_right(n, buffer);
    for (i = buf_cursor_pos(n, TEST);
            buffer[i] && (isspace(buffer[i])); i++)
        cursor_right(n, buffer);
    if (ispunc(buffer[i++])) {
        cursor_right(n, buffer);
        for ( ; buffer[i] && isspace(buffer[i]); i++)
            cursor_right(n, buffer);
    }
    return TRUE;
}   /* word_right */


/*
home() moves the cursor:
    to the beginning of the current line,
    to the leftmost position in the window, or
    up one line,
```

```
depending on the cursor's current position.  It must accommodate
tabs and "null" columns at the leftmost window position.
*/

int home(int n, char *buffer)
{
    if (c_pos(n) == 0) {
        up(n, buffer);
        return FALSE;
    }
    else if (adjacent_to_leftmost_column(n, buffer)) {
        go_line_start(n, buffer);
        window_restore_shift(n, buffer);
        return TRUE;
    }
    else {
        go_line_start(n, buffer);
        window_adjust_cursor_position(n, buffer,
                                       window_offset(n, TEST));
        return TRUE;
    }
}   /* home */


/*
endd() moves the cursor:
    to the end of the current line,
    to the rightmost position in the window, or
    down one line, plus another endd() operation,
depending on the cursor's current position.  It must accommodate
tabs and "null" columns at the rightmost window position.
*/

int endd(int n, char *buffer)
{
    if (buffer[buf_cursor_pos(n, TEST)] == LF)
        down(n, buffer);
    else if (adjacent_to_rightmost_column(n))
        window_shift_right(n, buffer,
                window_line_length(n, buffer) - c_pos(n) - 1);
    else
        ;   /* cursor is within the window */
    return go_right_as_far_as_possible(n, buffer);
}   /* endd */
```

```
/*
page_up() moves up one page.  The cursor is
positioned in the middle of the screen (vertically).
*/

int page_up(int n, char *buffer)
{
    if (buf_cursor_pos(n, TEST) == 0)
        return FALSE;
    else {
        move_backward_x_lines(n, buffer, PAGE);
        redisplay_window(n, buffer, c_pos(n));
        return TRUE;
    }
}   /* page_up */


/*
page_down() moves down one page.  The cursor is
positioned in the middle of the screen (vertically).
*/

int page_down(int n, char *buffer)
{
    if (buf_cursor_pos(n, TEST) == edit_buf_len(n, TEST))
        return FALSE;
    else {
        move_forward_x_lines(n, buffer, PAGE);
        redisplay_window(n, buffer, c_pos(n));
        return TRUE;
    }
}   /* page_down */


/*
top_of_buffer() moves the cursor to the beginning
of the file/buffer.
*/

int top_of_buffer(int n, char *buffer)
{
    if (buf_cursor_pos(n, TEST) == 0)
```

```
        return FALSE;
    else {
        buf_cursor_pos(n, RESET);
        top_left_pos(n, RESET);
        window_offset(n, RESET);
        window_fill(n, 0, 0, buffer, 0);
        return TRUE;
    }
}   /* top_of_buffer */


/*
bottom_of_buffer() moves the cursor to the last displayable
character of the last line in the file/buffer.
*/

int bottom_of_buffer(int n, char *buffer)
{
    if (buf_cursor_pos(n, TEST) == edit_buf_len(n, TEST))
        return FALSE;
    else {
        buf_cursor_pos(n, edit_buf_len(n, TEST));
        redisplay_window(n, buffer,
                            window_line_length(n, buffer) - 1);
        return TRUE;
    }
}   /* bottom_of_buffer */


/*
top_of_window() moves the cursor to the top-left position
of the window.
*/

int top_of_window(int n, char *buffer)
{
    if (buf_cursor_pos(n, TEST) == 0)
        return FALSE;
    else {
        buf_cursor_pos(n, top_left_pos(n, TEST));
        window_go_rc(n, 0, 0);
        window_restore_shift(n, buffer);
        return TRUE;
    }
```

```
}   /* top_of_window */


/*
bottom_of_window() moves the cursor to the bottom-left
position of the window.
*/

int bottom_of_window(int n, char *buffer)
{
    int cur_r, lines_moved;

    cur_r = r_pos(n);
    window_cursor_bottom(n);
    lines_moved = move_forward_x_lines(n, buffer, r_pos(n) - cur_r);
    window_restore_shift(n, buffer);
    window_go_rc(n, cur_r + lines_moved, 0);
    return TRUE;
}   /* bottom_of_window */


/*
cut_and_paste() manages cut and paste operations.  The clipboard
is maintained internal to this function.  Clipboard operations are
performed by calling cut_and_paste() with the proper "operation"
argument.
*/

int cut_and_paste(int n, char *buffer, int operation)
{
    static char *clipboard;

    if (operation == CUT_CLIPBOARD || operation == COPY_CLIPBOARD)
        return cut_or_copy(n, buffer, clipboard, operation);
    else if (operation == PASTE_CLIPBOARD)
        return paste(n, buffer, clipboard, MAX_BUF_SIZE);
    else if (operation == CREATE_CLIPBOARD) {
        clipboard = create_buffer(MAX_CLIP_SIZE);
        *clipboard = EOS;
        return (clipboard != NULL) ? TRUE : FALSE;
    }
    else if (operation == DESTROY) {
        free(clipboard);
        return TRUE;
```

```
    }
    else
        return FALSE;
}   /* cut_and_paste */


/*
cut_or_copy() performs clipboard cut operations for cut_and_paste().
All text between the cursor and the tag is cut--the tag does NOT
have to precede the cursor in the buffer.  Alternatively, if a
"copy" operation is requested, the tagged text is copied to the
clipboard, but not cut from the edit buffer.
*/

int cut_or_copy(int n, char *buffer, char *clipboard, int operation)
{
    int tag_column;
    long clip_length, cursor, tag;

    cursor = buf_cursor_pos(n, TEST);
    if ((tag = tag_pos(n, TEST)) == UNDEFINED || tag == cursor) {
        *clipboard = EOS;
        message_query(ATTN_WIN, "", "** nothing to cut/copy **");
        return FALSE;
    }
    else {
        if (tag > cursor) {                             /* swap 'em */
            exch_tag_cursor(n);
            tag = tag_pos(n, TEST);
            cursor = buf_cursor_pos(n, TEST);
        }
        if ((clip_length = cursor - tag) >= MAX_CLIP_SIZE) {
            message_query(ATTN_WIN, "",
                    "** too large for clipboard **");
            return FALSE;
        }
        else {
            tag_column = get_tag_column(n, buffer);
            tag_pos(n, UNDEFINED);
            memcpy(clipboard, &buffer[tag], clip_length);
            clipboard[clip_length] = EOS;
            if (operation == COPY_CLIPBOARD) /* just a simple copy  */
                return TRUE;                 /* operation--finished */
```

```
            buffer_modified(n, TRUE);
            undo_op(n, buffer, -clip_length, UPDATE_UNDO_OFF_CUT);
            memmove(&buffer[tag], &buffer[cursor],
                    edit_buf_len(n, TEST) - cursor + 1);
            edit_buf_len(n, edit_buf_len(n, TEST) - clip_length);
            buf_cursor_pos(n, tag);
            if (linefeed_free(clipboard, clip_length)) {
                window_go_rc(n, r_pos(n), tag_column);
                redisplay_rest_of_line(n, buffer, UNDEFINED);
            }
            else
                redisplay_window(n, buffer,
                          current_column_offset(n, buffer));
            return TRUE;
        }   /* end else not-too-large */
    }   /* end tag defined */
}   /* cut_or_copy */


/*
paste() inserts the contents of a generic buffer at the
current cursor position in the edit buffer.  It is used
by both cut_and_paste() and undo_op().
*/

int paste(int n, char *buffer, char *from_buffer, long max_area)
{
    long cursor, from_length;

    cursor = buf_cursor_pos(n, TEST);
    from_length = strlen(from_buffer);
    if (from_length > 0 &&
            from_length <= max_area - edit_buf_len(n, TEST) - 1) {
        buffer_modified(n, TRUE);
        undo_op(n, buffer, from_length, UPDATE_UNDO_OFFSET);
        memmove(&buffer[cursor + from_length], &buffer[cursor],
                    edit_buf_len(n, TEST) - cursor + 1);
        edit_buf_len(n, edit_buf_len(n, TEST) + from_length);
        memcpy(&buffer[cursor], from_buffer, from_length);
        if (linefeed_free(from_buffer, from_length))
            redisplay_rest_of_line(n, buffer, 0);
        else
            if (window_offset(n, TEST) == 0)
                window_fill(n, r_pos(n), c_pos(n), buffer, cursor);
```

```
            else
                window_shift_right(n, buffer, 0);
        return TRUE;
    }
    else {
        if (from_length == 0)
            message_query(ATTN_WIN, "",
                    "** clipboard is empty **");
        else
            message_query(ATTN_WIN, "",
                    "** not enough space to paste/insert **");
        return FALSE;
    }
}   /* paste */


/*
undo_op() manages a small, internal "clipboard" that is used for
del_word(), del_eol(), and del_line() operations.
*/

int undo_op(int n, char *buffer, long value, int operation)
{
    static char *un_buffer;
    static long cursor_when_cut = UNDEFINED;

    if (operation == CUT_UNDO) {
        cursor_when_cut = buf_cursor_pos(n, TEST);
        return cut_to_undo(n, buffer, un_buffer, value);
    }
    else if (operation == PASTE_UNDO) {
        return paste_from_undo(n, buffer, un_buffer, cursor_when_cut);
    }
    else if (operation == CREATE_UNDO) {
        un_buffer = create_buffer(MAX_UNDO_SIZE);
        *un_buffer = EOS;
        return (un_buffer != NULL) ? TRUE : FALSE;
    }
    else if (operation == CANCEL_UNDO) {
        cursor_when_cut = UNDEFINED;
        *un_buffer = EOS;
    }
    else if (operation == UPDATE_UNDO_OFFSET) {
        return update_undo_offset(n, un_buffer,
```

```
                            &cursor_when_cut, value);
    }
    else if (operation == UPDATE_UNDO_OFF_CUT) {
        return update_undo_offset_for_cut(n, un_buffer,
                            &cursor_when_cut, value);
    }
    else if (operation == DESTROY) {
        free(un_buffer);
        return TRUE;
    }
    else
        return FALSE;
}   /* undo_op */


/*
paste_from_undo() handles the process of repositioning the
cursor and performing the undo uperation.
*/

int paste_from_undo(int n, char *buffer, char *un_buffer,
                        long cursor_when_cut)
{
    if (strlen(un_buffer) > 0) {
        if (buf_cursor_pos(n, TEST) != cursor_when_cut) {
            buf_cursor_pos(n, cursor_when_cut);
            redisplay_window(n, buffer,
                        current_column_offset(n, buffer));
        }
        return paste(n, buffer, un_buffer, MAX_BUF_SIZE);
    }
    else {
        message_query(ATTN_WIN, "", "** nothing to undo **");
        return FALSE;
    }
}   /* paste_from_undo */


/*
cut_to_undo() performs "clipboard" cut operations for undo_op().  All
text between start and end is clipped.
*/

int cut_to_undo(int n, char *buffer, char *un_buffer, long end)
```

```
{
    long clip_length, start;

    start = buf_cursor_pos(n, TEST);
    clip_length = end - start;
    if (clip_length <= 0) {
        message_query(ATTN_WIN, "", "** nothing to delete **");
        return FALSE;
    }
    else if (clip_length >= MAX_UNDO_SIZE) {
        message_query(ATTN_WIN, "", "** too large to delete **");
        return FALSE;
    }
    else {
        buffer_modified(n, TRUE);
        memcpy(un_buffer, &buffer[start], clip_length);
        un_buffer[clip_length] = EOS;
        memmove(&buffer[start], &buffer[end],
                edit_buf_len(n, TEST) - end + 1);
        edit_buf_len(n, edit_buf_len(n, TEST) - clip_length);
        if (linefeed_free(un_buffer, clip_length))
            redisplay_rest_of_line(n, buffer, UNDEFINED);
        else
            if (window_offset(n, TEST) == 0)
                window_fill(n, r_pos(n), c_pos(n), buffer, start);
            else
                window_shift_right(n, buffer, 0);
        return TRUE;
    }
} /* cut_to_undo */


/*
update_undo_offset() modifies the buffer offset for
the undo marker.  If a buffer modification is made at an
offset less than the undo marker, the undo marker must be
updated accordingly.
*/

int update_undo_offset(int n, char *un_buffer,
                       long *cursor_when_cut, long adjustment)
{
    if (buf_cursor_pos(n, TEST) <= *cursor_when_cut) {
        if (adjustment < 0 &&
```

```
                (buf_cursor_pos(n, TEST) + -adjustment >
                    *cursor_when_cut)) {     /* text spans undo marker*/
            un_buffer[0] = EOS;
            *cursor_when_cut = UNDEFINED;
        }
        else
            *cursor_when_cut += adjustment;
        return TRUE;
    }
    else
        return FALSE;
}   /* update_undo_offset */


/*
update_undo_offset_for_cut() modifies the buffer offset
for the undo marker.  If a cut operation is made at an
offset less than the undo marker, the undo marker must
be updated accordingly.
*/

int update_undo_offset_for_cut(int n, char *un_buffer,
                    long *cursor_when_cut, long adjustment)
{
    if (tag_pos(n, TEST) <= *cursor_when_cut) {
        if (tag_pos(n, TEST) + -adjustment > *cursor_when_cut) {
            un_buffer[0] = EOS;
            *cursor_when_cut = UNDEFINED;
        }
        else
            *cursor_when_cut += adjustment;
        return TRUE;
    }
    else
        return FALSE;
}   /* update_undo_offset_for_cut */


/*
exch_tag_and_cursor_redisplay() swaps the tag and the cursor in
the buffer and then redisplays the edit buffer.
*/

void exch_tag_cursor_redisplay(int n, char *buffer)
```

```
{
    long cur_c;

    if (tag_pos(n, TEST) == UNDEFINED)
        message_query(ATTN_WIN, "", "** no tag has been set **");
    else {
        cur_c = get_tag_column(n, buffer);
        exch_tag_cursor(n);
        redisplay_window(n, buffer, cur_c);
    }
}   /* exch_tag_cursor_redisplay */


/*
exch_tag_cursor() is a generic routine that physically swaps the tag
and the cursor without updating the display.  See, for example,
cut_or_copy() and exch_tag_cursor_redisplay().
*/

long exch_tag_cursor(int n)
{
    long tag;

    if ((tag = tag_pos(n, TEST)) != UNDEFINED) {
        tag_pos(n, buf_cursor_pos(n, TEST));
        return buf_cursor_pos(n, tag);
    }
    else
        return UNDEFINED;
} /* exch_tag_cursor */


/*
get_tag_column() computes the window offset (on-screen
column) for the tag.
*/

int get_tag_column(int n, char *buffer)
{
    int column;

    long old_cursor_offset = buf_cursor_pos(n, TEST);
    buf_cursor_pos(n, tag_pos(n, TEST));
    column = current_column_offset(n, buffer);
```

```
    buf_cursor_pos(n, old_cursor_offset);
    return column;
}   /* get_tag_column */


/*
find_and_change manages simple text find (search) and change
(replace) operations.  Previous find-and-change activity is
recorded within find_and_change() to allow the user to repeat
the command.
*/

int find_and_change(int n, char *buffer, int operation)
{
    static char find_text[MAX_STR] = "";
    static char change_text[MAX_STR] = "";
    static int last_operation = FALSE;
    long offset;

    if (operation == REPEAT_IT && !last_operation)
        return FALSE;                       /* nothing to repeat */

    if (operation != REPEAT_IT)
        if (!prompt_for_pattern(FIND_WIN, last_operation = operation,
                                find_text, change_text)) {
            deactivate_window(FIND_WIN);
            return FALSE;                   /* user pressed <Esc> */
        }
    offset = (operation == REPEAT_IT) ? 1 : 0;/* don't find it again */
    if ((offset = string_search(buffer, find_text,
            buf_cursor_pos(n, TEST) + offset)) == -1) {
        display_not_found(FIND_WIN, operation, find_text);
        return FALSE;
    }
    else {
        deactivate_window(FIND_WIN);
        buf_cursor_pos(n, offset);
        redisplay_window(n, buffer, current_column_offset(n, buffer));
        if (operation == CHANGE_IT || last_operation == CHANGE_IT)
            replace_text(n, buffer, offset, find_text, change_text);
        return TRUE;
    }
}   /* find_and_change */
```

```
/*
prompt_for_pattern() prompts the user for the search pattern, and
optionally, a replacement pattern.  It activates, but does not
deactivate, the "find" window.  It returns FALSE, if <Esc> was
pressed.
*/

int prompt_for_pattern(int n, int operation, char *find_text,
                            char *change_text)
{
    char find_txt[MAX_STR], change_txt[MAX_STR];

    activate_window(n, "", rev_border_color, rev_border_color);
    window_puts(n, " Find: ");
    if (!window_gets_filter(n, find_txt, MAX_STR))
        return FALSE;
    if (operation == CHANGE_IT) {
        window_go_rc(n, 1, 0);
        window_puts(n, " Change to: ");
        if (!window_gets_filter(n, change_txt, MAX_STR))
            return FALSE;
        strcpy(change_text, change_txt);
    }
    strcpy(find_text, find_txt);
    return TRUE;
}   /* prompt_for_pattern */


/*
display_not_found() displays a "pattern not found" message for the
user, and then deactivates the "find" window.
*/

void display_not_found(int n, int operation, char *find_text)
{
    if (operation == REPEAT_IT) {
        activate_window(n, "", rev_border_color, rev_border_color);
        window_puts(n, " Find: ");
        window_puts(n, find_text);
    }
    window_cursor_bottom(n);
    window_puts(n, " Pattern not found -- press any key...");
    window_getche(n);
```

```
    deactivate_window(n);
}   /* display_not_found */


/*
string_search() searches search_string for the first occurrence of
search_text.  If search_text is null, it returns -1, instead of
entering the search loop; otherwise, it returns the buffer offset
where search_text begins.
*/

long string_search(char *search_ptr, char *search_text,
                    register long offset)
{
    register int next;
    register long begin_match_offset = offset;

    if (*search_text)
        for (next = 0; search_ptr[offset]; offset++)
            if (search_ptr[offset] == search_text[next]) {
                begin_match_offset = offset;
                while (search_text[next] &&
                        search_ptr[offset++] == search_text[next++])
                    ;
                if (!search_text[next] &&
                        search_ptr[--offset] == search_text[--next])
                    return begin_match_offset;
                offset = begin_match_offset;
                next = 0;
            }
    return -1;
}   /* string_search */


/*
replace_text() performs the replacement of text
for the find-and-change operation.
*/

void replace_text(int n, char *buffer, long offset,
                    char *find_text, char *change_text)
{
    int find_length = strlen(find_text);
    char cut_to_buffer[MAX_STR];
```

```
    cut_to_undo(n, buffer, cut_to_buffer,
                offset + find_length);
    cut_to_buffer[find_length] = EOS;
    undo_op(n, buffer, DUMMY, CANCEL_UNDO);
    if (!paste(n, buffer, change_text, MAX_BUF_SIZE)) {
        paste(n, buffer, cut_to_buffer, MAX_BUF_SIZE);
        message_query(ATTN_WIN, "", "** not enough edit space **");
    }
}   /* replace_text */


/*
redisplay_window() redisplays the edit buffer in the edit window
with the cursor positioned (vertically) in the middle of the window.
*/

int redisplay_window(int n, char *buffer, int current_c)
{
    int lines_moved;
    long old_buf_pos;

    old_buf_pos = go_line_start(n, buffer);
    lines_moved = move_backward_x_lines(n, buffer, HALF_PAGE);
    top_left_pos(n, buf_cursor_pos(n, TEST));
    buf_cursor_pos(n, old_buf_pos);
    window_go_rc(n, lines_moved, DUMMY);
    if (!window_adjust_cursor_position(n, buffer, current_c))
        window_shift_right(n, buffer, 0);
    return lines_moved;
}   /* redisplay_window */


/*
redisplay_rest_of_line() redisplays the remainder of the line,
beginning at the current cursor position.  Based on the second
argument, it clears the remaining part of the line previously
occupied by text.
*/

void redisplay_rest_of_line(int n, char *buffer, int num_blanks)
{
    register long i;
    register int cur_c, last_c, next_c;
```

```
    if ((cur_c = c_pos(n)) < window_offset(n, TEST)) {
        window_restore_shift(n, buffer);
        window_go_rc(n, r_pos(n), cur_c);
    }
    for (i = buf_cursor_pos(n, TEST), next_c = cur_c,
            last_c = rightmost_col(n);
            buffer[i] && buffer[i] != LF && next_c <= last_c; i++)
        if (buffer[i] == TAB)
            next_c += fill_tabs(n, tab_fill_size(c_pos(n)));
        else {
            window_putchar(n, buffer[i]);
            next_c++;
        }
    if (num_blanks == UNDEFINED)
        for ( ; next_c <= last_c; next_c++)
            window_putchar(n, BLANK);
    else
        for ( ; next_c <= last_c && num_blanks > 0;
                next_c++, num_blanks--)
            window_putchar(n, BLANK);
    window_go_rc(n, r_pos(n), cur_c);
}   /* redisplay_rest_of_line */


/*
window_scroll_up() is used to move the cursor down one line (closer
to the END of the buffer) and redisplay the buffer.  It is a secon-
dary function, and is called by, for example, down(), when the
cursor is already on the bottom line.
*/

int window_scroll_up(int n, char *buffer, int current_c)
{
    long old_buf_pos;

    if (last_char_on_line(n, buffer) == EOS)
        return FALSE;
    else {
        old_buf_pos = buf_cursor_pos(n, TEST);
        buf_cursor_pos(n, top_left_pos(n, TEST));
        go_line_end(n, buffer);
        top_left_pos(n, buf_cursor_pos(n, INCR));
        buf_cursor_pos(n, old_buf_pos);
```

```
        window_cursor_bottom(n);
        if (!buffer_down_line(n, buffer, current_c)) {
            window_scroll(n, SCROLL_UP);            /* didn't have  */
            go_line_start(n, buffer);               /* to redisplay */
            window_go_rc(n, r_pos(n), 0);           /* just scroll  */
            redisplay_rest_of_line(n, buffer, 0);
            window_adjust_cursor_position(n, buffer, current_c);
        }
        return TRUE;
    }
}   /* window_scroll_up */


/*
window_scroll_down() is used to move the cursor up one line (closer to
the BEGINNING of the buffer) and redisplay the buffer.  It is a secon-
dary function, and is called by, for example, up(), when the cursor is
already on the top line.
*/

int window_scroll_down(int n, char *buffer, int current_c)
{
    if (top_left_pos(n, TEST) > 0) {
        buf_cursor_pos(n, top_left_pos(n, TEST) - 1);
        top_left_pos(n, go_line_start(n, buffer));
        if (!window_adjust_cursor_position(n, buffer, current_c)) {
            window_scroll(n, SCROLL_DOWN);      /* didn't have  */
            go_line_start(n, buffer);           /* to redisplay */
            window_go_rc(n, r_pos(n), 0);       /* just scroll  */
            redisplay_rest_of_line(n, buffer, 0);
            window_adjust_cursor_position(n, buffer, current_c);
        }
        return TRUE;
    }
    else
        return FALSE;
}   /* window_scroll_down */


/*
buffer_up_line() shifts the cursor up one line, maintaining its
previous column position, if possible.  This routine does NOT
perform screen management.
*/
```

```
int buffer_up_line(int n, char *buffer, int ideal_c)
{
    if (go_line_start(n, buffer) > 0) {
        buf_cursor_pos(n, DECR);
        go_line_start(n, buffer);
        window_adjust_cursor_position(n, buffer, ideal_c);
    }
    return buf_cursor_pos(n, TEST);
}   /* buffer_up_line */


/*
buffer_down_line() shifts the cursor down one line, maintaining
its previous column position, if possible.  This routine does NOT
perform screen management.
*/

int buffer_down_line(int n, char *buffer, int ideal_c)
{
    if (go_line_end(n, buffer) < edit_buf_len(n, TEST)) {
        buf_cursor_pos(n, INCR);
        return window_adjust_cursor_position(n, buffer, ideal_c);
    }
    else
        return FALSE;
}   /* buffer_down_line */


/*
window_adjust_cursor_position() places the cursor in the specified
column, if possible; otherwise, it places the cursor at the end of
the line.  It returns Boolean true, if it was necessary to redisplay
the screen.  This routine assumes that the cursor is at the begin-
ning of the line (in the buffer).
*/

int window_adjust_cursor_position(int n, char *buffer, int ideal_c)
{
    int actual_c, len, had_to_redisplay = FALSE;

    len = window_line_length(n, buffer);
    actual_c = (ideal_c > len - 1) ? len - 1 : ideal_c;
    if (actual_c < window_offset(n, TEST) ||
```

```
            actual_c > rightmost_col(n)) {
        window_restore_offset_and_column(n);
        if (actual_c > rightmost_col(n))
            window_shift_right(n, buffer,
                actual_c - rightmost_col(n) + tab_size(TEST) * 2);
        else
            window_shift_right(n, buffer, 0);
        had_to_redisplay = TRUE;
    }
    adjust_onscreen_position(n, buffer, actual_c);
    return had_to_redisplay;
}   /* window_adjust_cursor_position */


/*
adjust_onscreen_position() moves the cursor to the specified column.
If the desired position is beyond the rightmost onscreen position,
the cursor is adjusted backward within the window, taking into con-
sideration any tab characters.  adjust_onscreen_position() assumes
that the cursor is at the beginning of the line (in the buffer).  If
the specifed column, is "null," due to tabbing, the cursor is adjusted
accordingly.
*/

void adjust_onscreen_position(int n, char *buffer, int ideal_c)
    {
    register int column, prev_column;
    register long i;

    for (column = 0, i = buf_cursor_pos(n, TEST);
            column < ideal_c; i++) {
        prev_column = column;
        column += (buffer[i] == TAB) ? tab_fill_size(column) : 1;
    }
    if (column > ideal_c && column <= rightmost_col(n))
        ;
    else if (column > rightmost_col(n) || column > ideal_c) {
        column = prev_column;
        i--;
        }
    window_go_rc(n, r_pos(n), column);
    buf_cursor_pos(n, i);
}   /* adjust_onscreen_position */
```

```
/*
adjacent_to_leftmost_column() returns TRUE if the cursor is posi-
tioned at the leftmost column in the window, or, if the leftmost
column is "null," it returns TRUE if the cursor is positioned on
a tab just right of the leftmost column.
*/

int adjacent_to_leftmost_column(int n, char *buffer)
{
    return c_pos(n) == window_offset(n, TEST) ||
            previous_column(n, buffer) < window_offset(n, TEST);
}   /* adjacent_to_leftmost_column */


/*
adjacent_to_rightmost_column() returns TRUE if the cursor is posi-
tioned at the rightmost column in the window, or, if the rightmost
column is "null," it returns TRUE if the cursor is positioned on a
TAB just left of the rightmost column.
*/

int adjacent_to_rightmost_column(int n)
{
    return c_pos(n) == rightmost_col(n) ||
            next_tab_column(n) > rightmost_col(n);
}   /* adjacent_to_rightmost_column */


/*
window_buffer_forward() increments both the buffer and window
positions.  It must take tabbing into consideration.  Note: this
procedure performs no error checking--it must be called in the
proper context.
*/

void window_buffer_forward(int n, char *buffer)
{
    if (buffer[buf_cursor_pos(n, TEST)] == TAB)
        window_go_rc(n, r_pos(n), next_tab_column(n));
    else
        window_go_rc(n, r_pos(n), c_pos(n) + 1);
    buf_cursor_pos(n, INCR);
}   /* window_buffer_forward */
```

```
/*
window_buffer_backward() decrements both the buffer and window
positions.  It must take tabbing into consideration.  Note: this
procedure performs no error checking--it must be called in the
proper context.
*/

void window_buffer_backward(int n, char *buffer)
{
    if (buffer[buf_cursor_pos(n, TEST) - 1] == TAB)
        window_go_rc(n, r_pos(n), previous_column(n, buffer));
    else
        window_go_rc(n, r_pos(n), c_pos(n) - 1);
    buf_cursor_pos(n, DECR);
}   /* window_buffer_backward */


/*
go_right_as_far_as_possible() moves the cursor to either the end of
the line, or to the rightmost onscreen position, if the line extends
beyond the last screen position.
*/

int go_right_as_far_as_possible(int n, char *buffer)
{
    if (window_line_length(n, buffer) - 1 > rightmost_col(n)) {
        go_line_start(n, buffer);
        adjust_onscreen_position(n, buffer, rightmost_col(n));
        return FALSE;
    }
    else {
        window_go_rc(n, r_pos(n), window_line_length(n, buffer) - 1);
        go_line_end(n, buffer);
        return TRUE;
    }
}   /* go_right_as_far_as_possible */


/*
move_forward_x_lines() moves the cursor forward in the buffer the
specified number of lines.  It leaves the cursor at the beginning of
the line.  It returns the number of lines that were moved.  The
```

```
actual number of lines moved may be less than that requested, if the
cursor is near the beginning or end of the buffer.
*/

int move_forward_x_lines(int n, char *buffer, int num_lines)
{
    register int lines_moved;
    register long i;

    if (num_lines == 0) {
        go_line_start(n, buffer);
        return 0;
    }
    else {
        i = buf_cursor_pos(n, TEST);
        for (lines_moved = 0; buffer[i] && num_lines > 0;) {
            for ( ; buffer[i] && buffer[i] != LF; i++)
                ;
            if (buffer[i]) {
                i++;
                num_lines--;
                lines_moved++;
            }
        }
        buf_cursor_pos(n, i);
        go_line_start(n, buffer);
        return lines_moved;
    }
}   /* move_forward_x_lines */


/*
move_backward_x_lines() moves the cursor backward in the buffer the
specified number of lines.  It leaves the cursor at the beginning of
the line.  It returns the number of lines that were moved.  The
actual number of lines moved may be less than that requested, if the
cursor is near the beginning or end of the buffer.
*/

int move_backward_x_lines(int n, char *buffer, int num_lines)
{
    register int lines_moved;
    register long i;
```

```
    if (num_lines == 0) {
        go_line_start(n, buffer);
        return 0;
    }
    else {
        i = buf_cursor_pos(n, TEST);
        for (lines_moved = 0; i > 0 && num_lines > 0;) {
            if ((i = go_line_start(n, buffer)) > 0) {
                buf_cursor_pos(n, DECR);
                num_lines--;
                lines_moved++;
            }
        }
        go_line_start(n, buffer);
        return lines_moved;
    }
}   /* move_backward_x_lines */


/*
go_line_start() moves the cursor to the beginning of the current line
in the buffer; it does NOT update the cursor position in the window.
*/

long go_line_start(int n, char *buffer)
{
    register long i;

    if ((i = buf_cursor_pos(n, TEST)) == 0)
        return FALSE;
    else if (buf_line_length(n, buffer) == 1)
        return i;
    else {
        if (buffer[i] == LF)
            i--;
        for ( ; i >= 0 && buffer[i] != LF; i--)
            ;
        i++;
        return buf_cursor_pos(n, i);
    }
}   /* go_line_start */


/*
```

```
go_line_end() moves the cursor to the end of the current line in
the buffer; it does NOT update the cursor position in the window.
*/

long go_line_end(int n, char *buffer)
{
    register long i;

    i = buf_cursor_pos(n, TEST);
    if (!buffer[i] || buffer[i] == LF)
        return i;
    else {
        for ( ; buffer[i] && buffer[i] != LF; i++)
            ;
        return buf_cursor_pos(n, i);
    }
}   /* go_line_end */


/*
last_char_on_line() returns the last character on the specified line.
Typically, this will be a LF; however, it may be an EOS.
*/

char last_char_on_line(int n, char *buffer)
{
    long i;

    for (i = buf_cursor_pos(n, TEST); buffer[i] && buffer[i] != LF; i++)
        ;
    return buffer[i];
}   /* last_char_on_line */


/*
linefeed_free() determines whether or not an array of characters is
completely free of linefeed characters.
*/

int linefeed_free(char *ch_array, register long index)
{
    while (ch_array[--index] != LF && index > 0)
        ;
    return (ch_array[index] != LF) ? TRUE : FALSE;
```

```
}   /* linefeed_free */


/*
buf_line_length() returns the length of the
current line in the buffer.
*/

int buf_line_length(int n, char *buffer)
{
    register long end, start;

    for (end = buf_cursor_pos(n, TEST); buffer[end]
            && buffer[end] != LF; end++)
        ;
    for (start = end - 1; start > 0 && buffer[start] != LF; start--)
        ;
    if (start == 0)
        return end - start + 1;
    else
        return end - start;
}   /* buf_line_length */


/*
window_line_length() calculates the on-screen distance between
the first and last columns of the current line.
*/

int window_line_length(int n, char *buffer)
{
    register int column;
    register long i;

    if (buffer[i = buf_cursor_pos(n, TEST)] == LF)
        i--;
    for ( ; i >= 0 && buffer[i] != LF; i--)
        ;
    i++;
    for (column = 0; buffer[i] && buffer[i] != LF; i++)
        column += (buffer[i] == TAB) ? tab_fill_size(column) : 1;
    return column + 1;
}   /* window_line_length */
```

```
/*
previous_column() backs up one column; tab characters must be
considered.  Since all line and column positions are relative,
previous_column() must do its calculations from the beginning
of the line.
*/

int previous_column(int n, char *buffer)
{
    register int col, cur_col, prev_col;
    register long i;

    if (buffer[i = buf_cursor_pos(n, TEST)] == LF)
        i--;
    for ( ; i >= 0 && buffer[i] != LF; i--)
        ;
    i++;
    for (col = 0, cur_col = c_pos(n); col < cur_col; i++) {
        prev_col = col;
        col += (buffer[i] == TAB) ? tab_fill_size(col) : 1;
    }
    return prev_col;
}   /* previous_column */


/*
next_tab_column() determines the first column following the
current column that coincides with a tab increment.
*/

int next_tab_column(int n)
{
    int increment;

    increment = tab_fill_size(c_pos(n));
    return c_pos(n) + ((increment == 0) ?
                tab_size(TEST) : increment);
}   /* next_column */


/*
tab_fill_size() calculates the distance in columns between the
current column and the next tab increment.
```

```
*/

int tab_fill_size(int current_col)
{
    return tab_size(TEST) - (current_col % tab_size(TEST));
}   /* tab_fill_size */


/*
fill_tabs() expands tab characters--onscreen only.
*/

int fill_tabs(int n, int num_blanks)
{
    int i, last;

    for (i = 0, last = rightmost_col(n);
            i < num_blanks && c_pos(n) <= last; i++)
        window_putchar(n, BLANK);
    return i;
}   /* fill_tabs */


/*
strlen_with_tabs() determines the length of a substring, including
any embedded tabs.  The substring is assumed to begin at a tab stop.
*/

int strlen_with_tabs(char *str, register int substring_len)
{
    register int i, pos;

    for (i = 0, pos = 0; str[i] && i < substring_len; i++)
        pos += (str[i] == TAB) ? tab_fill_size(pos) : 1;
    return pos;
}   /* strlen_with_tabs */


/*
current_column_offset() determines the on-screen offset of the
current buffer position relative to the previous linefeed character.
*/

int current_column_offset(int n, char *buffer)
```

```
{
    register long i;

    if (buffer[i = buf_cursor_pos(n, TEST)] == LF)
        i--;
    for ( ; i >= 0 && buffer[i] != LF; i--)
        ;
    i++;
    return strlen_with_tabs(&buffer[i], buf_cursor_pos(n, TEST) - i);
}   /* current_column_offset */


/****  editwin.c  ****  edit-specific window management routines ****/

#include "editc.h"
#include "windowsc.h"
#include "vidconc.h"
#include "ed.h"
#include "edit.h"
#include "editwin.h"
#include "windows.h"


/*
window_fill() clears and then fills a window with the contents of
a buffer.  The fill operation begins with the specified window
coordinates, based on the specified offset within the buffer.
*/

int window_fill(int n, int r, int c, char *buffer, long buf_offset)
{
    register int column, last_r, last_c, win_offset;

    if (!wframe[n].is_active)
        return FALSE;
    else {
        window_go_rc(n, r, c);
        window_clr_rest(n);
        window_go_rc(n, r, c);
        for (column = 0, win_offset = window_offset(n, TEST),
                last_r = wframe[n].end_r - wframe[n].start_r - 2,
                last_c = rightmost_col(n);
                buffer[buf_offset] && (wframe[n].cursor_r <= last_r);
                buf_offset++) {
```

```
            if (buffer[buf_offset] == LF) {
                column = 0;
                wframe[n].virtual_c = win_offset;
                wframe[n].cursor_r++;
            }
            else if (column < win_offset)
                column += skip_offset(n, &buffer[buf_offset],
                                            column, win_offset);
            else if (wframe[n].virtual_c > last_c)
                ;
            else
                put_text(n, &buffer[buf_offset]);
        }
        window_go_rc(n, r, c);
        return TRUE;
    }
}   /* window_fill */


/*
skip_offset() skips over those characters in the buffer that
would be output to the left of the leftmost column, given the
currently active window offset.  If a tab advances the cursor into
the window beyond the leftmost column, the window column coordinate
(virtual_c) must be updated accordingly.
*/

int skip_offset(int n, char *buf_ptr, int current_pos, int win_offset)
{
    int offset_adjustment, padding;

    if (*buf_ptr == TAB) {
        padding = tab_fill_size(current_pos);
        offset_adjustment = current_pos + padding - win_offset;
        if (offset_adjustment > 0)
            wframe[n].virtual_c += offset_adjustment;
        return padding;
    }
    else
        return 1;
}   /* skip_offset */


/*
```

```
put_text() outputs the text to the window, taking into
consideration any tab characters that are encountered.
*/

void put_text(int n, char *buf_ptr)
{

    if (*buf_ptr == TAB)
        fill_tabs(n, tab_fill_size(wframe[n].virtual_c));
    else
        window_putchar(n, *buf_ptr);
}   /* put_text */


/*
window_offset() manages the current window offset.
*/

int window_offset(int n, int new_value)
{
    if (new_value == TEST)
        return wframe[n].offset;
    else
        return wframe[n].offset = new_value;
}   /* window_offset */


/*
window_shift_right() shifts the window to the right the specified
number of columns.  If possible, the cursor (window coordinates only)
is also shifted by the same amount.  Some routines may need to
readjust the cursor.
*/

void window_shift_right(int n, char *buffer, int num_columns)
{
    int cur_r, cur_c;

    wframe[n].offset += num_columns;
    cur_c = (wframe[n].virtual_c += num_columns);
    if (cur_c >= window_line_length(n, buffer))
        cur_c = window_line_length(n, buffer) - 1;
    cur_r = r_pos(n);
    window_go_rc(n, 0, wframe[n].offset);
```

```
    window_fill(n, 0, wframe[n].offset, buffer,
                    top_left_pos(n, TEST));
    window_go_rc(n, cur_r, cur_c);
}   /* window_shift_right */


/*
window_restore_shift() repositions/redisplays the text
without any text offset in the window.
*/

void window_restore_shift(int n, char *buffer)
{
    if (window_offset(n, TEST) > 0) {
        window_restore_offset_and_column(n);
        window_shift_right(n, buffer, 0);
    }
}   /* window_restore_shift */


/*
window_restore_offset_and_column() restores/resets two window
shift-related variables without redisplaying the text.
*/

int window_restore_offset_and_column(int n)
{
    if (window_offset(n, TEST) > 0)
        wframe[n].offset = wframe[n].virtual_c = 0;
    return wframe[n].virtual_c;
}   /* window_restore_offset_and_column */


/****  keyboard.c  ****  keyboard routines  ****/

#include <dos.h>
#include "scrnprnc.h"
#include "keyboard.h"


/*
get_keystroke() reads and returns the 16-bit scan code for a key.
*/
```

```
int get_keystroke(void)
{
    union REGS r;

    r.h.ah = KEYBOARD_READ;
    int86(KEYBOARD_INT, &r, &r);
    return r.x.ax;
}   /* get_keystroke */


/*
keyboard_alt_depressed_() determines whether or not the <Alt> key
is depressed--this can be used to allow a signal from the user.
*/

int keyboard_alt_depressed(void)
{
    union REGS r;

    r.h.ah = 0x2;
    int86(KEYBOARD_INT, &r, &r);
    return (r.h.al & 0x08);

}   /* keyboard_alt_depressed */


/*
set_cntl_break() stores the current status of the break flag, and
then turns it off.  It can also be used to restore the break status.
*/

void set_cntl_break(int operation)
{
    static int break_status;
    union REGS r;

    if (operation == OFF) {
        r.h.ah = CONTROL_BREAK_FUNC;
        r.h.al = 0;                /* get status function */
        int86(DOS_FUNCTION, &r, &r);
        break_status = r.h.dl;
        r.h.ah = CONTROL_BREAK_FUNC;
        r.h.al = 1;                /* set status function */
        r.h.dl = OFF;
```

```
        int86(DOS_FUNCTION, &r, &r);
    }
    else {
        r.h.ah = CONTROL_BREAK_FUNC;
        r.h.al = 1;              /* set status function */
        r.h.dl = break_status;
        int86(DOS_FUNCTION, &r, &r);
    }
}   /* set cntl break */


/****  screen.c  ****  screen handling routines  ****/

#include <dos.h>
#include "scrnprnc.h"
#include "screen.h"


/*
globals:
*/

static char far *screen;                 /* private ptr. to video RAM */
static char exit_screen[SCREEN_SIZE];    /* private screen buffer */


/*
clrscn() clears the screen.
*/

void clrscn(void)
{
    union REGS r;

    r.h.ah = SCROLL_UP;
    r.h.al = 0;              /* clear screen */
    r.h.ch = 0;              /* start row    */
    r.h.cl = 0;              /* start column */
    r.h.dh = 24;             /* end row      */
    r.h.dl = 79;             /* end column   */
    r.h.bh = NORMAL_VIDEO;
    int86(VIDEO_INT, &r, &r);
}   /* clrscn */
```

```
/*
dos_level_cursor() handles cursor operations.  It saves the current
cursor size and position in four internal static variables, or re-
stores the cursor size and position previously saved, depending on the
value of "operation."
*/

void dos_level_cursor(int op)
{
    union REGS r;
    static int row, column, start, end;

    if (op == CURSOR_RESTORE) {           /* restore the cursor */
        r.h.ah = SET_CURSOR_POS;
        r.h.dh = row;
        r.h.dl = column;
        r.h.bh = 0;
        int86(VIDEO_INT, &r, &r);
        r.h.ah = SET_CURSOR_SIZE;
        r.h.ch = start;
        r.h.cl = end;
        r.h.bh = PAGE_0;
        int86(VIDEO_INT, &r, &r);
    }
    else {                                /* save the cursor */
        r.h.ah = READ_CURSOR_POS;
        r.h.bh = PAGE_0;
        int86(VIDEO_INT, &r, &r);
        row = r.h.dh;
        column = r.h.dl;
        start = r.h.ch;
        end = r.h.cl;
    }
}   /* dos_level_cursor */


/*
video_initialize() determines the screen address and saves the
screen buffer in the exit_screen array (global); it returns the
video_mode.  (restore_exit_screen() recovers the old screen.)
*/

int video_initialize(void)
```

```
{
    int i;

    set_screen_addr();
    for (i = 0; i < SCREEN_SIZE; i++)
        exit_screen[i] = screen[i];
/*  memcpy(exit_screen, screen, SCREEN_SIZE);*/
    dos_level_cursor(CURSOR_SAVE);  /* record its characteristics */
    return get_video_mode();
}   /* video_initialize */


/*
get_screen_addr() returns the start of video memory.
*/

char far *get_screen_addr(void)
{
    return screen;
}   /* get_screen_addr */


/*
set_screen_addr() sets the screen pointer to the
appropriate video buffer address.
*/

void set_screen_addr(void)
{
    screen = (char far *) ((get_video_mode() == MONO_MODE) ?
                              MONO_SCREEN : COLOR_SCREEN);
}   /* set_screen_addr */


/*
get_video_mode() returns the screen mode.
*/

int get_video_mode(void)
{
    union REGS r;

    r.h.ah = GET_VIDEO_MODE;
    int86(VIDEO_INT, &r, &r);
```

```
    return r.h.al;
}   /* get_video_mode */


/*
restore_exit_screen() restores the user's screen that existed prior to
the current program's execution.  The user's screen was saved by
video_initialize().
*/

void restore_exit_screen(void)
{
    int i;

    for (i = 0; i < SCREEN_SIZE; i++)
        screen[i] = exit_screen[i];
/*  memcpy(screen, exit_screen, SCREEN_SIZE);*/
    dos_level_cursor(CURSOR_RESTORE);    /* reset cursor size/posn. */
}   /* restore_exit_screen */


/*
cursor_rc positions the cursor at the specified coordinates.
*/

void cursor_rc(int row, int column)
{
    union REGS r;

    r.h.ah = SET_CURSOR_POS;
    r.h.dh = row;
    r.h.dl = column;
    r.h.bh = PAGE_0;
    int86(VIDEO_INT, &r, &r);
}   /* cursor_rc */


/****  windows.c  ****  several pop-up window routines  ****/


/*
These window routines were influenced by those provided with Turbo C,
Borland International, 1988, and by several routines found in "C: Power
User's Guide", by Herbert Schildt, Osborne McGraw-Hill, 1988.  However,
```

```
beyond the overall design, there are many significant differences,
including the use of a virtual column position to support horizontal
scrolling.  See the file windowsc.h.
*/

#include <stdio.h>
#include <dos.h>
#include <stdlib.h>
#include <string.h>
#include <ctype.h>
#include "windowsc.h"
#include "scrnprnc.h"
#include "windows.h"
#include "screen.h"
#include "keyboard.h"
#include "display.h"


/*
make_window() establishes a window.  Each window is referenced by
number.  make_window() returns TRUE, if no errors occur; it returns
a special code, if memory can't be allocated, and it returns
FALSE otherwise.
*/

int make_window(int n, char *header, int start_r, int start_c,
                int end_r, int end_c)
{
    char *save_ptr;

    if ((start_r > 23) || (start_r < 0) ||
        (start_c > 78) || (start_c < 0))
        return FALSE;
    if ((end_r > 24) || (end_c > 79))
        return FALSE;
    if ((save_ptr =
            (char *) malloc((end_r - start_r + 1) *
                            (end_c - start_c + 1) * 2)) == NULL)
        return CANT_ALLOCATE_WIN;

    wframe[n].window_save_buffer = save_ptr;
    wframe[n].start_r = start_r;        /* window boundaries */
    wframe[n].end_r = end_r;
    wframe[n].start_c = start_c;
```

```
    wframe[n].end_c = end_c;
    wframe[n].header = header;
    wframe[n].is_active = FALSE;
    wframe[n].offset = 0;              /* see windowsc.h */
    wframe[n].cursor_r = 0;            /* see windowsc.h */
    wframe[n].virtual_c = 0;           /* see windowsc.h */
    return TRUE;
}   /* make_window */


/*
activate_window() switches to a particular window.
*/

void activate_window(int n, char *header, int header_attr,
                        int border_attr)
{
    if (!wframe[n].is_active) {
        window_save_screen_area(n);
        wframe[n].is_active = TRUE;
        window_display_border(n, border_attr);
        window_display_header(n, header, header_attr);
    }
}   /* activate_window */


/*
deactivate_window() clears a window, restoring the previous screen.
*/

void deactivate_window(int n)
{
    if (wframe[n].is_active) {
        wframe[n].offset = 0;
        wframe[n].cursor_r = 0;
        wframe[n].virtual_c = 0;
        wframe[n].is_active = FALSE;
        window_restore_screen_area(n);
    }
}   /* deactivate_window */


/*
window_display_header() displays a header, centered on the top line
```

```
of a window border.
*/

void window_display_header(int n, char *alt_header, int attr)
{
    char *hdr_ptr;
    int hdr_start, hdr_len;

    hdr_ptr = (*alt_header == EOS) ? wframe[n].header : alt_header;
    hdr_len = strlen(hdr_ptr);
    hdr_start = ((wframe[n].end_c - wframe[n].start_c - 1 - hdr_len)
                / 2) + 1 + wframe[n].start_c;
    if (hdr_start < wframe[n].start_c)
        return;
    display_string(wframe[n].start_r, hdr_start, hdr_ptr, attr);
    if (hdr_len > 0) {
        display_char(wframe[n].start_r, hdr_start - 1, BLANK, attr);
        display_char(wframe[n].start_r, hdr_start + hdr_len, BLANK,
                        attr);
    }
}   /* window_display_header */


/*
window_display_border() puts a border around a window.
*/

void window_display_border(int n, int attr)
{
    register int i;

    for (i = wframe[n].start_r + 1; i < wframe[n].end_r; i++) {
        display_char(i, wframe[n].start_c, VERTICAL_BAR, attr);
        display_char(i, wframe[n].end_c, VERTICAL_BAR, attr);
    }
    for (i = wframe[n].start_c + 1; i < wframe[n].end_c; i++) {
        display_char(wframe[n].start_r, i, HORIZON_BAR, attr);
        display_char(wframe[n].end_r, i, HORIZON_BAR, attr);
    }
    display_char(wframe[n].start_r, wframe[n].start_c,
                    TOP_LEFT_CORNER, attr);
    display_char(wframe[n].start_r, wframe[n].end_c,
                    TOP_RIGHT_CORNER, attr);
    display_char(wframe[n].end_r, wframe[n].start_c,
```

```
                    BOT_LEFT_CORNER, attr);
    display_char(wframe[n].end_r, wframe[n].end_c,
                    BOT_RIGHT_CORNER, attr);
}   /* window_display_border */


/*
window_puts() prints a string in a window.
*/

int window_puts(int n, char *str)
{
    if (!wframe[n].is_active)
        return FALSE;
    for ( ; *str; str++)
        window_putchar(n, *str);
    return TRUE;
}   /* window_puts */


/*
window_puts_center() pads a string with blanks, and then calls
window_puts() to output the text in a window.
*/

int window_puts_center(int n, char *str)
{
    int num_blanks;

    if (!wframe[n].is_active)
        return FALSE;
    else {
        num_blanks = ((wframe[n].end_c - wframe[n].start_c - 1 -
                        strlen(str)) / 2) - 1;
        while (num_blanks-- > 0)
            window_putchar(n, BLANK);
        return window_puts(n, str);
    }
}   /* window_puts_center */


/*
window_putchar() prints a character in a window.
*/
```

```
int window_putchar(int n, char ch)
{
    register int r, c;
    char far *win_ptr;

    if (!wframe[n].is_active)
        return FALSE;
    /*
    no error checking
    */
    r = wframe[n].cursor_r + wframe[n].start_r + 1;
    c = wframe[n].virtual_c + wframe[n].start_c + 1 -
            wframe[n].offset;
    if (ch == LF) {
        wframe[n].cursor_r++;
        wframe[n].virtual_c = 0;
        wframe[n].offset = 0;
    }
    else {
        win_ptr = char_addr(get_screen_addr(), r, c);
        *win_ptr++ = ch;
        *win_ptr++ = NORMAL_VIDEO;
        wframe[n].virtual_c++;
    }
    window_go_rc(n, wframe[n].cursor_r, wframe[n].virtual_c);
    return TRUE;
}   /* window_putchar */


/*
window_clr_eol() clears/overwrites the current line of a window
from the current position to the end of the line.
*/

void window_clr_eol(int n)
{
    register int i, last_c;
    int r, c;

    r = wframe[n].cursor_r;
    c = wframe[n].virtual_c;
    for (i = wframe[n].virtual_c,
            last_c = wframe[n].end_c - 1 - wframe[n].start_c +
```

```
                              wframe[n].offset;
                i < last_c; i++)
            window_putchar(n, BLANK);
    window_go_rc(n, r, c);
}   /* window_clr_eol */


/*
window_go_rc() sets the coordinates within a window.
*/

int window_go_rc(int n, int r, int c)
{
    if ((r < 0) || ((r + wframe[n].start_r) >= (wframe[n].end_r - 1)))
        return FALSE;
    if ((c < 0) || ((c + wframe[n].start_c - wframe[n].offset) >=
                        (wframe[n].end_c - 1)))
        return FALSE;
    wframe[n].cursor_r = r;
    wframe[n].virtual_c = c;
    cursor_rc(wframe[n].start_r + x + 1,
                    wframe[n].start_c + y + 1 - wframe[n].offset);
    return TRUE;
}   /* window_go_rc */


/*
window_gets_filter() reads a string from a window, up to some maximum
limit, as long as printable ASCII characters are entered.  If <Esc> is
pressed, it returns FALSE.
*/

int window_gets_filter(int n, char *str, int limit)
/*
limit is the limit for number of characters that can be read.
*/
{
    char ch, *temp, *start;
    int i;

    temp = start = str;
    for (i = 0, limit--; i < limit; ) {
        ch = window_getche(n);          /* truncate returned value */
        switch (ch) {
```

```
            case ESC:
                *start = EOS;        /* return a null string */
                return FALSE;
            case RETURN:
                *str = EOS;
                return TRUE;
            case BKSP:
                if (str > temp) {
                    str--;
                    i--;
                    backspace_char(n);
                }
                break;
            default:
                if (!isprint(ch)) {
                    *str = EOS;
                    return TRUE;
                }
                *str = ch;
                str++;
                i++;
        }
    }
    if (i == limit)       /* reached limit, terminate string */
        *str = EOS;
    return TRUE;
}   /* window_gets_filter */


/*
backspace_char() attempts to remove the previously entered
character from the "buffer."
*/

void backspace_char(int n)
{
    wframe[n].virtual_c--;
    if (wframe[n].virtual_c < 0)
        wframe[n].virtual_c = wframe[n].offset = 0;
    window_go_rc(n, wframe[n].cursor_r, wframe[n].virtual_c);
    display_char(wframe[n].start_r + wframe[n].cursor_r + 1,
            wframe[n].start_c + wframe[n].virtual_c + 1
                - wframe[n].offset,
            BLANK, NORMAL_VIDEO);
```

```
}    /* backspace_char */


/*
window_getche() reads a character from a window, with echo.
*/

int window_getche(int n)
{
    union keystroke key;

    if (!wframe[n].is_active)
        return FALSE;
    window_go_rc(n, wframe[n].cursor_r, wframe[n].virtual_c);
    key.word = get_keystroke();
    if (!key.byte[0] || key.byte[0] == RETURN || key.byte[0] == BKSP
            || key.byte[0] == TAB || key.byte[0] == EOF_CHAR)
        return key.word;
    echo_char(n, key.byte[0]);
    return key.word;
}    /* window_getche */


/*
echo_char() echos a character to the screen.
*/

void echo_char(int n, char ch)
{
    if ((wframe[n].virtual_c + wframe[n].start_c -
            wframe[n].offset) < (wframe[n].end_c - 1)) {
        display_char(wframe[n].start_r + wframe[n].cursor_r + 1,
                        wframe[n].start_c + wframe[n].virtual_c + 1
                            - wframe[n].offset,
                        ch, NORMAL_VIDEO);
        wframe[n].virtual_c++;
        window_go_rc(n, wframe[n].cursor_r, wframe[n].virtual_c);
    }
}    /* echo_char */


/*
window_clr_rest() clears the remainder of a window, relative to
the cursor, that is, current (x,y) coordinates.
```

```
*/

void window_clr_rest(int n)
{
    register int i, j;
    char far *win_ptr, far *win_ptr_2;

    win_ptr = get_screen_addr();
    for (i = wframe[n].start_c + 1 + wframe[n].virtual_c -
            wframe[n].offset,
            j = wframe[n].start_r + 1 + wframe[n].cursor_r;
            i < wframe[n].end_c; i++) {
        win_ptr_2 = char_addr(win_ptr, j, i);
        *win_ptr_2++ = BLANK;
        *win_ptr_2 = NORMAL_VIDEO;
    }
    for (i = wframe[n].start_c + 1; i < wframe[n].end_c; i++)
        for (j = wframe[n].start_r + 1 + wframe[n].cursor_r + 1;
                j < wframe[n].end_r; j++) {
            win_ptr_2 = char_addr(win_ptr, j, i);
            *win_ptr_2++ = BLANK;
            *win_ptr_2 = NORMAL_VIDEO;
        }
}   /* window_clr_rest */


/*
window_up_line() moves up one line in a window.
*/

int window_up_line(int n)
{
    if (wframe[n].cursor_r > 0) {
        wframe[n].cursor_r--;
        window_go_rc(n, wframe[n].cursor_r, wframe[n].virtual_c);
        return TRUE;
    }
    return FALSE;
}   /* window_up_line */


/*
window_down_line() advances to the next line in a window.
*/
```

```
int window_down_line(int n)
{
    if (wframe[n].cursor_r < wframe[n].end_r -
            wframe[n].start_r - 2) {
        wframe[n].cursor_r++;
        window_go_rc(n, wframe[n].cursor_r, wframe[n].virtual_c);
        return TRUE;
    }
    return FALSE;
}   /* window_down_line */


/*
window_cursor_bottom() takes the cursor to the bottom line of
the window, column 0;
*/

void window_cursor_bottom(int n)
{
    window_go_rc(n, wframe[n].end_r - wframe[n].start_r - 2, 0);
}   /* window_cursor_bottom */


/*
window_scroll() scrolls a window up, or down, one line, depending
on the value of the second argument, operation.
*/

void window_scroll(int n, int operation)
{
    union REGS r;

    r.h.ah = operation;
    r.h.al = 1;
    r.h.ch = wframe[n].start_r + 1;
    r.h.cl = wframe[n].start_c + 1;
    r.h.dh = wframe[n].end_r - 1;
    r.h.dl = wframe[n].end_c - 1;
    r.h.bh = NORMAL_VIDEO;
    int86(VIDEO_INT, &r, &r);
}   /* window_scroll */
```

```
/*
r_pos() returns the current row (y-coordinate) within
a given window.
*/

int r_pos(int n)
{
    return wframe[n].cursor_r;
}   /* r_pos */


/*
c_pos() returns the current column (x-coordinate) within
a given window.
*/

int c_pos(int n)
{
    return wframe[n].virtual_c;
}   /* c_pos */


/*
rightmost_col() returns the rightmost column of a window,
not including the border column.
*/

int rightmost_col(int n)
{
    return wframe[n].end_c - wframe[n].start_c - 2 +
        wframe[n].offset;
}   /* rightmost_col */


/*
window_save_screen_area() saves the screen area to a buffer.
*/

void window_save_screen_area(int n)
{
    register int i, j, k = 0;
    char *win_buf;
    char far *win_ptr, far *win_ptr_2;
```

```
    win_buf = wframe[n].window_save_buffer;
    win_ptr = get_screen_addr();
    for (i = wframe[n].start_c; i < wframe[n].end_c + 1; i++)
        for (j = wframe[n].start_r; j < wframe[n].end_r + 1; j++) {
            win_ptr_2 = char_addr(win_ptr, j, i);
            win_buf[k++] = *win_ptr_2;
            win_buf[k++] = *(win_ptr_2 + 1);
            *win_ptr_2 = BLANK;
        }
}   /* window save screen area */


/*
window_restore_screen_area() recovers the screen area
used by a window.
*/

void window_restore_screen_area(int n)
{
    register int i, j, k = 0;
    char *win_buf;
    char far *win_ptr, far *win_ptr_2;

    win_buf = wframe[n].window_save_buffer;
    win_ptr = get_screen_addr();
    for (i = wframe[n].start_c; i < wframe[n].end_c + 1; i++)
        for (j = wframe[n].start_r; j < wframe[n].end_r + 1; j++) {
            win_ptr_2 = char_addr(win_ptr, j, i);
            *win_ptr_2++ = win_buf[k++];
            *win_ptr_2 = win_buf[k++];
        }
}   /* window_restore_screen_area */


/****    edhelp.hlp    ****/

/*
This file contains the text for ed's help screens.  See the file
edhelp.c.  Each help screen is split into two strings to accommo-
date some compilers' limits on the length of string constants.
*/

#define MAX_HELP    8           /* number of help screens * 2 */
```

```
    static char *help[MAX_HELP] = {
" Commands:\n\
\n\
   F1 (Help)   - invokes this help system.\n\
   F2 (Tag)    - sets a tag at the cursor.\n\
   F3 (Cut)    - moves tagged text to the clipboard.\n\
   F4 (Paste) - inserts the clipboard's contents at the cursor.\n\
   F5 (DW)     - deletes the next/current word.\n\
   F6 (DEOL)   - deletes all characters from the cursor to end of line.\n\
   F7 (DL)     - deletes the entire line.\n",

"    F8 (Undo)  - recovers text from the previous DW, DEOL, or DL.\n\
   F9 (Quit)  - abandons current edit session - edited text not saved.\n\
   F10 (End)  - saves edited text to disk and ends the current edit.\n\
   Alt-F2 - exchanges the tag and the cursor.\n\
   Alt-F3 - copies tagged text to the clipboard.\n\
   Alt-F5 - deletes the previous word (to the left of the cursor).\n\
   Alt-F8 - removes (undoes) a tag (set by F2).",

" Commands (cont.):\n\
\n\
   Alt-C - finds and changes a pattern.\n\
   Alt-F - finds a pattern in the text.\n\
   Alt-I - inserts (reads in) an alternate file at the cursor.\n",

"    Alt-R - repeats the previous find or find and change.\n\
   Alt-S - saves/overwrites the current file - no warning given.\n\
   Alt-T - sets a new tab size.\n\
   Alt-W - writes the tagged text to an alternate disk file.",

" Cursor Movement and Keypad Commands:\n\
   Ins        - toggles insert/overstrike mode\n\
   Del        - deletes character under cursor\n\
   Backspace - deletes character to left of cursor\n\
   \x18          - moves cursor up one line\n\
   \x19          - moves cursor down one line\n\
   <-         - moves cursor left one character\n\
   ->         - moves cursor right one character\n\
   PgUp       - moves cursor up one page (toward beginning of file)\n\
   PgDn       - moves cursor down one page (toward end of file)\n",

"    Home       - moves cursor to beginning of line (with repeat action)\n\
   End        - moves cursor to end of line (with repeat action)\n\
   Ctrl-Home - moves cursor to top-left position of window\n\
```

```
   Ctrl-End  - moves cursor to bottom-left position of window\n\
   Ctrl-PgUp - moves cursor to beginning of file\n\
   Ctrl-PgDn - moves cursor to end of file\n\
   Ctrl- <-  - moves cursor left one word\n\
   Ctrl- ->  - moves cursor right one word\n",

" Miscellaneous:\n\
\n The bottom, rightmost two positions of the screen:\n\
   \"I\" = Insert mode\n\
   \"O\" = Overtype mode\n\
   \"M\" = Modifications have been made\n\
\n Notes:\n\
\n  To clear a pop-up message window:  press any key, e.g., <Esc>.\n",

"  To improve start-up time, ed does not maintain backups.\n\
\n  Maximum sizes (chars.):  edit areas and clipboard = 64000; undo = 5000."
};
```

B

The C++ Version of ed

At the time of this writing, Zortech C++ is the only available C++ system for DOS environments. We have not, however, tailored the source code to Zortech C++, since this could inhibit you from porting **ed** to other C++ compilers as they become available. In order to make the editor "more like a commercial product," we've used Zortech-specific code to check for floppy disk errors. It's fairly easy to strip out this code. You must: (1) strip out the section of code that installs the interrupt in **main()** (in *ed.c*), (2) comment out the function **floppy_handler()** (in *edfile.c*), and (3) replace the function body of **floppy_error()** (in *edfile.c*) with "return FALSE;".

The source code for **ed** is listed in alphabetical order using the module names given in the chapters. "*.h" files are listed first, followed by interface files, and then implementation files. The help text is listed last. The source code begins immediately after this sentence:

```
////  buffers.h  ////  constants for buffer-related operations  ////

#ifndef BUFFER_CONSTANTS
#define BUFFER_CONSTANTS     1

#ifndef BOOLEANS
#define BOOLEANS          1
```

```
enum boolean {FALSE, TRUE};           // logical constants
#endif

enum inits {RESET, SET};

enum buf_errors {NO_MATCH = -1,       // arbitrary error constants */
                CANT_READ = -2,
                CANT_WRITE = -3,
                TOO_LARGE = -4,
                CANT_ALLOCATE_BUFS= -5};


enum find_consts {                    // used by rw_edit_buffers
        FIND_IT =           -1,
        CHANGE_IT =         -2,
        REPEAT_IT =         -3};


#ifndef ARB_CONSTANTS
#define ARB_CONSTANTS
#define DUMMY               0         // constants denoting some
#define TEST                -1        // action where the specific
#define UNDEFINED           -2        // value is arbitrary
#endif

#ifndef SPEC_CHARS
#define SPEC_CHARS          1
#define EOS                 '\0'      // special characters
#define CR                  '\r'
#define LF                  '\n'
#define TAB                 '\t'
#define BKSP                '\b'
#define FORMFEED            '\f'
#define BLANK               ' '
#define EOF_CHAR            26
#define ESC                 27
#endif

#endif


////  colors.h  ////

#include "vidconc.h"                  // video color constants
```

```
#ifndef NORMAL_COLORS
#define NORMAL_COLORS            1
#define REVERSE_VIDEO            0x70
#define NORMAL_VIDEO             0x07
#endif

//#define REVERSE_EDIT  1

#ifndef WINDOW_COLORS
#ifdef REVERSE_EDIT
#define WINDOW_COLORS            1
#define NOR_BORDER_COLOR         REVERSE_VIDEO
#define REV_BORDER_COLOR         NORMAL_VIDEO
#define BACK_ATTR                REVERSE_VIDEO
#else
#define WINDOW_COLORS            1
#define NOR_BORDER_COLOR         NOR_CYAN_LOW
#define REV_BORDER_COLOR         REV_CYAN_LOW
#define BACK_ATTR                NORMAL_VIDEO
#endif
#endif


////  editintc.h  ////  constants for the edit interface  ////

#ifndef EDIT_CONSTANTS
#define EDIT_CONSTANTS  1

#include "colors.h"


enum spec_rows {TOP_ROW =       0,          // used during display
                BOT_ROW =       24};        // operations only

enum spec_cols {MODIFIED_COLUMN =       77,
                INSERT_MODE_COLUMN =    78};



#ifndef LIMIT_CONSTANTS
#define LIMIT_CONSTANTS 1
#define MAX_BUF_SIZE             64000      // "limit" constants,
```

```
#define MAX_CLIP_SIZE             64000       // plus miscellany
#define MAX_UNDO_SIZE             5000
#define MAX_WINDOWS               5
#endif

#define PROMPT_STR                57
#define MAX_STR                   45
#define MIN_STR                   7
#define MAX_NAME                  80
#define TAB_SIZE                  4
#define MAX_TAB                   40


#define BREAK_PROMPT              48              // Alt-B keystroke
#define PUNCTUATION               "()!_:;\"',.?+-*/"

#define HELP_SPEC                 "\\ed.hlp"
#endif


////  keys.h  ////  key definitions for the editor  ////

#ifndef KEY_CONSTANTS
#define KEY_CONSTANTS   1

/*
keyboard-and function-related constants appear next.  Note that
a function is represented by its keyboard extended code.  That is,
the (decimal) extended byte code for F1 is 59, which is used to
represent the HELP function.
*/

#ifndef SPEC_KEYS
#define SPEC_KEYS           1
enum keys {HELP =           59,             // F1
            TAG =           60,             // F2
            CUT =           61,             // F3
            PASTE =         62,             // F4
            DWORD =         63,             // F5
            DEOL =          64,             // F6
            DLINE =         65,             // F7
            UNDO =          66,             // F8
            QUIT =          67,             // F9
            EXIT =          68,             // F10
```

```
                TAG_CURSOR =    105,            // Alt-F2
                COPY =          106,            // Alt-F3
                DWORD_LEFT =    108,            // Alt-F5
                UNTAG =         111,            // Alt-F8
                CHANGE_TEXT =   46,             // Alt-C
                DOS_CMD =       32,             // Alt-D
                EDIT_FILE =     18,             // Alt_E
                FIND_TEXT =     33,             // Alt-F
                INSERT_FILE =   23,             // Alt-I
                REPEAT FC =     19,             // Alt-R
                SAVE_FILE =     31,             // Alt-S
                SET_TABS =      20,             // Alt-T
                WRITE_FILE =    17,             // Alt-W
                FIRST_WIN =     120,            // Alt-1
                SECOND_WIN =    121,            // Alt-2
                INS =           82,
                DEL =           83,
                UP =            72,
                DOWN =          80,
                LEFT =          75,
                RIGHT =         77,
                PGUP =          73,
                PGDN =          81,
                HOME =          71,             // beginning of line
                END =           79,             // end of line
                CTRL_HOME =     119,            // top of screen
                CTRL_END =      117,            // bottom of screen
                CTRL_PGUP =     132,            // top of file
                CTRL_PGDN =     118,            // end of file
                CTRL_LEFT =     115,            // left one word
                CTRL_RIGHT =    116};           // right one word
#endif

#endif


////  spkdos.h  ////  various DOS-related constants  ////

#ifndef DOS_CONSTANTS
#define DOS_CONSTANTS   1

#ifndef BOOLEANS
#define BOOLEANS    1
enum boolean {FALSE, TRUE};
```

```
#endif

#ifndef SPEC_CHARS
#define SPEC_CHARS          1
#define EOS                 '\0'        // special characters
#define CR                  '\r'
#define LF                  '\n'
#define TAB                 '\t'
#define BKSP                '\b'
#define BLANK               ' '
#define FORMFEED            '\f'
#define EOF_CHAR            26
#define ESC                 27
#endif


#define VIDEO_INT           0x10        // interrupts
#define KEYBOARD_INT        0x16
#define DOS_FUNCTION        0x21

#define KEYBOARD_READ       0           // interrupt parameters
#define KEYBOARD_STATUS     1
#define PAGE_0              0
#define SET_CURSOR_SIZE     0x01        // Int 10 function 1
#define SET_CURSOR_POS      0x02        // Int 10 function 2
#define READ_CURSOR_POS     0x03        // Int 10 function 3
#define SCROLL_UP           6           // Int 10 function 6
#define SCROLL_DOWN         7           // Int 10 function 7
#define READ_CHAR           8           // Int 10 function 8
#define WRITE_CHAR          9           // Int 10 function 9
#define GET_VIDEO_MODE      0x0f        // Int 10 function F


#define SCREEN_SIZE         4000        // screen size @ 4000 bytes
#define MONO_MODE           7           // monochrome video mode #
#define CURSOR_SAVE         0           // cursor save operation
#define CURSOR_RESTORE      1           // cursor restore operation

#define MONO_SCREEN         0xb0000000  // address of mono screen
#define COLOR_SCREEN        0xb8000000  // address of color screen

#define ON                  1
#define OFF                 0
```

```
#ifndef ARB_CONSTANTS
#define ARB_CONSTANTS
#define DUMMY               0          // constants denoting some
#define TEST                -1         // action where the specific
#define UNDEFINED           -2         // value is arbitrary
#endif


#ifndef NORMAL_COLORS
#define NORMAL_COLORS       1
#define NORMAL_VIDEO        0x07
#define REVERSE_VIDEO       0x70
#endif

#endif


////  vidconc.h  ////  some video attribute constants  ////

#ifndef VID_COLORS
#define VID_COLORS          1

#define NOR_WHITE_HIGH      0x07    // normal video -- white on black
#define REV_WHITE_HIGH      0x70    // reverse video -- black on white
#define REV_BLUE_BLINK_HIGH 0x9f    // blue background, blink, & high
#define REV_RED_BLINK_HIGH  0xcf    // red background, blink, & high
#define REV_BLUE_BLINK_LOW  0x97    // blue background, blink, & low
#define REV_RED_BLINK_LOW   0xc7    // red background, blink, & low
#define REV_BLUE_HIGH       0x1f    // blue background, high intensity
#define REV_RED_HIGH        0x4f    // red background, high intensity
#define REV_BLUE_LOW        0x17    // blue background, low intensity
#define REV_RED_LOW         0x47    // red background, low intensity
#define REV_RED_BLACK_HIGH  0x48
#define REV_RED_BLACK_LOW   0x40
#define NOR_BLUE_HIGH       0x09    // blue foreground, high intensity
#define NOR_RED_HIGH        0x0c    // red foreground, high intensity
#define NOR_BLUE_LOW        0x01    // blue foreground, low intensity
#define NOR_RED_LOW         0x04    // red foreground, low intensity

#define NOR_CYAN_LOW        0x03
#define REV_CYAN_LOW        0x30

#define NOR_YEL_LOW         0x0e
```

```
#ifndef NORMAL_COLORS
#define NORMAL_COLORS       1
#define NORMAL_VIDEO        0x07
#define REVERSE_VIDEO       0x70
#endif

#endif


////  windows.h  ////  constants for windows.cpp  ////

#include "colors.h"


#ifndef WIN_CONSTANTS
#define WIN_CONSTANTS   1

#ifndef BOOLEANS
#define BOOLEANS    1
enum boolean {FALSE, TRUE};              // logical constants
#endif

#define MAX_PROMPT_INPUT    500

#ifndef SPEC_CHARS
#define SPEC_CHARS          1
#define EOS                 '\0'         // special characters
#define CR                  '\r'
#define LF                  '\n'
#define TAB                 '\t'
#define BKSP                '\b'
#define FORMFEED            '\f'
#define BLANK               ' '
#define EOF_CHAR            26
#define ESC                 27
#endif

enum lines {VERTICAL_BAR =       179,    // 186  "double lines"
            HORIZON_BAR =        196,    // 205
            TOP_LEFT_CORNER =    218,    // 201
            BOT_LEFT_CORNER =    192,    // 200
            TOP_RIGHT_CORNER =   191,    // 187
            BOT_RIGHT_CORNER =   217};   // 188
```

```
#endif


////  browser.hpp  ////  interface for class:  browser  ////

#ifndef BROWSERHPP
#define BROWSERHPP  1

#include "winbufs.hpp"


class browser : public buf_window {
public:
    browser(int, char *, int, int, int, int, long, int = BACK_ATTR);
    int dispatcher();
    int process_cmd(union keystroke);
    int page_up();
    int page_down();
    int top_of_buffer();
    int bottom_of_buffer();
    int redisplay_window();
};

#endif


////  buffers.hpp  ////  interface for class:  char_buffer  ////

#ifndef BUFFERSHPP
#define BUFFERSHPP  1

#include <stdio.h>
#include <dos.h>
#include "buffers.h"
#include "spkdos.h"
#include "editintc.h"


class char_buffer {
    int error_state;
protected:
    long max_buf_size;
    char *buffer;
public:
```

```
    char_buffer(long);
    ~char_buffer() {
        delete buffer;
    }
    int get_error_state() {
        return error_state;
    }
    long get_max_size() {
        return max_buf_size;
    }
    char *get_buffer() {
        return buffer;
    }
    long read_from_disk(char *);
    int write_to_disk(char *, long = 0, long = 0);
    long line_count();
    long line_count(long, long);
};

class clipboard : public char_buffer {
    friend class edit_window;
public:
    clipboard(long buf_size) : (buf_size) {
    }
};


class undo_buffer : public char_buffer {
    friend class edit_window;
private:
    long cursor_when_cut[MAX_WINDOWS + 1];
public:
    undo_buffer(long buf_size) : (buf_size) {
        for (int i = 0; i <= MAX_WINDOWS; i++)
            cursor_when_cut[i] = UNDEFINED;
    }
};

#endif


////  ed.hpp  ////  interface for the editor application  ////

#ifndef EDHPP
```

```
#define EDHPP   1

#include <stdio.h>
#include <dos.h>
#include <int.h>
#include <stream.hpp>

#include "editintc.h"
#include "edfile.hpp"
#include "edhelp.hpp"


/*
functions:
*/

extern int main(int, char **);
extern char *check_args(int, char **);
extern void issue_error_messages(int, char *);
extern int edit_main(int, char *);
extern int edit_text(edit_window &, char *);
extern void dispatch_extended_code(edit_window &,
                                    unsigned char, char *);
extern void display_edit_info();
extern void display_filename(int, char *);
extern void execute_dos_command();


extern help *ed_help;
extern prompt_window *dos_cmd;

#endif


////  edfile.hpp    ////  supplemental file system  ////
                    ////  interface for ed.cpp      ////

#ifndef EDFILEHPP
#define EDFILEHPP   1

#include <stdio.h>
#include <dos.h>
#include <direct.h>
#include <int.h>
```

```
#include "querybox.hpp"
#include "numbox.hpp"
#include "winprmt.hpp"
#include "winedit.hpp"


extern screen dos_screen;
extern keyboard dos_keybd;


extern int write_from_buffer(edit_window &, char *,
                             long = 0, long = 0);
extern int alt_edit_window();
extern void insert_file(edit_window &, char *);
extern void write_alt_file(edit_window &, char *);
extern void execute_dos_command();
extern char *get_alt_file_spec();
extern char *get_drive_path(char *);
extern int get_drive(char *);
extern long get_free_space(char *);
extern int file_exists(char *);
extern long file_size(char *);
extern int ok_to_overwrite(char *);
extern int delete_and_check_space(long, char *);
extern int floppy_ready_query(char *);
extern int floppy_error(char *);
extern "C" int floppy_handler(struct INT_DATA *pd);

#endif


////  edhelp.hpp  ////  interface for class:  help  ////

#ifndef EDHELPHPP
#define EDHELPHPP   1

#include "editintc.h"
#include "browser.hpp"


class help {
    int error_state;
    browser help_win;
```

```
public:
    help(int, char *, int, int, int, int, int);
    get_error_state() {
        return error_state;
    }
    void present_help_screens();
};

#endif


////  keyboard.hpp  ////  interface for class:  keyboard  ////

#ifndef KEYBOARDHPP
#define KEYBOARDHPP 1
#include <dos.h>
#include "spkdos.h"


/*
a data structure for keystrokes
*/

union keystroke {                    // represents a key's
    unsigned char byte[2];           // data and scan code
    int word;
};


class keyboard {
    int break_status;
public:
    keyboard();
    ~keyboard();
    int get_keystroke();
    int alt_key_depressed();
};

#endif


////  numbox.hpp  ////  interface for class:  num_box  ////

#ifndef NUMBOXHPP
```

```
#define NUMBOXHPP   1

#include "winmsgs.hpp"


class num_box : public msg_window {
    long user_response;
public:
    num_box(char *, int, int, int, int = BACK_ATTR);
    long get_user_response() {
        return user_response;
    }
    long message(char *, char *, int = REV_BORDER_COLOR,
                    int = REV_BORDER_COLOR);
};

#endif


////  querybox.hpp  ////  interface for class:  query_box  ////

#ifndef QUERYBOXHPP
#define QUERYBOXHPP 1

#include "winmsgs.hpp"


class query_box : public msg_window {
    int user_response;
public:
    query_box(char *, int, int, int, int = BACK_ATTR);
    get_user_response() {
        return user_response;
    }
    int message(char *, char *, int = REV_BORDER_COLOR,
                    int = REV_BORDER_COLOR);
};

#endif


////  screen.hpp  ////  interface for class:  screen  ////

#ifndef SCREENHPP
```

```
#define SCREENHPP   1

#include <dos.h>
#include "colors.h"
#include "spkdos.h"         // assorted DOS-related constants


class screen {
    int video_mode;
    int row, column, start, end;
    int attr;                            // background attribute
    char far *screen_ptr;
    char exit_screen[SCREEN_SIZE];       // a "screen buffer"

    char far *char_addr(char far *base, int r, int c) {
        return base + (r * 160) + (c * 2);
    }
public:
    screen(int = BACK_ATTR);
    ~screen();
    int get_video_mode();
    char far *get_screen_addr();
    void save_dos_level_cursor();
    void restore_dos_level_cursor();
    void clrscn(int = BACK_ATTR);
    void restore_exit_screen();
    void cursor_rc(int, int);
    void display_string(int, int, char*, int = BACK_ATTR);
    void display_blanks(int, int, int, int = BACK_ATTR);
    void display_char(int, int, char, int = BACK_ATTR);
};

#endif


////  winbufs.hpp  ////  interface for class:  buf_window  ////

#ifndef WINBUFSHPP
#define WINBUFSHPP  1

#include "buffers.h"
#include "keys.h"
#include "windows.hpp"
#include "querybox.hpp"
```

```
#include "numbox.hpp"
#include "editintc.h"


extern query_box attn_win;


class buf_window : public window {
protected:
    char *buffer;
    long buf_length, buf_cursor_pos, top_left_pos, max_buf_size;
    int tab_width, page_size;
public:
    buf_window(int, char *, int, int, int, int, long, int);
    ~buf_window() {
        delete buffer;
    }
    long get_max_size() {
        return max_buf_size;
    }
    long set_buf_length(long);
    long get_buf_length();
    long get_cursor_pos();
    int change_tab_width();
    int move_forward_x_lines(int);
    int move_backward_x_lines(int);
    long go_line_start();
    long go_line_end();
    char last_char_on_line();
    int linefeed_free(char *, register long);
    int buf_line_length();
    int window_line_length();
    int previous_column();
    int next_tab_column();
    int tab_fill_size(int);
    int fill_tabs(int);
    int strlen_with_tabs(char *, register int);
    int current_column_offset();
    int window_fill(int, int, long);
    int skip_offset(char *, int);
    void put_text(char *);
    void window_shift_right(int);
    void window_restore_shift();
    int window_restore_offset_and_column();
```

```
    long read_from_disk(char *);
    int write_to_disk(char *, long = 0, long = 0);
    long line_count();
    long line_count(long, long);
};

#endif


////  windows.hpp  ////  interface for class:  window  ////

#ifndef WINDOWSHPP
#define WINDOWSHPP  1

#include <stdio.h>
#include <dos.h>
#include <stdlib.h>
#include <string.h>
#include <ctype.h>
#include "spkdos.h"
#include "windows.h"
#include "keyboard.hpp"
#include "screen.hpp"


extern screen dos_screen;
extern keyboard dos_keybd;


/*
In window, a physical row coordinate is adequate for vertical
cursor movement.  However, in order to provide horizontal scrolling
within a window, the column position is "virtualized."  In this case,
the physical column is a function of the current offset within the
window and the virtual column coordinate.
*/

class window {
protected:
    int error_state;
    int win_no;          // for external, nominal usage
    int offset;          // physical column = virtual column - offset
    int cursor_r;        // physical row for the cursor
    int virtual_c;       // virtual column for the cursor
```

```
    int start_r, end_r;
    int start_c, end_c;
    char *window_save_buffer;
    char *header;
    int is_active;
    int attr;           // background attribute
    char far *char_addr(char far *base, int r, int c) {
        return base + (r * 160) + (c * 2);
    }
public:
    window(int, char *, int, int, int, int, int);
    ~window();
    int get_error_state() {
        return error_state;
    }
    int get_win_no() {
        return win_no;
    }
    void set_background_attr(int color) {
        window::attr = color;
    }
    int activate(char *, int = REV_BORDER_COLOR,
                     int = REV_BORDER_COLOR);
    int deactivate();
    void display_header(char *, int);
    void display_border(int);
    int wputchar(char);
    int wgetche();
    void echo_char(char);
    void clr_rest();
    void clr_eol();
    int up_line();
    int down_line();
    void cursor_bottom();
    void scroll(int);
    int go_rc(int, int);
    int rightmost_col();
    int bottommost_row();
    void save_screen_area();
    void restore_screen_area();
};


#endif
```

```
////  winedit.hpp  ////  interface for class:  edit_window  ////

#ifndef WINEDITHPP
#define WINEDITHPP  1

#include "buffers.hpp"
#include "wintext.hpp"


class edit_window : public text_window {
protected:
    int buf_mod_state;
public:
    edit_window(int, char *, int, int, int, int, long,
                    int = BACK_ATTR);
    int dispatcher();
    int process_cmd(keystroke);
    int buffer_modified(int);
    int buffer_modified();
    int set_insert_mode(int);
    int insert_char(char);      // variation of parent method
    int del_char();             // variation of parent method
    int backspace();            // variation of parent method
    int del_word();
    int del_word_left();
    int del_eol();
    int del_line();
    int paste(char *);
    int paste_from_buffer(char_buffer &);
    int copy_to_clipboard();
    int cut_to_clipboard();
    int cut_to_undo(long);
    int paste_from_undo();
    int find_and_change(int);
    int prompt_for_pattern(int, char *, char *);
    int replace_text(char *, char *, long);
    void display_not_found(int, char *);
    long string_search(char *, char *, register long);
    int update_undo_dependent_offset(long);
    int update_undo_dependent_offset_for_cut(long);
};
```

```
#endif


//// winmsgs.hpp //// interface for class: msg_window ////

#ifndef WINMSGSHPP
#define WINMSGSHPP 1

#include "windows.hpp"


class msg_window : public window {
public:
    msg_window(int, char *, int, int, int, int, int = BACK_ATTR);
    int deactivate();
    int wputs(char *);
    int wputs_center(char *);
    int wgets_filter(char *, int);
    void backspace_char();
};

#endif


//// winprmt.hpp //// interface for class: prompt_window ////

#ifndef WINPRMTHPP
#define WINPRMTHPP 1

#include "wintext.hpp"


class prompt_window : public text_window {
public:
    prompt_window(int, char *, int, int, int, int, long,
                  int = BACK_ATTR);
    int dispatcher(int = BREAK_PROMPT);
    int dispatcher();
    int process_cmd(keystroke);
    char *get_line(char *put_to, int len) {
        strncpy(put_to, buffer, len);
        return put_to;
    }
    int set_insert_mode(int);
```

```
    int del_rest_of_line();
};

#endif


//// wintext.hpp //// interface for class: text_window ////

#ifndef WINTEXTHPP
#define WINTEXTHPP 1

#include "winbufs.hpp"


class text_window : public buf_window {
protected:
    long tag_pos;
    int insert_mode;
public:
    text_window(int, char *, int, int, int, int, long, int);
    int process_cmd(keystroke);
    int get_insert_mode();
    long set_tag_pos();
    long set_tag_pos(int);
    long get_tag_pos();
    int insert_char(char);
    int insertion_special_conditions(char);
    void advance_cursor_to_next_tab();
    void insert_window_update(char, long);
    int del_char();
    int backspace();
    int up();
    int down();
    int cursor_left();
    int cursor_right();
    int word_left();
    int word_right();
    int home();
    int endd();
    int page_up();
    int page_down();
    int top_of_buffer_redisplay();
    int top_of_buffer();
    int bottom_of_buffer();
```

```
    int top_of_window();
    int bottom_of_window();
    void exch_tag_cursor_redisplay();
    long exch_tag_cursor();
    int get_tag_column();
    int redisplay_window(int);
    void redisplay_rest_of_line(int);
    int window_scroll_up(int);
    int window_scroll_down(int);
    int buffer_up_line(int);
    int buffer_down_line(int);
    int window_adjust_cursor_position(int);
    void adjust_onscreen_position(int);
    int adjacent_to_leftmost_column();
    int adjacent_to_rightmost_column();
    void window_buffer_forward();
    void window_buffer_backward();
    int go_right_as_far_as_possible();
    int ispunc(char);
};

#endif


////  browser.cpp  ////  implementation of class:  browser  ////
////
////  classes used:  buf_window

#include "browser.hpp"


/*
browser() passes initialization values to the parent constructor.
*/

browser::browser(int win_no, char *hdr, int start_r, int start_c,
            int end_r, int end_c, long buf_size, int attr) :
            (win_no, hdr, start_r, start_c, end_r, end_c,
                buf_size, attr)
{
}   /* browser */


/*
```

```
dispatcher() dispatches keystroke commands to process_cmd(),
as long as process_cmd() can continue to process them.
*/

int browser::dispatcher()
{
    keystroke key;

    if (buf_cursor_pos != 0)
        top_of_buffer();
    else
        window_fill(0, 0, 0);
    do
        key.word = wgetche();
    while (process_cmd(key));
    return key.word;
}   /* dispatcher */


/*
process_cmd() processes keystroke commands.  It returns FALSE
if it can't do anything with a command.
*/

int browser::process_cmd(keystroke key)
{
    if (key.byte[0])            // ASCII character, so just return
        return FALSE;
    switch (key.byte[1]) {
        case PGUP:
            page_up();
            break;
        case PGDN:
            page_down();
            break;
        case CTRL_PGUP:
            top_of_buffer();
            break;
        case CTRL_PGDN:
            bottom_of_buffer();
            break;
        default:
            return FALSE;           // can't process command
    }
```

```
    return key.word;
}   /* process_cmd */


/*
page_up() moves up one page.  The cursor remains
in the top-left corner.
*/

int browser::page_up()
{
    if (buf_cursor_pos == 0)
        return FALSE;
    else {
        move_backward_x_lines(page_size);
        redisplay_window();
        return TRUE;
    }
}   /* page_up */


/*
page_down() moves down one page.  The cursor remains
in the top-left corner.
*/

int browser::page_down()
{
    if (buf_cursor_pos == buf_length)
        return FALSE;
    else {
        move_forward_x_lines(page_size);
        redisplay_window();
        return TRUE;
    }
}   /* page_down */


/*
top_of_buffer() moves the cursor to the beginning of the file/buffer.
*/

int browser::top_of_buffer()
{
```

```
    if (buf_cursor_pos == 0)
        return FALSE;
    else {
        buf_cursor_pos = top_left_pos = RESET;
        offset = RESET;
        window_fill(0, 0, 0);
        return TRUE;
    }
}   /* top_of_buffer */


/*
bottom_of_buffer() moves the cursor to the last displayable
line in the file/buffer.
*/

int browser::bottom_of_buffer()
{
    if (buf_cursor_pos == buf_length)
        return FALSE;
    else {
        buf_cursor_pos = buf_length;
        go_line_start();
        redisplay_window();
        return TRUE;
    }
}   /* bottom_of_buffer */


/*
redisplay_window() redisplays the buffer in the window.
*/


int browser::redisplay_window()
{
    top_left_pos = buf_cursor_pos;
    go_rc(0, 0);
    window_shift_right(0);
}   /* redisplay_window */


////  buffers.cpp  ////  implementation of class:  char_buffer  ////
```

```
#include "buffers.hpp"


/*
char_buffer() allocates and initializes a character buffer.
*/

char_buffer::char_buffer(long buf_size) {
    max_buf_size = buf_size;
    buffer = new char[buf_size];
    if (buffer == NULL)
        error_state = TRUE;
    else {
        error_state = FALSE;
        buffer[0] = EOS;
    }
}   /* char_buffer */


/*
read_from_disk() loads a buffer from a disk file.
*/

long char_buffer::read_from_disk(char *filename)
{
    FILE *buf_file;

    if ((buf_file = fopen(filename, "rt")) == NULL)
        return CANT_READ;
    else {
        for (register long len = 0; (len < max_buf_size) &&
                ((buffer[len] = fgetc(buf_file)) != EOF); len++)
            ;
        if (len == max_buf_size) {      // file is too large
            fclose(buf_file);
            return TOO_LARGE;
        }
        else {                          // OK to process it
            buffer[len] = EOS;
            fclose(buf_file);
            return len;
        }
    }
}   /* read_from_disk */
```

```
/*
write_to_disk() writes a buffer to disk and returns TRUE
if no errors occur.
*/

int char_buffer::write_to_disk(char *filename, long start,
                                long num_chars)
{
    FILE *buf_file;
    register int write_ok = TRUE;
    register long i;

    if ((buf_file = fopen(filename, "wt")) == NULL)
        return CANT_WRITE;
    else {
        if (num_chars != DUMMY)
            for (i = start; buffer[i] && write_ok == TRUE
                                && num_chars--; i++)
                write_ok = (fputc(buffer[i], buf_file) != EOF);
        else
            for (i = 0; buffer[i] && write_ok == TRUE; i++)
                write_ok = (fputc(buffer[i], buf_file) != EOF);
        if (write_ok == TRUE)
            write_ok = (fputc(EOF_CHAR, buf_file) != EOF);
        fclose(buf_file);
        return write_ok;
    }
}   /* write_to_disk */


/*
line_count() counts the number of lines in a buffer.
*/

long char_buffer::line_count()
{
    register long i, num_lines;

    for (i = 0, num_lines = 0; buffer[i]; i++)
        if (buffer[i] == LF)
            num_lines++;
    return num_lines;
```

```
}   /* line_count */


/*
line_count() counts the number of lines in a buffer segment.
*/

long char_buffer::line_count(long start, long num_chars)
{
    register long i, num_lines;

    for (i = start, num_lines = 0; buffer[i] && num_chars--; i++)
        if (buffer[i] == LF)
            num_lines++;
    return num_lines;
}   /* line_count */


////  ed.cpp  ////  contains primary routines for ed  ////

/*
    Programmer:     J. Smith
    Date:           2/13/89

    Copyright (c) 1989 Iris Computing Laboratories
*/

/*
ed is a simple, full-screen editor.  It provides the
following basic features:

     - cursor movement from the numeric keypad;
     - simple deletion of a character, word, line, or
       all characters to end-of-line;
     - simple undo (undelete) capabilities;
     - cut and paste;
     - find and/or change next occurrence of specified text;
     - processing of files of arbitrary size, based on a
       program constant.
*/


#include "ed.hpp"
```

```
/*
globals:
*/

help *ed_help;
prompt_window *dos_cmd;


/*
main() sets up a pointer variable for the incoming file
specification, performs some screen handling, and invokes
a file specification routine, check_args().
*/

int main(int argc, char *argv[])
{
    char *file_spec;

    int_intercept(0x24, floppy_handler, 256);    // set up an int. handler
                                                 // for floppy disk errors

    if ((file_spec = check_args(argc, argv)) == NULL)
        exit(1);

    // initialize the help system and a line-edit prompt box //

    ed_help = new help(DUMMY, "ed 1.0 - Help", 2, 1, 22, 78,
                       int(file_size(HELP_SPEC)));
    dos_cmd = new prompt_window(DUMMY, "", 20, 10, 22,
                         10 + PROMPT_STR + 3, MAX_PROMPT_INPUT);

    // check buffer allocations (OK to continue if help file error) //

    if (dos_cmd->get_error_state() || ed_help->get_error_state()) {
        issue_error_messages(CANT_ALLOCATE_BUFS, file_spec);
        exit(1);
    }

    dos_screen.clrscn();
    display_edit_info();
    int edit_status = edit_main(1, file_spec);

    delete ed_help;
```

```
    delete dos_cmd;
    dos_screen.restore_exit_screen();
    if (edit_status == QUIT || edit_status == EXIT)
        exit(0);
    else {
        issue_error_messages(edit_status, file_spec);
        exit(1);
    }
}   /* main */


/*
check_args() checks to make sure that the proper number of
arguments is present.  It returns NULL for an error, or a char-
acter pointer to the file specification if the argument list is OK.
*/

char *check_args(int arg_count, char *arg_vector[])
{
    if (arg_count != 2) {                       // file_spec present?
        cerr <<"Usage: ED <file_spec>";
        return NULL;
    }
    if (floppy_error(arg_vector[1])) {          // open drive door?
        cerr << "Disk drive not ready for:  " << arg_vector[1];
        return NULL;
    }
    return arg_vector[1];
}   /* check_args */


/*
issue_error_messages() issues messages for a number of errors
that can occur during file initialization.
*/

void issue_error_messages(int edit_status, char *file_spec)
{
    if (edit_status == NO_MATCH)
        cerr << "Couldn't find any files:  " << file_spec;
    else if (edit_status == CANT_WRITE)
        cerr << "Couldn't write file:  " << file_spec;
    else if (edit_status == CANT_ALLOCATE_BUFS)
        cerr << "Couldn't allocate memory for editing space.";
```

```
    else
        cerr << "File is too large (64K max) OR can't be opened:  "
            << file_spec;
}   /* issue_error_messages */


/*
edit_main() processes the active edit buffer.  In addition, it
reports/returns error codes for a number of file errors that can
occur during editor initialization.
*/

int edit_main(int win_no, char *filename)
{
    int edit_status;
    edit_window edwin(win_no, "", 1, 0, 23, 79, MAX_BUF_SIZE);

    if (edwin.get_error_state())
        return CANT_ALLOCATE_BUFS;
    long file_length = edwin.read_from_disk(filename);
    if (file_length == TOO_LARGE)
        edit_status = TOO_LARGE;
    else {
        edwin.activate("", NOR_BORDER_COLOR, NOR_BORDER_COLOR);
        if (file_length == CANT_READ)                   // a new file
            edwin.set_buf_length(0);
        else
            edwin.set_buf_length(file_length);
        display_filename(win_no, strupr(filename));
        edit_status = edit_text(edwin, filename);
        if (edit_status == EXIT)
            write_from_buffer(edwin, filename);
        edwin.deactivate();
    }
    return edit_status;
}   /* edit_main */


/*
edit_text() analyzes incoming characters and calls the
appropriate routines.
*/

int edit_text(edit_window &edwin, char *filename)
```

```
{
    keystroke key;

    edwin.window_fill(0, 0, 0);
    do {
        do {
            key.word = edwin.wgetche();
            if (!edwin.process_cmd(key))
                dispatch_extended_code(edwin, key.byte[1], filename);
        } while (key.byte[0] || !(key.byte[1] == QUIT ||
                                   key.byte[1] == EXIT));
    } while (key.byte[1] == QUIT &&
            edwin.buffer_modified() &&
            !attn_win.message("", "Abandon changed text (y/n): "));
    return key.byte[1];
}   /* edit_text */


/*
dispatch_extended_code() processes commands by calling the
appropriate routines.
*/

void dispatch_extended_code(edit_window &edwin,
                            unsigned char command, char *filename)
{
    switch (command) {          // 8-bit command codes ==> unsigned
        case HELP:
            ed_help->present_help_screens();
            break;
        case SAVE_FILE:
            if (write_from_buffer(edwin, filename))
                edwin.buffer_modified(FALSE);
            break;
        case WRITE_FILE:
            write_alt_file(edwin, get_alt_file_spec());
            break;
        case INSERT_FILE:
            insert_file(edwin, get_alt_file_spec());
            break;
        case SECOND_WIN:
            if (alt_edit_window()) {
                display_filename(1, filename);
                edwin.buffer_modified(edwin.buffer_modified());
```

```
                edwin.set_insert_mode(edwin.get_insert_mode());
            }
            break;
        case DOS_CMD:
            execute_dos_command();
            break;
        default:
            break;
    }
}   /* dispatch extended code */


/*
display_edit_info() displays miscellaneous, editor-related
information on the screen.
*/

void display_edit_info()
{
    dos_screen.display_blanks(TOP_ROW, 0, 80, REV_BORDER_COLOR);
    dos_screen.display_string(BOT_ROW, 0,
" F1-Help F2-Tag F3-Cut F4-Paste F5-DW F6-DEOL F7-DL F8-Undo \
F9-Quit F10-End     ", REV_BORDER_COLOR);
    dos_screen.display_string(TOP_ROW, 71, "ed - 1.0",
                              REV_BORDER_COLOR);
}   /* display_edit_info */


/*
display_filename() shows the filename along the top line,
along with the number of the current edit buffer.
*/

void display_filename(int win_no, char *filename)
{
    char temp_str[MIN_STR];

    dos_screen.display_blanks(TOP_ROW, 0, 71, REV_BORDER_COLOR);
    dos_screen.display_string(TOP_ROW, 3, "File: ",
                              REV_BORDER_COLOR);
    dos_screen.display_string(TOP_ROW, 9, filename,
                              REV_BORDER_COLOR);
    itoa(win_no, temp_str, 10);
    dos_screen.display_char(TOP_ROW, 1, temp_str[0],
```

```
                                    REV_BORDER_COLOR);
}   /* display_filename */


////  edfile.cpp    ////  supplement file system    ////
                    ////  implementation of ed.cpp  ////

#include "ed.hpp"
#include "edfile.hpp"


/*
globals:
*/

static int alt_edit_active = FALSE;
static int critical_floppy_error = FALSE;


/*
write_from_buffer() stores a buffer as a disk file. It does not
check for the existence of the file.  Another routine can be used
to perform the latter check.
*/

int write_from_buffer(edit_window &edwin, char *filename, long start,
                        long num_chars)
{
    int write_status;
    char *alt_file = filename;

    long total_chars = (num_chars == DUMMY) ?
                edwin.get_buf_length() + edwin.line_count() :
                num_chars + edwin.line_count(start, num_chars);
    if (*alt_file == EOS)
        return FALSE;
    while ((write_status =
                delete_and_check_space(total_chars, alt_file))
                == TOO_LARGE &&
                attn_win.message(alt_file,
                    "Insufficient space; try another disk (y/n): "))
        alt_file = get_alt_file_spec();
    if (*alt_file == EOS)
        return FALSE;
```

```
    if (write_status == TRUE) {
        if ((write_status =
                edwin.write_to_disk(alt_file, start, num_chars))
                != TRUE) {
            if (write_status == CANT_WRITE)
                write_status = attn_win.message(alt_file,
                        "Can't write file; try again (y/n): ");
            else
                write_status = FALSE;
            if (write_status && floppy_ready_query(alt_file))
                write_status = edwin.write_to_disk(
                                    alt_file = get_alt_file_spec(),
                                                start, num_chars);
            else
                write_status = FALSE;
        }
    }
    if (!write_status)
        attn_win.message(alt_file, "** write abandoned **");
    return write_status;
}   /* write_from_buffer */


/*
alt_edit_window() is used to open an additional, alternative
edit window.
*/

int alt_edit_window()
{
    if (alt_edit_active) {
        attn_win.message("Alternate Edit Window",
                            "** can't open more edit windows **");
        return FALSE;
    }
    char *file_spec = get_alt_file_spec();
    if (*file_spec == EOS)
        return FALSE;

    alt_edit_active = TRUE;
    int edit_status = edit_main(2, file_spec);
    if (edit_status == CANT_ALLOCATE_BUFS)
        attn_win.message("Alternate Edit Window",
                            "** can't allocate memory **");
```

```
    else if (edit_status == TOO_LARGE)
        attn_win.message(file_spec, "** file is too large **");
    else
        edit_status = TRUE;
    attn_win.message("Alternate Edit Window",
                     "** returning to primary edit window **");
    alt_edit_active = FALSE;
    return edit_status;
}   /* alt_edit_window */


/*
insert_file() manages the insertion of the contents of an alternative
file in the edit area at the current cursor location.  insert_file()
allocates a separate buffer, in order to take advantage of the
existing editor paste facilities.
*/

void insert_file(edit_window &edwin, char *filename)
{
    long read_status;        // read_from_disk() and file_size()
                             // return the file length here

    if (*filename == EOS)
        return;
    if ((read_status = file_size(filename)) == -1) {
        attn_win.message(filename, "** file not found **");
        return;
    }
    char_buffer ins_buf(read_status + 1);
    if (!ins_buf.get_error_state()) {
        if ((read_status = ins_buf.read_from_disk(filename))
                == CANT_READ)
            attn_win.message(filename,
                        "** unknown error; can't read file **");
        else if (read_status == TOO_LARGE)
            attn_win.message(filename, "** file is too large **");
        else
            if (read_status > 0)
                edwin.paste_from_buffer(ins_buf);
    }
    else
        attn_win.message("Insert", "** not enough memory **");
}   /* insert_file */
```

```
/*
write_alt_file() writes the edit buffer to the specified file.
*/

void write_alt_file(edit_window &edwin, char *filename)
{
    long len, tag;

    if (*filename == EOS)
        return;
    if (ok_to_overwrite(filename)) {
        if ((tag = edwin.get_tag_pos()) == UNDEFINED)
            write_from_buffer(edwin, filename);
        else {
            if ((len = edwin.get_cursor_pos() - tag) == 0)
                attn_win.message("", "** nothing to write **");
            else {
                if (len < 0) {
                    edwin.exch_tag_cursor();
                    len = -len;
                }
                write_from_buffer(edwin, filename,
                                    edwin.get_tag_pos(), len);
            }
        }
    }
}   /* write_alt_file */


/*
execute_dos_command() temporarily suspends execution of the current
program and executes the DOS command given in the pop-up window.
*/

void execute_dos_command()
{
    char cmd_spec[MAX_PROMPT_INPUT], *temp_screen;
    char far *dos_scrn = dos_screen.get_screen_addr();
    keystroke key;
    int dos_error = FALSE, go_dos = FALSE;

    dos_cmd->activate("<Alt-D> invokes a DOS shell",
```

```
                                NOR_BORDER_COLOR, NOR_BORDER_COLOR);
    dos_cmd->top_of_buffer_redisplay();
    do {
        key.word = dos_cmd->wgetche();
        dos_cmd->process_cmd(key);
    } while (!((!key.byte[0] && key.byte[1] == DOS_CMD) ||
                key.byte[0] == CR || key.byte[0] == ESC));
    dos_cmd->deactivate();
    if (key.byte[0] == ESC)              // abandon the prompt box
        return;
    if ((temp_screen = new char[SCREEN_SIZE]) == NULL) {
        attn_win.message("DOS",
                            "** can't allocate necessary memory **");
        return;
    }
    if (!key.byte[0] && key.byte[1] == DOS_CMD) // second Alt-D, so
        go_dos = TRUE;                          // go out to DOS
    else
        go_dos = FALSE;
    memcpy(temp_screen, dos_scrn, SCREEN_SIZE);
    dos_screen.clrscn(NORMAL_VIDEO);
    dos_screen.cursor_rc(0, 0);
    if (go_dos || dos_cmd->get_buf_length() == 0) {
        dos_screen.display_string(0, 0,
            "Type \"exit\" to return to ed", NORMAL_VIDEO);
        dos_error = system("command");
    }
    else
        dos_error =
            system(dos_cmd->get_line(cmd_spec, MAX_PROMPT_INPUT));
    dos_screen.display_string(24, 64, "Press any key...",
                                REVERSE_VIDEO);
    dos_keybd.get_keystroke();
    memcpy(dos_scrn, temp_screen, SCREEN_SIZE);
    delete temp_screen;
    if (dos_error)
        attn_win.message("DOS",
                  "** unknown error; can't invoke command **");
}   /* execute_dos_command */


/*
get_alt_file_spec() prompts the user for a filename/file_spec.
*/
```

```
char *get_alt_file_spec()
{
    static char file_spec[MAX_STR];

    attn_win.activate("Enter a Filename");
    attn_win.go_rc(0, 1);
    attn_win.wputs("File: ");
    attn_win.wgets_filter(file_spec, MAX_STR);
    attn win.deactivate();
    return file_spec;
}   /* get_alt_file_spec */


/*
get_drive_path() uses a for loop to search the file_spec backward in
order to extract "[drive:]pathname" from the pathname plus filename.
*/

char *get_drive_path(char *file_spec)
{
    int i;
    static char path_spec[MAX_NAME];

    strcpy(path_spec, file_spec);

    for (i = strlen(path_spec) - 1;
            i > -1 && path_spec[i] != '\\' && path_spec[i] != ':';
            i--)
        ;
    path_spec[++i] = EOS;
    return path_spec;           // including search character
}   /* get_drive_path */


/*
get_drive() returns the drive associated with file_spec; it
returns 1 for A:, 2 for B:, etc.
*/

int get_drive(char *file_spec)
{
    char current_drive_path[MAX_NAME];
```

```
    if (file_spec[1] == ':')
        return toupper(file_spec[0]) - 64;              // A == 65
    else
        if (getcwd(current_drive_path, MAX_NAME) != NULL)
            return toupper(current_drive_path[0]) - 64; // A == 65
        else
            return FALSE;
}   /* get_drive */


/*
get_free_space() returns the disk free space on the drive
associated with file_spec.
*/

long get_free_space(char *file_spec)
{
    REGS r;

    r.h.ah = 0x36;              // get drive allocation information
    r.h.dl = get_drive(file_spec);
    int86(0x21, &r, &r);
    return long(r.x.ax) * long(r.x.bx) * long(r.x.cx);
}   /* get_free_space */


/*
file_exists() determines whether or not a file exists.
*/

int file_exists(char *file_spec)
{
    if (file_size(file_spec) != -1)
        return TRUE;
    else
        return FALSE;
}   /* file_exists */


/*
file_size() determines the size of a file.  It returns -1, if
the file doesn't exist.
*/
```

```
long file_size(char *file_spec)
{
    FIND *file_ptr;

    if (!floppy_ready_query(file_spec))
        return -1;
    if ((file_ptr = findfirst(file_spec, 0)) != NULL)
        return file_ptr->size;
    else
        return -1;
}   /* file_size */


/*
ok_to_overwrite() makes sure it's OK to overwrite an existing
file.
*/

int ok_to_overwrite(char *filename)
{
    if (!file_exists(filename))
        return TRUE;
    else
        return attn_win.message(filename,
                                "File exists; overwrite (y/n): ");
}   /* ok_to_overwrite */


/*
delete_and_check_space() deletes the old version of a file
and tests the remaining space.
*/

int delete_and_check_space(long num_chars, char *filename)
{
    int write_ok = TRUE;

    if (floppy_ready_query(filename)) {
        if (file_exists(filename))
            remove(filename);
        if (get_free_space(filename) < num_chars + 1)
            write_ok = TOO_LARGE;
    }
    else
```

```
        write_ok = FALSE;
    return write_ok;
}   /* delete_and_check_space */


/*
floppy_ready_query() handles disk-not-ready queries.
*/

int floppy_ready_query(char *filename)
{
    int disk_error = FALSE;

    if ((disk_error = floppy_error(filename)) != FALSE) {
        if (!attn_win.message(filename,
                        "Drive not ready; try again (y/n): "))
            disk_error = TRUE;
        else
            disk_error = floppy_error(filename);
    if (disk_error)
        attn_win.message(filename,
                "** disk error; disk operation abandoned **");
    }
    return !disk_error;
}   /* floppy_ready_query */


/*
floppy_error() attempts to detect a critical error, such as
an open drive door.
*/

int floppy_error(char *filename)
{
    FILE *fp;
    int error;

    fp = fopen(filename, "r");
    if ((error = critical_floppy_error) == FALSE) {
        critical_floppy_error = FALSE;
        fclose(fp);
        return FALSE;
    }
    else {
```

```
        critical_floppy_error = FALSE;
        for (int i = 2; i < 22; i++)
            dos_screen.display_char(i, 0, VERTICAL_BAR,
                                            NOR_BORDER_COLOR);
        return error;
    }
}   /* floppy_error */


/*
floppy_handler() sets the global variable critical_floppy_error, if
a critical floppy disk error occurs.  For critical_floppy_error:
    0 ==> no error
    1 ==> A: drive error
    2 ==> B: drive error
    etc.
*/

int floppy_handler(struct INT_DATA *pd)
{
    if (pd->regs.x.ax < 0)
        return 0;
    else {
        critical_floppy_error = (pd->regs.x.ax & 0x00ff) + 1;
        pd->regs.h.al = 0;
        return critical_floppy_error;
    }
}   /* floppy_handler */


////  edhelp.cpp  ////  implementation of class:  help  ////

#include "edfile.hpp"
#include "edhelp.hpp"


/*
help() sets up a read-only edit buffer (browser) for the help system.
*/

help::help(int win_no, char *hdr, int start_r, int start_c, int end_r,
    int end_c, int buf_size) :
    help_win(win_no, hdr, start_r, start_c, end_r, end_c, buf_size)
{
```

```
    long buf_len = help_win.read_from_disk(HELP_SPEC);
    help_win.set_buf_length(buf_len);
    error_state = help_win.get_error_state();
}   /* help */


/*
present_help_screens() displays help information in a window.
*/

void help::present_help_screens()
{
    keystroke key;

    if (help_win.get_buf_length() <= 0) {
        attn_win.message(HELP_SPEC, "** can't read help file **");
        return;
    }
    help_win.activate("");
    if (help_win.get_cursor_pos() != 0)
        help_win.top_of_buffer();
    else
        help_win.window_fill(0, 0, 0);
    do
        key.word = help_win.wgetche();
    while (help_win.process_cmd(key));
    help_win.deactivate();
}   /* present_help_screens */


////  keyboard.cpp  ////  implementation of class:  keyboard  ////

#include "keyboard.hpp"


/*
keyboard stores the current status of the break flag, and
then turns keyboard break off.
*/

keyboard::keyboard()
{
    REGS r;
```

```
    r.h.ah = 0x33;           // control break function
    r.h.al = 0;              // get status function
    int86(0x21, &r, &r);
    break_status = r.h.dl;
    r.h.ah = 0x33;
    r.h.al = 1;              // set status function
    r.h.dl = OFF;
    int86(0x21, &r, &r);
}   /* keyboard */


/*
~keyboard restores the break status.
*/

keyboard::~keyboard()
{
    REGS r;

    r.h.ah = 0x33;
    r.h.al = 1;              // set status function
    r.h.dl = break_status;
    int86(0x21, &r, &r);
}   /* ~keyboard */


/*
get_keystroke() reads and returns the 16-bit scan code of a key.
*/

int keyboard::get_keystroke()
{
    REGS r;

    r.h.ah = KEYBOARD_READ;
    int86(KEYBOARD_INT, &r, &r);
    return r.x.ax;
}   /* get_keystroke */


/*
alt_key_depressed() determines whether or not the <Alt> key
is depressed--this can be used to allow a signal from the user.
*/
```

```
int keyboard::alt_key_depressed()
{
    REGS r;

    r.h.ah = 0x2;
    int86(KEYBOARD_INT, &r, &r);
    return (r.h.al & 0x08);

}   /* alt_key_depressed */



////  numbox.cpp  ////  implementation of class:  num_box  ////
////
////  classes used:  msg_window

#include "numbox.hpp"


/*
num_box() constructs the query window.  Since it is a one-line
window, it must fill two additional initialization values needed
by the window constructor.
*/

num_box::num_box(char *hdr, int start_r, int start_c, int end_c,
    int attr) : (DUMMY, hdr, start_r, start_c, start_r + 2,
                    end_c, attr)
{
}   /* num_box */


/*
message() issues a request for a numeric quantity.
*/

long num_box::message(char *hdr, char *msg, int hdr_attr,
                          int bdr_attr)
{
    char temp_str[15];

    activate(hdr, hdr_attr, bdr_attr);
    go_rc(0, 1);
```

```
    wputs_center(msg);
    wgets_filter(temp_str, 14);
    user_response = atol(temp_str);
    deactivate();
    return user_response;
}   /* message */


////  querybox.cpp  ///implementation of class:  query_box  ////
////
////  classes used:  msg_window

#include "querybox.hpp"


/*
query_box() constructs the query window.  Since it is a one-line
window, it must fill two additional initialization values needed
by the window constructor.
*/

query_box::query_box(char *hdr, int start_r, int start_c,
                     int end_c, int attr) : (DUMMY, hdr,
                     start_r, start_c, start_r + 2, end_c, attr)
{
}   /* query_box */


/*
message() issues a message and queries the user.
*/

int query_box::message(char *hdr, char *msg, int hdr_attr,
                         int bdr_attr)
{
    activate(hdr, hdr_attr, bdr_attr);
    go_rc(0, 1);
    wputs_center(msg);
    char ch = wgetche();
    deactivate();
    return (user_response = (toupper(ch) == 'Y') ? TRUE : FALSE);
}   /* message */
```

```
////  screen.cpp  ////  implementation of class:  screen  ////

#include "screen.hpp"


/*
screen() determines the screen address and saves the screen
buffer in the exit_screen array.  Also, it set the video_mode.
*/

screen::screen(int attr)
{
    screen::attr = attr;
    video_mode = get_video_mode();
    screen_ptr = (char far *) ((video_mode == MONO_MODE) ?
                                MONO_SCREEN : COLOR_SCREEN);
    for (register int i = 0; i < SCREEN_SIZE; i++)
        exit_screen[i] = screen_ptr[i];
    save_dos_level_cursor();     // record its characteristics
}   /* screen */


/*
~screen() does nothing but clean-up at present.  In some cases, a
call to restore_exit_screen() would be appropriate here.
*/

int screen::~screen()
{
}   /* ~screen */


/*
restore_exit_screen() restore the DOS (exit) screen and cursor.
*/

void screen::restore_exit_screen()
{
    for (register int i = 0; i < SCREEN_SIZE; i++)
        screen_ptr[i] = exit_screen[i];
    restore_dos_level_cursor();     // reset cursor size/position
}   /* restore_exit_screen */
```

```
/*
get_video_mode() returns the screen mode.
*/

int screen::get_video_mode()
{
    REGS r;

    r.h.ah = GET_VIDEO_MODE;
    int86(VIDEO_INT, &r, &r);
    return r.h.al;
}   /* get_video_mode */


/*
get_screen_addr() returns the physical screen address.
*/

char far *screen::get_screen_addr()
{
    return screen_ptr;
}   /* get_screen_addr */


/*
save_dos_level_cursor() saves the current cursor size and position.
*/

void screen::save_dos_level_cursor()
{
    REGS r;

    r.h.ah = READ_CURSOR_POS;
    r.h.bh = PAGE_0;
    int86(VIDEO_INT, &r, &r);
    row = r.h.dh;
    column = r.h.dl;
    start = r.h.ch;
    end = r.h.cl;
}   /* save_dos_level_cursor */


/*
restore_dos_level_cursor() restores the cursor size and position
```

```
previously saved.
*/

void screen::restore_dos_level_cursor()
{
    REGS r;

    r.h.ah = SET_CURSOR_POS;
    r.h.dh = row;
    r.h.dl = column;
    r.h.bh = 0;
    int86(VIDEO_INT, &r, &r);
    r.h.ah = SET_CURSOR_SIZE;
    r.h.ch = start;
    r.h.cl = end;
    r.h.bh = PAGE_0;
    int86(VIDEO_INT, &r, &r);
}   /* restore_dos_level_cursor */


/*
clrscn() clears the screen.
*/

void screen::clrscn(int attr)
{
    REGS r;

    r.h.ah = SCROLL_UP;
    r.h.al = 0;             // clear screen
    r.h.ch = 0;             // start row
    r.h.cl = 0;             // start column
    r.h.dh = 24;            // end row
    r.h.dl = 79;            // end column
    r.h.bh = attr;
    int86(VIDEO_INT, &r, &r);
}   /* clrscn */


/*
cursor_rc positions the cursor at the specified coordinates.
*/

void screen::cursor_rc(int row, int column)
```

```
{
    REGS r;

    r.h.ah = SET_CURSOR_POS;
    r.h.dh = row;
    r.h.dl = column;
    r.h.bh = PAGE_0;
    int86(VIDEO_INT, &r, &r);
}   /* cursor_rc */


/*
display_string() displays a string on the screen with the
specified attribute.
*/

void screen::display_string(int row, int col, char *str, int attr)
{
    char far *scrn_ptr = screen_ptr;
    scrn_ptr = char_addr(scrn_ptr, row, col);
    for (register int i = 0; str[i]; i++) {
        *scrn_ptr++ = str[i];
        *scrn_ptr++ = attr;
    }
}   /* display_string */


/*
display_blanks displays a series of blanks at the
specified row and column.
*/

void screen::display_blanks(int row, int col, int count, int attr)
{
    char far *scrn_ptr = screen_ptr;
    scrn_ptr = char_addr(scrn_ptr, row, col);
    while (count-- > 0) {
        *scrn_ptr++ = BLANK;
        *scrn_ptr++ = attr;
    }
}   /* display_blanks */


/*
```

```
display_char() displays a character with the specified
attribute at a particular coordinate on the screen.
*/

void screen::display_char(int row, int col, char ch, int attr)
{
    char far *scrn_ptr = screen_ptr;
    scrn_ptr = char_addr(scrn_ptr, row, col);
    *scrn_ptr++ = ch;
    *scrn_ptr = attr;
}   /* display_char */


////  winbufs.cpp  ////  implementation of class:  buf_window  ////
////
////  classes used:  window

#include "winbufs.hpp"


/*
globals:
*/

// For reasons of economy, the attention window is made available
// to routines throughout the editor system.

query_box attn_win("Attention", 11, 16, 16 + POPUP_WIDTH, BACK_ATTR);


/*
buf_window() establishes initial values for a number of
critical window and buffer variables.
*/

buf_window::buf_window(int win_no, char *hdr, int start_r,
        int start_c, int end_r, int end_c, long buf_size, int attr) :
        (win_no, hdr, start_r, start_c, end_r, end_c, attr)
{
    buffer = new char[buf_size];
    max_buf_size = buf_size;
    if (buf_size <= 0)
        error_state = FALSE;
    else if (buffer == NULL)
```

```
        error_state = TRUE;
    else {
        error_state = FALSE;
        buffer[0] = EOS;
    }
    if (attn_win.get_error_state())
        error_state = TRUE;
    buf_length = RESET;
    buf_cursor_pos = top_left_pos = RESET;
    tab_width = TAB_STOP;
    page_size = end_r - start_r - 1;     // no page overlap
    go_rc(0, 0);                         // with this setting
}   /* buf_window */


/*
set_buf_length() updates buf_length.
*/

long buf_window::set_buf_length(long new_length)
{
    return (buf_length = new_length);
}   /* set_buf_length */


/*
get_buf_length() returns the current length of the buffer.
*/

long buf_window::get_buf_length()
{
    return buf_length;
}   /* get_buf_length */


/*
get_cursor_pos() determines the current cursor position.
*/

long buf_window::get_cursor_pos()
{
    return buf_cursor_pos;
}   /* get_cursor_pos */
```

```
/*
change_tab_width() manages changes to the tab size.
*/

int buf_window::change_tab_width()
{
    num_box get_tab("", 11, 16, 16 + POPUP_WIDTH, BACK_ATTR);
    int new_width;

    get_tab.message("change takes effect with next screen update",
                    "Enter tab size: ");
    if ((new_width = int(get_tab.get_user_response())) > 0 &&
            new_width <= MAX_TAB)
        tab_width = new_width;
    return tab_width;
}   /* change_tab_width */


/*
move_forward_x_lines() moves the cursor forward in the buffer the
specified number of lines.  It leaves the cursor at the beginning of
the line.  It returns the number of lines that were moved.  The
actual number of lines moved may be less than that requested, if the
cursor is near the beginning or end of the buffer.
*/

int buf_window::move_forward_x_lines(int num_lines)
{
    register int lines_moved;

    if (num_lines == 0) {
        go_line_start();
        return 0;
    }
    else {
        register long i = buf_cursor_pos;
        for (lines_moved = 0; buffer[i] && num_lines > 0;) {
            for ( ; buffer[i] && buffer[i] != LF; i++)
                ;
            if (buffer[i]) {
                i++;
                num_lines--;
                lines_moved++;
```

```
            }
        }
        buf_cursor_pos = i;
        go_line_start();
        return lines_moved;
    }
}   /* move_forward_x_lines */


/*
move_backward_x_lines() moves the cursor backward in the buffer the
specified number of lines.  It leaves the cursor at the beginning of
the line.  It returns the number of lines that were moved.  The
actual number of lines moved may be less than that requested, if the
cursor is near the beginning or end of the buffer.
*/

int buf_window::move_backward_x_lines(int num_lines)
{
    register int lines_moved;

    if (num_lines == 0) {
        go_line_start();
        return 0;
    }
    else {
        register long i = buf_cursor_pos;
        for (lines_moved = 0; i > 0 && num_lines > 0;) {
            if ((i = go_line_start()) > 0) {
                buf_cursor_pos--;
                num_lines--;
                lines_moved++;
            }
        }
        go_line_start();
        return lines_moved;
    }
}   /* move_backward_x_lines */


/*
go_line_start() moves the cursor to the beginning of the current line
in the buffer; it does NOT update the cursor position in the window.
*/
```

```
long buf_window::go_line_start()
{
    register long i;

    if ((i = buf_cursor_pos) == 0)
        return FALSE;
    else if (buf_line_length() == 1)
        return i;
    else {
        if (buffer[i] == LF)
            i--;
        for ( ; i >= 0 && buffer[i] != LF; i--)
            ;
        i++;
        return (buf_cursor_pos = i);
    }
}   /* go_line_start */


/*
go_line_end() moves the cursor to the end of the current line in
the buffer; it does NOT update the cursor position in the window.
*/

long buf_window::go_line_end()
{
    register long i = buf_cursor_pos;
    if (!buffer[i] || buffer[i] == LF)
        return i;
    else {
        for ( ; buffer[i] && buffer[i] != LF; i++)
            ;
        return (buf_cursor_pos = i);
    }
}   /* go_line_end */


/*
last_char_on_line() returns the last character on the specified line.
Typically, this will be a LF; however, it may be an EOS.
*/

char buf_window::last_char_on_line()
```

```
{
    for (long i = buf_cursor_pos; buffer[i] && buffer[i] != LF; i++)
        ;
    return buffer[i];
}   /* last_char_on_line */


/*
linefeed_free() determines whether or not an array of characters is
completely free of linefeed characters.
*/

int buf_window::linefeed_free(char *ch_array, register long index)
{
    while (ch_array[--index] != LF && index > 0)
        ;
    return (ch_array[index] != LF) ? TRUE : FALSE;
}   /* linefeed_free */


/*
buf_line_length() returns the length of the current
line in the buffer.
*/

int buf_window::buf_line_length()
{
    register long end, start;

    for (end = buf_cursor_pos; buffer[end]
            && buffer[end] != LF; end++)
        ;
    for (start = end - 1; start > 0 && buffer[start] != LF; start--)
        ;
    if (start == 0)
        return end - start + 1;
    else
        return end - start;
}   /* buf_line_length */


/*
window_line_length() calculates the ON-SCREEN distance between
the first and last columns of the current line.
```

```
*/

int buf_window::window_line_length()
{
    register long i;

    if (buffer[i = buf_cursor_pos] == LF)
        i--;
    for ( ; i >= 0 && buffer[i] != LF; i--)
        ;
    i++;
    for (register int column = 0; buffer[i] && buffer[i] != LF; i++)
        column += (buffer[i] == TAB) ? tab_fill_size(column) : 1;
    return column + 1;
}   /* window_line_length */


/*
previous_column() backs up one column; tab characters must be
considered.  Since all line and column positions are relative,
previous_column() must do its calculations from the beginning
of the line.
*/

int buf_window::previous_column()
{
    register int col, cur_col, prev_col;
    register long i;

    if (buffer[i = buf_cursor_pos] == LF)
        i--;
    for ( ; i >= 0 && buffer[i] != LF; i--)
        ;
    i++;
    for (col = 0, cur_col = virtual_c; col < cur_col; i++) {
        prev_col = col;
        col += (buffer[i] == TAB) ? tab_fill_size(col) : 1;
    }
    return prev_col;
}   /* previous_column */


/*
next_tab_column() determines the first column following the current
```

```
column that coincides with a tab increment.
*/

int buf_window::next_tab_column()
{
    int increment = tab_fill_size(virtual_c);
    return virtual_c + ((increment == 0) ? tab_width : increment);
}   /* next_column */


/*
tab_fill_size() calculates the distance in columns between the
current column and the next tab increment.
*/

int buf_window::tab_fill_size(int current_col)
{
    return tab_width - (current_col % tab_width);
}   /* tab_fill_size */


/*
fill_tabs() expands tab characters--on-screen only.
*/

int buf_window::fill_tabs(int num_blanks)
{
    for (int i = 0, last = rightmost_col();
            i < num_blanks && virtual_c <= last; i++)
        wputchar(BLANK);
    return i;
}   /* fill_tabs */


/*
strlen_with_tabs() determines the length of a substring, including
any embedded tabs.  The substring is assumed to begin at a tab stop.
*/

int buf_window::strlen_with_tabs(char *str,
                                    register int substring_len)
{
    for (register int i = 0, pos = 0;
            str[i] && i < substring_len; i++)
```

```
        pos += (str[i] == TAB) ? tab_fill_size(pos) : 1;
    return pos;
}   /* strlen_with_tabs */


/*
current_column_offset() determines the on-screen offset of the
current buffer position relative to the previous linefeed character.
*/

int buf_window::current_column_offset()
{
    register long i;

    if (buffer[i = buf_cursor_pos] == LF)
        i--;
    for ( ; i >= 0 && buffer[i] != LF; i--)
        ;
    i++;
    return strlen_with_tabs(&buffer[i], buf_cursor_pos - i);
}   /* current_column_offset */


/*
window_fill() clears and then fills the window with the contents of
a buffer.  The fill operation begins with the specified window
coordinates, based on the specified offset within the buffer.
*/

int buf_window::window_fill(int r, int c, long buf_offset)
{
    register int column, last_r, last_c;

    go_rc(r, c);
    clr_rest();
    go_rc(r, c);
    for (column = 0, last_r = bottommost_row(),
            last_c = rightmost_col(); buffer[buf_offset] &&
            (cursor_r <= last_r); buf_offset++) {
        if (buffer[buf_offset] == LF) {
            column = 0;
            virtual_c = offset;
            cursor_r++;
        }
```

```
        else if (column < offset)
            column += skip_offset(&buffer[buf_offset], column);
        else if (virtual_c > last_c)
            ;
        else
            put_text(&buffer[buf_offset]);
    }
    go_rc(r, c);
    return TRUE;
}   /* window fill */


/*
skip_offset() skips over those characters in the buffer that
would be output to the left of the leftmost column, given the
currently active window offset.  If a tab advances the cursor into
the window beyond the leftmost column, the window column coordinate
(virtual_c) must be updated accordingly.
*/

int buf_window::skip_offset(char *buf_ptr, int current_pos)
{
    if (*buf_ptr == TAB) {
        int padding = tab_fill_size(current_pos);
        int offset_adjustment = current_pos + padding - offset;
        if (offset_adjustment > 0)
            virtual_c += offset_adjustment;
        return padding;
    }
    else
        return 1;
}   /* skip_offset */


/*
put_text() outputs the text to the window, taking into consideration
any tab characters that are encountered.
*/

void buf_window::put_text(char *buf_ptr)
{

    if (*buf_ptr == TAB)
        fill_tabs(tab_fill_size(virtual_c));
```

```
    else
        wputchar(*buf_ptr);
}   /* put_text */


/*
window_shift_right() shifts the window to the right the specified
number of columns.  If possible, the cursor (window coordinates
only) is also shifted by the same amount.  Some routines may need
to readjust the cursor.
*/

void buf_window::window_shift_right(int num_columns)
{
    offset += num_columns;
    virtual_c += num_columns;
    int cur_c = virtual_c;
    if (cur_c >= window_line_length())
        cur_c = window_line_length() - 1;
    int cur_r = cursor_r;
    go_rc(0, offset);
    window_fill(0, offset, top_left_pos);
    go_rc(cur_r, cur_c);
}   /* window_shift_right */


/*
window_restore_shift() repositions/redisplays the text
without any text offset in the window.
*/

void buf_window::window_restore_shift()
{
    if (offset > 0) {
        window_restore_offset_and_column();
        window_shift_right(0);
    }
}   /* window_restore_shift */


/*
window_restore_offset_and_column() restores/resets two window
shift-related variables without redisplaying the text.
*/
```

```
int buf_window::window_restore_offset_and_column()
{
    if (offset > 0)
        offset = virtual_c = 0;
    return virtual_c;
}   /* window_restore_offset_and_column */


/*
read_from_disk() loads a buffer from a disk file.
*/

long buf_window::read_from_disk(char *filename)
{
    FILE *buf_file;

    if ((buf_file = fopen(filename, "rt")) == NULL)
        return CANT_READ;
    else {
        for (register long len = 0; (len < max_buf_size) &&
                ((buffer[len] = fgetc(buf_file)) != EOF); len++)
            ;
        if (len == max_buf_size) {      // file is too large
            fclose(buf_file);
            return TOO_LARGE;
        }
        else {                          // OK to process it
            buffer[len] = EOS;
            fclose(buf_file);
            return len;
        }
    }
}   /* read_from_disk */


/*
write_to_disk() writes a buffer to disk and returns TRUE, if no
errors occur.
*/

int buf_window::write_to_disk(char *filename, long start,
                                long num_chars)
{
```

```
    FILE *buf_file;
    register int write_ok = TRUE;
    register long i;

    if ((buf_file = fopen(filename, "wt")) == NULL)
        return CANT_WRITE;
    else {
        if (num_chars != DUMMY)
            for (i = start; buffer[i] && write_ok == TRUE
                                && num_chars--; i++)
                write_ok = (fputc(buffer[i], buf_file) != EOF);
        else
            for (i = 0; buffer[i] && write_ok == TRUE; i++)
                write_ok = (fputc(buffer[i], buf_file) != EOF);
        if (write_ok == TRUE)
            write_ok = (fputc(EOF_CHAR, buf_file) != EOF);
        fclose(buf_file);
        return write_ok;
    }
}   /* write_to_disk */


/*
line_count() counts the number of lines in a buffer.
*/

long buf_window::line_count()
{
    register long i, num_lines;

    for (i = 0, num_lines = 0; buffer[i]; i++)
        if (buffer[i] == LF)
            num_lines++;
    return num_lines;
}   /* line_count */


/*
line_count() counts the number of lines in a buffer segment.
*/

long buf_window::line_count(long start, long num_chars)
{
    register long i, num_lines;
```

```
    for (i = start, num_lines = 0; buffer[i] && num_chars--; i++)
        if (buffer[i] == LF)
            num_lines++;
    return num_lines;
}   /* line_count */


////  windows.cpp  //// implementation of class:  window  ////
////
////  classes used:  screen and keyboard

#include "windows.hpp"


/*
These window routines were influenced by those provided with Turbo C,
Borland International, 1988, and by several routines found in "C: Power
User's Guide", by Herbert Schildt, Osborne McGraw-Hill, 1988.  However,
there are many significant differences, including the use of a virtual
column position to support horizontal scrolling.  See the file
windows.hpp.
*/


/*
globals:
*/

screen dos_screen(BACK_ATTR);    // used by almost any module
keyboard dos_keybd;              // that uses windows


/*
window() initializes the window and sets up a buffer where the
existing screen area can be saved during the window's activation.
*/

window::window(int win_no, char *header, int start_r, int start_c,
                int end_r, int end_c, int attr)
{
    error_state = FALSE;
    if ((start_r > 23) || (start_r < 0) ||
            (start_c > 78) || (start_c < 0))
```

```
        error_state = TRUE;
    if ((end_r > 24) || (end_c > 79))
        error_state = TRUE;
    char *save_ptr = new char[(end_r - start_r + 1) *
                              (end_c - start_c + 1) * 2];
    if (save_ptr == NULL)
        error_state = TRUE;

    window_save_buffer = save_ptr;
    window::win_no = win_no;
    window::header = header;
    window::start_r = start_r;           // window boundaries
    window::end_r = end_r;
    window::start_c = start_c;
    window::end_c = end_c;
    window::attr = attr;
    is_active = FALSE;
    offset = 0;              // see windows.hpp for an explanation
    cursor_r = 0;            // see windows.hpp for an explanation
    virtual_c = 0;           // see windows.hpp for an explanation
}   /* window */


/*
~window releases the screen save area for each window.
*/

window::~window()
{
    delete window_save_buffer;
}   /* ~window */


/*
activate() makes the window active.
*/

int window::activate(char *header, int header_attr, int border_attr)
{
    if (!is_active) {
        save_screen_area();
        is_active = TRUE;
        display_border(border_attr);
        display_header(header, header_attr);
```

```
        return TRUE;
    }
    return FALSE;
}   /* activate */


/*
deactivate() clears the window, restoring the previous screen.
*/

int window::deactivate()
{
    if (is_active) {
        is_active = FALSE;
        restore_screen_area();
        return TRUE;
    }
    else
        return FALSE;
}   /* deactivate */


/*
display_header() displays a header, centered on the top line of
the window border.
*/

void window::display_header(char *alt_header, int h_attr)
{
    char *hdr_ptr = (*alt_header == EOS) ? header : alt_header;
    int hdr_len = strlen(hdr_ptr);
    int hdr_start =
            ((end_c - start_c - 1 - hdr_len) / 2) + 1 + start_c;
    if (hdr_start < start_c)
        return;
    dos_screen.display_string(start_r, hdr_start, hdr_ptr, h_attr);
    if (hdr_len > 0) {
        dos_screen.display_char(start_r, hdr_start - 1,
                                BLANK, h_attr);
        dos_screen.display_char(start_r, hdr_start + hdr_len,
                                BLANK, h_attr);
    }
}   /* display_header */
```

```
/*
display_border() puts a border around the window.
*/

void window::display_border(int b_attr)
{
    for (register int i = start_r + 1; i < end_r; i++) {
        dos_screen.display_char(i, start_c, VERTICAL_BAR, b_attr);
        dos_screen.display_char(i, end_c, VERTICAL_BAR, b_attr);
    }
    for (i = start_c + 1; i < end_c; i++) {
        dos_screen.display_char(start_r, i, HORIZON_BAR, b_attr);
        dos_screen.display_char(end_r, i, HORIZON_BAR, b_attr);
    }
    dos_screen.display_char(start_r, start_c, TOP_LEFT_CORNER, b_attr);
    dos_screen.display_char(start_r, end_c, TOP_RIGHT_CORNER, b_attr);
    dos_screen.display_char(end_r, start_c, BOT_LEFT_CORNER, b_attr);
    dos_screen.display_char(end_r, end_c, BOT_RIGHT_CORNER, b_attr);
}   /* display_border */


/*
wputchar() prints a character in the window.
*/

int window::wputchar(char ch)
{
    if (!is_active)
        return FALSE;
    /*
    no error checking
    */
    int r = cursor_r + start_r + 1;
    int c = virtual_c + start_c + 1 - offset;
    if (ch == LF) {
        cursor_r++;
        virtual_c = 0;
        offset = 0;
    }
    else {
        char far *win_ptr = dos_screen.get_screen_addr();
        win_ptr = char_addr(win_ptr, r, c);
        *win_ptr++ = ch;
```

```
        *win_ptr++ = attr;
        virtual_c++;
    }
    go_rc(cursor_r, virtual_c);
    return TRUE;
}   /* wputchar */


/*
wgetche() reads a character from the window, with echo.
*/

int window::wgetche()
{
    keystroke key;

    if (!is_active)
        return FALSE;
    go_rc(cursor_r, virtual_c);
    key.word = dos_keybd.get_keystroke();
    if (!key.byte[0] || key.byte[0] == CR || key.byte[0] == BKSP
            || key.byte[0] == TAB || key.byte[0] == EOF_CHAR)
        return key.word;
    echo_char(key.byte[0]);
    return key.word;
}   /* wgetche */


/*
echo_char() echos a character to the screen.
*/

void window::echo_char(char ch)
{
    if ((virtual_c + start_c - offset) < (end_c - 1)) {
        dos_screen.display_char(start_r + cursor_r + 1,
                        start_c + virtual_c + 1 - offset,
                        ch, attr);
        go_rc(cursor_r, ++virtual_c);
    }
}   /* echo_char */


/*
```

```
clr_rest() clears the remainder of the window--relative to the
cursor, that is, current (x,y) coordinates--NOT window coordinates.
*/

void window::clr_rest()
{
    char far *win_ptr = dos_screen.get_screen_addr();
    char far *win_ptr_2;
    for (register int i = start_c + 1 + virtual_c - offset,
            j = start_r + 1 + cursor_r;
            i < end_c; i++) {
        win_ptr_2 = char_addr(win_ptr, j, i);
        *win_ptr_2++ = BLANK;
        *win_ptr_2 = attr;
    }
    for (i = start_c + 1; i < end_c; i++)
        for (j = start_r + 1 + cursor_r + 1; j < end_r; j++) {
            win_ptr_2 = char_addr(win_ptr, j, i);
            *win_ptr_2++ = BLANK;
            *win_ptr_2 = attr;
        }
}   /* clr_rest */


/*
clr_eol() clears/overwrites the current line of the window
from the current position to the end of the line.
*/

void window::clr_eol()
{
    register int r = cursor_r, c = virtual_c,
                last_c = end_c - 1 - start_c + offset;
    for (register int i = virtual_c; i < last_c; i++)
        wputchar(BLANK);
    go_rc(r, c);
}   /* clr_eol */


/*
up_line() moves up one line in the window.
*/

int window::up_line()
```

```
{
    if (cursor_r > 0) {
        cursor_r--;
        go_rc(cursor_r, virtual_c);
        return TRUE;
    }
    return FALSE;
}   /* up_line */


/*
down_line() advances to the next line in the window.
*/

int window::down_line()
{
    if (cursor_r < end_r - start_r - 2) {
        cursor_r++;
        go_rc(cursor_r, virtual_c);
        return TRUE;
    }
    return FALSE;
}   /* down_line */


/*
cursor_bottom() takes the cursor to the bottom line of
the window, column 0;
*/

void window::cursor_bottom()
{
    go_rc(end_r - start_r - 2, 0);
}   /* cursor_bottom */


/*
scroll() scrolls the window up, or down, one line, depending on
the value of the second argument, operation.
*/

void window::scroll(int operation)
{
    REGS r;
```

```
    r.h.ah = operation;
    r.h.al = 1;
    r.h.ch = start_r + 1;
    r.h.cl = start_c + 1;
    r.h.dh = end_r - 1;
    r.h.dl = end_c - 1;
    r.h.bh = attr;
    int86(VIDEO_INT, &r, &r);
}   /* scroll */


/*
go_rc() sets the coordinates within the window, and goes there.
*/

int window::go_rc(int r, int c)
{
    if ((r < 0) || ((r + start_r) >= (end_r - 1)))
        return FALSE;
    if ((c < 0) || ((c + start_c - offset) >= (end_c - 1)))
        return FALSE;
    cursor_r = r;
    virtual_c = c;
    dos_screen.cursor_rc(start_r + r + 1, start_c + c + 1 - offset);
    return TRUE;
}   /* go_rc */


/*
rightmost_col() returns the rightmost column of the window, not
including the border column--this is a zero-based, relative position.
*/

int window::rightmost_col()
{
    return end_c - start_c - 2 + offset;
}   /* rightmost_col */


/*
bottommost_row() returns the bottommost row of the window, not
including the border row--this is a zero-based, relative position.
*/
```

```
int window::bottommost_row()
{
    return end_r - start_r - 2;
}   /* bottommost_row */


/*
save_screen_area() saves the screen area to a buffer.
*/

void window::save_screen_area()
{
    char *win_buf = window_save_buffer;
    char far *win_ptr = dos_screen.get_screen_addr();
    register int k = 0;
    for (register int i = start_c; i < end_c + 1; i++)
        for (register int j = start_r; j < end_r + 1; j++) {
            char far *win_ptr_2 = char_addr(win_ptr, j, i);
            win_buf[k++] = *win_ptr_2;
            win_buf[k++] = *(win_ptr_2 + 1);
            *win_ptr_2 = BLANK;
        }
}   /* save_screen_area */


/*
restore_screen_area() recovers the screen area used by the window.
*/

void window::restore_screen_area()
{
    char *win_buf = window_save_buffer;
    char far *win_ptr = dos_screen.get_screen_addr();
    register int k = 0;
    for (register int i = start_c; i < end_c + 1; i++)
        for (register int j = start_r; j < end_r + 1; j++) {
            char far *win_ptr_2 = char_addr(win_ptr, j, i);
            *win_ptr_2++ = win_buf[k++];
            *win_ptr_2 = win_buf[k++];
        }
}   /* restore_screen_area */
```

```
//// winedit.cpp //// implementation of class: edit_window ////
////
//// classes used: text_window

#include "winedit.hpp"


/*
globals: these data should be available to all r/w edit windows
*/

static msg_window find_win(0, "Find/Change", 3, 16, 7,
                           16 + POPUP_WIDTH, BACK_ATTR);
static clipboard clip_bd(MAX_BUF_SIZE);
static undo_buffer undo_buf(MAX_UNDO_SIZE);


/*
edit_window() establishes initial values for a number of
critical window variables.
*/

edit_window::edit_window(int win_no, char *hdr, int start_r,
    int start_c, int end_r, int end_c, long buf_size, int attr) :
    (win_no, hdr, start_r, start_c, end_r, end_c, buf_size, attr)
{
    buffer_modified(FALSE);
    set_insert_mode(SET);
    if (find_win.get_error_state() || clip_bd.get_error_state() ||
            undo_buf.get_error_state())
        error_state = TRUE;     // can't use the editor w/o these
}   /* edit_window */


/*
dispatcher() dispatches keystroke commands to process_cmd(),
as long as process_cmd() can continue to process them.
*/

int edit_window::dispatcher()
{
    keystroke key;

    do {
```

```
        key.word = wgetche();
    } while (process_cmd(key));
    return key.word;
}   /* dispatcher */


/*
process_cmd() processes keystroke commands.
*/

int edit_window::process_cmd(keystroke key)
{
    if (key.byte[0])
        switch (key.byte[0]) {
            case EOF_CHAR:          // don't allow the user to
                break;              // enter an EOF character
            case BKSP:
                backspace();
                break;
            default:
                insert_char(key.byte[0]);
                break;
        }
    else
        switch (key.byte[1]) {
            case DEL:
                del_char();
                break;
            case DWORD:
                del_word();
                break;
            case DWORD_LEFT:
                del_word_left();
                break;
            case DEOL:
                del_eol();
                break;
            case DLINE:
                del_line();
                break;
            case CUT:
                cut_to_clipboard();
                break;
            case COPY:
```

```
                copy_to_clipboard();
                break;
            case PASTE:
                paste_from_buffer(clip_bd);
                break;
            case FIND_TEXT:
                find_and_change(FIND_IT);
                break;
            case CHANGE_TEXT:
                find_and_change(CHANGE_IT);
                break;
            case REPEAT_FC:
                find_and_change(REPEAT_IT);
                break;
            case UNDO:
                paste_from_undo();
                break;
            case INS:
                set_insert_mode(get_insert_mode() ? RESET : SET);
                break;
            default:
                return text_window::process_cmd(key);    // submit to
        }                                                // a higher authority
    return key.word;
}   /* process_cmd */


/*
buffer_modified() records whether or not the buffer has been
modified, and displays an indicator of this condition on screen,
each time that it changes.
*/

int edit_window::buffer_modified(int change_state)
{
    buf_mod_state = change_state;
    if (buf_mod_state)
        set_tag_pos(UNDEFINED);
    dos_screen.display_char(BOT_ROW, MODIFIED_COLUMN,
                (buf_mod_state ? 'M' : BLANK), REV_BORDER_COLOR);
    return buf_mod_state;
}   /* buffer_modified */
```

```
/*
buffer_modified(void) simply tests whether or not a buffer
has been modified.
*/

int edit_window::buffer_modified()
{
    return buf_mod_state;
}   /* buffer_modified */


/*
set_insert_mode() sets insert/overwrite mode and displays
an indicator of the current state.
*/

int edit_window::set_insert_mode(int change_state)
{
    insert_mode = change_state;
    dos_screen.display_char(BOT_ROW, INSERT_MODE_COLUMN,
                (insert_mode ? 'I' : 'O'), REV_BORDER_COLOR);
    return insert_mode;
}   /* set_insert_mode */


/*
insert_char() inserts characters into the buffer and updates
the screen as necessary.  It must take into consideration the
fact that window::wgetche() has already updated the current
screen coordinates--for displayable characters.
*/

int edit_window::insert_char(char ch)
{
    text_window::insert_char(ch);
    if (insert_mode)
        update_undo_dependent_offset(1);
    buffer_modified(TRUE);
}   /* insert_char */


/*
del_char() deletes a character from the buffer
and updates the screen.
```

```
*/

int edit_window::del_char()
{
    if (text_window::del_char())
        update_undo_dependent_offset(-1);
    buffer_modified(TRUE);
}   /* del_char */


/*
backspace() moves the cursor to the left one column
and then deletes that character.
*/

int edit_window::backspace()
{
    if (text_window::backspace())
        update_undo_dependent_offset(-1);
    buffer_modified(TRUE);
}   /* backspace */


/*
del_word() deletes a "word," or string of characters.  Leading
blanks are also deleted.  Punctuation characters serve as
word delimiters also.  del_word() determines the location of
the to-be-deleted characters and calls cut_to_undo() to perform
the deletion.  Deletions performed by cut_to_undo() can be undone.
*/

int edit_window::del_word()
{
    long last_pos;      // the last/final character to be deleted

    if ((last_pos = buf_cursor_pos) == buf_length)
        return FALSE;
    else {
        if (buffer[last_pos] == LF)
            last_pos++;
        else if (buffer[last_pos] == BLANK || buffer[last_pos] == TAB)
            while (buffer[last_pos] == BLANK ||
                    buffer[last_pos] == TAB)
                last_pos++;
```

```
        else {
            if (ispunc(buffer[last_pos]))
                last_pos++;
            while (buffer[last_pos] && !isspace(buffer[last_pos]) &&
                    !ispunc(buffer[last_pos]))
                last_pos++;
            if (buffer[last_pos] == BLANK)
                last_pos++;
        }
        return cut_to_undo(last_pos);
    }
}   /* del_word */


/*
del_word_left() deletes the word to the left of the cursor.
*/

int edit_window::del_word_left()
{
    if (word_left())
        return del_word();
    else
        return FALSE;
}   /* del_word_left */


/*
del_eol() deletes all characters between the cursor and the end of
the line by first determining the respective buffer offsets, and
then calling cut_to_undo().  As with del_word(), this operation can
be undone.
*/

int edit_window::del_eol()
{
    long last_pos;       // the last/final character to be deleted

    if (buffer[last_pos = buf_cursor_pos] == LF ||
            buffer[last_pos] == EOS) {
        attn_win.message("", "** already at end of line **");
        return FALSE;
    }
    else {
```

```
        while (buffer[last_pos] && buffer[last_pos] != LF)
            last_pos++;
        return cut_to_undo(last_pos);
    }
}   /* del_eol */


/*
del_line() deletes an entire line using cut_to_undo(); hence, this
operation can be undone.
*/

int edit_window::del_line()
{
    long last_pos;      // the last/final character to be deleted

    go_line_start();
    window_restore_shift();
    go_rc(cursor_r, 0);
    last_pos = buf_cursor_pos;
    while (buffer[last_pos] && buffer[last_pos] != LF)
        last_pos++;
    if (buffer[last_pos])       // don't delete EOS character
        last_pos++;
    return cut_to_undo(last_pos);
}   /* del_line */


/*
paste() inserts the contents of a generic buffer at the current
cursor position in the edit buffer.  It can be used by a number
of routines.
*/

int edit_window::paste(char *from_buffer)
{
    long from_length = strlen(from_buffer);
    if (from_length > 0 &&
            from_length <= max_buf_size - buf_length - 1) {
        buffer_modified(TRUE);
        memmove(&buffer[buf_cursor_pos + from_length],
                    &buffer[buf_cursor_pos],
                    buf_length - buf_cursor_pos + 1);
        buf_length += from_length;
```

```
        memcpy(&buffer[buf_cursor_pos], from_buffer, from_length);
        if (linefeed_free(from_buffer, from_length))
            redisplay_rest_of_line(0);
        else
            if (offset == 0)
                window_fill(cursor_r, virtual_c, buf_cursor_pos);
            else
                window_shift_right(0);
        return TRUE;
    }
    else {
        if (from_length == 0)
            attn_win.message("", "** clipboard is empty **");
        else
            attn_win.message("",
                    "** not enough space to paste/insert **");
        return FALSE;
    }
}   /* paste */


/*
paste_from_buffer() provides a mechanism for performing a top-level
paste operation, hiding the details of the necessary call to paste(),
where the proper buffer must be given as an argument.
*/

int edit_window::paste_from_buffer(char_buffer &gen_buf)
{
    update_undo_dependent_offset(strlen(gen_buf.get_buffer()));
    return paste(gen_buf.get_buffer());
}   /* paste_from_buffer */


/*
copy_to_clipboard() copies a portion of the edit buffer to
the clipboard.  NOTE:  the tag is left "as is."  The clipboard
must be a friend.
*/

int edit_window::copy_to_clipboard()
{
    long clip_length;
```

```
    if (tag_pos == UNDEFINED || tag_pos == buf_cursor_pos) {
        attn_win.message("", "** nothing to cut/copy **");
        return FALSE;
    }
    else {
        if (tag_pos > buf_cursor_pos)
            exch_tag_cursor();
        if ((clip_length = buf_cursor_pos - tag_pos)
                >= clip_bd.get_max_size()) {
            attn_win.message("", "** too large for clipboard **");
            return FALSE;
        }
        else {
            memcpy(clip_bd.buffer, &buffer[tag_pos], clip_length);
            clip_bd.buffer[clip_length] = EOS;
            return TRUE;
        }
    }
}   /* copy_to_clipboard */


/*
cut_to_clipboard() cuts a portion of the edit buffer to the
clipboard.  To do so, it uses copy_to_clipboard() to perform the
first half of the operation.  NOTE:  the tag is removed.  The
clipboard must be a friend.
*/

int edit_window::cut_to_clipboard()
{
    if (copy_to_clipboard()) {
        long clip_length = buf_cursor_pos - tag_pos;
        update_undo_dependent_offset_for_cut(-clip_length);
        memmove(&buffer[tag_pos], &buffer[buf_cursor_pos],
                buf_length - buf_cursor_pos + 1);
        buf_length -= clip_length;
        buf_cursor_pos = tag_pos;
        if (linefeed_free(clip_bd.buffer, clip_length)) {
            go_rc(cursor_r, get_tag_column());
            redisplay_rest_of_line(UNDEFINED);
        }
        else
            redisplay_window(current_column_offset());
        buffer_modified(TRUE);
```

```
        set_tag_pos(UNDEFINED);
        return TRUE;
    }
}   /* cut_to_clipboard */


/*
cut_to_undo() cuts a portion of the edit buffer to the undo buffer.
The cut operation begins at the cursor and ends with the location
passed in the parameter end.  The undo buffer must be a friend
*/

int edit_window::cut_to_undo(long end)
{
    undo_buf.cursor_when_cut[win_no] = buf_cursor_pos;
    long start = buf_cursor_pos;
    long clip_length = end - start;
    if (clip_length <= 0) {
        attn_win.message("", "** nothing to delete **");
        return FALSE;
    }
    else if (clip_length >= undo_buf.get_max_size()) {
        attn_win.message("", "** too large to delete **");
        return FALSE;
    }
    else {
        buffer_modified(TRUE);
        memcpy(undo_buf.buffer, &buffer[start], clip_length);
        undo_buf.buffer[clip_length] = EOS;
        memmove(&buffer[start], &buffer[end], buf_length - end + 1);
        buf_length -= clip_length;
        if (linefeed_free(undo_buf.buffer, clip_length))
            redisplay_rest_of_line(UNDEFINED);
        else
            if (offset == 0)
                window_fill(cursor_r, virtual_c, start);
            else
                window_shift_right(0);
        return TRUE;
    }
} /* cut_to_undo */


/*
```

```
paste_from_undo() accesses the undo buffer and pastes it into
the edit buffer at the cursor.  The undo buffer must be a friend.
*/

int edit_window::paste_from_undo()
{
    if (strlen(undo_buf.buffer) > 0) {
        if (buf_cursor_pos != undo_buf.cursor_when_cut[win_no]) {
            buf_cursor_pos = undo_buf.cursor_when_cut[win_no];
            redisplay_window(current_column_offset());
        }
        return paste(undo_buf.buffer);
    }
    else {
        attn_win.message("", "** nothing to undo **");
        return FALSE;
    }
}   /* paste_from_undo */


/*
find_and_change manages simple text find (search) and change (replace)
operations.  Previous find-and-change activity is recorded within
find_and_change() to allow the user to repeat the command.
*/

int edit_window::find_and_change(int operation)
{
    static char find_text[MAX_STR] = "";
    static char change_text[MAX_STR] = "";
    static int last_operation = FALSE;

    if (operation == REPEAT_IT && !last_operation)
        return FALSE;                               // nothing to repeat

    if (operation != REPEAT_IT)
        if (!prompt_for_pattern(last_operation = operation,
                                find_text, change_text)) {
            find_win.deactivate();
            return FALSE;                           // user pressed <Esc>
        }
    long offset = (operation == REPEAT_IT) ? 1 : 0; // don't find the
                                                    // same text
    if ((offset = string_search(buffer, find_text,
```

```
                                buf_cursor_pos + offset)) == -1) {
            display_not_found(operation, find_text);
            return FALSE;
        }
        else {
            find_win.deactivate();
            buf_cursor_pos = offset;
            redisplay_window(current_column_offset());
            if (operation == CHANGE_IT || last_operation == CHANGE_IT)
                replace_text(find_text, change_text, offset);
            return TRUE;
        }
}   /* find_and_change */


/*
prompt_for_pattern() prompts the user for the search pattern, and
optionally, a replacement pattern.  It activates, but does not
deactivate, the "find" window.  It returns FALSE, if <Esc> was
pressed.
*/

int edit_window::prompt_for_pattern(int operation, char *find_text,
                            char *change_text)
{
    char find_txt[MAX_STR], change_txt[MAX_STR];

    find_win.activate("");
    find_win.wputs(" Find: ");
    if (!find_win.wgets_filter(find_txt, MAX_STR))
        return FALSE;
    if (operation == CHANGE_IT) {
        find_win.go_rc(1, 0);
        find_win.wputs(" Change to: ");
        if (!find_win.wgets_filter(change_txt, MAX_STR))
            return FALSE;
        strcpy(change_text, change_txt);
    }
    strcpy(find_text, find_txt);
    return TRUE;
}   /* prompt_for_pattern */


/*
```

```
replace_text() performs the exchange of text.
*/

int edit_window::replace_text(char *find_text, char *change_text,
                              long offset)
{
    cut_to_undo(offset + strlen(find_text));
    if (!paste(change_text)) {
        paste(undo_buf.buffer);
        attn_win.message("", "** not enough edit space **");
    }
    undo_buf.buffer[0] = EOS;
    undo_buf.cursor_when_cut[win_no] = UNDEFINED;
}   /* replace_text */


/*
display_not_found() displays a "pattern not found" message for the
user, and then deactivates the "find" window.
*/

void edit_window::display_not_found(int operation, char *find_text)
{
    if (operation == REPEAT_IT) {
        find_win.activate("");
        find_win.wputs(" Find: ");
        find_win.wputs(find_text);
    }
    find_win.cursor_bottom();
    find_win.wputs(" Pattern not found -- press any key...");
    find_win.wgetche();
    find_win.deactivate();
}   /* display_not_found */


/*
string_search() searches search_string for the first occurrence of
search_text.  If search_text is null, it returns -1, instead of
entering the search loop; otherwise, it returns the buffer offset
where search_text begins.
*/

long edit_window::string_search(char *search_ptr, char *search_text,
                        register long offset)
```

```
{
    register int next;
    register long begin_match_offset = offset;

    if (*search_text)
        for (next = 0; search_ptr[offset]; offset++)
            if (search_ptr[offset] == search_text[next]) {
                begin_match_offset = offset;
                while (search_text[next] &&
                        search_ptr[offset++] == search_text[next++])
                    ;
                if (!search_text[next] &&
                        search_ptr[--offset] == search_text[--next])
                    return begin_match_offset;
                offset = begin_match_offset;
                next = 0;
            }
    return -1;
}   /* string_search */


/*
update_undo_dependent_offset() modifies the buffer offset for
the undo marker.  If a buffer modification is made at an
offset less than the undo marker, the undo marker must be
updated accordingly.
*/

int edit_window::update_undo_dependent_offset(long adjustment)
{
    if (buf_cursor_pos <= undo_buf.cursor_when_cut[win_no]) {
        if (adjustment < 0 &&
                (buf_cursor_pos + -adjustment >
                    undo_buf.cursor_when_cut[win_no])) {// "cut" spans
            undo_buf.buffer[0] = EOS;                  // undo marker
            undo_buf.cursor_when_cut[win_no] = UNDEFINED;
        }
        else
            undo_buf.cursor_when_cut[win_no] += adjustment;
        return TRUE;
    }
    else
        return FALSE;
}   /* update_undo_dependent_offset */
```

```
int edit_window::update_undo_dependent_offset_for_cut(long adjustment)
{
    if (tag_pos <= undo_buf.cursor_when_cut[win_no]) {
        if (tag_pos + -adjustment > undo_buf.cursor_when_cut[win_no]) {
            undo_buf.buffer[0] = EOS;
            undo_buf.cursor_when_cut[win_no] = UNDEFINED;
        }
        else
            undo_buf.cursor_when_cut[win_no] += adjustment;
        return TRUE;
    }
    else
        return FALSE;
}   /* update_undo_dependent_offset_for_cut */


////  winmsgs.cpp  //// implementation of class:  msg_window  ////
////
////  classes used:  window

#include "winmsgs.hpp"


/*
msg_window() initializes the window and sets up a buffer where the
existing screen area can be saved during the window's activation.
*/

msg_window::msg_window(int win_no, char *header, int start_r,
        int start_c, int end_r, int end_c, int attr) :
        (win_no, header, start_r, start_c, end_r, end_c, attr)
{
}   /* msg_window */


/*
deactivate() calls the related parent function to restore the
previous screen text, and, in addition, resets the cursor
position.
*/

int msg_window::deactivate()
```

```
{
    if (window::deactivate()) {
        cursor_r = virtual_c = offset = 0;
        return TRUE;
    }
    else
        return FALSE;
}   /* deactivate */


/*
wputs() prints a string in the window.
*/

int msg_window::wputs(char *str)
{
    if (!is_active)
        return FALSE;
    for ( ; *str; str++)
        wputchar(*str);
    return TRUE;
}   /* wputs */


/*
wputs_center() pads a string with blanks, and then calls
wputs() to output the text in the window.
*/

int msg_window::wputs_center(char *str)
{
    if (!is_active)
        return FALSE;
    else {
        int num_blanks =
                ((end_c - start_c - 1 - strlen(str)) / 2) - 1;
        while (num_blanks-- > 0)
            wputchar(BLANK);
        return wputs(str);
    }
}   /* wputs_center */


/*
```

```
wgets_filter() reads a string from the window, up to some maximum
limit, as long as printable ASCII characters are entered.  If
<Esc> is pressed, it returns FALSE.
*/

int msg_window::wgets_filter(char *str, int limit)

// limit is the limit for number of characters that can be read.

{
    char *temp = str;
    char *start = str;
    for (int i = 0, max_len = limit - 1; i < max_len; ) {
        char ch = wgetche();            // truncate returned value
        switch (ch) {
            case ESC:
                *start = EOS;           // return a null string
                return FALSE;
            case CR:
                *str = EOS;
                return TRUE;
            case BKSP:
                if (str > temp) {
                    str--;
                    i--;
                    backspace_char();
                }
                break;
            default:
                if (!isprint(ch)) {
                    *str = EOS;
                    return TRUE;
                }
                *str = ch;
                str++;
                i++;
        }
    }
    if (i == max_len)           // reached limit, terminate string
        *str = EOS;
    return TRUE;
}   /* wgets_filter */
```

```
/*
backspace_char() attempts to remove the previously entered
character from the "buffer."
*/

void msg_window::backspace_char()
{
    virtual_c--;
    if (virtual_c < 0)
        virtual_c = offset = 0;
    go_rc(cursor_r, virtual_c);
    dos_screen.display_char(start_r + cursor_r + 1,
                start_c + virtual_c + 1 - offset,
                BLANK, BACK_ATTR);
}   /* backspace_char */


////  winprmt.cpp  ////  implementation of class:  prompt_window  ////
////
////  classes used:  text_window

#include "winprmt.hpp"


/*
prompt_window() passes window initialization values to the
parent constructor.
*/

prompt_window::prompt_window(int win_no, char *hdr, int start_r,
        int start_c, int end_r, int end_c, long buf_size, int attr) :
        (win_no, hdr, start_r, start_c, end_r, end_c, buf_size, attr)
{
    set_insert_mode(SET);
}   /* prompt_window */


/*
dispatcher() dispatches keystroke commands.  A programmer-defined
"break key" can be used to abandon the prompt box, in addition to
the <Enter> and <Esc> keys.
*/

int prompt_window::dispatcher(int break_prompt)
```

```
{
    keystroke key;

    top_of_buffer_redisplay();
    do {
        key.word = wgetche();
        process_cmd(key);
    } while (!((!key.byte[0] && key.byte[1] == break_prompt) ||
                key.byte[0] == CR || key.byte[0] == ESC));
    return key.word;
}   /* dispatcher */


/*
dispatcher() dispatches keystroke commands.  The prompt box is
terminated when the user presses either <Enter> and <Esc>.
*/

int prompt_window::dispatcher()
{
    keystroke key;

    top_of_buffer_redisplay();
    do {
        key.word = wgetche();
        process_cmd(key);
    } while (!(key.byte[0] == CR || key.byte[0] == ESC));
    return key.word;
}   /* dispatcher */


/*
process_cmd() processes keystroke commands.
*/

int prompt_window::process_cmd(keystroke key)
{
    if (key.byte[0])
        switch (key.byte[0]) {
            case ESC:                   // terminate the prompt editing
            case CR:
                return key.word;
            case EOF_CHAR:              // don't allow the user to
                break;                  // enter an EOF character
```

```
            case BKSP:
                backspace();
                break;
            default:
                insert_char(key.byte[0]);
                break;
        }
    else
        switch (key.byte[1]) {
            case DEL:
                del_char();
                break;
            case DEOL:
                    del_rest_of_line();
                break;
            case INS:
                set_insert_mode(get_insert_mode() ? RESET : SET);
                break;
            default:
                return text_window::process_cmd(key);   // submit to
        }                                               // a higher authority
    return key.word;
}   /* process_cmd */


/*
set_insert_mode() sets insert/overwrite mode and displays
an indicator of the current state.
*/

int prompt_window::set_insert_mode(int change_state)
{
    return (insert_mode = change_state);
}   /* set_insert_mode */


/*
del_rest_of_line() deletes the remaining characters on
a line without the possibility of undelete.
*/
int prompt_window::del_rest_of_line()
{
    if (buffer[buf_cursor_pos] == LF ||
            buffer[buf_cursor_pos] == EOS)
```

```
        return FALSE;
    else {
        long start = buf_cursor_pos;
        long end = go_line_end();
        memmove(&buffer[start], &buffer[end], buf_length - end + 1);
        buf_length -= end - start;
        buf_cursor_pos = start;
        redisplay_rest_of_line(UNDEFINED);
        return TRUE;
    }
}   /* del_rest_of_line */


////  wintext.cpp  ////  implementation of class:  text_window  ////
////
////  classes used:  buf_window

#include "wintext.hpp"


/*
text_window() establishes initial values for a number of
critical editor variables.
*/

text_window::text_window(int win_no, char *hdr, int start_r,
    int start_c, int end_r, int end_c, long buf_size, int attr) :
    (win_no, hdr, start_r, start_c, end_r, end_c, buf_size, attr)
{
    set_tag_pos(UNDEFINED);
}   /* text_window */


/*
process_cmd() processes keystroke commands.  It returns FALSE if it
can't do anything with a command.
*/

int text_window::process_cmd(keystroke key)
{
    if (key.byte[0])
        return FALSE;           // can't process read-write commands
    switch (key.byte[1]) {
        case LEFT:
```

```
            cursor_left();
            break;
        case RIGHT:
            cursor_right();
            break;
        case UP:
            up();
            break;
        case DOWN:
            down();
            break;
        case CTRL_LEFT:
            word_left();
            break;
        case CTRL_RIGHT:
            word_right();
            break;
        case HOME:
            home();
            break;
        case END:
            endd();
            break;
        case PGUP:
            page_up();
            break;
        case PGDN:
            page_down();
            break;
        case CTRL_PGUP:
            top_of_buffer();
            break;
        case CTRL_PGDN:
            bottom_of_buffer();
            break;
        case CTRL_HOME:
            top_of_window();
            break;
        case CTRL_END:
            bottom_of_window();
            break;
        case TAG:
            set_tag_pos();
            break;
```

```
        case UNTAG:
            set_tag_pos(UNDEFINED);
            break;
        case TAG_CURSOR:
            exch_tag_cursor_redisplay();
            break;
        case SET_TABS:
            change_tab_width();
            break;
        default:
            return FALSE;           // can't process command
    }
    return key.word;
}   /* process_cmd */


/*
get_insert_mode() determines the insert/overwrite state.
*/

int text_window::get_insert_mode()
{
    return insert_mode;
}   /* get_insert_mode */


/*
set_tag_pos() sets a tag; it uses buf_cursor_pos to
set the tag position.
*/

long text_window::set_tag_pos()
{
    return (tag_pos = buf_cursor_pos);
}   /* set_tag_pos */


/*
set_tag_pos() allows a tag to be turned off.
*/

long text_window::set_tag_pos(int new_pos)
{
    if (new_pos == UNDEFINED)
```

```
        tag_pos = UNDEFINED;
    return tag_pos;
}   /* set_tag_pos */


/*
get_tag_pos() determines the current tag position.
*/

long text_window::get_tag_pos()
{
    return tag_pos;
}   /* get_tag_pos */


/*
insert_char() inserts characters into the buffer and updates
the screen as necessary.  It must take into consideration the
fact that window::wgetche() has already updated the current
screen coordinates--for displayable characters.
*/

int text_window::insert_char(char ch)
{
    if (insertion_special_conditions(ch))
        return FALSE;
    else {
        if (ch == CR)
            ch = LF;
        long insert_point = buf_cursor_pos;
        if (insert_mode || buffer[insert_point] == LF) {
            memmove(&buffer[insert_point + 1], &buffer[insert_point],
                        buf_length - insert_point + 1);
            buf_length++;
        }
        else
            if (buffer[insert_point] == EOS) {  // in overwrite mode
                buffer[insert_point + 1] = EOS; // don't destroy EOS
                buf_length++;
            }
        int tab_overwrite =
                !insert_mode && buffer[insert_point] == TAB;
        buffer[insert_point] = ch;
        if (!insert_mode && !tab_overwrite &&
```

```
                !adjacent_to_rightmost_column())// a simple overwrite,
            buf_cursor_pos++;                   // so just increment
        else
            insert_window_update(ch, insert_point);
        return TRUE;
    }
}   /* insert_char */


/*
insertion_special_conditions() handles a number of special
conditions that can occur relative to insertion of characters.
*/

int text_window::insertion_special_conditions(char ch)
{
    if (buf_length + 1 >= max_buf_size) {
        if (ch != CR)
            go_rc(cursor_r, virtual_c - 1);
        redisplay_rest_of_line(1);
        attn_win.message("** edit space is full **", "");
        return TRUE;
    }
    else if (!insert_mode && ch == CR) {
        down();
        home();
        return TRUE;                        // do "local" CR only
    }
    else if (!insert_mode && ch == TAB) {
        advance_cursor_to_next_tab();
        return TRUE;                        // do "local" TAB only
    }
    else
        return FALSE;
}   /* insertion_special_conditions */


/*
advance_cursor_to_next_tab() moves the cursor to the next tab stop.
*/

void text_window::advance_cursor_to_next_tab()
{
    int tab_stop;
```

```
    long i;

    for (i = buf_cursor_pos, tab_stop = next_tab_column();
            buffer[i] && buffer[i] != LF && virtual_c < tab_stop; i++)
        cursor_right();
}   /* advance_cursor_to_next_tab */


/*
insert_window_update() performs the screen related updates for
the text window subsequent to character insertion.  Also, it
increments the buffer position.
*/

void text_window::insert_window_update(char ch, long insert_point)
{
    if (ch == LF) {
        clr_eol();
        window_restore_shift();
        if (down_line()) {
            buf_cursor_pos++;
            window_fill(cursor_r, 0, insert_point + 1);
        }
        else
            window_scroll_up(0);
    }
    else {
        int cur_c = virtual_c;
        if (ch != TAB)                      // back up--wgetche()
            go_rc(cursor_r, --cur_c);       // incremented position
        if (adjacent_to_rightmost_column()) {
            window_shift_right(tab_width * 2);
            go_rc(cursor_r, cur_c);
        }
        else
            redisplay_rest_of_line(0);
        window_buffer_forward();
    }
}   /* insert_window_update */


/*
del_char() deletes a character from the buffer and updates the screen.
*/
```

```
int text_window::del_char()
{
    if (buf_cursor_pos == buf_length)
        return FALSE;
    else {
        char ch = buffer[buf_cursor_pos];
        memmove(&buffer[buf_cursor_pos], &buffer[buf_cursor_pos + 1],
                      buf_length - buf_cursor_pos);
        buf_length--;
        if (ch != LF)
            redisplay_rest_of_line(tab_width);
        else
            if (offset == 0)
                window_fill(cursor_r, virtual_c, buf_cursor_pos);
            else
                window_shift_right(0);
        return TRUE;
    }
}   /* del_char */


/*
backspace() moves the cursor to the left one column
and then deletes that character.
*/

int text_window::backspace()
{
    if (cursor_left())
        return del_char();
    else
        return FALSE;
}   /* backspace */


/*
up() moves the cursor up one line.  If possible, the previous
cursor column position is retained.  Scrolling may be required.
*/

int text_window::up()
{
    if (!up_line())
```

```
        return window_scroll_down(virtual_c);
    else
        return buffer_up_line(virtual_c);
}   /* up */


/*
down() moves the cursor down one line.  If possible, the previous
cursor column position is retained.  Scrolling may be required.
*/

int text_window::down()
{
    if (last_char_on_line() == EOS)
        return FALSE;
    else
        if (!down_line())
            return window_scroll_up(virtual_c);
        else
            return buffer_down_line(virtual_c);
}   /* down */


/*
cursor_left() moves left one column.  If necessary, the cursor wraps
around to the end of the previous line--at the top of the screen this
operation requires scrolling.
*/

int text_window::cursor_left()
{
    int cur_c;

    if (buf_cursor_pos == 0)
        return FALSE;
    else {
        if (adjacent_to_leftmost_column())
            if ((cur_c = virtual_c) > 0) {
                home();
                window_adjust_cursor_position(cur_c - 1);
            }
            else {
                up();
                if (!go_right_as_far_as_possible())
```

```
                    endd();
                }
            else
                window_buffer_backward();
            return TRUE;
        }
}   /* cursor_left */


/*
cursor_right() advances one column.  If necessary, the cursor wraps
around to the next line--at the bottom of the screen this operation
requires scrolling.
*/

int text_window::cursor_right()
{
    long pos;

    if ((pos = buf_cursor_pos) == buf_length)
        return FALSE;
    else if (buffer[pos] != LF && adjacent_to_rightmost_column()) {
        int cur_c = virtual_c;
        window_shift_right(tab_width * 2);
        go_rc(cursor_r, cur_c);
        window_buffer_forward();
        return TRUE;
    }
    else {
        if (buffer[pos] == LF) {
            window_restore_shift();
            if (down_line())
                go_rc(cursor_r, 0);
            else
                window_scroll_up(0);
            buf_cursor_pos++;
        }
        else
            window_buffer_forward();
        return TRUE;
    }
}   /* cursor_right */
```

```
/*
word_left() moves the cursor left to the beginning of the previous
"word," that is, to the beginning of the previous "run" of characters.
Punctuation characters serve as word delimiters also.
*/

int text_window::word_left()
{
    long i;

    if ((i = buf_cursor_pos) == 0)
        return FALSE;
    else {
        if (isspace(buffer[i - 1]) || ispunc(buffer[i - 1])) {
            cursor_left();
            i = buf_cursor_pos;
        }
        for ( ; isspace(buffer[i]); i--)
            cursor_left();
        for (i = buf_cursor_pos;
                i > 0 && !isspace(buffer[i - 1]) &&
                !ispunc(buffer[i - 1]); i--)
            cursor_left();
        if (ispunc(buffer[i - 1]))
            cursor_left();
        return TRUE;
    }
}   /* word_left */


/*
word_right() advances the cursor to the beginning of the next
"word," that is, to the beginning of the next "run" of characters.
Punctuation characters serve as word delimiters also.
*/

int text_window::word_right()
{
    for (long i = buf_cursor_pos;
            buffer[i] && !isspace(buffer[i]) && !ispunc(buffer[i]);
            i++)
        cursor_right();
    for (i = buf_cursor_pos; buffer[i] && (isspace(buffer[i])); i++)
        cursor_right();
```

```
    if (ispunc(buffer[i++])) {
        cursor_right();
        for ( ; buffer[i] && isspace(buffer[i]); i++)
            cursor_right();
    }
    return TRUE;
}   /* word_right */


/*
home() moves the cursor:
    to the beginning of the current line,
    to the leftmost position in the window, or
    up one line,
depending on the cursor's current position.  It must accommodate
tabs and "null" columns at the leftmost window position.
*/

int text_window::home()
{
    if (virtual_c == 0) {
        up();
        return FALSE;
    }
    else if (adjacent_to_leftmost_column()) {
        go_line_start();
        window_restore_shift();
        return TRUE;
    }
    else {
        go_line_start();
        window_adjust_cursor_position(offset);
        return TRUE;
    }
}   /* home */


/*
endd() moves the cursor:
    to the end of the current line,
    to the rightmost position in the window, or
    down one line, plus another endd() operation,
depending on the cursor's current position.  It must accommodate
tabs and "null" columns at the rightmost window position.
```

```
*/

int text_window::endd()
{
    if (buffer[buf_cursor_pos] == LF)
        down();
    else if (adjacent_to_rightmost_column())
        window_shift_right(window_line_length() - virtual_c - 1);
    else
        ;   // cursor is within the window
    return go_right_as_far_as_possible();
}   /* endd */


/*
page_up() moves up one page.  The cursor is
positioned in the middle of the screen (vertically).
*/

int text_window::page_up()
{
    if (buf_cursor_pos == 0)
        return FALSE;
    else {
        move_backward_x_lines(page_size);
        redisplay_window(virtual_c);
        return TRUE;
    }
}   /* page_up */


/*
page_down() moves down one page.  The cursor is
positioned in the middle of the screen (vertically).
*/

int text_window::page_down()
{
    if (buf_cursor_pos == buf_length)
        return FALSE;
    else {
        move_forward_x_lines(page_size);
        redisplay_window(virtual_c);
        return TRUE;
```

```
    }
}   /* page_down */


/*
top_of_buffer_redisplay() advances to the top of the buffer
before doing a redisplay.
*/

int text_window::top_of_buffer_redisplay()
{
    buf_cursor_pos = top_left_pos = RESET;
    offset = RESET;
    window_fill(0, 0, 0);
    return TRUE;
}   /* top_of_buffer_redisplay */


/*
top_of_buffer() checks to see if the top-most character is
on-screen before doing a redisplay.
*/

int text_window::top_of_buffer()
{
    if (top_left_pos == 0)
        return top_of_window();
    else
        return top_of_buffer_redisplay();
}   /* top_of_buffer */


/*
bottom_of_buffer() moves the cursor to the last displayable character
of the last line in the file/buffer.
*/

int text_window::bottom_of_buffer()
{
    if (buf_cursor_pos == buf_length)
        return FALSE;
    else {
        buf_cursor_pos = buf_length;
        redisplay_window(window_line_length() - 1);
```

```
        return TRUE;
    }
}   /* bottom_of_buffer */


/*
top_of_window() moves the cursor to the top-left position
of the window.
*/

int text_window::top_of_window()
{
    if (buf_cursor_pos == 0)
        return FALSE;
    else {
        buf_cursor_pos = top_left_pos;
        go_rc(0, 0);
        window_restore_shift();
        return TRUE;
    }
}   /* top_of_window */


/*
bottom_of_window() moves the cursor to the bottom-left
position of the window.
*/

int text_window::bottom_of_window()
{
    int cur_r = cursor_r;
    cursor_bottom();
    int lines_moved = move_forward_x_lines(cursor_r - cur_r);
    window_restore_shift();
    go_rc(cur_r + lines_moved, 0);
    return TRUE;
}   /* bottom_of_window */


/*
exch_tag_and_cursor_redisplay() swaps the tag and the cursor in
the buffer and then redisplays the edit buffer.
*/
```

```
void text_window::exch_tag_cursor_redisplay()
{
    if (tag_pos == UNDEFINED)
        attn_win.message("", "** no tag has been set **");
    else {
        int cur_c = get_tag_column();
        exch_tag_cursor();
        redisplay_window(cur_c);
    }
}   /* exch_tag_cursor_redisplay */


/*
exch_tag_cursor() is a generic routine that physically swaps the tag
and the cursor without updating the display.  See, for example,
exch_tag_cursor_redisplay().
*/

long text_window::exch_tag_cursor()
{
    if (tag_pos != UNDEFINED) {
        long temp = tag_pos;
        tag_pos = buf_cursor_pos;
        return (buf_cursor_pos = temp);
    }
    else
        return UNDEFINED;
}   /* exch_tag_cursor */


/*
get_tag_column() computes the window offset (on-screen
column) for the tag.
*/

int text_window::get_tag_column()
{
    long old_cursor_offset = buf_cursor_pos;
    buf_cursor_pos = tag_pos;
    int column = current_column_offset();
    buf_cursor_pos = old_cursor_offset;
    return column;
}   /* get_tag_column */
```

```
/*
redisplay_window() redisplays the buffer in the text window with
the cursor positioned (vertically) in the middle of the window.  It
assumes that the cursor is positioned at the beginning of the line
(in the buffer).
*/

int text_window::redisplay_window(int current_c)
{
    long old_buf_pos = go_line_start();
    int lines_moved = move_backward_x_lines(page_size / 2);
    top_left_pos = buf_cursor_pos;
    buf_cursor_pos = old_buf_pos;
    go_rc(lines_moved, DUMMY);
    if (!window_adjust_cursor_position(current_c))
        window_shift_right(0);
    return lines_moved;
}   /* redisplay_window */


/*
redisplay_rest_of_line() redisplays the remainder of the line,
beginning at the current cursor position.  Based on the second
argument, it clears the remaining part of the line previously
occupied by text.
*/

void text_window::redisplay_rest_of_line(int num_blanks)
{
    register long i;
    register int cur_c, last_c, next_c;

    if ((cur_c = virtual_c) < offset) {
        window_restore_shift();
        go_rc(cursor_r, cur_c);
    }
    for (i = buf_cursor_pos, next_c = cur_c, last_c = rightmost_col();
            buffer[i] && buffer[i] != LF && next_c <= last_c; i++)
        if (buffer[i] == TAB)
            next_c += fill_tabs(tab_fill_size(virtual_c));
        else {
            wputchar(buffer[i]);
            next_c++;
```

```
        }
    if (num_blanks == UNDEFINED)
        for ( ; next_c <= last_c; next_c++)
            wputchar(BLANK);
    else
        for ( ; next_c <= last_c && num_blanks > 0;
                next_c++, num_blanks--)
            wputchar(BLANK);
    go_rc(cursor_r, cur_c);
}   /* redisplay_rest_of_line */


/*
window_scroll_up() is used to move the cursor down one line (closer
to the END of the buffer) and redisplay the buffer.  It is a
secondary function, and is called by, for example, down(), when the
cursor is already on the bottom line.
*/

int text_window::window_scroll_up(int current_c)
{
    if (last_char_on_line() == EOS)
        return FALSE;
    else {
        long old_buf_pos = buf_cursor_pos;
        buf_cursor_pos = top_left_pos;
        go_line_end();
        top_left_pos = ++buf_cursor_pos;
        buf_cursor_pos = old_buf_pos;
        cursor_bottom();
        if (!buffer_down_line(current_c)) {     // didn't have
            scroll(SCROLL_UP);                  // to redisplay
            go_line_start();                    // just scroll
            go_rc(cursor_r, 0);
            redisplay_rest_of_line(0);
            window_adjust_cursor_position(current_c);
        }
        return TRUE;
    }
}   /* window_scroll_up */


/*
window_scroll_down() is used to move the cursor up one line (closer
```

```
to the BEGINNING of the buffer) and redisplay the buffer.  It is a
secondary function, and is called by, for example, up(), when the
cursor is already on the top line.
*/

int text_window::window_scroll_down(int current_c)
{
    if (top_left_pos > 0) {
        buf_cursor_pos = top_left_pos - 1;
        top_left_pos = go_line_start();
        if (!window_adjust_cursor_position(current_c)) {
            scroll(SCROLL_DOWN);            // didn't have
            go_line_start();                // to redisplay
            go_rc(cursor_r, 0);             // just scroll
            redisplay_rest_of_line(0);
            window_adjust_cursor_position(current_c);
        }
        return TRUE;
    }
    else
        return FALSE;
}   /* window_scroll_down */


/*
buffer_up_line() shifts the cursor up one line, maintaining its
previous column position, if possible.  This routine does NOT
perform screen management.
*/

int text_window::buffer_up_line(int ideal_c)
{
    if (go_line_start() > 0) {
        buf_cursor_pos--;
        go_line_start();
        window_adjust_cursor_position(ideal_c);
    }
    return buf_cursor_pos;
}   /* buffer_up_line */


/*
buffer_down_line() shifts the cursor down one line, maintaining
its previous column position, if possible.  This routine does NOT
```

```
perform screen management.
*/

int text_window::buffer_down_line(int ideal_c)
{
    if (go_line_end() < buf_length) {
        buf_cursor_pos++;
        return window_adjust_cursor_position(ideal_c);
    }
    else
        return FALSE;
}   /* buffer_down_line */


/*
window_adjust_cursor_position() places the cursor in the specified
column, if possible; otherwise, it places the cursor at the end of
the line.  It returns Boolean true, if it was necessary to redisplay
the screen.  This routine assumes that the cursor is at the beginning
of the line (in the buffer).
*/

int text_window::window_adjust_cursor_position(int ideal_c)
{
    int had_to_redisplay = FALSE;

    int len = window_line_length();
    int actual_c = (ideal_c > len - 1) ? len - 1 : ideal_c;
    if (actual_c < offset || actual_c > rightmost_col()) {
        window_restore_offset_and_column();
        if (actual_c > rightmost_col())
            window_shift_right(actual_c - rightmost_col() + tab_width * 2);
        else
            window_shift_right(0);
        had_to_redisplay = TRUE;
    }
    adjust_onscreen_position(actual_c);
    return had_to_redisplay;
}   /* window_adjust_cursor_position */


/*
adjust_onscreen_position() moves the cursor to the specified column.
If the desired position is beyond the rightmost on-screen position,
```

```
the cursor is adjusted backward within the window, taking into con-
sideration any tab characters.  adjust_onscreen_position() assumes
that the cursor is at the beginning of the line (in the buffer).
If the specified column, is "null" due to tabbing the cursor is
adjusted accordingly.
*/

void text_window::adjust_onscreen_position(int ideal_c)
{
    register int column, prev_column;
    register long i;

    for (column = 0, i = buf_cursor_pos; column < ideal_c; i++) {
        prev_column = column;
        column += (buffer[i] == TAB) ? tab_fill_size(column) : 1;
    }
    if (column > ideal_c && column <= rightmost_col())
        ;
    else if (column > rightmost_col() || column > ideal_c) {
        column = prev_column;
        i--;
        }
    go_rc(cursor_r, column);
    buf_cursor_pos = i;
}   /* adjust_onscreen_position */


/*
adjacent_to_leftmost_column() returns TRUE if the cursor is positioned
at the leftmost column in the window, or, if the leftmost column is
"null," it returns TRUE if the cursor is positioned on a tab just right
of the leftmost column.
*/

int text_window::adjacent_to_leftmost_column()
{
    return virtual_c == offset ||
            previous_column() < offset;
}   /* adjacent_to_leftmost_column */


/*
adjacent_to_rightmost_column() returns TRUE if the cursor is posi-
tioned at the rightmost column in the window, or, if the rightmost
```

```
column is "null," it returns TRUE if the cursor is positioned on a
TAB just left of the rightmost column.
*/

int text_window::adjacent_to_rightmost_column()
{
    return virtual_c == rightmost_col() ||
            next_tab_column() > rightmost_col();
}   /* adjacent_to_rightmost_column */


/*
window_buffer_forward() increments both the buffer and window
positions.  It must take tabbing into consideration.  Note: this
procedure performs no error checking--it must be called in the
proper context.
*/

void text_window::window_buffer_forward()
{
    if (buffer[buf_cursor_pos] == TAB)
        go_rc(cursor_r, next_tab_column());
    else
        go_rc(cursor_r, virtual_c + 1);
    buf_cursor_pos++;
}   /* window_buffer_forward */


/*
window_buffer_backward() decrements both the buffer and window
positions.  It must take tabbing into consideration.  Note: this
procedure performs no error checking--it must be called in the
proper context.
*/

void text_window::window_buffer_backward()
{
    if (buffer[buf_cursor_pos - 1] == TAB)
        go_rc(cursor_r, previous_column());
    else
        go_rc(cursor_r, virtual_c - 1);
    buf_cursor_pos--;
}   /* window_buffer_backward */
```

```
/*
go_right_as_far_as_possible() moves the cursor to either the end of
the line, or to the rightmost onscreen position, if the line extends
beyond the last screen position.
*/

int text_window::go_right_as_far_as_possible()
{
    if (window_line_length() - 1 > rightmost_col()) {
        go_line_start();
        adjust_onscreen_position(rightmost_col());
        return FALSE;
    }
    else {
        go_rc(cursor_r, window_line_length() - 1);
        go_line_end();
        return TRUE;
    }
}   /* go_right_as_far_as_possible */


/*
ispunc determines if a character qualifies as a punctuation
character, according to the string constant PUNCTUATION.
ispunc() is called by, for example, del_word().
*/

int text_window::ispunc(char ch)
{
    return (strchr(PUNCTUATION, ch) != NULL) ? TRUE : FALSE;
}   /* ispunc */
```

The text for the help file begins immediately after this sentence with no spacing before " Commands":

```
 Commands:

   F1 (Help)    invokes this help system.
   F2 (Tag)     sets a tag at the cursor.
   F3 (Cut)     moves tagged text to the clipboard.
   F4 (Paste)   inserts the clipboard's contents at the cursor.
   F5 (DW)      deletes the next/current word.
   F6 (DEOL)    deletes all characters from the cursor to end of line.
```

```
  F7 (DL)      deletes the entire line.
  F8 (Undo)    recovers text from the previous DW, DEOL, or DL.
  F9 (Quit)    abandons current edit session  edited text not saved.
  F10 (End)    saves edited text to disk and ends the current edit.
  Alt-F2   exchanges the tag and the cursor.
  Alt-F3   copies tagged text to the clipboard.
  Alt-F5   deletes the previous word (to the left of the cursor).
  Alt-F8   removes (undoes) a tag (set by F2).


                                      *** <PgDn>, <Ctrl>-<PgDn>, or press any key ***
Commands (cont.):

  Alt-C  finds and changes a pattern.
  Alt-D  executes a DOS command.
  Alt-F  finds a pattern in the text.
  Alt-I  inserts (reads in) an alternate file at the cursor.
  Alt-R  repeats the previous find or find and change.
  Alt-S  saves/overwrites the current file  no warning given.
  Alt-T  sets a new tab size.
  Alt-W  writes the tagged text to an alternate disk file.
  Alt-2  opens a second (alternative) edit area.


    *** <PgUp>, <PgDn>, <Ctrl>-<PgUp>, <Ctrl>-<PgDn>, or press any key ***
Cursor Movement and Keypad Commands:
  Ins         toggles insert/overstrike mode
  Del         deletes character under cursor
  Backspace   deletes character to left of cursor
             moves cursor up one line
             moves cursor down one line
  <          moves cursor left one character
  >          moves cursor right one character
  PgUp        moves cursor up one page (toward beginning of file)
  PgDn        moves cursor down one page (toward end of file)
  Home        moves cursor to beginning of line (with repeat action)
  End         moves cursor to end of line (with repeat action)
  Ctrl-Home   moves cursor to top-left position of window
  Ctrl-End    moves cursor to bottom-left position of window
```

```
  Ctrl-PgUp  moves cursor to beginning of file
  Ctrl-PgDn  moves cursor to end of file
  Ctrl- <   moves cursor left one word
  Ctrl- >   moves cursor right one word
    *** <PgUp>, <PgDn>, <Ctrl>-<PgUp>, <Ctrl>-<PgDn>, or press any key ***
Miscellaneous:

  The bottom, rightmost two positions of the screen:
  "I" = Insert mode
  "O" = Overtype mode
  "M" = Modifications have been made

Notes:
 * To clear a pop-up message window:  press any key, e.g., <Esc>.
 * To improve start-up time, ie does not maintain backups.

Maximum sizes (chars.):  edit areas and clipboard = 64000; undo = 5000.




                           *** <PgUp>, <Ctrl>-<PgUp>, or press any key ***
******* end of help system *** <PgUp>, <Ctrl>-<PgUp>, or press any key ***
```

The C++ Source Code for the Multi-window Version of ed

The source code for the multi-window version of **ed** is listed in alphabetical order by module. This appendix contains replacement source code for specific modules from Appendix B; modules that aren't given here are the same as in Appendix B. Note that the header file *editintc.h* is different, and that the help file specification is "edd.hlp", not "ed.hlp", to avoid confusion. The text for the help file is listed last.

```
////  editintc.h  ////  constants for the edit interface  ////


#ifndef EDIT_CONSTANTS
#define EDIT_CONSTANTS  1

#include "colors.h"


enum spec_rows {TOP_ROW =        0,           // used during display
```

```
                BOT_ROW =       24};          // operations only

enum spec_cols {MODIFIED_COLUMN =       77,
                INSERT_MODE_COLUMN =    78};



#ifndef LIMIT_CONSTANTS
#define LIMIT_CONSTANTS 1
#define MAX_BUF_SIZE            64000         // "limit" constants,
#define MAX_CLIP_SIZE           64000         // plus miscellany
#define MAX_UNDO_SIZE           5000
#define MAX_WINDOWS             5
#endif

#define PROMPT_STR              57
#define MAX_STR                 45
#define POPUP_WIDTH             48            // must be MAX_STR + 3
#define MIN_STR                 7
#define MAX_NAME                80
#define TAB_SIZE                4
#define MAX_TAB                 40


#define BREAK_PROMPT            48                // Alt-B keystroke
#define PUNCTUATION             "()!_:;\"',.?+-*/"

#define HELP_SPEC               "\\edd.hlp"       // note extra "d"
#endif


////  keys.h  ////  key definitions for the editor  ////

#ifndef KEY_CONSTANTS
#define KEY_CONSTANTS   1

/*
keyboard-and function-related constants appear next.  Note that
a function is represented by its keyboard extended code.  That is,
the (decimal) extended byte code for F1 is 59, which is used to
represent the HELP function.
*/

#ifndef SPEC_KEYS
```

```
#define SPEC_KEYS           1
enum keys {HELP =           59,             // F1
           TAG =            60,             // F2
           CUT =            61,             // F3
           PASTE =          62,             // F4
           DWORD =          63,             // F5
           DEOL =           64,             // F6
           DLINE =          65,             // F7
           UNDO =           66,             // F8
           QUIT =           67,             // F9
           EXIT =           68,             // F10
           TAG_CURSOR =     105,            // Alt-F2
           COPY =           106,            // Alt-F3
           DWORD_LEFT =     108,            // Alt-F5
           UNTAG =          111,            // Alt-F8
           CHANGE_TEXT =    46,             // Alt-C
           DOS_CMD =        32,             // Alt-D
           EDIT_FILE =      18,             // Alt_E
           FIND_TEXT =      33,             // Alt-F
           INSERT_FILE =    23,             // Alt-I
           REPEAT_FC =      19,             // Alt-R
           SAVE_FILE =      31,             // Alt-S
           SET_TABS =       20,             // Alt-T
           WRITE_FILE =     17,             // Alt-W
           ALT_EXIT =       45,             // Alt-X
           FIRST_WIN =      120,            // Alt-1
           SECOND_WIN =     121,            // Alt-2
           THIRD_WIN =      122,            // Alt-3
           FOURTH_WIN =     123,            // Alt-4
           FIFTH_WIN =      124,            // Alt-5
           INS =            82,
           DEL =            83,
           UP =             72,
           DOWN =           80,
           LEFT =           75,
           RIGHT =          77,
           PGUP =           73,
           PGDN =           81,
           HOME =           71,             // beginning of line
           END =            79,             // end of line
           CTRL_HOME =      119,            // top of screen
           CTRL_END =       117,            // bottom of screen
           CTRL_PGUP =      132,            // top of file
           CTRL_PGDN =      118,            // end of file
```

```
            CTRL_LEFT =      115,               // left one word
            CTRL_RIGHT =     116};              // right one word
#endif

#endif


////  ed.hpp  ////  primary file for ed, a simple editor  ////

#ifndef EDHPP
#define EDHPP   1

#include <stdio.h>
#include <dos.h>
#include <int.h>
#include <stream.hpp>

#include "editor.hpp"


/*
functions:
*/

extern int main(int, char **);
extern char *check_args(int, char **);
extern int issue_error_messages(int, char *);

#endif


////  edfile.hpp     ////  supplemental file system  ////
                     ////  interface for ed.cpp      ////

#ifndef EDFILEHPP
#define EDFILEHPP   1

#include <stdio.h>
#include <dos.h>
#include <direct.h>
#include <int.h>

#include "querybox.hpp"
#include "numbox.hpp"
```

```
#include "winprmt.hpp"
#include "winedit.hpp"


extern screen dos_screen;
extern keyboard dos_keybd;


extern int write_from_buffer(edit_window *, char *, long = 0,
                              long = 0);
extern void insert_file(edit_window *, char *);
extern void write_alt_file(edit_window *, char *);
extern char *get_alt_file_spec();
extern char *get_drive_path(char *);
extern int get_drive(char *);
extern long get_free_space(char *);
extern int file_exists(char *);
extern long file_size(char *);
extern int ok_to_overwrite(char *);
extern int delete_and_check_space(long, char *);
extern int floppy_ready_query(char *);
extern int floppy_error(char *);
extern "C" int floppy_handler(struct INT_DATA *pd);

#endif


////  edhelp.hpp  ////  interface for class:  help  ////

#ifndef EDHELPHPP
#define EDHELPHPP   1

#include "browser.hpp"
#include "editintc.h"


class help {
    int error_state;
    browser help_win;
public:
    help(int, char *, int, int, int, int, int);
    get_error_state() {
        return error_state;
    }
```

```
    void present_help_screens();
};

#endif


////  editor.hpp  ////  interface for class:  editor  ////

#ifndef EDITORHPP
#define EDITORHPP   1
#include "edhelp.hpp"
#include "edfile.hpp"
#include "editintc.h"


class editor {
    int error_state;
    int cur_win;    // the current editor window--an array position
    help *ed_help;
    prompt_window *dos_box;
    edit_window *ed[MAX_WINDOWS];   // array of ptrs. to edit_windows
    char filename[MAX_WINDOWS][MAX_STR];
public:
    editor();
    ~editor();
    int dispatcher(char *);
    int init_edit(char *);
    int edit_file();
    int close_current_window();
    int close_active_windows();
    int file_active();
    int file_spec_ok(char *);
    void alt_edit_window(int);
    void switch_edit_window(int);
    void execute_dos_command();
    void display_edit_info();
    void display_filename(int, char *);
};

#endif


////  ed.cpp  ////  contains primary routines for ed  ////
```

```
/*
    Programmer:     J. Smith
    Date:           2/13/89

    Copyright (c) 1989 Iris Computing Laboratories
*/

/*
ed is a simple, full-screen editor.  It provides the
following basic features:

    - cursor movement from the numeric keypad;
    - simple deletion of a character, word, line, or
      all characters to end-of-line;
    - simple undo (undelete) capabilities;
    - cut and paste;
    - find and/or change next occurrence of specified text;
    - processing of files of an arbitrary size.
*/


#include "ed.hpp"


/*
main() sets up a pointer variable for the incoming file specification,
performs some screen handling, and invokes a file specification routine,
check_args().
*/

int main(int argc, char *argv[])
{
    char *file_spec;

    int_intercept(0x24, floppy_handler, 256);// set up an int. handler
                                             // for floppy disk errors

    if ((file_spec = check_args(argc, argv)) == NULL)
        exit(1);
    dos_screen.clrscn();
    editor ed;
    int edit_status = ed.dispatcher(file_spec);
    dos_screen.restore_exit_screen();
    if (issue_error_messages(edit_status, file_spec))
```

```
        exit(1);
    else
        exit(0);
}   /* main */


/*
check_args() checks to make sure that the proper number of arguments
is present.  It returns NULL for an error, or a character pointer
to the file specification if the argument list is OK.
*/

char *check_args(int arg_count, char *arg_vector[])
{
    if (arg_count > 2) {                          // illegal arg. count
        cerr <<"Usage: ED [<file_spec>]";
        return NULL;
    }
    else if (arg_count == 2) {
        if (floppy_error(arg_vector[1])) {        // open drive door?
            cerr << "Disk drive not ready for:  " << arg_vector[1];
            return NULL;
        }
        else
            return arg_vector[1];
    }
    else if (arg_count == 1)                      // "empty" file spec.
        return "";                                // is OK
    else
        return arg_vector[1];
}   /* check_args */


/*
issue_error_messages() issues messages for a number of errors
that can occur during file initialization.
*/

int issue_error_messages(int edit_status, char *file_spec)
{
    switch (edit_status) {
        case NO_MATCH:
            cerr << "Couldn't find any files:  " << file_spec;
            break;
```

```
        case CANT_WRITE:
            cerr << "Couldn't write file:  " << file_spec;
            break;
        case CANT_ALLOCATE_BUFS:
            cerr << "Couldn't allocate memory for editing space.";
            break;
        case TOO_LARGE:
            cerr << "File is too large (64K max):  " << file_spec;
            break;
        case QUIT:                  // indicate all non-error
        case EXIT:                  // conditions here
        case ALT_EXIT:
            return FALSE;           // no errors so return FALSE
        default:
            cerr << "Unknown error";
            break;
    }
    return TRUE;
}   /* issue_error_messages */


////  edfile.cpp    ////  supplement file system    ////
                    ////  implementation of ed.cpp  ////


#include "edfile.hpp"


/*
globals:
*/

static int alt_edit_active = FALSE;
static int critical_floppy_error = FALSE;


/*
write_from_buffer() stores a buffer as a disk file. It does not
check for the existence of the file.  Another routine can be used
to perform the latter check.
*/

int write_from_buffer(edit_window *edwin, char *filename, long start,
                        long num_chars)
```

```
{
    int write_status;
    char *alt_file = filename;

    long total_chars = (num_chars == DUMMY) ?
                edwin->get_buf_length() + edwin->line_count() :
                num_chars + edwin->line_count(start, num_chars);
    if (*alt_file == EOS)
        return FALSE;
    while ((write_status =
                    delete_and_check_space(total_chars, alt_file))
                    == TOO_LARGE && attn_win.message(alt_file,
                    "Insufficient space; try another disk (y/n): "))
        alt_file = get_alt_file_spec();
    if (*alt_file == EOS)
        return FALSE;
    if (write_status == TRUE) {
        if ((write_status =
                edwin->write_to_disk(alt_file, start, num_chars))
                != TRUE) {
            if (write_status == CANT_WRITE)
                write_status = attn_win.message(alt_file,
                        "Can't write file; try again (y/n): ");
            else
                write_status = FALSE;
            if (write_status && floppy_ready_query(alt_file))
                write_status = edwin->write_to_disk(
                                alt_file = get_alt_file_spec(),
                                        start, num_chars);
            else
                write_status = FALSE;
        }
    }
    if (!write_status)
        attn_win.message(alt_file, "** write abandoned **");
    return write_status;
}   /* write_from_buffer */


/*
insert_file() manages the insertion of the contents of an alternative
file in the edit area at the current cursor location.  insert_file()
allocates a separate buffer, in order to take advantage of the
existing editor paste facilities.
```

```
*/

void insert_file(edit_window *edwin, char *filename)
{
    long read_status;        // read_from_disk() and file_size()
                             // return the file length here

    if (*filename == EOS)
        return;
    if ((read_status = file_size(filename)) == -1) {
        attn_win.message(filename, "** file not found **");
        return;
    }
    char_buffer ins_buf(read_status + 1);
    if (!ins_buf.get_error_state()) {
        if ((read_status = ins_buf.read_from_disk(filename))
                == CANT_READ)
            attn_win.message(filename,
                            "** unknown error; can't read file **");
        else if (read_status == TOO_LARGE)
            attn_win.message(filename, "** file is too large **");
        else
            if (read_status > 0)
                edwin->paste_from_buffer(ins_buf);
    }
    else
        attn_win.message("Insert", "** not enough memory **");
}   /* insert_file */


/*
write_alt_file() writes the edit buffer to the specified file.
*/

void write_alt_file(edit_window *edwin, char *filename)
{
    long len, tag;

    if (*filename == EOS)
        return;
    if (ok_to_overwrite(filename)) {
        if ((tag = edwin->get_tag_pos()) == UNDEFINED)
            write_from_buffer(edwin, filename);
        else {
```

```
            if ((len = edwin->get_cursor_pos() - tag) == 0)
                attn_win.message("", "** nothing to write **");
            else {
                if (len < 0) {
                    edwin->exch_tag_cursor();
                    len = -len;
                }
                write_from_buffer(edwin, filename,
                                    edwin->get_tag_pos(), len);
            }
        }
    }
}   /* write_alt_file */


/*
get_alt_file_spec() prompts the user for a filename/file_spec.
*/

char *get_alt_file_spec()
{
    static char file_spec[MAX_STR];

    attn_win.activate("Enter a Filename");
    attn_win.go_rc(0, 1);
    attn_win.wputs("File: ");
    attn_win.wgets_filter(file_spec, MAX_STR);
    attn_win.deactivate();
    return file_spec;
}   /* get_alt_file_spec */


/*
get_drive_path() uses a for loop to search the file_spec backward in
order to extract "[drive:]pathname" from the pathname plus filename.
*/

char *get_drive_path(char *file_spec)
{
    int i;
    static char path_spec[MAX_NAME];

    strcpy(path_spec, file_spec);
```

```
    for (i = strlen(path_spec) - 1;
            i > -1 && path_spec[i] != '\\' && path_spec[i] != ':'; i--)
        ;
    path_spec[++i] = EOS;
    return path_spec;            // including search character
}   /* get_drive_path */


/*
get_drive() returns the drive associated with file spec; it
returns 1 for A:, 2 for B:, etc.
*/

int get_drive(char *file_spec)
{
    char current_drive_path[MAX_NAME];

    if (file_spec[1] == ':')
        return toupper(file_spec[0]) - 64;                  // A == 65
    else
        if (getcwd(current_drive_path, MAX_NAME) != NULL)
            return toupper(current_drive_path[0]) - 64;     // A == 65
        else
            return FALSE;
}   /* get_drive */


/*
get_free_space() returns the disk free space on the drive
associated with file_spec.
*/

long get_free_space(char *file_spec)
{
    REGS r;

    r.h.ah = 0x36;               // get drive allocation information
    r.h.dl = get_drive(file_spec);
    int86(0x21, &r, &r);
    return long(r.x.ax) * long(r.x.bx) * long(r.x.cx);
}   /* get_free_space */


/*
```

```
file_exists() determines whether or not a file exists.
*/

int file_exists(char *file_spec)
{
    if (file_size(file_spec) != -1)
        return TRUE;
    else
        return FALSE;
}   /* file_exists */


/*
file_size() determines the size of a file.  It returns -1, if
the file doesn't exist.
*/

long file_size(char *file_spec)
{
    FIND *file_ptr;

    if (!floppy_ready_query(file_spec))
        return -1;
    if ((file_ptr = findfirst(file_spec, 0)) != NULL)
        return file_ptr->size;
    else
        return -1;
}   /* file_size */


/*
ok_to_overwrite() makes sure it's OK to overwrite an existing
file.
*/

int ok_to_overwrite(char *filename)
{
    if (!file_exists(filename))
        return TRUE;
    else
        return attn_win.message(filename,
                                "File exists; overwrite (y/n): ");
}   /* ok_to_overwrite */
```

```
/*
delete_and_check_space() deletes the old version of a file
and tests the remaining space.
*/

int delete_and_check_space(long num_chars, char *filename)
{
    int write_ok = TRUE;

    if (floppy_ready_query(filename)) {
        if (file_exists(filename))
            remove(filename);
        if (get_free_space(filename) < num_chars + 1)
            write_ok = TOO_LARGE;
    }
    else
        write_ok = FALSE;
    return write_ok;
}   /* delete_and_check_space */


/*
floppy_ready_query() handles disk-not-ready queries.
*/

int floppy_ready_query(char *filename)
{
    int disk_error = FALSE;

    if ((disk_error = floppy_error(filename)) != FALSE) {
        if (!attn_win.message(filename,
                            "Drive not ready; try again (y/n): "))
            disk_error = TRUE;
        else
            disk_error = floppy_error(filename);
    if (disk_error)
        attn_win.message(filename,
                        "** disk error; disk operation abandoned **");
    }
    return !disk_error;
}   /* floppy_ready_query */
```

```
/*
floppy_error() attempts to detect a critical error, such a
an open drive door.
*/

int floppy_error(char *filename)
{
    FILE *fp;
    int error;

    fp = fopen(filename, "r");
    if ((error = critical_floppy_error) == FALSE) {
        critical_floppy_error = FALSE;
        fclose(fp);
        return FALSE;
    }
    else {
        critical_floppy_error = FALSE;
        for (int i = 2; i < 22; i++)
            dos_screen.display_char(i, 0, VERTICAL_BAR,
                                           NOR_BORDER_COLOR);
        return error;
    }
}   /* floppy_error */


/*
floppy_handler() sets the global variable critical_floppy_error, if
a critical floppy disk error occurs.  For critical_floppy_error:
    0 ==> no error
    1 ==> A: drive error
    2 ==> B: drive error
    etc.
*/

int floppy_handler(struct INT_DATA *pd)
{
    if (pd->regs.x.ax < 0)
        return 0;
    else {
        critical_floppy_error = (pd->regs.x.ax & 0x00ff) + 1;
        pd->regs.h.al = 0;
        return critical_floppy_error;
    }
```

```
}   /* floppy_handler */


////  edhelp.cpp  ////  implementation of class:  help  ////


#include "edfile.hpp"
#include "edhelp.hpp"


/*
help() sets up a read-only edit buffer (browser) for the help system.
*/

help::help(int win_no, char *hdr, int start_r, int start_c, int end_r,
        int end_c, int buf_size) :
        help_win(win_no, hdr, start_r, start_c, end_r, end_c,
                buf_size, BACK_ATTR)
{
    long buf_len = help_win.read_from_disk(HELP_SPEC);
    help_win.set_buf_length(buf_len);
    error_state = help_win.get_error_state();
}   /* help */


/*
present_help_screens() displays help information in a window.
*/

void help::present_help_screens()
{
    keystroke key;

    if (help_win.get_buf_length() <= 0) {
        attn_win.message(HELP_SPEC, "** can't read help file **");
        return;
    }
    help_win.activate("");
    help_win.dispatcher();
    help_win.deactivate();
}   /* present_help_screens */


////  editor.cpp  ////  implementation of class:  editor  ////
```

```
#include "editor.hpp"


/*
editor() initializes the data structures needed
for the editor system.
*/

editor::editor()
{
    ed_help = new help(0, "ed 1.0 - Help", 2, 1, 22, 78,
                        int(file_size(HELP_SPEC)));
    dos_box = new prompt_window(0, "", 20, 10, 22,
                    10 + PROMPT_STR + 3, MAX_PROMPT_INPUT,
                    BACK_ATTR);
    if (dos_box->get_error_state() || ed_help->get_error_state())
        error_state = TRUE;
    else {
        error_state = FALSE;
        display_edit_info();
        cur_win = 0;
        for (int i = 0; i < MAX_WINDOWS; i++)
            ed[i] = NULL;
    }
}   /* editor */


/*
~editor() must delete the help and prompt box systems.
*/

editor::~editor()
{
    delete ed_help;
    delete dos_box;
}   /* ~editor */


/*
dispatcher() dispatches keystrokes to the appropriate routines.
First, keystrokes are handed over to the edit_window's own dis-
patcher.  If the edit_window dispatcher can't process a keystroke,
```

```
it simply returns and the editor dispatcher takes over.
*/

int editor::dispatcher(char *file_spec)
{
    int terminate_edit;
    keystroke key;

    if (error_state)
        return CANT_ALLOCATE BUFS;
    strcpy(filename[0], file_spec);
    if ((terminate_edit = init_edit(filename[0])) < 0) // use the
        return terminate_edit;                         // "passed" file
    else                                               // spec., if possible
        terminate_edit = FALSE;
    do {
        dos_screen.cursor_rc(1, 0);          // an arbitrary location
        if (ed[cur_win] != NULL)
            key.word = ed[cur_win]->dispatcher();
        else
            key.word = dos_keybd.get_keystroke();
        switch (key.byte[1]) {
            case FIRST_WIN:
            case SECOND_WIN:
            case THIRD_WIN:
            case FOURTH_WIN:
            case FIFTH_WIN:
                alt_edit_window(key.byte[1] - FIRST_WIN);
                break;
            case EDIT_FILE:
                edit_file();
                break;
            case SAVE_FILE:
                if (file_active())
                    if (write_from_buffer(ed[cur_win],
                            filename[cur_win]))
                        ed[cur_win]->buffer_modified(FALSE);
                break;
            case WRITE_FILE:
                if (file_active())
                    write_alt_file(ed[cur_win], get_alt_file_spec());
                break;
            case INSERT_FILE:
                if (file_active())
```

```
                insert_file(ed[cur_win], get_alt_file_spec());
            break;
        case HELP:
            ed_help->present_help_screens();
            break;
        case DOS_CMD:
            execute_dos_command();
            break;
        case EXIT:
            if (file_active())
                if (write_from_buffer(ed[cur_win],
                        filename[cur_win]))
                    ed[cur_win]->buffer_modified(FALSE);
            close_current_window();
            break;
        case QUIT:
            close_current_window();
            break;
        case ALT_EXIT:
            terminate_edit = close_active_windows();
            break;
        default:
        break;
        }
    } while (!terminate_edit);
    return key.byte[1];
}   /* dispatcher */


/*
init_edit() checks for a number of errors.  If possible, it creates
an edit_window object and assigns it to the array set up to hold
pointers to edit_window objects.  Next, init_edit() loads the edit
window's buffer.
*/

int editor::init_edit(char *filename)
{
    if (*filename == EOS || !file_spec_ok(filename)) {
        display_filename(cur_win + 1, "");
        return FALSE;
    }
    ed[cur_win] = new edit_window(cur_win + 1, "", 1, 0, 23, 79,
                                        MAX_BUF_SIZE, BACK_ATTR);
```

```
    if (ed[cur_win]->get_error_state()) {
        close_current_window();
        attn_win.message("", "** can't allocate memory **");
        return CANT_ALLOCATE_BUFS;
    }
    long file_length = ed[cur_win]->read_from_disk(filename);
    if (file_length == TOO_LARGE) {
        close_current_window();
        attn_win.message(filename, "** file is too large **");
        return TOO_LARGE;
    }
    ed[cur_win]->activate("", NOR_BORDER_COLOR, NOR_BORDER_COLOR);
    if (file_length == CANT_READ)                 // a new file
        ed[cur_win]->set_buf_length(0);
    else
        ed[cur_win]->set_buf_length(file_length);
    display_filename(cur_win + 1, strupr(filename));
    ed[cur_win]->window_fill(0, 0, 0);
    return TRUE;
}   /* init_edit */


/*
edit_file() prompts for a filename and then begins an edit session
in the current window.  If the edit window is already active, it is
closed first.
*/

int editor::edit_file()
{
    if (close_current_window()) {
        strcpy(filename[cur_win], get_alt_file_spec());
        return init_edit(filename[cur_win]);
    }
    else
        return FALSE;
}   /* edit_file */


/*
close_current_window() closes the current edit window, if it
is active.  The user is given an opportunity to abandon the
close operation, if the window contains unsaved changes.
*/
```

```
int editor::close_current_window()
{
    if (ed[cur_win] != NULL) {
        if (ed[cur_win]->buffer_modified())
            if (!attn_win.message("", "Abandon changed text (y/n): "))
                return FALSE;
        ed[cur_win]->deactivate();
        delete ed[cur_win];
        ed[cur_win] = NULL;
        display_filename(cur_win + 1, "");
    }
    return TRUE;
}   /* close_current_window */


/*
close_active_windows() scans all windows.  It attempts to close each
active window.  If the buffer has unsaved changes, the user can
abandon that close operation.  In this case, close operations are
abandoned on all remaining active buffers.
*/

int editor::close_active_windows()
{
    if (!close_current_window())
        return FALSE;
    for (int i = 0; i < MAX_WINDOWS; i++)
        if (ed[i] != NULL)
            if (ed[i]->buffer_modified()) {
                switch_edit_window(i);
                if (!close_current_window())
                    return FALSE;
            }
            else
                close_current_window();
    return TRUE;
}   /* close_active_windows */


/*
file_active() reminds the user that certain operations
require an active edit window.
*/
```

```
int editor::file_active()
{
    if (ed[cur_win] == NULL) {
        attn_win.message("",
                        "** operation requires an active file **");
        return FALSE;
    }
    else
        return TRUE;
}   /* file_active */


/*
file_spec_ok() ensures that file specifications are OK.
*/

int editor::file_spec_ok(char *file_spec)
{
    FILE *file_ptr;

    if (floppy_ready_query(file_spec)) {
        if ((file_ptr = fopen(file_spec, "r")) != NULL) {
            fclose(file_ptr);
            return TRUE;
        }
        else
            if ((file_ptr = fopen(file_spec, "w")) == NULL) {
                attn_win.message(file_spec,
                                "** couldn't create file **");
                return FALSE;
            }
            else {
                fclose(file_ptr);
                remove(file_spec);
                return TRUE;
            }
    }
    else
        return FALSE;
}   /* file_spec_ok */


/*
```

```
alt_edit_win() deactivates the current window and switches
to the specified window (makes it active).
*/

void editor::alt_edit_window(int cur_win)
{
    if (ed[editor::cur_win] != NULL)
        ed[editor::cur_win]->deactivate();
    switch_edit_window(cur_win);
}   /* alt_edit_window */


/*
switch_edit_window() activates the specified window, performing
related operations, such as displaying the filename.
*/

void editor::switch_edit_window(int cur_win)
{
    if (ed[cur_win] != NULL) {
        display_filename(cur_win + 1, filename[cur_win]);
        ed[cur_win]->buffer_modified(ed[cur_win]->buffer_modified());
        ed[cur_win]->set_insert_mode(
                            ed[editor::cur_win]->get_insert_mode());
        ed[cur_win]->activate("", NOR_BORDER_COLOR, NOR_BORDER_COLOR);
        ed[cur_win]->redisplay_window(
                            ed[cur_win]->current_column_offset());
    }
    else {
        display_edit_info();
        display_filename(cur_win + 1, "");
    }
    editor::cur_win = cur_win;
}   /* switch_edit_window */


/*
execute_dos_command() temporarily suspends execution of the current
program and executes the DOS command given in the pop-up window.
The pop-up window can be edited.
*/

void editor::execute_dos_command()
{
```

```
    keystroke key;
    char cmd_spec[MAX_PROMPT_INPUT], *temp_screen;

    char far *dos_scrn = dos_screen.get_screen_addr();
    int dos_error = FALSE, go_dos = FALSE;
    dos_box->activate("<Alt-D> invokes a DOS shell",
                        NOR_BORDER_COLOR, NOR_BORDER_COLOR);
    key.word = dos_box->dispatcher(DOS_CMD);
    dos_box->deactivate();
    if (key.byte[0] == ESC)             // abandon the prompt box
        return;
    if ((temp_screen = new char[SCREEN_SIZE]) == NULL) {
        attn_win.message("DOS",
                            "** can't allocate necessary memory **");
        return;
    }
    if (!key.byte[0] && key.byte[1] == DOS_CMD) // second Alt-D, so
        go_dos = TRUE;                          // go out to DOS
    else
        go_dos = FALSE;
    memcpy(temp_screen, dos_scrn, SCREEN_SIZE);
    dos_screen.clrscn(NORMAL_VIDEO);
    dos_screen.cursor_rc(0, 0);
    if (go_dos || dos_box->get_buf_length() == 0) {
        dos_screen.display_string(0, 0,
            "Type \"exit\" to return to ed", NORMAL_VIDEO);
        dos_error = system("command");
    }
    else
        dos_error = system(dos_box->get_line(cmd_spec,
                            MAX_PROMPT_INPUT));
    dos_screen.display_string(24, 64, "Press any key...",
                                REVERSE_VIDEO);
    dos_keybd.get_keystroke();
    memcpy(dos_scrn, temp_screen, SCREEN_SIZE);
    delete temp_screen;
    if (dos_error)
        attn_win.message("DOS",
                "** unknown error; can't invoke command **");
}   /* execute_dos_command */


/*
display_edit_info() displays miscellaneous, editor-related
```

```
information on the screen.
*/

void editor::display_edit_info()
{
    dos_screen.display_blanks(TOP_ROW, 0, 80, REV_BORDER_COLOR);
    dos_screen.display_string(BOT_ROW, 0,
" F1-Help F2-Tag F3-Cut F4-Paste F5-DW F6-DEOL F7-DL F8-Undo \
F9-Quit F10-End     ", REV_BORDER_COLOR);
    dos_screen.display_string(TOP_ROW, 71, "ed - 1.0",
                              REV_BORDER_COLOR);
}   /* display_edit_info */


/*
display_filename() shows the filename along the top line,
along with the number of the current edit window.
*/

void editor::display_filename(int win_no, char *filename)
{
    char temp_str[MIN_STR];

    dos_screen.display_blanks(TOP_ROW, 0, 71, REV_BORDER_COLOR);
    dos_screen.display_string(TOP_ROW, 3, "File: ", REV_BORDER_COLOR);
    dos_screen.display_string(TOP_ROW, 9, filename, REV_BORDER_COLOR);
    itoa(win_no, temp_str, 10);
    dos_screen.display_char(TOP_ROW, 1, temp_str[0], REV_BORDER_COLOR);
}   /* display_filename */
```

The text for the help file begins immediately after this sentence with no spacing before " Commands":

```
 Commands:

   F1 (Help)    invokes this help system.
   F2 (Tag)     sets a tag at the cursor.
   F3 (Cut)     moves tagged text to the clipboard.
   F4 (Paste)   inserts the clipboard's contents at the cursor.
   F5 (DW)      deletes the next/current word.
   F6 (DEOL)    deletes all characters from the cursor to end of line.
   F7 (DL)      deletes the entire line.
   F8 (Undo)    recovers text from the previous DW, DEOL, or DL.
   F9 (Quit)    closes the current edit window  edited text not saved.
```

```
  F10 (End)   saves edited text to disk and closes the current window.
  Alt-F2  exchanges the tag and the cursor.
  Alt-F3  copies tagged text to the clipboard.
  Alt-F5  deletes the previous word (to the left of the cursor).
  Alt-F8  removes (undoes) a tag (set by F2).


                                      *** <PgDn>, <Ctrl>-<PgDn>, or press any key ***
 Commands (cont.):

  Alt-C  finds and changes a pattern.
  Alt-D  executes a DOS command.
  Alt-E  initiates an edit session in the current window.
  Alt-F  finds a pattern in the text.
  Alt-I  inserts (reads in) an alternate file at the cursor.
  Alt-R  repeats the previous find or find and change.
  Alt-S  saves/overwrites the current file  no warning given.
  Alt-T  sets a new tab size.
  Alt-W  writes the tagged text to an alternate disk file.
  Alt-X  terminates ed  prompts you regarding any unsaved files.
  Alt-n  switches to edit window n, where 1 <= n <= 5.



    *** <PgUp>, <PgDn>, <Ctrl>-<PgUp>, <Ctrl>-<PgDn>, or press any key ***
 Cursor Movement and Keypad Commands:
  Ins         toggles insert/overstrike mode
  Del         deletes character under cursor
  Backspace   deletes character to left of cursor
             moves cursor up one line
             moves cursor down one line
  <          moves cursor left one character
  >          moves cursor right one character
  PgUp        moves cursor up one page (toward beginning of file)
  PgDn        moves cursor down one page (toward end of file)
  Home        moves cursor to beginning of line (with repeat action)
  End         moves cursor to end of line (with repeat action)
  Ctrl-Home   moves cursor to top-left position of window
  Ctrl-End    moves cursor to bottom-left position of window
  Ctrl-PgUp   moves cursor to beginning of file
  Ctrl-PgDn   moves cursor to end of file
  Ctrl- <    moves cursor left one word
```

```
  Ctrl- >   moves cursor right one word
    *** <PgUp>, <PgDn>, <Ctrl>-<PgUp>, <Ctrl>-<PgDn>, or press any key ***
Miscellaneous:

  The bottom, rightmost two positions of the screen:
  "I" = Insert mode
  "O" = Overtype mode
  "M" = Modifications have been made

Notes:
 * To clear a pop-up message window:  press any key, e.g., <Esc>.
 * You don't have to close a window to switch to an alternate
   window  ed keeps track of each window so that you can move
   among them freely.
 * To improve start-up time, ed does not maintain backups.

Maximum sizes (chars.):  edit areas and clipboard = 64000; undo = 5000.



                           *** <PgUp>, <Ctrl>-<PgUp>, or press any key ***
******* end of help system *** <PgUp>, <Ctrl>-<PgUp>, or press any key ***
```

References

Berry, J. *C++ Programming*. Indianapolis, IN: The Waite Group, Inc., Howard W. Sams & Company, 1988.

Biggerstaff, T.J. and Perlis, A.J. *Software Reusability, Volume I: Concepts and Models*. Reading, MA: Addison-Wesley, 1989.

Borland. *Turbo C®*. Scotts Valley, CA: Borland International, 1988.

Carroll, M. References in C++. *The C++ Report*, *1*, No. 1, 8-9, 1989.

CNS. *C_talk™ User Guide*. Eden Prarie, MN: CNS, Inc., 1987.

Coggins, J.M. and Bollella, G. Managing C++ libraries. *SIGPLAN Notices*, *24*, No. 6, 37-48, 1989a.

Coggins, J. and Bollella, G. Managing C++ libraries: subdirectories and .c files. *The C++ Report*, *1*, No. 6, 6-8, 1989b.

Cox, B.J. *Object-oriented Programming: An Evolutionary Approach*. Reading, MA: Addison-Wesley, 1986.

Dahl, O. and Nygaard, K. SIMULA: An ALGOL-based simulation language. *Communications of the ACM*, *9*, No. 9, 671-678, 1966.

Duncan, R. *Advanced MS-DOS Programming*. Redmond, WA: Microsoft Press, 1988.

Duntemann, J. Structured programming. *Dr. Dobbs's Journal*, *14*, No. 2, 130-135, 1989.

Goldberg, A. and Robson, D. *Smalltalk-80: The Language and its Implementation*. Reading, MA: Addison-Wesley, 1983.

Goldstein, T. The object-oriented programmer, Part two: composition. *The C++ Report*, *1*, No. 5, 4-6.

Harbison, S.P. and Steele, G.L., Jr. *C: A Reference Manual*. Englewood Cliffs, NJ: Prentice Hall, 1987.

Hayes-Roth, F., Waterman, D.A., and Lenat, D.B. *Building Expert Systems*. Reading, MA: Addison-Wesley, 1983.

Johnson, R.E. The importance of being abstract. *The C++ Report*, *1*, No. 3, 1-5, 1989.

Johnson, R.E. and Foote B. Designing reusable classes. *Journal of Object-oriented Programming*, *1*, No. 2, 22-35, 1988.

Kernighan, B.W. and Ritchie, D.M. *The C Programming Language*. Englewood Cliffs, NJ: Prentice Hall, 1978.

Koenig, A. How virtual functions work. *Journal of Object-oriented Programming*, *1*, No. 5, 73-74, 1989.

Lippman, S. *C++ Primer*. Reading, MA: Addison-Wesley, 1989.

Maier, D. and Warren, D.S. *Computing with Logic: Logic Programming with Prolog*. Menlo Park, CA: Benjamin/Cummings, 1988.

McIlroy, M.D. Mass-produced software components. In *Software Engineering Concepts and Techniques* (republication of materials from the 1968 NATO conference on software engineering), eds. Buxton, J.M., Naur, P., and Randell, B., 1976.

Meyer, B. Harnessing multiple inheritance. *Journal of Object-oriented Programming*, *1*, No. 4, 48-51, 1988a.

Meyer, B. *Object-oriented software construction*. Englewood Cliffs, NJ: Prentice Hall, 1988b.

Microsoft. *Microsoft® C*. Redmond, WA: Microsoft Corporation, 1988.

Moon, D.A. Object-oriented programming with Flavors. In *Object-oriented Programming Systems, Languages, and Applications: 1986 Conference Proceedings*, Association for Computing Machinery, 1986. Portland, Oregon.

ParcPlace Systems. *Objectworks™ for C++*. Mountain View, CA: ParcPlace Systems, Inc., 1989.

Rafter, M. Using inline functions effectively. *The C++ Report*, *1*, No. 4, 1-10, 1989a.

Rafter, M. Using inline functions effectively. *The C++ Report*, *1*, No. 5, 1-3, 1989b.

Rochkind, M.J. *Advanced C Programming for Displays*. Englewood Cliffs, NJ: Prentice Hall, 1988.

Schildt, H. *C Power User's Guide*. Berkeley, CA: Osborne McGraw-Hill, 1988.

Schwarz, J. Initializing static variables in C++ libraries. *The C++ Report*, *1*, No. 2, 1-4, 1989.

Stroustrup, B. *The C++ Programming Language*. Reading, MA: Addison-Wesley, 1986.

Sun Microsystems. *SunView™ 1 Programmer's Guide*. Part Number: 800-1783-10, Mountain View, CA: Sun Microsystems, Inc., 1988.

Wiener, R.S. and Pinson, L.J. *An Introduction to Object-oriented Programming and C++*. Reading, MA: Addison-Wesley, 1988.

Wiener, R.S. and Sincovec, R. *Software Engineering with Modula-2 and Ada*. New York: John Wiley & Sons, 1984.

Zortech. *Zortech C++ Compiler V2.0: Compiler Reference*. Arlington, MA: Zortech, Inc., 1989.

Index

!

& (Reference parameter operator), 137
-> (Selection operator), 232
... (Ellipsis), 138
// (Comment delimiter), 134
:: (Scope resolution operator), 135
<< (Output stream operator), 140
>> (Input stream operator), 140

A

Abstract classes, 172, 175 - 176, 181, 205, 214, 222, 224, 283
Abstract data structures, 42
Abstract data types, 278
Abstraction, 3
  Class, 175
  Data, 4 - 5, 74, 144
  Procedural, 14, 52, 62, 251
Access functions, 17, 43, 280
Access methods, 150, 157, 274
activate(), 182, 185
activate_window(), 51, 78, 81, 85
Ada, 5
Address arithmetic, 25, 27, 114
adjacent_to_leftmost_column(), 129
adjacent_to_rightmost_column(), 122
ALGOL, 5
allocate_windows(), 49, 73, 77
<Alt>, 37, 60
alt_edit_window(), 233, 241, 245
alt_panel, 156
Arguments, 9
  Unspecified number, 258
AT&T, 6, 133
atol(), 191
Attention window
  See **ed**, Message window
Attribute bytes, 23

B

backspace(), 124, 213
Base class constructors, 187

Basic disk operating system (BDOS)
 See BDOS
Basic input/output system (BIOS)
 See BIOS
BDOS, 21
 See also Kernel
Bell Laboratories, 133
Berry, J., 141, 197
Biggerstaff, T.J., 7
BIOS, 20
 Functions, 58
 See also ROM-BIOS
Black-box designs, 230, 244
Bollella, G., 160
Borland International, 20
bottom_of_buffer(), 200
break_status, 62
browser, 177, 199, 226 - 227, 251, 265, 267
browser(), 200
browzr, 267
buf_cursor_pos(), 126
buf_window, 176, 193, 265
buf_window(), 195
buffer, 217
Buffer I/O operations, 197
buffer_modified(), 102, 212
buffer_up_line(), 128
Buffers
 Character, 93
buffers.cpp, 217
buffers.hpp, 214 - 215
BYTEREGS, 28

C

C, 4 - 6, 13, 15, 17, 19, 25 - 26, 73, 137, 140
C++, 5 - 6, 17, 73, 132 - 133, 150, 224, 267, 275, 279
C_talk, 6, 172
Call by address, 9 - 10
Call by value, 137
Callback function table, 269
Callback functions, 272 - 273
Callback objects, 258, 264
Callback procedures, 254, 257
callback_command(), 258
callback_object, 258
Carroll, M., 232
Case analysis, 4
Cast, 136
change_tab_width(), 196
char_addr, 23
char_addr(), 165
char_buffer, 214, 217
char_buffer(), 215
Characters
 Line-drawing, 82
check_args(), 48
check_with_callback_objects(), 259, 261, 265
check_with_exit_functions(), 270
cin, 140
Class, 4, 135, 149, 172, 275
Class derivation, 144
Class design, 224
Class hierarchies, 152, 173, 175, 222, 224, 280, 283
 Advantages of, 171
 Fine tuning, 284
 Iterative refinement, 172
Class implementations, 162
Class instances, 156
Class interfaces, 162
Class member access, 155
Class nesting, 226
Class variables, 221, 281
Classes
 High-level, 284
 Low-level, 284
clip_bd, 210
Clipboard, 108, 113, 216 - 217, 222
Clipboard operations, 214, 238
close_current_window(), 246
CNS, 6, 172

COBOL, 5
Code generation, 26
Coggins, J.M., 160
Color monitors, 66
Command dispatching
    See Dispatching operations
// (Comment delimiter), 134
Compilers, 133
Composition, 180, 223, 226, 240
Computing hardware, 3
Concrete classes, 173, 181, 283
const, 17, 136, 167 - 168, 279
Constants, 136
Constructors, 150, 222
    Base class, 154
    Derived class, 154
    Global, 221 - 222
    Hiding, 181
    Multiple, 282
countdown(), 138
cout, 140
Cox, B.J., 6, 8
create_buffer(), 107
Critical variables, 13
Cursor operations, 125, 127
    Paging, 200
cursor_left(), 129
cursor_rc(), 69
cut_and_paste(), 107

D

Dahl, O., 5
Data hiding, 4
deactivate(), 185, 188
deactivate_window(), 81
Declarative programming, 3
Default attributes, 184, 187
Default headers, 84
#define, 46, 64, 104
del_char(), 122, 213
del_eol(), 124, 213
del_line(), 124
del_rest_of_line(), 220
del_word(), 123
del_word_left(), 124
delete, 139, 184
Deletion
    Characters, 93, 122
    Words, 123
Dependency files, 160
Derivation, 3 - 4, 180
Derived class constructors, 187
Destructors, 156, 184
Development environments, 133
dispatch_extended_code(), 53, 231
dispatcher(), 203, 212, 219, 237, 242, 249, 252, 263, 267
Dispatching commands, 249
Dispatching operations, 263, 274, 284
display.c, 39 - 40, 63 - 64
display.h, 64
display_blanks(), 65
display_char(), 87, 167
display_edit_info(), 45
display_filename(), 234
display_header(), 185
display_not_found(), 116
display_string(), 64, 69 - 70
DOS interrupts, 58
DOS shell, 225, 235
dos_cmd, 228
dos_keybd, 164, 179, 244
dos_level_cursor(), 67, 168
dos_screen, 169, 179, 185
Duncan, R., 29 - 30, 61, 68, 71
Duntemann, J., 67
Dynamic binding, 4 - 5, 173 - 174, 214, 266, 285
Dynamic method selection, 173

E

echo_char(), 87
ed, 35, 42 - 43, 63, 65 - 66, 77, 149, 225, 235,

ed (cont.), 237, 240, 251
  Bottom status line, 36
  Clipboard, 38
  Cursor operations, 37
  Delete operations, 37
  DOS command window, 235
  Edit window, 36, 74
  Help window, 36
  Message window, 36, 84, 110
  Search-and-replace operations, 38
  Search-and-replace window, 36, 77
  Tab operations, 38
  Top status line, 36
ed.c, 39 - 40, 44, 62
ed.cpp, 251
ed.h, 43
ed_help, 232
edc.h, 46
edfile.c, 39 - 40, 55
edfile.cpp, 252
edhelp.c, 39 - 40, 54
edhelp.hlp, 54
edhelp.hpp, 226
Edit buffers
  Line-based, 198
  String-based, 198
edit.c, 39 - 40, 149
edit.h, 149
edit_buf_len(), 101
edit_file(), 246
edit_main(), 45, 50, 106, 229, 234
edit_text(), 51, 53, 230
edit_window, 177, 235, 265
edit_window(), 208 - 209
edit_window_count(), 45, 49, 106
editintc.h, 49, 103, 130, 218, 227, 252
editor, 240, 251, 257 - 258
  Bottom status line, 240, 246
  Top status line, 240, 246
editor(), 241 - 242, 271
editor.cpp, 240
editor.hpp, 240, 259, 269
Editors
  Line-based, 100
  String-based, 101
editwin.c, 39 - 40, 91
edwin, 230, 232
Efficiency, 39
Eiffel, 6
... (Ellipsis), 138
Encapsulation, 4, 144
endd(), 129 - 130
enum, 135
error_state, 182, 184, 195, 210
<Esc>, 89, 116, 219, 237
Events
  Registering, 254
execute_dos_command(), 235 - 236, 249
Expert systems, 3
Extensibility, 8 - 9, 12, 39, 70, 284
External factors, 7 - 8
External variables, 9, 11, 15, 42, 47, 51, 271
  See also Global variables

F

far, 26, 66
File operations, 232
fill_tabs(), 95
find_and_change(), 115
find_win, 210
findfirst(), 238
findnext(), 238
Flavors, 5 - 6
Floppy disk errors, 229
Foote, B., 173, 194, 222, 224
FORTRAN, 3, 5
fprintf(), 48
friend, 157, 216
Function, 8 - 9
Function calls
  Data passage, 9
  Missing arguments, 32

Function interface, 8
Function overhead, 13
Function prototypes, 32 - 33
Function registration system, 274
Function return, 9 - 10
Functional programming, 3, 7
Functions
    BIOS, 58
    Kernel, 59

G

Generalizability, 7, 9, 20, 102
get_error_state(), 182, 196, 210, 227, 230
get_insert_mode(), 207
get_keystroke(), 59 - 60, 87, 164
get_line(), 218, 237
get_screen_addr(), 64 - 66, 166
get_ssn(), 136
get_user_response(), 189, 191, 196
get_video_mode(), 66
Global constructors, 221 - 222
Global objects, 179, 221 - 222, 227
Global variables, 4, 7, 42, 74, 180, 258, 279, 282
    See also External variables
go_line_start(), 125
go_right_as_far_as_possible(), 129
Goldberg, A., 5, 172
Goldstein, T., 180

H

Harbison, S.P., 114, 282
Hayes-Roth, F., 3
Header data, 30
Header files, 30, 44, 57 - 58, 72, 162
help, 226, 250
help(), 226
Heterogeneous pointers, 174
Hierarchical class design, 171 - 172
    See also Class hierarchies
home(), 129
Horizontal scrolling, 79, 130

I

IBM-compatible PCs, 19, 28, 82
#ifndef, 31, 159
Implementation file, 151
#include, 30, 32
Information hiding, 8, 12 - 14, 62, 74
    See also Data hiding
Inheritance, 4 - 5, 182, 223
init_edit(), 217
initialize_edit(), 108
Inline methods, 151
Input stream, 140
insert_char(), 52, 119, 212
insert_window_update(), 121
insertion_special_conditions(), 118
Instance variables, 279
Instances of a class, 156
int86(), 20, 28 - 29, 59
Interface files, 150, 162
Internal factors, 8
Is-a links, 223
ispunc(), 124
issue_error_messages(), 45, 48
Iterative class refinement, 274

J

Johnson, R.E., 173, 175, 194, 222, 224

K

Kernel, 21, 28
key, 53, 60, 244
Keyboard operations, 21, 63
keyboard(), 163
keyboard.c, 39 - 40, 87
keyboard.cpp, 163
keyboard.hpp, 161, 163
keyboard_alt_depressed(), 60 - 61
keystroke, 60, 62, 87, 162
Keystroke operations, 228
Keystrokes, 21, 31

Keystrokes (cont.)
  Dispatching, 203
Koenig, A., 267

L

Latent typing, 214
Lexical scope, 11, 15
Library management, 160
line_count(), 198
Linear address spaces, 24
Lippman, S., 133, 267
LISP, 3, 6
Local object definitions, 196
Local objects, 221 - 222
Local variables, 128, 134, 274, 277

M

Maier, D., 3
main(), 44, 48, 228, 251, 268
Maintainability, 8 - 9, 12
make_window(), 49, 76 - 77
malloc(), 76, 78, 107, 139
McIlroy, M.D., 2
Member functions
  See Methods
Member name clashes, 223
memcpy(), 69, 217
memmove(), 114, 123
Memory models, 26
message(), 190 - 191, 196
message_query(), 111
Method overloading, 198 - 199, 207
Methods, 3, 145
Meyer, B., 6, 8, 14, 223
Microsoft C, 20
Microsoft, Inc., 20
minimal_dispatcher(), 263
Modula-2, 5 - 6
Modules, 8
  Compiled, 8, 15, 20, 30 - 31
  Interface, 53
Monochrome monitor, 28, 45
Monochrome monitors, 66
Moon, D.A., 5
MS-DOS, 19 - 20, 28 - 29, 58, 71
msg_window, 176, 182, 186
msg_window(), 187
Multiple constructors, 283
Multiple edit buffers, 110
Multiple inheritance, 223
Multiple undo markers, 110

N

Nested interface files, 159
new, 139, 184
Normal video, 24
Notification-based control, 254, 258
Notifier, 254
num_box, 176, 191, 217
numbox.hpp, 191
Nygaard, K., 5

O

Object registration system, 274
Object-oriented languages, 4 - 6, 174, 214, 279
Object-oriented programming (OOP)
  See OOP
Object-oriented programming system (OOPS)
  See OOPS
Objective-C, 6
Objects, 3
  Pointers to, 228
  Self-control, 204
ObjectWorks, 172
ok_to_overwrite(), 112
OOP, 3 - 6, 134, 172, 226, 274 - 275, 279
OOPS, 3, 6
Output stream, 140
overload, 139, 146
Overloaded functions, 138

P

page_down(), 202
page_up(), 201
panel, 144 - 145, 152
panel_create_item(), 256
Panels, 256
Parameters, 10
ParcPlace Systems, 172
Pascal, 5
Paste operations, 112
paste(), 109, 112
paste_from_undo(), 109
Perlis, A.J., 7
Pinson, L.J., 133, 283
PL/I, 5
Pluggable pointers, 180
  Disadvantages of, 180
Pointer arithmetic, 26
  See also Address arithmetic
Pointers
  As place-holders, 180
  Far, 26
  Near, 26
  Normalization, 27 - 28
  Public, 228
  To objects, 228
  To void functions, 269
Polymorphism, 146, 188
Portability, 8, 19 - 20
Prelude file, 160
present_help_screens(), 227
print_panel_color(), 145
print_stats(), 142, 146
printf(), 48
private, 157
Private methods, 280
Private variables, 16, 278
process_cmd(), 202, 206, 210, 212, 219, 228, 231, 249
Programming by difference, 4, 146, 152, 173
PROLOG, 3
prompt_for_pattern(), 116
prompt_window, 177, 218, 235, 265
prompt_window(), 218
protected, 157, 162, 181, 222, 249, 275, 280
public, 145, 153, 156 - 157, 162, 249
Public variables, 16
put_length(), 142
put_text(), 94
put_width(), 142
puts(), 48

Q

query_box, 176, 189, 217
querybox.cpp, 190
querybox.hpp, 189
quit_proc(), 256

R

r_pos(), 89
Rafter, M., 151
Read-only browser, 267
read_from_disk(), 51, 197, 230
Readability, 8 - 9, 12, 42, 188
rectangl.cpp, 151
rectangl.hpp, 151
rectangle, 142, 149
rectangle(), 143
redisplay_rest_of_line(), 122
redisplay_window(), 126, 201, 208
& (Reference parameter operator), 137
Reference parameters, 137, 217
register_callback_objects(), 259 - 260, 265
register_exit_functions(), 270
REGS, 28, 60
restore_dos_level_cursor(), 169
restore_exit_screen(), 68, 167
return, 136
Reusability, 3, 7 - 8, 12, 20, 31 - 32, 42, 66, 74, 132, 146, 188, 253, 268, 273, 277, 279, 284
Reverse video, 24
Robson, D., 5, 172

Rochkind, M.J., 72 - 73
ROM-BIOS, 20 - 21, 28, 61, 66, 80

S

save_dos_level_cursor(), 168
Scan codes, 21, 62, 258
Schildt, H., 71 - 73
Schwarz, J., 222
:: (Scope resolution operator), 135
Scope resolution operator, 135
screen, 66, 165, 179, 278, 281
Screen buffer
    See Video RAM
screen(), 166
screen.c, 39 - 40, 65
screen.h, 64
screen.hpp, 164
screen_ptr, 167 - 168
scrnprnc.h, 57 - 58
Scrolling
    Horizontal, 79, 130
    Vertical, 80
Search-and-replace operations, 115
Search-and-replace window, 74
Segment-offset pairs, 26 - 27, 114
Segmented memory, 24, 27
Segments, 25 - 26
-> (Selection operator), 232
set_background_attr(), 184
set_cntl_break(), 61 - 62
set_insert_mode(), 221
set_screen_addr(), 67
set_tag_pos(), 207
set_up_buf_window(), 262
Shared objects, 179 - 180
Side-effects, 9
Simula 67, 5
Sincovec, R., 2
Single inheritance
    See Inheritance
skip_offset(), 94
Small interfaces, 53, 267, 273
Smalltalk, 5 - 6, 172, 175, 214, 224
Software construction, 2 - 3, 14
Software crisis, 1, 3, 5
Software engineering, 2 - 3
Software maintenance, 3 - 4, 39
Specialization, 223
spkdos.h, 162
Stand-alone editor, 240
Standard protocols, 188, 257, 263 - 264, 284
Static method replacement, 173
Static methods, 175
Static variables, 4, 277
Steele, G.L., 114, 282
stream.hpp, 151
string_search(), 117
strncpy(), 218
Stroustrup, B., 5, 133, 141, 267, 280
strstr(), 117
struct, 135, 141
Structured programming, 5
Sun Microsystems, 74, 254
SunView, 74, 254 - 255, 257, 260, 271, 274
Surface area, 8
Surface-level complexity, 4, 7 - 8, 15, 43
swap(), 137
switch_edit_window(), 241, 245
system(), 236 - 237

T

Tab characters, 95, 119
tab_fill_size(), 95
tab_size(), 105, 119
Tag operations, 207
tag_pos(), 105
Tagging operations, 105
text_window, 177, 204 - 205
text_window(), 206
top_left_pos(), 105
top_of_buffer(), 131, 200, 228
Traditional languages, 3, 5

Traditional programming, 226
Translators, 133
Turbo C, 20
Type conversion, 136
typedef, 270

U

Undo buffer, 108, 216
Undo operations, 214
undo_buf, 210
undo_buffer, 216 - 217
undo_op(), 108, 123
union, 135
UNIX, 20
Unspecified number of arguments, 258, 260
up(), 127, 129
User interface, 20
User-defined types, 135
User-interface toolkits, 20

V

va_arg(), 261
va_end(), 261
va_list, 261
va_start(), 261
vararg, 138, 260
Vertical scrolling, 80
Video memory, 22, 28, 66
Video mode, 66
Video RAM, 22, 24
  See also Video memory
video_initialize(), 68
virtual, 266
Virtual functions
  See Virtual methods
Virtual method table, 267
Virtual methods, 173 - 174, 215, 224, 258, 267, 285
  Pure, 267, 285
Void functions, 269
vtbl, 267

W

Warren, D.S., 3
wframe, 74
White-box designs, 230
Whitespace characters, 141
Wiener, R.S., 2, 133, 283
Wildcard file specifications, 237
winbufs.cpp, 195, 214, 217
winbufs.hpp, 193, 266, 275
window, 176 - 177, 181
Window handles, 50
  Array-based, 72 - 73
  Pointer-based, 73
Window hierarchy, 175
window(), 183 - 184
window_adjust_cursor_position(), 129, 208
window_buffer_backward(), 122, 129
window_buffer_forward(), 122, 126
window_create(), 255
window_destroy(), 256
window_display_border(), 83 - 84
window_display_header(), 84
window_down_line(), 122
window_fill(), 52, 92, 228
window_fit(), 257
window_frame, 42, 72, 74 - 75, 79
window_getche(), 52 - 53, 87, 119
window_gets_filter(), 87, 116
window_go_rc(), 80, 126
window_line_length(), 96
window_offset(), 95
window_putchar(), 85
window_puts(), 86
window_puts_center(), 86
window_restore_offset_and_column(), 97
window_restore_screen_area(), 82
window_restore_shift(), 97
window_save_buffer, 76, 182, 196
window_save_screen_area(), 76
window_scroll(), 80
window_scroll_down(), 128 - 129

window_scroll_up(), 122
window_set(), 256
window_shift_right(), 96
window_up_line(), 128
Windows
  Graphics-based, 82
  Text-based, 82
windows.c, 39 - 40, 63, 72
windows.cpp, 182
windows.hpp, 177
windowsc.h, 82
winedit.cpp, 222
winedit.hpp, 209
winmsgs.hpp, 186
winprmt.hpp, 218
wintext.cpp, 205
wintext.hpp, 204
word_right(), 130
WORDREGS, 28
Workstations, 20, 172, 254
write_from_buffer(), 51
write_to_disk(), 197

X

X Windows, 254

Z

Zortech C, 20
Zortech C++, 150, 229, 241
Zortech, Inc., 20, 150, 241